# VISUAL QUICKSTART GUIDE

# MAC OS 8.6

**Maria Langer**

 **Peachpit Press**

Visual QuickStart Guide
# Mac OS 8.6
Maria Langer

Peachpit Press
1249 Eighth Street
Berkeley, CA 94710
510-524-2178 · 800-283-9444
510-524-2221 (fax)

Find us on the World Wide Web at: http://www.peachpit.com/

Peachpit Press is a division of Addison Wesley Longman

Editor: Clifford Colby
Indexer: Emily Glossbrenner
Cover Design: The Visual Group
Production: Maria Langer, Kate Reber

## Colophon

This book was produced with Adobe PageMaker 6.5 on a Power Macintosh G3/300. The fonts used were Kepler Multiple Master, Meta Plus, and PIXymbols Command. Screenshots were created using Snapz Pro on a Power Macintosh 8500/180, PowerBook 3400/180c, and original iMac.

## Notice of Rights

## Notice of Liability

## Trademarks

ISBN 0-201-35472-1

9 8 7 6 5 4 3 2

Printed and bound in the United States of America.

 Printed on recycled paper.

## Dedication

To Janet and Steve,
two new members of the
Macintosh user community

# Thanks!

To Cliff Colby, for helping me fine-tune this third edition of my Mac OS VQS. Cliff pointed out a few things that I overlooked, enabling me to make this book clearer and more complete.

To Nancy Ruenzel and the other powers-that-be at Peachpit Press, for letting me revise *Mac OS 8.5: Visual QuickStart Guide*.

To Kate Reber, for not coming up with a single major production complaint while I laid out this book. I just wonder how many changes she made when she received the "final" files…

To Victor Gavenda, for getting me the software I needed to write this book, sparing me (and my computer) hours of frustrating FTP download time.

To the rest of the folks at Peachpit Press—especially Gary-Paul, Trish, Hannah, Paula, Zigi, Jimbo, and Keasley—for doing what they do so well.

To Emily Glossbrenner for yet another excellent indexing job.

To Apple Computer, Inc., for continuing to hone the world's best operating system.

And to Mike, for the usual reasons.

# Author Note

I've been working with Mac OS for ten years and sometimes I forget that troubleshooting minor problems can be a scary mystery for new users. My friends Janet and Steve, new iMac owners, reminded me.

Because of this, I've added a troubleshooting section to the last chapter of this book. Other than necessary modifications to cover new Mac OS 8.6 features, this new section is the most significant difference between this book and *Mac OS 8.5: Visual QuickStart Guide*.

For the benefit of the folks who already have one of my Mac OS VQS books and don't think they need this one, I've included an Adobe Acrobat PDF file of the new troubleshooting information on the book's companion Web site, http://www.gilesrd.com/macosvqs/. I hope you'll download it and share it with your friends.

— Maria

http://www.gilesrd.com/mlanger/

# TABLE OF CONTENTS

TABLE OF CONTENTS

**TABLE OF CONTENTS**

# INTRODUCTION TO MAC OS 8.6

## Introduction

Mac OS 8.6 is the latest version of the computer operating system that put the phrase *graphic user interface* in everyone's vocabulary. With Mac OS, you can point, click, and drag to work with files, applications, and utilities. Because the same intuitive interface is utilized throughout the system, you'll find that a procedure that works in one program works in virtually all the others.

This Visual QuickStart Guide will help you learn Mac OS 8.6 by providing step-by-step instructions, plenty of illustrations, and a generous helping of tips. On these pages, you'll find everything you need to know to get up and running quickly with Mac OS 8.6—and more!

This book was designed for page flipping. Use the thumb tabs, index, or table of contents to find the topics for which you need help. If you're brand new to Mac OS, however, I recommend that you begin by reading at least the first two chapters. In them, you'll find basic information about techniques you'll use every day with your computer.

If you're interested in information about features added in Mac OS 8.5 and 8.6 and the components of Mac OS 8.6, be sure to browse through this **Introduction**. It'll give you a good idea of what you can expect to see on your computer.

START HERE

# Features Added in Mac OS 8.6

Mac OS 8.6, which was released in the spring of 1999, is a minor revision to Mac OS. Here is a list of its new features:

◆ Sherlock now includes more search site files. Its Search Internet tab now has a Uncheck All button that you can click to clear all check boxes (**Figure 1**).

◆ The LaserWriter print driver has additional options for documenting and downloading fonts (**Figure 2**) and for logging PostScript print jobs (**Figure 3**).

◆ A number of Mac OS components were updated to make them faster or more reliable, including AppleScript, UDF, FireWire, PlainTalk, Multi-Language Text Editor, Help Viewer, and Desktop Printer Utility.

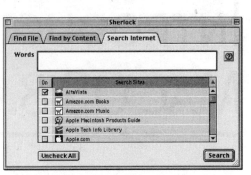

**Figure 1** Sherlock now offers more Internet search sites and an Uncheck All button.

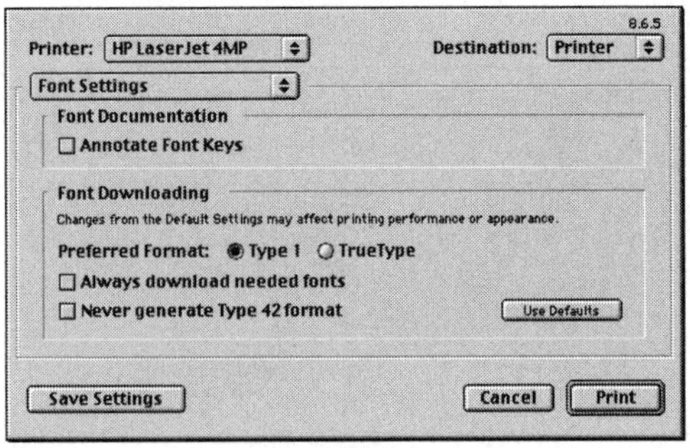

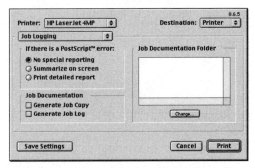

**Figure 2** The LaserWriter printer driver now offers Font Settings...

**Figure 3** ...and Job Logging options in the Print dialog box.

*Icon in title bar*   *Proportional scroll box*

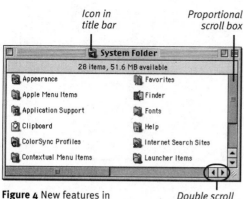

*Double scroll arrows*

**Figure 4** New features in Finder windows.

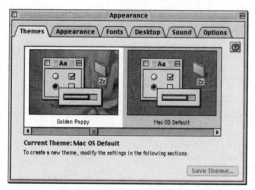

**Figure 5** The improved Appearance control panel offers more settings, including predefined themes and sounds.

# Features Added in Mac OS 8.5

Mac OS 8.5, a major revision to the Macintosh System software, was released in the autumn of 1998. It added many new features to the Mac OS Finder and system. Here's a list:

## New appearance & Finder window features

◆ An icon in a window's title bar (**Figure 4**) enables you to move or copy a window's contents without selecting icons or closing the window.

◆ Proportional scroll boxes (**Figure 4**) enable you to estimate how much of a window's contents are visible.

◆ Double scroll arrows (**Figure 4**) make it easier to scroll window contents.

◆ The Appearance control panel (**Figure 5**) now includes predefined, customizable *themes* that can include sound effects and other options.

◆ Anti-aliasing smooths the appearance of text characters on screen.

◆ You can now define a set of standard view options for icon, button, and list view windows. Options automatically apply to all windows other than the ones for which you have customized view options.

◆ You can now change the width and order of columns in list view windows.

◆ New icons clearly identify aliases, locked files, shared folders, and folders with AppleScript scripts attach to them.

## New file management features

◆ Open (**Figure 6**) and Save As dialog boxes now available in some applications offer an improved interface for opening and saving documents. Future versions of all applications will take advantage of the Navigation Services features of these dialog boxes.

◆ The Application menu now displays both the icon and name of the active application (**Figure 7**).

◆ You can drag the Application menu away from the menu bar to display the floating Application Switcher window (**Figure 8**); clicking an application name in this window switches to it.

◆ The Favorites submenu under the Apple menu offers easy access to the documents, applications, network items, and Internet locations you use most.

◆ Info windows now include a pop-up menu to view or set general, memory, or sharing (**Figure 9**) options. You can even use the Info window to get information about a desktop printer's configuration and installed fonts.

◆ Sherlock (**Figure 10**), a major revision to the old Find File program, enables you to search for files by file attribute or content.

◆ Document translation features formerly found in a number of control panels— including those that enable you to open PC files—are now handled by the new File Exchange control panel.

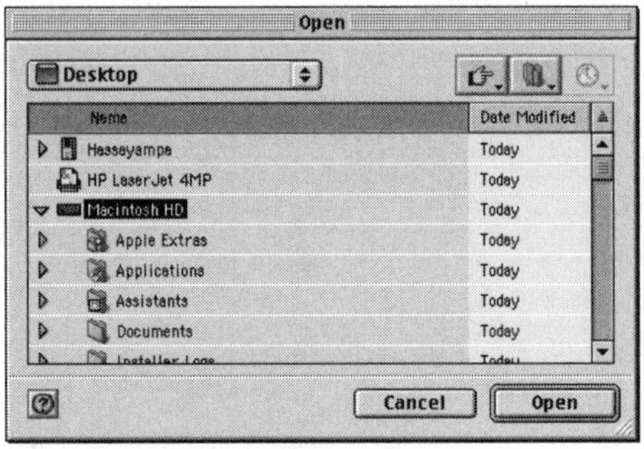

**Figure 6** The new Open dialog box.

**Figure 7** The Application menu now includes the name of the active application—not just the icon.

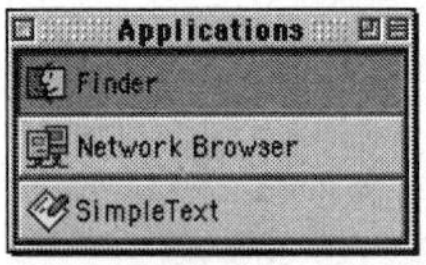

**Figure 8**
The Application Switcher appears when you drag the Application menu away from the menu bar.

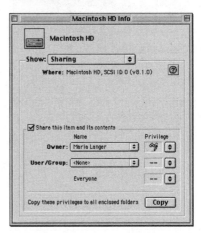

**Figure 9** The Info window includes a pop-up menu for various types of options.

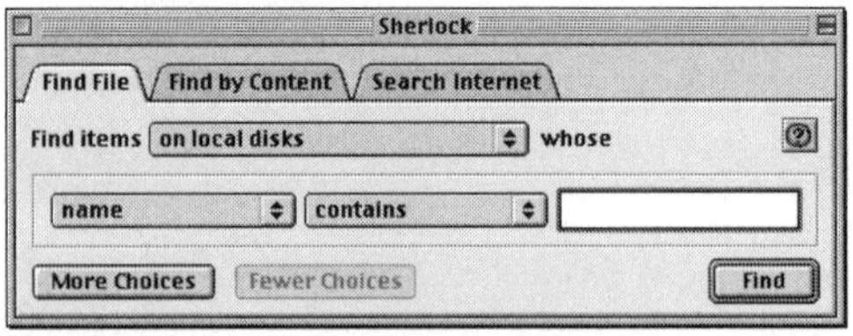

**Figure 10** Sherlock has far more searching capabilities than Find File ever had.

**Figure 11** The Remote Access control panel now does the job of the old PPP control panel.

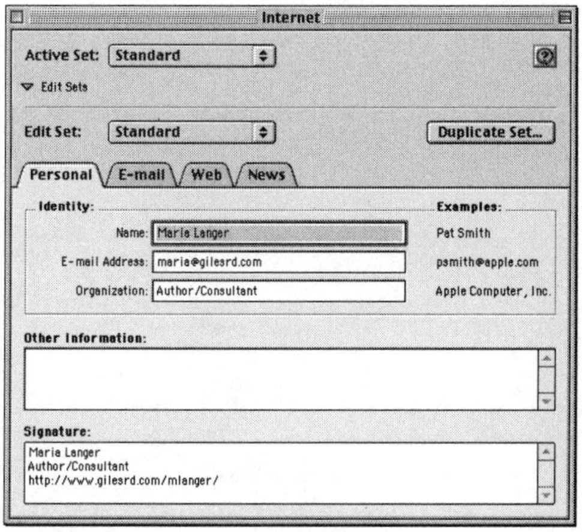

**Figure 12** The Internet control panel makes it easier than ever to set Internet preferences.

**Figure 13** When you drag a URL to the Desktop or a Finder window, you create an Internet location document.

www.gilesrd.com

# New networking & Internet features

◆ The Network Browser offers a new interface for locating and connecting to AppleShare servers on a network.

◆ The Remote Access control panel (**Figure 11**) now includes the functionality of the old PPP control panel for dialing into an ISP.

◆ Sherlock, the Find File replacement, enables you to search the Internet.

◆ You can now display multilingual content in Web browser windows.

◆ The new Internet control panel (**Figure 12**) enables you to create sets of Internet configurations that are referenced by all Internet applications.

◆ New Internet access software includes Microsoft Internet Explorer for Web browsing and Microsoft Outlook Express for e-mail.

◆ You can create an Internet location file by dragging a selected Internet address to the Desktop. Double-clicking the file's icon (**Figure 13**) opens that location.

◆ You can set your system clock by accessing a network time server.

## New online help features

◆ Mac OS Help (**Figure 14**) is easier to use and provides clickable links to other help topics, Apple Guide instructions, installed applications, and Internet locations.

## Improved performance features

◆ Copying is now faster over networks and between hard disks, removable media such as Zip disks, and CD-ROMs.

◆ QuickDraw improvements display graphics faster on screen and speed up window scrolling.

◆ Disk First Aid can now repair your startup disk. Disk First Aid also automatically launches and checks disks if the computer was not shut down properly.

◆ QuickTime now supports more multimedia formats.

◆ The Monitor Calibration Assistant in the Monitors & Sound control panel enables you to set up ColorSync so the colors you see on your monitor closely match the colors you scan or print.

◆ AppleScript runs three to five times faster. More control panels are scriptable. You now can attach scripts to specific folders to automatically perform operations when you open or copy an item into the folder.

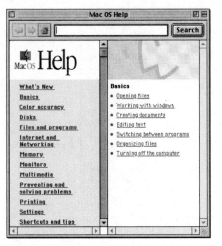

**Figure 14** Mac OS Help is now more user-friendly than ever.

# Mac OS 8.6 Components

Mac OS 8.6 includes the following software components:

◆ **Mac OS 8.6** is the basic collection of system software files, including the System file, Finder file, control panels, and extensions. This is the foundation of Mac OS; its various parts are covered throughout this book.

◆ **Internet Access** enables you to connect to the Internet. I tell you about accessing the Internet in **Chapter 12**.

◆ **Apple Remote Access** enables you to use your modem to connect to another computer or establish a PPP connection to the Internet. I discuss Apple Remote Access in **Chapters 11** and **12**.

◆ **Personal Web Sharing** enables you to build your own Web server for sharing information on an intranet or the Internet. I tell you about Personal Web Sharing in **Chapter 12**.

◆ **QuickDraw 3D** enables you to work with complex, three-dimensional graphics.

◆ **Text-to-Speech** enables your computer to read text and alerts with a synthesized voice. I cover speaking text in **Chapter 6** and setting Speech options in **Chapter 13**.

◆ **Mac OS Runtime for Java** enables you to run Java applets from the Finder.

◆ **ColorSync** helps ensure color accuracy when working with color images.

◆ **QuickDraw GX** offers enhanced printing and preview features.

◆ **English Speech Recognition** enables your computer to recognize and respond to human speech. I discuss speech recognition briefly in **Chapter 13**.

◆ **Multilingual Internet Access** allows Internet applications to display and edit multilingual text.

## ✔ Tip

■ The Mac OS 8.6 installer, which I discuss in **Chapter 1**, enables you to install any combination of these components.

# SETTING UP MAC OS 8.6

## Setting Up Mac OS 8.6

Before you can use Mac OS 8.6, you must install it on your computer and configure it to work the way you need it to. This is a three-step process:

1. Use the Mac OS 8.6 installer to install the components you want.

2. Restart your computer.

3. Use the Mac OS Setup Assistant, as well as other assistants, to configure the Mac OS 8.6 components you installed.

This chapter explains how to complete all three of these steps, so you can properly install and configure Mac OS 8.6 on your computer.

### ✔ Tips

■ Mac OS 8.6 offers many installation and configuration options—far too many to discuss in detail in this book. Although the figures and instructions in this chapter cover only the most common options, I think you'll find enough general information to help you complete virtually any combination of installation and configuration options.

■ I tell you how to use the Internet Setup Assistant in **Chapter 12**.

# The Mac OS 8.6 Installer

Mac OS 8.6 comes with an installer application that makes software installation easy. Simply launch the installer and follow the instructions that appear on screen to select a destination disk, learn more about the software, agree to a license agreement, and select the Mac OS 8.6 components you want installed. The installer builds the System and Finder files for your computer and copies the software you specified to your hard disk.

The Mac OS 8.6 installer can perform two types of installations:

◆ **Standard Installation** lets you select the Mac OS 8.6 components you want installed. The installer copies all standard parts of each selected component to your hard disk.

◆ **Customized Installation** lets you select the Mac OS 8.6 components you want installed and then lets you select the individual parts of each component to be installed.

The first half of this chapter explains how to use the Mac OS 8.6 installer to perform both a standard and a customized installation.

## ✔ Tips

■ The installation instructions in this chapter assume you know basic Mac OS techniques, such as pointing, clicking, double-clicking, dragging, and selecting items from a menu. If you're brand new to the Mac and don't know any of these techniques, skip ahead to **Chapter 2**, which discusses Mac OS basics.

■ A standard installation of Mac OS 8.6 includes the following components: Mac OS 8.6, Internet Access, Apple Remote Access, Personal Web Sharing, QuickDraw 3D, Text-to-Speech, Mac OS Runtime for Java, and ColorSync.

**Figure 1**
To launch the Mac OS 8.6 installer, double-click this icon.

*Install Mac OS 8.6*

**Figure 2** The Mac OS 8.6 installer's Welcome window appears when you launch it.

■ I tell you about the individual components of Mac OS 8.6 in the **Introduction** of this book.

■ You can click the Go Back button at any time during installation to change options in a previous window.

■ You can press [Return] or [Enter] to "click" a default button—a button with a dark border around it—such as the Continue button in **Figure 2**.

■ I explain how to use the Mac OS 8.6 updater, which updates an existing Mac OS 8.5 installation to Mac OS 8.6, later in this chapter.

THE MAC OS 8.6 INSTALLER

**Figure 3** Use the Select Destination window to select the disk on which to install Mac OS 8.6.

**Figure 4** Choose a disk from the Destination Disk pop-up menu.

**Figure 5** Turn on the Perform Clean Installation check box to create a brand new System Folder for Mac OS 8.6.

## ✔ Tips

- The destination disk is normally your internal hard disk but can be any disk that is turned on at startup.

- Only those hard disks and removable high-capacity media (such as Zip, Jaz, and SyQuest disks) that appear on your Desktop are listed in the Destination Disk pop-up menu (**Figure 4**).

- A status area beneath the Destination Disk pop-up menu indicates the version of Mac OS that is installed on the disk, as well as the available disk space and the amount of disk space required for a basic installation (**Figure 3**).

## To launch the installer

1. Start your computer from the Mac OS 8.6 CD-ROM disc.

   *or*

   Start your computer the usual way and insert the Mac OS 8.6 CD-ROM disc.

2. Locate and double-click the Install Mac OS 8.6 icon (**Figure 1**).

3. After a moment, the installer's Welcome window appears (**Figure 2**). Click Continue.

## ✔ Tip

- To start your computer from the Mac OS 8.6 CD-ROM disc, insert the disc, choose Special > Restart, and hold down [C] until the "Welcome to Mac OS" message appears. This is the recommended way to start your computer when installing OS software.

## To select a destination disk

1. In the installer's Select Destination window (**Figure 3**), use the Destination Disk pop-up menu (**Figure 4**) to select the disk on which you want to install Mac OS 8.6.

2. Click Select.

- To create a brand new System Folder for Mac OS 8.6, click the Options button. Turn on the Perform Clean Installation check box in the dialog box that appears (**Figure 5**). The old System Folder is renamed "Previous System Folder" and should be deleted after you move non-Apple control panels, extensions, and preferences files to their proper locations in the new System Folder.

## To read important information about Mac OS 8.6

1. Read the contents of the installer's Important Information window (**Figure 6**). Click the down arrow on the vertical scroll bar to scroll through the entire document.

2. When you have finished reading the information, click Continue.

## ✔ Tips

- Read the information in this window carefully! It provides important, late-breaking news about installing Mac OS, including compatibility information and special instructions not included in this book.

- To save a copy of the information for future reference, click the Save button. Then use the Save As dialog box that appears to select a disk location and enter a name for the file. Click Save to complete the save. (I tell you more about the Save As dialog box in **Chapter 5**.)

- To print a copy of the information for reference, click the Print button. Then click Print in the Print dialog box that appears to send the document to your printer. (I tell you about printing and using the Print dialog box in **Chapter 10**.)

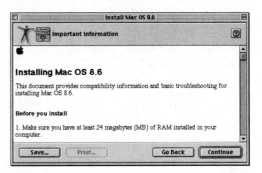

**Figure 6** The Important Information window contains late-breaking news about installing Mac OS 8.6.

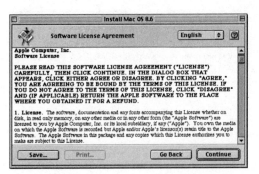

**Figure 7** The Software License Agreement tells you exactly what you're allowed to do with Mac OS 8.6 software.

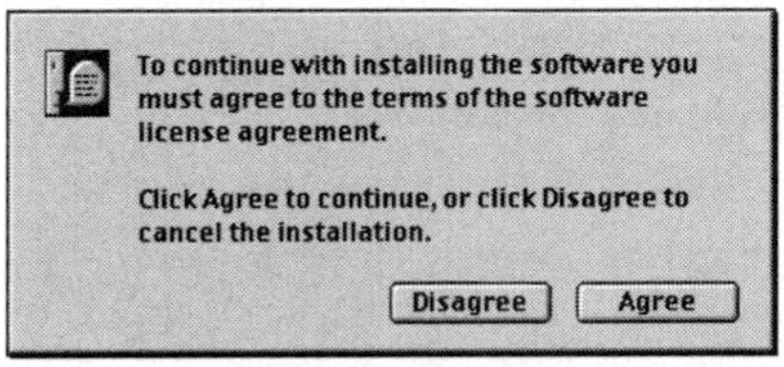

To continue with installing the software you must agree to the terms of the software license agreement.

Click Agree to continue, or click Disagree to cancel the installation.

Disagree    Agree

**Figure 8** To complete the installation of Mac OS 8, you must click Agree in this dialog box.

## To read and agree to the Software License Agreement

1. If desired, choose a language from the pop-up menu at the top-right of the Software License Agreement window (**Figure 7**).

2. Read the contents of the window. Click the down arrow on the vertical scroll bar to scroll through the entire document.

3. When you have finished reading the agreement, click Continue.

4. A dialog box appears, informing you that you must agree to the terms of the agreement you just read to continue (**Figure 8**). Click Agree.

## ✔ Tips

- To save a copy of the license agreement for future reference, click the Save button. Then use the Save As dialog box that appears to select a disk location and enter a name for the file. Click Save to complete the save. (I tell you more about the Save As dialog box in **Chapter 5**.)

- To print a copy of the license agreement for reference, click the Print button. Then click Print in the Print dialog box that appears to send the document to your printer. (I tell you about printing and using the Print dialog box in **Chapter 10**.)

- If you click Disagree in step 4, the installer returns you to its Welcome window (**Figure 2**).

## To customize an installation

1. In the Install Software window (**Figure 9**), click the Customize button. The window changes to the Custom Installation and Removal window (**Figure 10**), which displays a list of software components.

2. Toggle the check box settings to turn on only those for the components you want to install. Be sure to click the down arrow at the bottom of the vertical scroll bar to view all the options.

3. If desired, choose an installation mode from the pop-up menu beside each checked component.

   ▲ **Recommended Installation** installs the recommended parts of the component for your computer.

   ▲ **Customized Installation** displays a dialog box similar to the one in **Figure 11**. Use this option to specify which parts of the component should be installed, and click OK.

## ✔ Tips

- If you change your mind about making a custom installation, click the Don't Customize button (**Figure 10**) to go back to the Install Software window (**Figure 9**).

- To successfully use the Customized Installation option, you must be familiar with all parts of each component you want installed. This is a feature designed for Mac OS experts. If used improperly, it can cause erratic system behavior.

- You can click the triangle to the left of an item (**Figure 11**) to display individual items within it (**Figure 12**).

- You can click the info icon (or "i" button) to the right of an item to learn more about it (**Figure 13**). Click OK to dismiss the information dialog box.

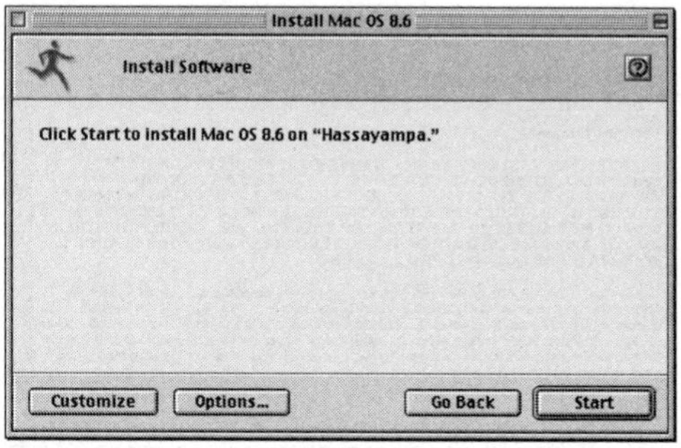

**Figure 9** Use the Install Software window to select the Mac OS components you want to install.

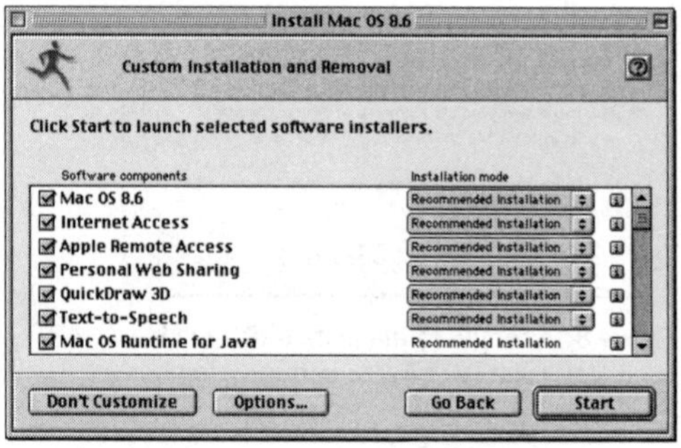

**Figure 10** Use the Custom Installation and Removal window to select Mac OS 8.6 components for a custom installation.

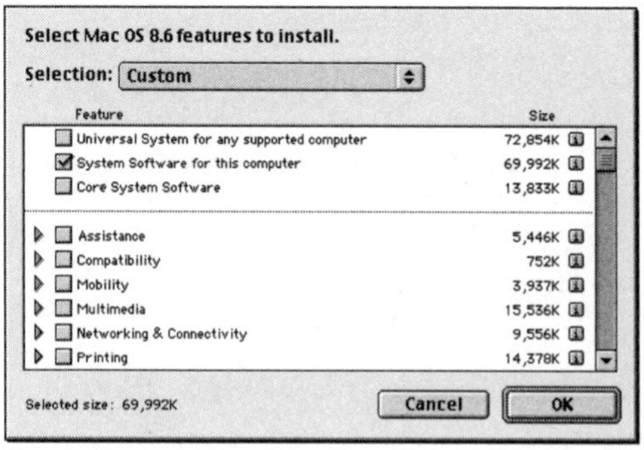

**Figure 11** Windows like these enable you to select the parts of a specific component that you want to install.

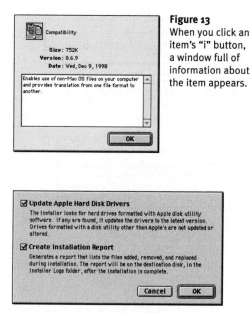

| | |
|---|---|
| ▽ ☐ Assistance | 5,446K |
| ▷ ☐ Apple Guide Files | 3,499K |
| ☐ Mac OS Help | 3,063K |
| ▽ ☐ Read Me Files | 127K |
| ☐ About AppleScript | 12K |
| ☐ About Automated Tasks | 4K |
| ☐ About FireWire Support | 4K |
| ☐ About Mac OS 8.5 | 14K |
| ☐ About More Automated Tasks | 3K |

**Figure 12** Clicking the triangle to the left of an item displays individual items within it.

**Figure 13**
When you click an item's "i" button, a window full of information about the item appears.

**Figure 14** You can use this dialog box to set two additional installation options.

## To set other installation options

1. Click the Options button in the Install Software or Custom Installation and Removal window to display a dialog box like the one in **Figure 14**.

2. To prevent the installer from attempting to update the hard disk driver of the destination disk, turn off the Update Apple Hard Disk Driver check box.

3. To prevent the installer from creating an installation log file, turn off the Create Installation Report check box.

4. Click OK.

## ✔ Tips

- As shown in **Figure 14**, both of these options are enabled by default. If you're not sure how to set these options, leave them both turned on.

- If you're not sure what to do in step 3, leave the check box turned on. The Mac OS 8.6 installer can only update the driver on an Apple-branded hard disk—one that comes with a Macintosh computer. It cannot affect a hard disk made by another manufacturer. If the installer cannot update your disk's driver, it will display a message saying so and provide additional information about updating your driver.

SETTING OTHER INSTALLATION OPTIONS

## To complete the installation

1. In the Install Software window (**Figure 9**) or Custom Installation and Removal window (**Figure 10**), click the Start button.

2. A dialog box like the one in **Figure 15** may appear, informing you that other applications cannot be running during the install process and that you will have to restart your computer when it's finished. Click Continue.

3. The installer performs some maintenance tasks, then begins installing the software you selected. A progress window like the one in **Figure 16** appears to show you how it's doing.

4. When the installation is complete, a dialog box like the one in **Figure 17** appears. Click Restart.

## ✔ Tips

- The amount of time it takes to install Mac OS 8.6 depends on the components you selected (if you customized the installation), the speed of your computer's CPU, and the speed of your CD-ROM drive (if applicable). A basic installation can take 15 minutes or more.

- To perform additional Mac OS 8.6 installations, click the Continue button in the dialog box that appears when installation is complete (**Figure 17**). This returns you to the Install Software window (**Figure 9**).

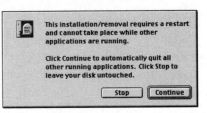

This installation/removal requires a restart and cannot take place while other applications are running.

Click Continue to automatically quit all other running applications. Click Stop to leave your disk untouched.

Stop    Continue

**Figure 15** A dialog box like this may appear after you click the Start button.

Installing Mac OS 8.6 onto "Hassayampa"

Estimated Time Remaining: About 10 minutes    Cancel

**Figure 16** The Mac OS 8.6 installer displays a progress window as it works.

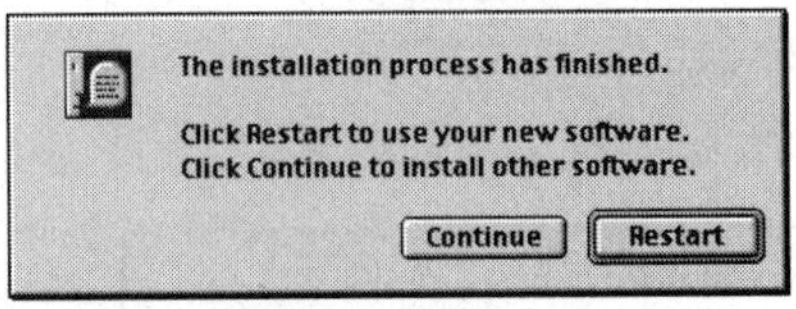

The installation process has finished.

Click Restart to use your new software. Click Continue to install other software.

Continue    Restart

**Figure 17** A dialog box like this appears when the installation is complete.

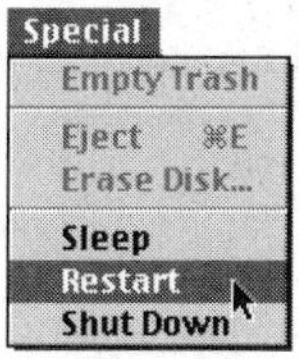

**Special**

Empty Trash

Eject ⌘E
Erase Disk...

Sleep
Restart
Shut Down

**Figure 18**
To restart your
computer,
choose Restart
from the Special
menu.

# Restarting Your Computer

To configure and use your newly installed Mac OS 8.6 software, you must restart your computer. This loads the new software into the computer's RAM and, if necessary, launches the Mac OS Setup Assistant.

## To restart your computer

If you are not prompted to restart your computer at the conclusion of the installation process (**Figure 17**), choose Special > Restart (**Figure 18**).

### ✔ Tips

- Do not restart your computer by turning off power and then turning it back on! This can cause file corruption. I tell you other ways to restart your computer in **Chapter 2**.

- If you have more than one disk with Mac OS software installed on it, you may have to use the Startup Disk control panel to specify which disk's operating system should be loaded at startup. I tell you about the Startup Disk control panel in **Chapter 12**.

RESTARTING YOUR COMPUTER

# Updating to Mac OS 8.6 from Mac OS 8.5

If Mac OS 8.5 is currently installed on your computer, you can use the Mac OS 8.6 updater to update it to Mac OS 8.6. This updater is available for free to Mac OS 8.5 users on Apple's Web site, http://www.apple.com/.

## ✔ Tip

■ The Mac OS 8.6 updater merely updates all installed Mac OS 8.5 features to Mac 8.6. It cannot install any additional features.

## To use the Mac OS 8.6 updater

1. Launch the updater, double-clicking the Update to Mac OS 8.6 icon (**Figure 19**).

2. Follow the instructions on pages 3 through 5 and 7 to select a destination disk, read important information about Mac OS 8.6, read and agree to the Software License Agreement, and set other options.

3. In the Install/Remove Software window (**Figure 20**), click the Start button.

4. Follow steps 2 through 4 on page 8 to complete the installation.

## ✔ Tip

■ If a dialog box like the one in **Figure 17** does not appear at the conclusion of the update, restart your computer by choosing Special>Restart (**Figure 18**).

**Figure 19**
To launch the updater, double-click the Update to Mac OS 8.6 icon.

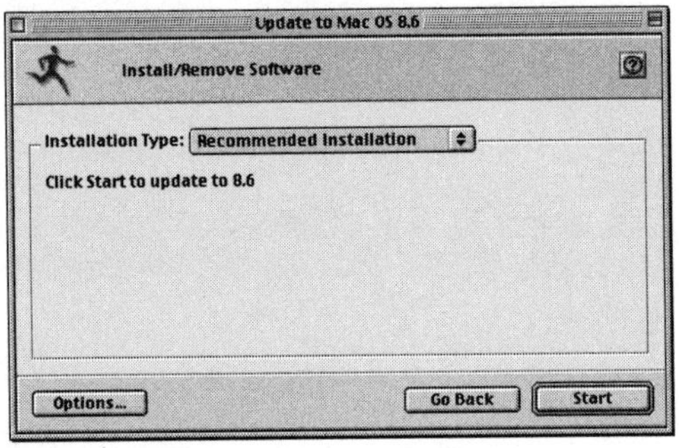

**Figure 20** Use the updater's Install/Remove window to start the update.

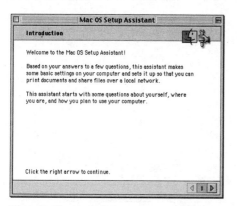

**Figure 21** The Mac OS Setup Assistant offers an easy way to configure Mac OS 8.6.

**Figure 22** When you first start your computer after installing Mac OS 8.6, it may automatically rebuild the invisible Desktop files on attached disks.

# The Mac OS Setup Assistant

When you restart your computer after installing Mac OS 8.6, the Mac OS Setup Assistant automatically appears (**Figure 21**). This program uses a simple question and answer process to get information about you and the way you use your computer. The information you provide is automatically entered into the appropriate control panels to configure Mac OS 8.6.

## ✔ Tips

- Your computer may automatically rebuild the Desktop file for attached disks when you restart after installing Mac OS 8.6. If so, a dialog box like the one in **Figure 22** appears. Do not stop this process. When it is finished, the dialog box will automatically disappear.

- If the Mac OS Setup Assistant does not automatically appear at startup, you can launch it by opening the Mac OS Setup Assistant icon in the Assistants folder on your hard disk. I explain how to work with files and folders in **Chapter 3**.

- I tell you about control panels and how you can use them to customize Mac OS in **Chapter 12**.

## Chapter 1

## To use the Mac OS Setup Assistant

1. Read the information in each Mac OS Setup Assistant window. Enter information or make selections when prompted.

2. Click the right arrow button or press $→$ to continue.

   *or*

   Click the left arrow button or press $←$ to go back and make changes in previous windows.

### ✔ Tip

■ The next few pages explain exactly how to enter information in each window that appears.

## To select regional preferences

1. If you haven't already done so, click the right arrow button in the Introduction window of the Mac OS Setup Assistant (**Figure 21**).

2. Read the information in the Regional Preferences window (**Figure 23**) to learn how Mac OS 8.6 uses your language version.

3. Click the language you prefer to select it.

4. Click the right arrow button.

### ✔ Tips

■ The languages that appear in this dialog box will vary depending on the language supported by your copy of Mac OS 8.6.

■ You can set the keyboard layout for a language in the Keyboard control panel, which I discuss in **Chapter 13**.

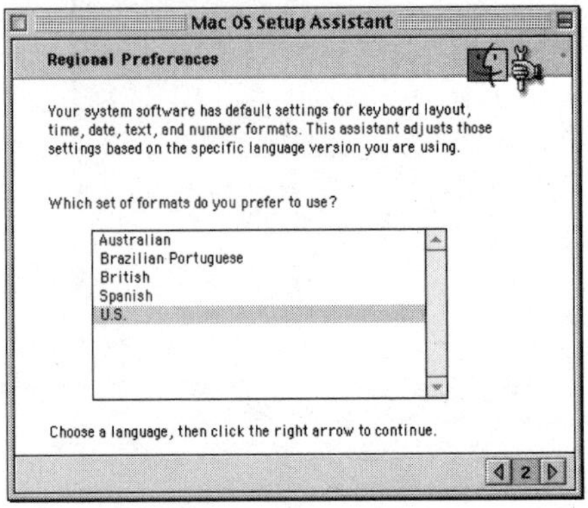

**Figure 23** Use the Regional Preferences window to select your language version.

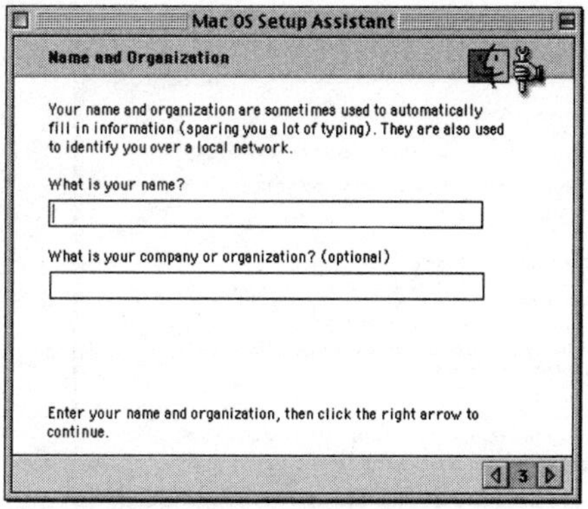

**Figure 24** Enter your name and organization in these edit boxes.

## To enter your name & organization

1. Read the information in the Name and Organization window (**Figure 24**) to learn how Mac OS 8.6 uses your name and company.

2. Enter your name in the What is your name? edit box.

3. Press ⌈Tab⌉ or click in the What is your company or organization? edit box to position the blinking insertion point.

4. Enter the name of your company or organization.

5. Click the right arrow button.

## ✔ Tips

- You must enter a name in the What is your name? box. You may, however, leave the What is your company or organization? box empty if desired.

- You can also enter your name in the File Sharing control panel, which I tell you about in **Chapter 10**.

**ENTERING YOUR NAME & ORGANIZATION**

## To set the time & date

1. Read the information in the Time and Date window of the Mac OS Setup Assistant (**Figure 25**) to learn how Mac OS 8.6 uses the time and date.

2. If daylight savings time is currently in effect, select the Yes radio button by clicking it.

3. If the time in the What time is it? box is not correct, change it. To do this, click an incorrect number in the time sequence to select it (**Figure 26**) and either type in the correct number or click the up or down arrow button beside the time until the correct number appears.

4. If the date in the What is today's date? box is not correct, change it. To do this, click an incorrect number in the date sequence to select it and either type in the correct number or click the up or down arrow button beside the date until the correct number appears.

5. Click the right arrow button.

## ✔ Tips

- ☑ The time and date, which are tracked by your computer's internal clock, may already be correct. If so, no changes will be necessary.

- ◼ You can also set the time and date in the Date & Time control panel, which I tell you about in **Chapter 13**.

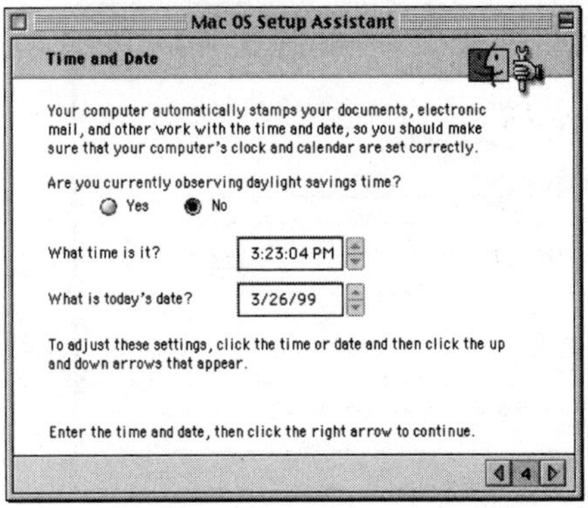

**Figure 25** Use the Time and Date window to check and, if necessary, change the time or date.

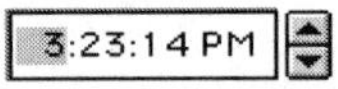

**Figure 26** To change the time (or date), click an incorrect number in the sequence to select it and then click the up or down arrow until the right number appears.

SETTING THE TIME & DATE

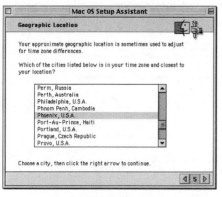

**Figure 27** The Geographic Location window lists cities all over the world—including one near you.

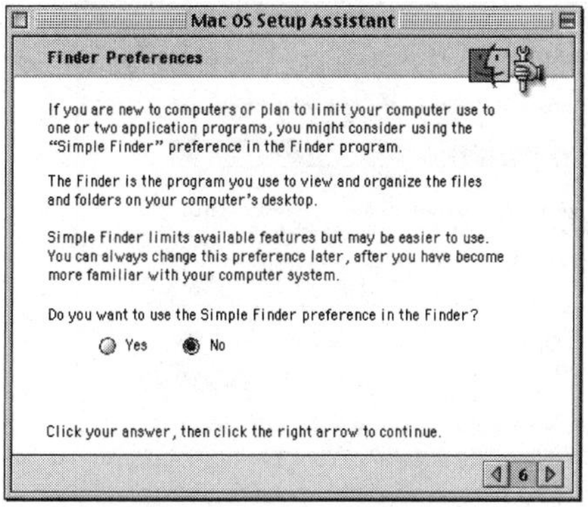

**Figure 28** Use the Finder Preferences window to turn Simple Finder on or off.

## To select your geographic location

1. Read the information in the Geographic Location window of the Mac OS Setup Assistant (**Figure 27**) to learn how Mac OS 8.6 uses your location.

2. Click the up or down arrow on the scroll bar until the name of a city in your time zone (preferably near you) appears. Click it once to select it.

3. Click the right arrow button.

## ✔ Tip

- You can also set your geographic location or time zone in the Date & Time control panel, which I tell you about in **Chapter 13**.

## To set Finder preferences

1. Read the information in the Finder Preferences window of the Mac OS Setup Assistant (**Figure 28**) to learn about the difference between the standard Finder and Simple Finder.

2. If you want fewer menu commands in the Finder, click the Yes radio button to select it.

3. Click the right arrow button.

## ✔ Tips

- The standard Finder—*not* Simple Finder—is used throughout this book.

- I illustrate both standard Finder and Simple Finder menus in **Appendix A**.

- You can also set Finder preferences in the Preferences dialog box, which I tell you about in **Chapter 4**.

## To set network options

1. Read the information in the Local Network Introduction window of the Mac OS Setup Assistant (**Figure 29**) to learn more about networks.

2. Click the right arrow button.

3. Read the information in the Computer Name and Password window (**Figure 30**) to learn how Mac OS uses your computer's name and password.

4. To change the default name that the Mac OS Setup Assistant has assigned to your computer, type it in the top edit box. (The name should be selected as shown in **Figure 30** so it is not necessary to click in the box first; simply type to overwrite the contents of the edit box.) Then press [Tab] or click in the bottom edit box to position the insertion point there.

   *or*

   To accept the default name that the Mac OS Setup Assistant has assigned to your computer, just press [Tab] or click in the bottom edit box to position the insertion point there.

5. In the bottom edit box, enter a password you want to use to protect your computer from unauthorized access by other network users.

6. Click the right arrow button.

7. Wait while the Mac OS Setup Assistant validates the computer name and password.

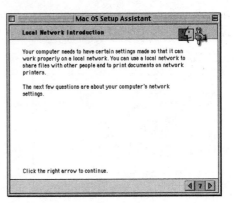

**Figure 29** The Local Network Introduction window tells you a little about networks.

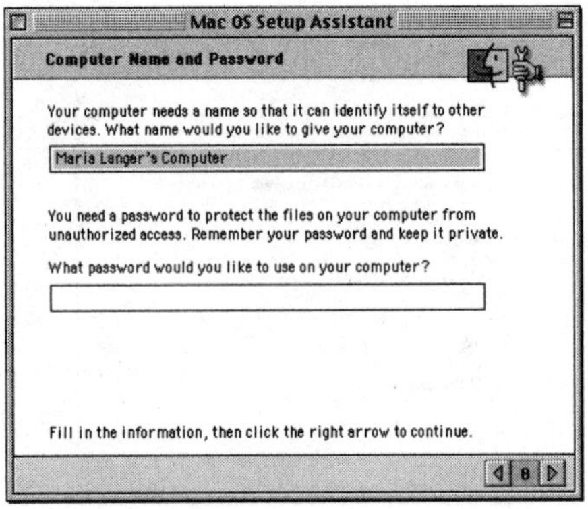

**Figure 30** Use this window to enter a name for your computer and a password to protect your files from unauthorized network users.

**SETTING NETWORK OPTIONS**

**Figure 31** Use this window to set up a shared folder—if you want one.

**8.** Read the information in the Shared Folder window (**Figure 31**) to learn what a shared folder is and how it is used.

**9.** If you do not want a shared folder on the network, select the No radio button by clicking it. Then skip to step 11.

**10.** To change the default name that the Mac OS Setup Assistant has assigned to your shared folder, type it in the edit box. (The name should be selected as shown in **Figure 31**, so it is not necessary to click in the box first; simply type to overwrite the contents of the box.)

**11.** Click the right arrow button.

## ✔ Tips

■ You must go through these steps even if your computer is not connected to a network.

■ You must provide both a name and password for your computer.

■ You can also set network settings in the File Sharing control panel, which I tell you about in **Chapter 11**.

SETTING NETWORK OPTIONS

## To set printer options

1. Turn on your printer and if necessary, let it warm up.

2. Read the information in the Printer Connection window of the Mac OS Setup Assistant (**Figure 32**) to learn the difference between a direct connection and a network connection.

3. Select the appropriate connection type by clicking its radio button.

4. Click the right arrow button.

5. If you selected Network connection in step 2, wait while the Mac OS Setup Assistant searches the network for connected printers. Then, in the Printer Selection window that appears (**Figure 33**), select the printer you use most often by clicking its name.

   *or*

   If you selected Direct connection in step 2, the Printer Type window appears (**Figure 34**). Select the type of printer connected to your computer by clicking its name in the list. Then select the port to which the printer is connected by clicking the Printer Port or Modem Port radio button.

6. Click the right arrow button.

## ✔ Tips

- You can also select a printer in the Chooser, which I tell you about in **Chapter 10**.

- If the type of printer you use does not appear in the Printer Type window (**Figure 34**), you may have to install a printer driver for it. I tell you about that in **Chapter 10**, too.

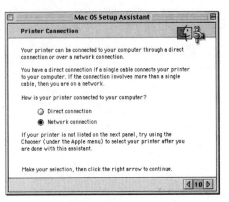

**Figure 32** Use the Printer Connection window to tell the Mac OS Setup Assistant how your printer is connected.

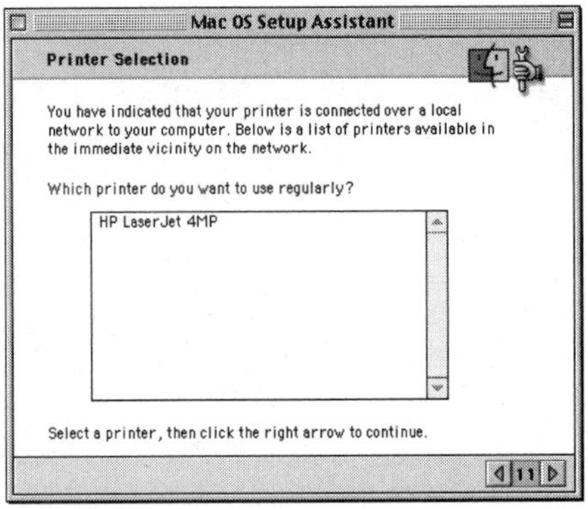

**Figure 33** If you printer is connected to your computer through a network connection, select it in this window.

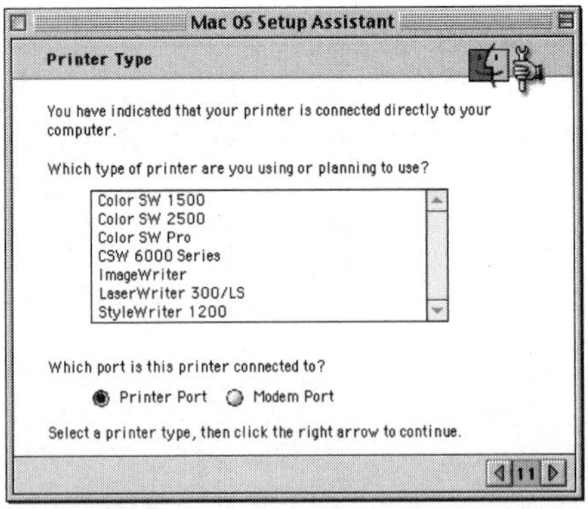

**Figure 34** If your printer is directly connected to your computer, select the type of printer you have in this window.

SETTING PRINTER OPTIONS

**Figure 35** When the Mac OS Setup Assistant is finished asking for information, it displays this window.

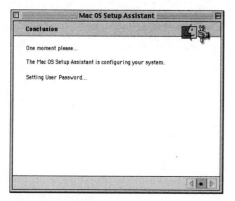

**Figure 36** The Conclusion window also indicates the configuration progress.

**Figure 37** Finally, the Conclusion window tells you when the configuration is done.

## To complete the setup process

1. Click the Go Ahead button in the Conclusion window of the Mac OS Setup Assistant (**Figure 35**).

2. Wait while the Mac OS Setup Assistant configures your system. The Conclusion window changes to indicate the configuration progress (**Figure 36**). When the configuration is complete, the Conclusion window tells you that the Mac OS Setup Assistant is done (**Figure 37**).

3. To stop configuring your computer, click the Quit button.

   *or*

   To go on to the Internet Setup Assistant, click the Continue button.

## ✔ Tips

- To check your settings one last time before they're written to your computer's configuration files, click the Show Details button (**Figure 35**). The Conclusion window changes to list all configuration options you entered or selected.

- If you have not installed the Internet Access component of Mac OS 8.6, the Continue button in the Conclusion window (**Figure 37**) will not appear.

- I explain how to use the Internet Setup Assistant in **Chapter 12**.

COMPLETING THE SETUP PROCESS

# FINDER BASICS

Finder

**Figure 1** The Finder is the program that provides a graphic user interface for working with files.

## The Finder & Desktop

The *Finder* (**Figure 1**) is a program that is part of Mac OS. It launches automatically when you start your computer.

The Finder provides a graphic user interface called the *Desktop* (**Figure 2**) that you can use to open, copy, delete, list, organize, and perform other operations on computer files.

This chapter provides important instructions for using the Finder and items that appear on the Mac OS Desktop. It's important that you understand how to use these basic Finder techniques, since you'll use them again and again every time you work with your computer.

Menu bar    Window    Desktop    Icons

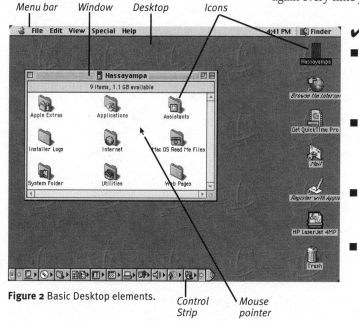

**Figure 2** Basic Desktop elements.    *Control Strip*    *Mouse pointer*

## ✔ Tips

- Do *not* move or delete the Finder! Doing so will prevent your computer from operating properly.

- You never have to manually launch the Finder; it always starts automatically.

- Under normal circumstances, you cannot Quit the Finder.

- If you're new to Mac OS, don't skip this chapter. It provides the basic information you'll need to use your computer successfully.

# The Mouse

Mac OS, like most graphic user interface systems, uses the mouse as an input device. There are several basic mouse techniques you must know to use your computer:

♦ **Point** to a specific item on screen.

♦ **Click** an item to select it.

♦ **Double-click** an item to open it.

♦ **Drag** to move an item or select multiple items.

## ✔ Tips

■ Some computers use either a trackball or a trackpad instead of a mouse.

■ You can customize the way the mouse works with the Mouse control panel, which I tell you about in **Chapter 12**.

## To point

1. Move the mouse on the work surface or mouse pad.

   *or*

   Use your fingertips to move the ball of the trackball.

   *or*

   Move the tip of *one* finger (usually your forefinger) on the surface of the trackpad.

   The mouse pointer, which usually looks like an arrow (**Figure 3**), moves on your computer screen.

2. When the tip of the mouse pointer's arrow is on the item to which you want to point (**Figure 4**), stop moving it.

## ✔ Tip

■ The tip of the mouse pointer is its "business end."

**Figure 3** The mouse pointer usually looks like an arrow pointer when you are working in the Finder.

System Folder

**Figure 4** Move the mouse pointer so the arrow's tip is on the item to which you want to point.

**Figure 5**
Click to select
an icon...

**Figure 6** ...or an item in a list.

**Figure 7**
Drag to move
items like folders.

## To click

1.  Point to the item on which you want to click.

2.  Press (and release) the mouse button once. The item on which you clicked becomes selected (**Figures 5** and **6**).

## To double-click

1.  Point to the item on which you want to double-click.

2.  Press (and release) the mouse button twice quickly. The item on which you double-clicked opens.

## ✔ Tip

■ It is vital that you keep the mouse pointer still while double-clicking. If you move the mouse pointer during the double-click process, you may move the item instead of double-clicking it.

## To drag

1.  Point to the item you want to drag.

2.  Press the mouse button down.

3.  While holding the mouse button down, move the mouse pointer. The item you are dragging moves (**Figure 7**).

**USING THE MOUSE**

# Menus

The Finder—and just about every other Mac OS-compatible program—offers menus full of options. There are four types of menus in Mac OS 8.6:

◆ A **pull-down menu** appears on the menu bar at the top of the screen (**Figure 8**).

◆ A **submenu** appears when a menu option with a right-pointing triangle is selected (**Figure 9**).

◆ A **pop-up menu**, which displays a pair of triangles (or double arrow), appears within a window (**Figures 10** and **11**).

◆ A **contextual menu** appears when you hold down (Control) while clicking on an item (**Figure 12**).

## ✔ Tips

■ A menu option followed by an ellipsis (…) (**Figure 8**) will display a dialog box when chosen. I tell you about dialog boxes in this **Chapter 5**.

■ A menu option that is dimmed or gray (**Figure 8**) cannot be chosen. The commands that are available vary depending on what is selected on the Desktop or in a window.

■ A menu option preceded by a check mark (**Figure 9**) is selected, or "turned on."

■ A menu option followed by a series of keyboard characters (**Figure 8**) has a keyboard command. I tell you about keyboard commands later in this chapter.

■ Contextual menus only display options that apply to the item to which you are pointing.

■ Depending on how menu preferences are set, a menu option should blink when chosen. You can set menu blinking preferences in the General Controls control panel, which I discuss in **Chapter 13**.

**Figure 8**
The menu bar offers pull-down menus.

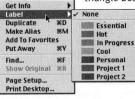

**Figure 9** A submenu appears when you select a menu option with a right-pointing triangle beside it.

**Figure 10** Pop-up menus can appear within dialog boxes.

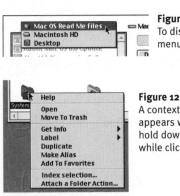

**Figure 11**
To display a pop-up menu, click it.

**Figure 12**
A contextual menu appears when you hold down (Control) while clicking.

**Figure 13** Point to the menu name.

**Figure 14**
Hold down the mouse
button or just click to
display the menu.

**Figure 15**
Drag to or just click
the menu option
you want.

## To use a menu

1. Point to the name of the menu (**Figure 13**).

2. Press and hold down the mouse button. The menu opens, displaying its options (**Figure 14**).

3. Drag to select the menu option you want (**Figure 15**).

4. Release the mouse button to choose the selected option. The menu disappears.

## ✔ Tips

- This is the standard way to choose an option from a menu. This method works in all versions of Mac OS.

- Throughout this book, I use the following notation to indicate menu commands: *Menu Name > Submenu Name* (if necessary) > *Command Name*. For example, to instruct you to choose the Essential command from the Label submenu under the File menu (**Figure 9**), I'd say, "choose File > Label > Essential."

## To use a sticky menu

1. Point to the name of the menu (**Figure 13**).

2. Click. The menu opens, displaying its options (**Figure 14**).

3. Point to the menu option you want (**Figure 15**).

4. Click to choose the selected option. The menu disappears.

## ✔ Tips

- This method of choosing a menu option works in Mac OS version 8 and later only.

- To close a sticky menu without choosing an option, click outside the menu.

- A sticky menu will close automatically by itself if no option is chosen after a few seconds.

USING MENUS

## To use a contextual menu

1. Point to the item on which you want to act.

2. Press and hold down [Control]. A tiny contextual menu icon appears beside the mouse pointer (**Figure 16**).

3. Press and hold down the mouse button.

    *or*

    Click.

    A contextual menu appears at the item (**Figure 17**).

4. Drag to select the menu option you want (**Figure 18**). Then release the mouse button to choose the option.

    *or*

    Click the menu option you want (**Figure 18**).

## To use a keyboard command

1. Hold down the modifier key(s) in the sequence. This is usually [⌃ ⌘] but can be [Option], [Control], or [Shift].

2. Press the letter, number, or symbol key in the sequence.

For example, to choose the Open command, which can be found under the File menu (**Figure 15**), hold down [⌃ ⌘] and press [O].

## ✔ Tips

■ You can learn keyboard commands by observing the key sequences that appear to the right of some menu commands (**Figure 8**).

■ Some commands include more than one modifier key. You must hold all modifier keys down while pressing the letter, number, or symbol key for the keyboard command.

■ I provide a list of all Finder keyboard commands in **Appendix A**.

**Figure 16**
Hold down [Control] while pointing to an item.

System Folder

**Figure 17**
A contextual menu appears when you click.

**Figure 18**
Drag or click to select the option you want.

Figure 19 Application icons.

Figure 20 Document icons, including two different SimpleText documents and a PageMaker document.

Figure 21 Folder icons.

Figure 22 Icons for System files including an extension, a control panel, and a printer driver (or Chooser extension).

Figure 23 Four different disk icons: hard disk, Mac OS floppy disk, PC floppy disk, and CD-ROM disc.

Figure 24 A Desktop printer icon and the Trash icon when the Trash is empty and full.

# Icons

Mac OS uses icons to graphically represent files and other items on the Desktop or within Finder windows:

◆ **Applications (Figure 19)** are programs you use to get work done. I tell you more about working with applications in **Chapter 5**.

◆ **Documents (Figure 20)** are the files created by applications. I tell you more about working with documents in **Chapter 5**.

◆ **Folders (Figure 21)** are used to organize files. I tell you more about using folders in **Chapters 3** and **4**.

◆ **System files (Figure 22)**, such as control panels, extensions, and drivers, are used by Mac OS to add capabilities to your computer and operate peripherals. I tell you about various System files in **Chapter 13** and elsewhere throughout this book.

◆ **Disks (Figure 23)** are used to store files. I tell you about working with disks in **Chapter 3**.

◆ **Desktop printers (Figure 24)** let you print documents from the Finder and check the status of documents scheduled to be printed. I tell you about printing in **Chapter 10**.

◆ The **Trash (Figure 24)** is for discarding items you no longer want. I explain how to use the Trash in **Chapter 3**.

## ✔ Tip

■ Icons can appear a number of different ways, depending on the view and view options chosen for a window. I tell you about windows later in this chapter and about views in **Chapter 3**.

ICONS

## To select an icon

Click the icon that you want to select. The icon darkens and its name becomes highlighted (**Figure 25**).

### ✔ Tip

■ You can also select an icon in an active window by pressing the keyboard key for the first letter of the icon's name or by pressing [Tab], [Shift][Tab], [←], [→], [↑], or [↓] until the icon is selected.

## To deselect an icon

Click anywhere in the window or on the Desktop other than on the selected icon.

### ✔ Tips

■ If you deselect an icon by clicking another icon, the originally selected icon is deselected and the icon you clicked becomes selected instead.

■ I tell you more about windows later in this chapter.

## To select multiple icons by clicking

1. Click the first icon that you want to select.

2. Hold down [Shift] and click on another icon that you want to select (**Figure 26**).

3. Repeat step 2 until all icons that you want to select have been selected.

### ✔ Tip

■ Icons that are part of a multiple selection must be in the same window. I tell you about windows later in this chapter.

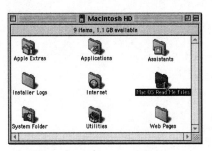

**Figure 25** To select an icon, click it.

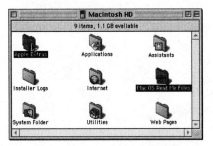

**Figure 26** Hold down [Shift] while clicking other icons to add them to a multiple selection.

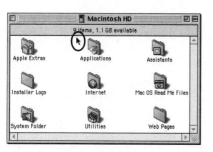

**Figure 27** Position the mouse pointer above and to the left of the first icon that you want to select.

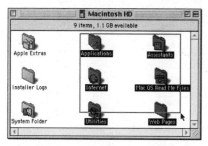

**Figure 28** Drag to draw a selection box around the icons that you want to select.

**Figure 29** Release the mouse button to complete the selection.

**Figure 30**
Choose Select All from the Edit menu.

## To select multiple icons by dragging

1. Position the mouse pointer slightly above and to the left of the first icon in the group that you want to select (**Figure 27**).

2. Press the mouse button down, and drag diagonally across the icons you want to select. A gray border appears to indicate the selection area, and the items within it become selected (**Figure 28**).

3. When all the icons that you want to select are included in the selection area, release the mouse button (**Figure 29**).

## ✔ Tip

- To select multiple icons by dragging, the icons must be adjacent.

## To select all icons in a window

Choose Edit > Select All (**Figure 30**).

*or*

Press ⌃ ⌘ A.

All icons in the active window are selected.

## ✔ Tip

- I tell you more about windows, including how to activate them, later in this chapter.

## To deselect one icon in a multiple selection

Hold down [Shift] while clicking the icon that you want to deselect. That icon is deselected while the others remain selected.

## To move an icon

1. Position the mouse pointer on the icon that you want to move (**Figure 31**).

2. Press the mouse button down, and drag the icon to the new location. As you drag, a shadowy image of the icon moves with the mouse pointer (**Figure 32**).

3. Release the mouse button when the icon is in the desired position. The icon moves (**Figure 33**).

## ✔ Tips

- You cannot drag to reposition icons within windows set to list view. I tell you about views in **Chapter 3**.

- You move icons to rearrange them in a window or on the Desktop, or to copy or move the items they represent to another folder or disk. I discuss copying and moving items in **Chapter 3**.

- You can also move multiple icons at once. Simply select the icons first, then position the mouse pointer on one of the selected icons and follow steps 2 and 3 above. All selected icons move together.

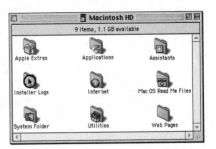

**Figure 31** Point to the icon that you want to move.

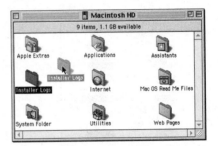

**Figure 32** Drag the icon to the new location.

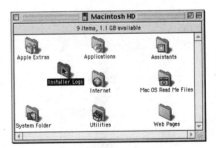

**Figure 33** When you release the mouse button, the icon moves.

**Figure 34** Select the icon.

**Figure 35** Choose Open from the File menu.

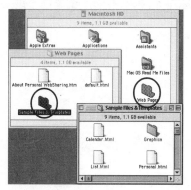

**Figure 36** Opening a folder icon opens a window that displays the contents of the folder.

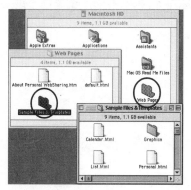

**Figure 37** Open folder icons appear shaded.

## To open an icon

1. Select the icon you want to open (**Figure 34**).

2. Choose File > Open (**Figure 35**) or press ⌃ ⌘ O.

*or*

Double-click the icon that you want to open.

## ✔ Tips

■ What happens when you open an icon depends on the type of icon you open. For example:

▲ Opening a folder icon opens a new Finder window that displays the contents of that folder (**Figure 36**). I tell you about windows later in this chapter.

▲ Opening an application icon launches the application so that you can work with it. I tell you about working with applications in **Chapter 5**.

▲ Opening a document icon launches the application that created that document and displays the document so you can view or edit it. I tell you about working with documents in **Chapter 5**.

▲ Opening a Desktop printer icon displays a list of files waiting to be printed so you can reschedule them or remove them from the print queue. I tell you about printing in **Chapter 10**.

▲ Opening the Trash displays items that will be deleted when you empty the Trash. I tell you about using and emptying the Trash in **Chapter 3**.

■ You can identify an open disk, folder, or application icon by its shaded appearance in a Finder window (**Figure 37**).

**OPENING ICONS**

# Windows

Mac OS makes extensive use of windows for displaying icons and other information in the Finder and documents in other applications. **Figures 38** and **39** show examples of Finder windows.

Each window includes a variety of controls you can use to manipulate it:

◆ The **title bar** displays the window's icon and name and can be used to move the window.

◆ The **close box** lets you close the window.

◆ The **zoom box** lets you toggle the window between full size and a custom size.

◆ The **collapse box** lets you toggle the window between collapsed and expanded views.

◆ The **size box** lets you resize the window by dragging.

◆ **Scroll bars** let you scroll the contents of the window into view.

◆ The **header** indicates the number of items in the window and the amount of space available on the disk.

◆ **Column headings** (in list view only) display the names of the columns and let you quickly sort by a column.

◆ **Sort direction button** (in list view only) enables you to change the sort direction to ascending or descending order.

## ✔ Tip

■ I tell you about views in **Chapter 3**.

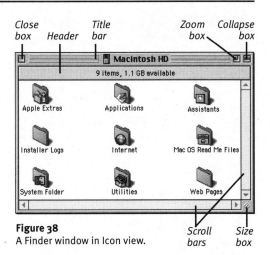

**Figure 38**
A Finder window in Icon view.

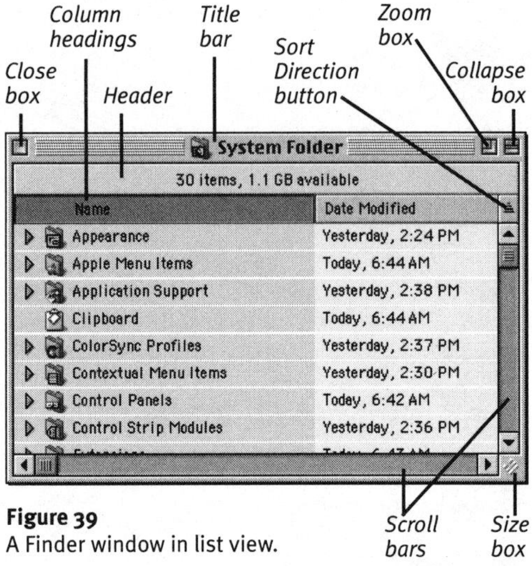

**Figure 39**
A Finder window in list view.

WINDOWS

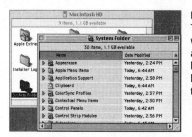

**Figure 40** The active window always has horizontal lines on its title bar.

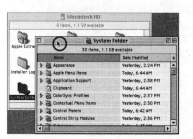

**Figure 41** Position the mouse pointer on the title bar.

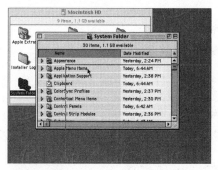

**Figure 42** As you drag, an outline of the window moves with the mouse pointer.

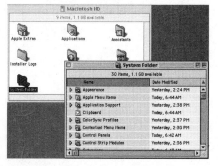

**Figure 43** When you release the mouse button, the window moves.

## To activate a window

Click anywhere in or on the window.

## ✔ Tips

- It's important to make sure that the window with which you want to work is open and active *before* using commands that work on the active window—like Print Window, Select All, and View menu options.

- You can distinguish between the active window and inactive windows by the appearance of their title bars; the active window's title bar always has horizontal lines (**Figure 40**).

- When two or more windows overlap, the active window will always be on top of the stack (**Figure 40**).

## To move a window

1. Position the mouse pointer on the window's title bar (**Figure 41**).

   *or*

   Position the mouse pointer on the border of the window.

2. Press the mouse button down and drag the window to a new location. As you drag, an outline of the window moves along with your mouse pointer (**Figure 42**).

3. When the outline of the window is in the desired position, release the mouse button. The window moves (**Figure 43**).

## ✔ Tip

- If you move a window to the very bottom of the screen, it becomes a pop-up window. I tell you more about pop-up windows in **Chapter 4**.

## To resize a window

1. Position the mouse pointer on the window's size box (**Figure 44**).

2. Press the mouse button down, and drag. As you drag, dotted lines indicating the right and bottom borders of the window move with the mouse pointer (**Figure 45**).

3. When the dotted lines indicate the desired borders for the window, release the mouse button. The window resizes (**Figure 46**).

## ✔ Tips

- The larger a window is, the more you can see inside it.

- By resizing and repositioning windows, you can see inside more than one window at a time. This comes in handy when moving or copying the icons for files and folders from one window to another. I tell you about moving and copying files and folders in **Chapter 3**.

**Figure 44**
Position the mouse pointer on the size box.

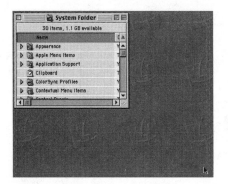

**Figure 45** As you drag, a dotted border moves with the mouse pointer.

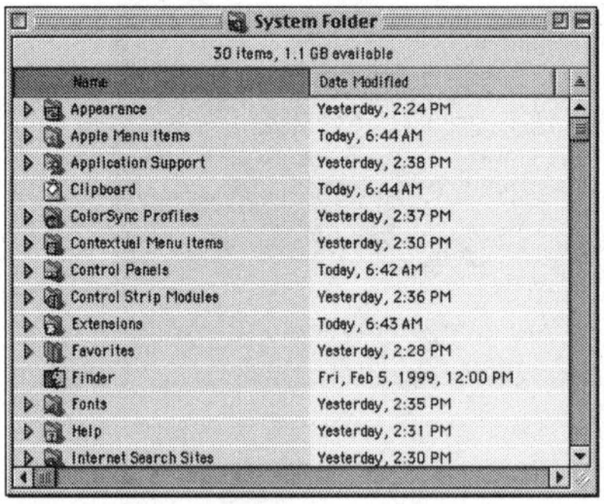

**Figure 46** When you release the mouse button, the window resizes.

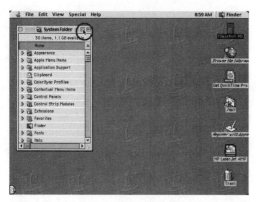

Figure 47 Click the window's zoom box...

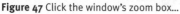

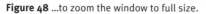

Figure 48 ...to zoom the window to full size.

Figure 49 Click on the collapse box...

Figure 50 ...to collapse the window so only its title bar shows.

## To zoom a window

Click the window's zoom box (**Figure 47**).

## ✔ Tips

- Each time you click the zoom box, the window's size toggles between full size (**Figure 48**) and the custom size you specified with the size box (**Figure 46**).

- The actual size of a window zoomed to full size varies based on its content. If a window contains only a few icons, zooming the window to full size will make it only as large as it needs to be to display the items it contains (**Figure 49**).

## To collapse or expand a window

Click the window's collapse box (**Figure 49**).

## ✔ Tips

- Each time you click the collapse box, the window either collapses to display just its title bar (**Figure 50**) or expands to display its contents (**Figure 49**).

- A collapsed window can be moved around the screen like any other window.

## To collapse or expand all open windows

Hold down (Option) while clicking the active window's collapse box (**Figure 49**).

## To scroll a window's contents

Click one of the scroll bar arrows (**Figure 51**) as follows:

◆ To scroll the window's contents up, click the down arrow on the vertical scroll bar.

◆ To scroll the window's contents down, click the up arrow on the vertical scroll bar.

◆ To scroll the window's contents to the left, click the right arrow on the horizontal scroll bar.

◆ To scroll the window's contents to the right, click the left arrow on the horizontal scroll bar.

## ✔ Tips

■ If you have trouble remembering which scroll arrow to click, think of it this way:

▲ Click down to see down.

▲ Click up to see up.

▲ Click right to see right.

▲ Click left to see left.

■ You can also scroll a window's contents by either clicking in the scroll bar between the scroll box and a scroll arrow or by dragging the scroll box to a new position on the scroll bar. Both of these techniques enable you to scroll a window's contents more quickly.

■ If all of a window's contents are displayed, you will not be able to scroll the window. A window that cannot be scrolled will have flat or empty looking scroll bars without scroll boxes (**Figure 49**).

■ You can change the appearance and functionality of scroll bars with the Appearance control panel, which I discuss in **Chapter 13**.

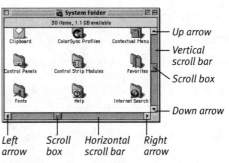

**Figure 51** Scroll bars, scroll bar arrows, and scroll boxes.

**Figure 52** Click in the window's close box.

**Figure 53**
Choose Close
Window from
the File menu.

## To close a window

Click the window's close box (**Figure 52**).

*or*

Choose File > Close Window (**Figure 53**).

*or*

Press ⌘ W.

## To close all open windows

Hold down Option while clicking the active window's close box (**Figure 52**).

*or*

Hold down Option while choosing File > Close Window (**Figure 53**).

*or*

Press ⌘ Option W.

## To automatically close the active window when you open an icon within it

1. Select the icon that you want to open.

2. Hold down Option while choosing File > Open (**Figure 35**).

   *or*

   Press ⌘ Option O.

*or*

Hold down Option while double-clicking the icon that you want to open.

# Sleeping, Restarting, & Shutting Down

The Special menu (**Figure 54**) offers several options that change the work state of your computer:

◆ **Sleep** puts the computer into a state where it uses very little power. The screen goes blank and the hard disk may stop spinning.

◆ **Restart** instructs the computer to shut down and immediately start back up.

◆ **Shut Down** closes all open documents and programs, clears memory, and either cuts power to the computer or tells you that it's safe to turn off the power switch.

## ✔ Tips

■ You can view a dialog box with buttons for Restart, Sleep, and Shut Down commands (**Figure 55**) by pressing the Power key (◁). This feature, however, does not work with all Mac OS-computer models.

■ The Energy Saver control panel, which I tell you about in **Chapter 13**, can automatically put a computer to sleep or shut it down after a specific period of inactivity.

■ Do *not* restart or shut down a computer by simply flicking off the power switch. Doing so prevents the computer from properly closing files, which may result in file corruption and related problems.

**Figure 54**
Three commands under the Special menu let you change the work state of your computer.

**Figure 55** Pressing the Power key on some Mac OS computers displays a dialog box like this one.

## To put your computer to sleep

Choose Special > Sleep (**Figure 54**).

*or*

1. Press ◁.

2. In the dialog box that appears (**Figure 55**), click Sleep or press Ⓢ.

## ✔ Tips

- Not all computers support sleep mode. If your computer does not support sleep mode, the Sleep command will not appear on the Special menu.

- When you put your computer to sleep, everything in memory is preserved. When you wake the computer, you can quickly continue working where you left off.

- Sleep mode is an effective way to conserve the battery life of a PowerBook without turning it off. I tell you more about special PowerBook considerations in **Appendix B**.

## To wake a sleeping computer

Press any keyboard key. Expect to wait from 10 to 30 seconds for the computer to fully wake.

## ✔ Tips

- It's much quicker to wake a sleeping computer than to restart a computer that has been shut down.

- On some computer models, pressing Caps Lock or certain other keys may not wake the computer. When in doubt, press a letter key—they always work.

PUTTING THE COMPUTER TO SLEEP

Chapter 2

## To restart your computer

Choose Special > Restart (**Figure 54**).

*or*

1. Press [◁].
2. In the dialog box that appears (**Figure 55**), click Restart or press [R].

### ✔ Tips

- Restarting the computer clears memory and reloads the System, Finder, and all system files.
- It's a good idea to restart your computer after a program unexpectedly quits so your computer's memory can start fresh.

## To shut down your computer

Choose Special > Shut Down (**Figure 54**).

*or*

1. Press [◁].
2. In the dialog box that appears (**Figure 55**), click Shut Down or press [S].

   *or*

   Press [Return] or [Enter].

### ✔ Tip

- On most computers, the Shut Down command will cut power to the computer as part of the shut down process. If it doesn't, a dialog box will appear on screen, telling you it's safe to turn off your computer. You can then use the power switch to cut power to the computer.

RESTARTING & SHUTTING DOWN

# FILE MANAGEMENT

## File Management

In Mac OS, you use the Finder to organize and manage your files.

- ◆ View the contents of your disks in windows in a variety of ways.

- ◆ Automatically sort items by name, kind, creation date, or other criteria in ascending or descending order.

- ◆ Assign colored labels to items.

- ◆ Rename items.

- ◆ Create folders to store related items.

- ◆ Move items stored on disk to organize them so they're easy to find and back up.

- ◆ Copy items to other disks to back them up or share them with others.

- ◆ Delete items you no longer need.

- ◆ Mount and eject disks.

- ◆ Format and erase floppy disks.

## ✔ Tip

- ■ If you're brand new to Mac OS, be sure to read the information in **Chapter 2** before working with this chapter. That chapter contains information and instructions about techniques that are used throughout this chapter.

# Views

Every Finder window's contents can be viewed a variety of ways:

◆ **As Icons** displays the window's contents as small or large icons (**Figure 1**).

◆ **As Buttons** displays the window's contents as clickable buttons (**Figure 2**).

◆ **As List** displays the window's contents as a sorted list (**Figure 3**).

In addition to setting a specific view for a Finder window, you can use the View Options dialog box (**Figures 6**, **7**, and **9**) to specify view options that fine tune the view.

## ✔ Tip

■ Button view works a little differently than icon and list views. I tell you about working with button view a little later in this chapter.

## To change a window's view

**1.** Activate the window whose view you want to change.

**2.** Choose the view option you want from the View menu (**Figure 4**). The view of the active window changes.

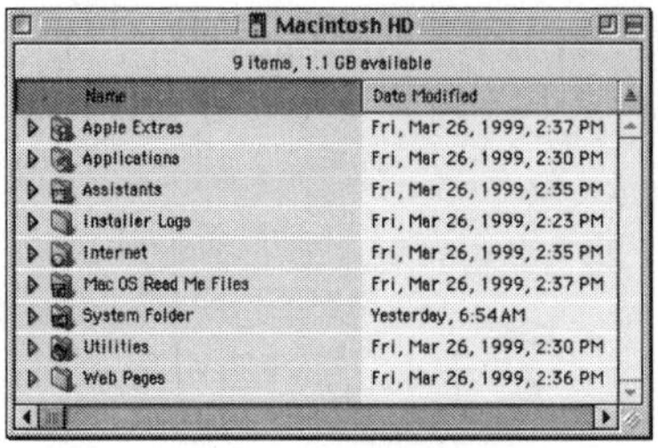

## ✔ Tips

■ Commands on the View menu (**Figure 4**) work on the active window only.

■ A check mark appears on the View menu beside the name of the view currently applied to the active window (**Figure 4**).

■ You can set the view for each window individually.

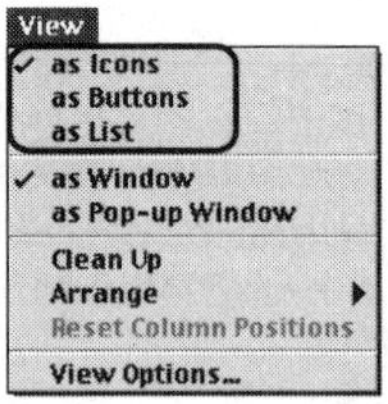

**Figure 1**
You can display a window's contents as icons...

**Figure 2**
...as clickable buttons...

**Figure 3**
...or as a list.

**Figure 4**
Choose one of the three window content view options from the View menu.

**Figure 5**
Choose View
Options from
the View menu.

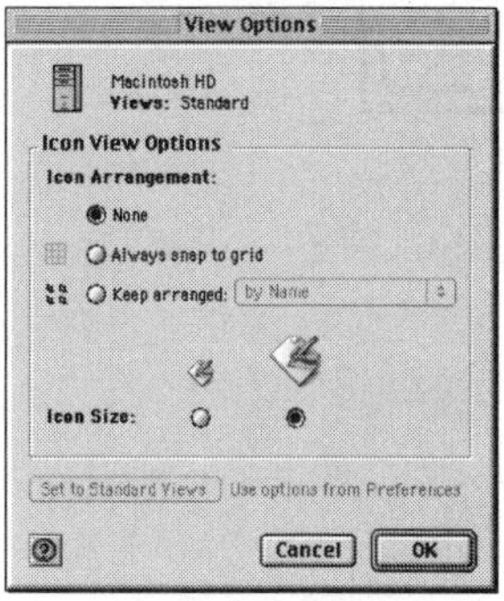

**Figure 6**
The View
Options dialog
box for an icon
view window.

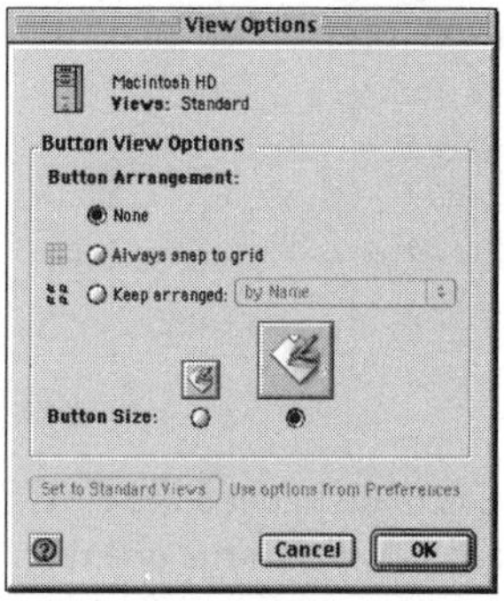

**Figure 7**
The View
Options dialog
box for a button
view window.

**Figure 8**
Use the Keep arranged
pop-up menu to
choose an automatic
arrangement option.

## To set View Options for icon or button view

1. Activate a window displayed in icon view (**Figure 1**) or button view (**Figure 2**).

2. Choose View > View Options (**Figure 5**). The View Options dialog box for icon view (**Figure 6**) or button view (**Figure 7**) appears.

3. Select an Icon Arrangement or Button Arrangement option:

   ▲ To remove any automatic icon or button arrangement, click the None radio button.

   ▲ To force icons or buttons to snap to an invisible grid within the window, click the Always snap to grid radio button.

   ▲ To automatically keep icons or buttons arranged in a certain order, turn on the Keep arranged radio button. Then choose an option from the pop-up menu beside it (**Figure 8**).

4. Select an Icon Size or Button Size option by clicking the radio button beneath the size you want.

5. Click OK to accept your changes.

## ✔ Tips

■ You can restore the window's settings to the standard settings for all windows by clicking the Set to Standard Views button. I explain how to set standard view options when I tell you about the Preferences window in **Chapter 4**.

■ You can set grid spacing options in the Preferences window, which I tell you about in **Chapter 4**.

■ I provide more details about working with dialog boxes in **Chapter 5**.

## To set View Options for list view

1. Activate a window displayed in list view
   (**Figure 3**).

2. Choose View > View Options (**Figure 5**).
   The View Options dialog box for list view
   appears (**Figure 9**).

3. To display the date in relative terms (that
   is, using the words "today" and "yesterday"),
   make sure the Use relative date check box
   is turned on.

4. To display the total disk space occupied by
   the contents of folders in the list, make
   sure the Calculate folder sizes check box is
   turned on.

5. Select the columns you want to appear in
   list view by turning Show Columns check
   boxes on or off:

   ▲ **Date Modified** is the date and time an
     item was last changed.

   ▲ **Date Created** is the date and time an
     item was first created.

   ▲ **Size** is the amount of disk space the
     item occupies.

   ▲ **Kind** is the type of item. I tell you
     about types of icons in **Chapter 2**.

   ▲ **Label** is the label assigned to the item.
     I tell you about labels later in this
     chapter.

   ▲ **Comments** is the information you
     entered in the comments field of the
     Info window. I tell you about the Info
     window in **Chapter 4**.

   ▲ **Version** is the item's version number.

6. Select an Icon Size option by clicking the
   radio button beneath the size you want.

7. Click OK to accept your changes.

**Figure 9**
The View
Options dialog
box for a list
view window.

## ✔ Tips

■ Turning on the Calculate folder sizes check
  box in step 4 could slow down the opening
  of list view windows.

■ You can restore the window's settings to
  the standard settings for all windows by
  clicking the Set to Standard Views button. I
  explain how to set standard view options
  when I tell you about the Preferences
  window in **Chapter 4**.

■ I provide more details about working with
  dialog boxes in **Chapter 5**.

**Figures 10 & 11**
Point to the *name* of the
button (left). When you
click, the button is
selected (right).

Apple Extras

Apple Extras

**Figure 12** Drag a button's name to move the button.

**Figure 13** When you release the mouse button, the button moves to its new position.

**Figure 14**
Choose Open
from the File
menu.

# Button View

Designed for novices and to give the Finder a more user-friendly look, button view works a bit differently from icon and list views. Here's a summary of the differences.

## To select a button

Click the name of the button (**Figure 10**). The button becomes selected (**Figure 11**).

## To move a button

1. Position the mouse pointer on the button name (**Figure 10**)—*not* the button itself.

2. Press the mouse button down and drag the button to a new position. As you drag, the shadow of the button moves with the mouse pointer (**Figure 12**).

3. Release the mouse button to complete the move (**Figure 13**).

## To open a button

Click the button once.

*or*

1. Select the button that you want to open (**Figure 11**).

2. Choose File > Open (**Figure 14**).

   *or*

   Press ⌘O.

# Cleaning Up & Arranging Icons & Buttons

Even if you're not a neat freak, you'll like the automatic clean-up and arrangement features that are part of the Finder.

◆ **Clean Up** neatly arranges icons or buttons in the window's invisible grid.

◆ **Arrange** lets you specify the order in which icons or buttons should appear in the window.

## To clean up a window

1. Activate the window that you want to clean up (**Figure 15**).

2. Choose View > Clean Up (**Figure 16**). The icons move into empty slots in the window's invisible grid (**Figure 17**).

## ✔ Tips

■ To have an icon you are moving automatically move into an empty grid slot, hold down ⌃ ⌘ as you drag it. When you release the mouse button, the icon's position adjusts automatically.

■ You can set the grid spacing in the Preferences window, which I tell you about in **Chapter 4**.

## To arrange a window's contents

1. Activate the window whose contents you want to arrange (**Figure 17**).

2. Choose an option from the Arrange submenu under the View menu (**Figure 18**). The icons are sorted by the option you selected (**Figure 19**).

## ✔ Tip

■ You can specify a default arrangement order for the window in the View Options dialog box, which I tell you about earlier in this chapter.

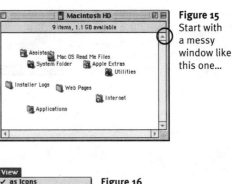

**Figure 15**
Start with a messy window like this one...

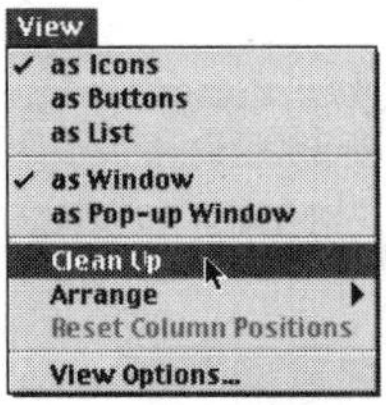

**Figure 16**
...then choose Clean Up from the View menu.

**Figure 17**
The icons are moved into empty slots of the window's invisible grid.

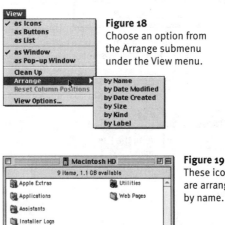

**Figure 18**
Choose an option from the Arrange submenu under the View menu.

**Figure 19**
These icons are arranged by name.

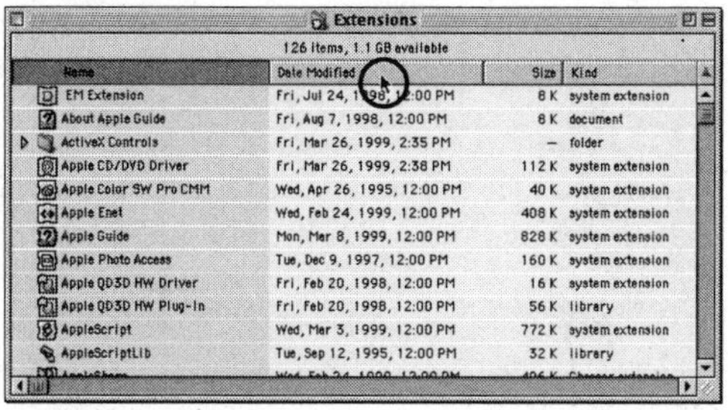

**Figure 20** Point to the heading for the column by which you want to sort.

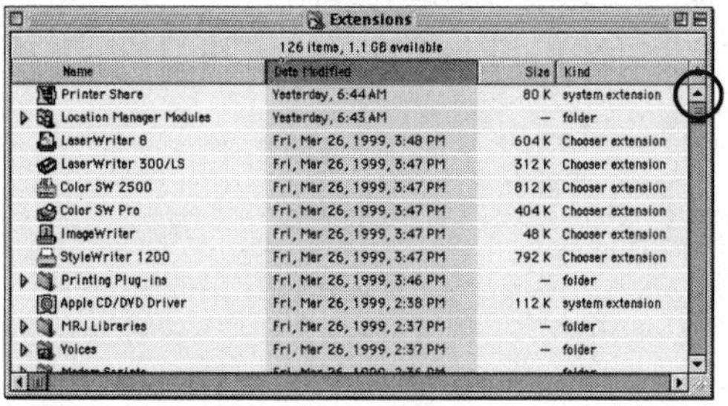

**Figure 21** The list view is sorted by the column you clicked.

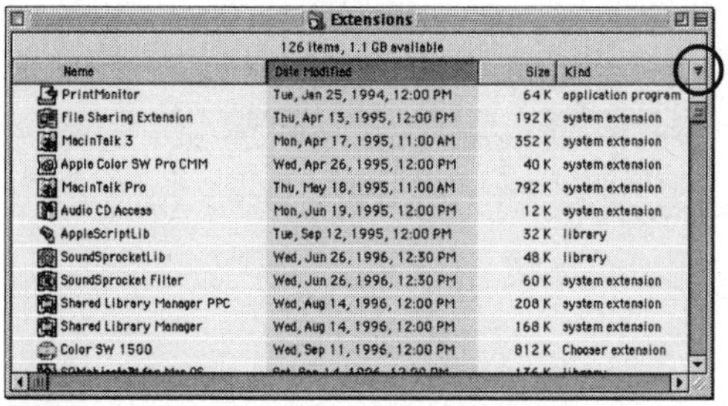

**Figure 22** Clicking the sort direction button reverses the sort order.

# List Views

A list view window can be modified in the following ways:

◆ Sort by any column in ascending or descending order.

◆ Change the width of columns.

◆ Change the order in which columns appear.

## To sort a window's contents

Click the column heading for the column by which you want to sort (**Figure 20**). The list is sorted by that column (**Figure 21**).

## ✔ Tips

■ You can always identify the column by which a list is sorted because its column heading is dark and its column is shaded (**Figures 20** and **21**).

■ To properly sort folders in a window sorted by size, you should turn on the Calculate folder sizes check box in the View Options dialog box (**Figure 9**) for that window. Otherwise, a folder has no size and is sorted to the top or bottom of the list.

## To reverse the sort order of a window's contents

Click the sort direction button at the top of the window's vertical scroll bar (**Figure 21**). The sort order reverses (**Figure 22**).

## ✔ Tip

■ When the sort direction button points up, the items are sorted in descending order. When it points down, the items are sorted in ascending order. You can see this in **Figures 21** and **22**.

## To change a column's width

1. Position the mouse pointer on the line between the heading for the column whose width you want to change and the column to its right. The mouse pointer turns into a vertical bar with two arrows (**Figure 23**).

2. Press the mouse button down and drag as follows:

   ▲ To make the column narrower, drag to the left (**Figure 24**).

   ▲ To make the column wider, drag to the right.

3. When the column is displayed at the desired width, release the mouse button.

### ✔ Tip

■ If you make a column too narrow to display all of its contents, information may be truncated or condensed.

## To change a column's position

1. Position the mouse pointer on the heading for the column you want to move.

2. Press the mouse button down and drag as follows:

   ▲ To move the column to the left, drag to the left (**Figure 25**).

   ▲ To move the column to the right, drag to the right.

   As you drag, the mouse pointer turns into a grabbing hand. Vertical lines indicate the column's position (**Figure 25**).

3. When the mouse pointer is on the column where you want to move the column you are dragging, release the mouse button. The column changes its position (**Figure 26**).

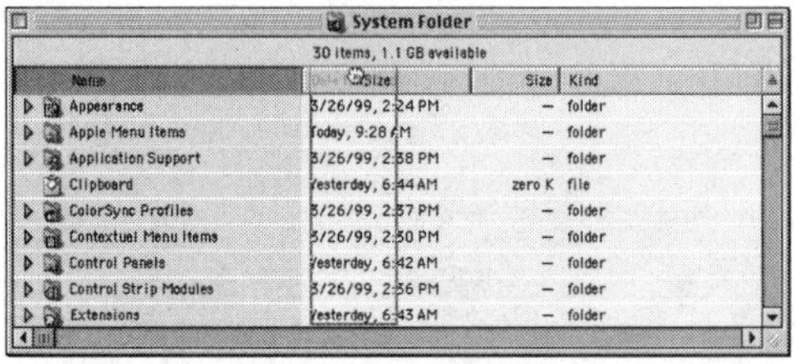

### ✔ Tip

■ You cannot change the position of the Name column.

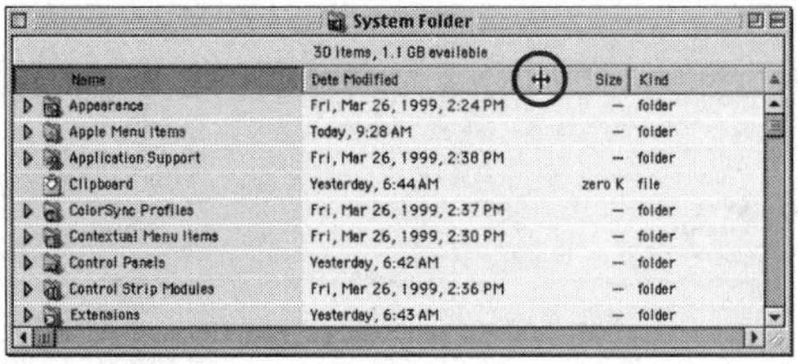

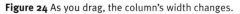

**Figure 23** Position the mouse pointer between two column headings.

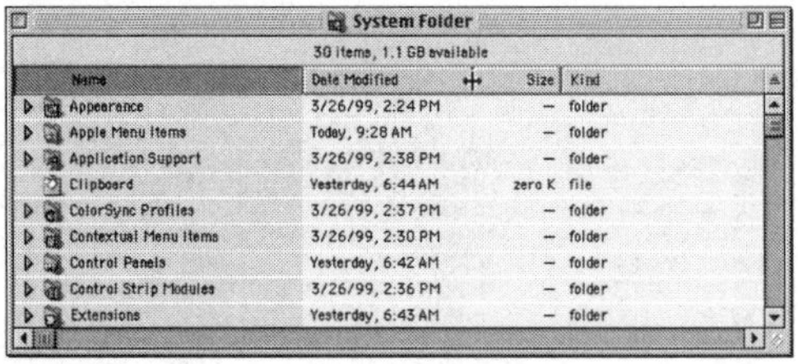

**Figure 24** As you drag, the column's width changes.

**Figure 25** Drag a column on top of the column where you want to move it.

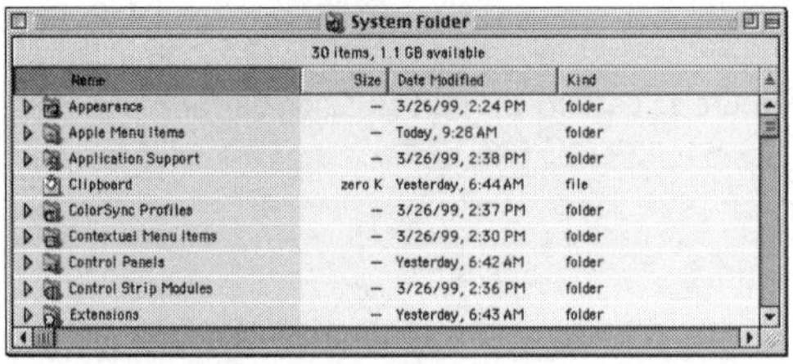

**Figure 26** When you release the mouse button, the column moves.

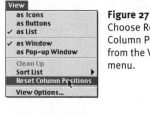

**Figure 27**
Choose Reset Column Positions from the View menu.

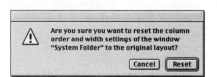

**Figure 28** Use this dialog box to confirm that you really do want to reset column width and positions.

## To reset the column widths & positions

1. Activate the window for which you want to reset column widths and positions.

2. Choose View > Reset Column Positions menu (**Figure 27**).

3. A dialog box like the one in **Figure 28** appears. Click the Reset button. The column widths and positions return to the default settings.

## ✔ Tips

■ Here are three things to keep in mind about the Reset Column Positions command:

▲ It works only on the active window.

▲ It resets both column widths and positions.

▲ It is only available if the active window's column widths, positions, or both have been changed.

# Labels

The label feature lets you assign a colored label to each icon. This makes it possible to:

◆ Visually identify items based on the color assigned.

◆ Arrange or sort items based on the label assigned.

## ✔ Tips

■ You can use labels to organize icons by project or importance.

■ I tell you how to arrange icon and button view windows and how to sort list view windows earlier in this chapter.

## To assign a label to an icon

1. Select the icon to which you want to assign a label (**Figure 29**).

2. Choose the desired label from the Labels submenu under the File menu (**Figure 30**).

## ✔ Tips

■ To see the color assigned to the selected icon, deselect the icon (**Figure 31**).

■ As shown in **Figures 29** and **31**, you can assign a label to more than one icon at a time.

■ You can also assign a label to an icon in the Info window, which I tell you about in **Chapter 4**.

■ You can use the Preferences window to change the labels and colors that are associated with each command in the Labels submenu. I tell you how in **Chapter 4**.

## To remove a label from an icon

1. Select the icon from which you want to remove a label.

2. Choose File > Labels > None (**Figure 32**).

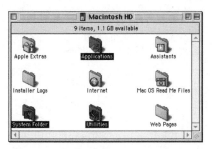

**Figure 29** Select the icon(s) to which you want to apply a color or label.

**Figure 30** Choose a label from the Labels submenu.

**Figure 31** The color of the selected icon(s) changes.

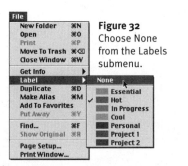

**Figure 32** Choose None from the Labels submenu.

ASSIGNING LABELS TO ICONS

**Figure 33**
Point to the name of
the icon.

**Figure 34**
When you click, an edit box
appears around the name.

**Figure 35**
Type a new name
for the icon.

**Figure 36**
When you press Return,
the name changes.

# Icon Names

Mac OS is very flexible when it comes to
names for files, folders, and disks.

◆ A file or folder name can be up to 31
characters long. A disk name can be up to
27 characters long.

◆ A name can contain any character except a
colon (:).

This makes it easy to give your files, folders,
and disks names that make sense to you.

## ✔ Tips

■ Normally, you name documents when you
save them. I tell you how to save documents
in **Chapter 5**.

■ No two documents in the same window
can have the same name.

■ I tell you about disks later in this chapter.

## To rename an icon

1. Point to the name of the icon (**Figure 33**)
and click. After a brief pause, an edit box
appears around the name and the name
becomes highlighted (**Figure 34**).

2. Type the new name. The text you type
automatically overwrites the highlighted
text (**Figure 35**).

3. Press Return or Enter or click anywhere
else in the window or on the Desktop. The
icon is renamed (**Figure 36**).

## ✔ Tips

■ Not all icons can be renamed. If the edit
box does not appear around an icon name
(**Figure 34**), that icon cannot be renamed.

■ Renaming some folders may remove their
special icons (**Figures 33** and **36**).

■ You can also rename an icon in the Info
window, which I tell you about in **Chapter 4**.

**RENAMING ICONS**

# Folders

Mac OS uses folders to organize files and other folders on disk. You can create a folder, give it a name that makes sense to you, and move files and other folders into it. It's a lot like organizing paper files and folders in a file cabinet.

## ✔ Tips

- A folder can contain any number of files and other folders.

- It's a very good idea to use folders to organize the files on your hard disk. Imagine a file cabinet without file folders—that's how your hard disk would appear if you never used folders to keep your files tidy.

## To create a folder

1. Choose File > New Folder (**Figure 37**).

   *or*

   Press ⌃ ⌘ N.

   A new untitled folder (**Figure 38**) appears in the active window.

2. While the edit box appears around the new folder's name (**Figure 38**), type a name for it (**Figure 39**) and press Return.

## ✔ Tips

- You can rename a folder the same way you rename any other icon. I tell you how on the previous page.

- I tell you more about windows, including how to activate them, in **Chapter 2**.

**Figure 37**
Choose New Folder from the File menu.

**Figure 38**
A new folder appears.

**Figure 39**
Enter a name for the folder while the edit box appears around it.

# Moving & Copying Items

In addition to moving icons around within a window or on the Desktop, which I discuss in **Chapter 2**, you can move or copy items to other locations on the same disk or to other disks by dragging them:

◆ When you drag an item to a location on the same disk, the item is moved to that location.

◆ When you drag an item to a location on another disk, the item is copied to that location.

◆ When you hold down (Option) while dragging an item to a location on the same disk, the item is copied to that location.

I provide instructions for of all these techniques, as well as instructions for duplicating items, on the next few pages.

## ✔ Tips

■ You can move or copy more than one item at a time. Begin by selecting all the items that you want to move or copy, then drag any one of them to the destination. All items will be moved or copied.

■ You can continue working with the Finder—even start more copy jobs—while a copy job is in progress.

## To move an item to another location on the same disk

1. Drag the icon for the item that you want to move as follows:

   ▲ To move the item into a specific folder on the disk, drag the icon to the icon for the folder. The icon becomes highlighted when the mouse pointer moves over it (**Figure 40**).

   ▲ To move the item into a specific window on the disk, drag the icon into the window (**Figure 41**).

2. Release the mouse button. The item moves.

## ✔ Tips

■ If the destination location is on another disk, the item you drag will be copied rather than moved. You can always delete the original after the copy is made. I tell you how to delete items later in this chapter.

■ You can also move a disk or folder whose window is open by dragging the icon in the title bar of the open window (**Figure 42**). This feature works with Mac OS 8.5 and later only.

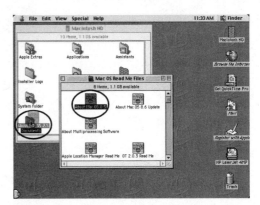

**Figure 40** Drag the icon onto the icon for the folder to which you want to move it...

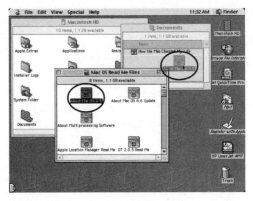

**Figure 41** ...or drag the icon into the window in which you want to move it.

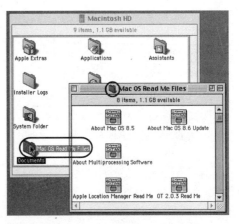

**Figure 42** You can drag a window's title bar icon to move a disk or folder whose window is open.

MOVING ITEMS TO ANOTHER DISK LOCATION

**Figure 43** Drag the icon to the destination disk's icon...

**Figure 44** ...or to an open window on the destination disk...

**Figure 45** ...or to a folder icon in a window on the destination disk.

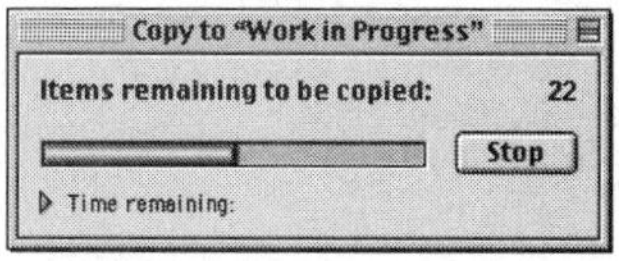

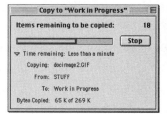

**Figure 46** A window like this indicates copy progress.

**Figure 47** You can expand the Copy window to show more information.

## To copy an item to another disk

1. Drag the icon for the item that you want to copy as follows:

   ▲ To copy the item to the top (or *root*) level of a disk, drag the icon to the icon for the destination disk (**Figure 43**).

   ▲ To copy the item into a specific window on the disk, drag the icon into the window (**Figure 44**).

   ▲ To copy the item into a folder on the disk, drag the icon to the icon for the folder on the destination disk (**Figure 45**).

   When the item you are dragging moves on top of the destination location, a plus sign appears beside the mouse pointer. If the destination is an icon, the icon becomes highlighted.

2. Release the mouse button. A Copy status window like the one in **Figure 46** appears. When it disappears, the copy operation is complete.

## ✔ Tips

■ You can also copy a disk or folder whose window is open by dragging the icon in the title bar of the open window.

■ You can expand the Copy status window (**Figure 46**) to show more information (**Figure 47**). Simply click the right-pointing triangle near the bottom of the window. You can collapse the window by clicking the triangle again.

■ You cannot copy items to a disk that is write protected. I tell you about write-protecting disks later in this chapter.

## To copy an item to another location on the same disk

1. Hold down Option while dragging the icon for the item that you want to copy onto a folder icon (**Figure 48**) or into a window (**Figure 49**).

   When the mouse pointer on the item you are dragging moves on top of the destination location a plus sign appears beside it. If the destination is an icon, the icon becomes highlighted.

2. Release the mouse button. A Copy status window like the one in **Figure 46** appears. When it disappears, the copy operation is complete.

## ✔ Tips

- When copying an item to a new location on the same disk, you *must* hold down Option. If you don't, the item will be moved rather than copied.

- You can expand the Copy status window (**Figure 46**) to show more information (**Figure 47**). Simply click the right-pointing triangle near the bottom of the window. You can collapse the window by clicking the triangle again.

## To duplicate an item

1. Select the item that you want to duplicate.

2. Choose File > Duplicate (**Figure 50**)

   *or*

   Press ⌘ ⌘ D.

*or*

Hold down Option while dragging the item that you want to duplicate to a different location in the same window.

A copy of the item you duplicated appears beside the original. The word *copy* appears at the end of the file name (**Figure 51**).

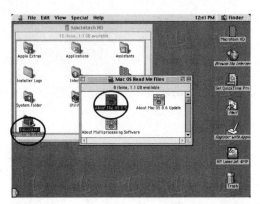

**Figure 48** Hold down Option while dragging the item onto a folder...

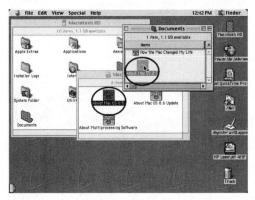

**Figure 49** ...or into a window on the same disk.

**Figure 50** Choose Duplicate from the File menu.

About Mac OS 8.5 copy

**Figure 51** A duplicate appears beneath the original.

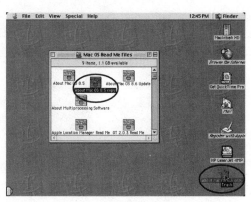

Figure 52 To move an item to the Trash, drag it there...

**Figure 53**
...or select the item and choose Move to Trash from the File menu.

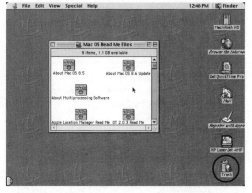

Figure 54 When an item has been moved to the Trash, the Trash icon looks full.

# The Trash & Deleting Items

The Trash is a special place on your hard disk where you place items you want to delete. Items in the Trash remain there until you empty the Trash, which permanently deletes them.

## To move an item to the Trash

1. Drag the icon for the item you want to delete to the Trash icon on the Desktop.

2. When the mouse pointer moves over the Trash icon, the Trash icon becomes selected (**Figure 52**). Release the mouse button.

*or*

1. Select the item that you want to delete.

2. Choose File > Move to Trash (**Figure 53**).

   *or*

   Press ⌃ ⌘ Delete.

## ✔ Tips

- The Trash icon's appearance indicates its status:
  - ▲ If the Trash is empty, the Trash icon looks like a covered trash can.
  - ▲ If the Trash is not empty, the Trash icon looks like an open trash can filled with papers (**Figure 54**).

- You can delete more than one item at a time. Begin by selecting all the items you want to delete, then drag any one of them to the Trash. All items will be moved to the Trash.

- Moving a disk icon to the Trash does not delete or erase it. Instead, it ejects or *unmounts* it. I tell you more about working with disks later in this chapter.

## To move an item out of the Trash

1. Open the Trash using one of these techniques:

   ▲ Double-click the Trash icon.

   ▲ Select the Trash icon, and choose File > Open (**Figure 14**) or press ⌘O.

   A Trash window opens (**Figure 55**).

2. Drag the item from the Trash window to the Desktop or to another window on your hard disk.

   *or*

   Select the item, and choose File > Put Away (**Figure 56**) or press ⌘Y.

## ✔ Tip

■ The Put Away command automatically moves a selected icon from the Desktop or Trash to the folder in which it was located before being moved to the Desktop or Trash.

## To empty the Trash

1. Choose Empty Trash from the Special menu (**Figure 57**).

2. A Trash warning dialog box like the one in **Figure 58** appears. Click OK to permanently remove all items that are in the Trash.

## ✔ Tips

■ You can disable the Trash warning dialog box by turning off the Warn before emptying check box in the Trash Info window (**Figure 59**). I tell you about the Info window in **Chapter 4**.

■ Technically speaking, it may be possible to recover accidently deleted items using utility software such as Norton Utilities for Macintosh. File recovery software is not included with Mac OS 8.6.

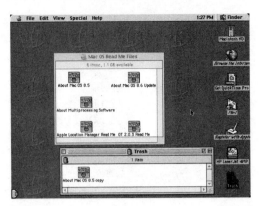

**Figure 55** Opening the Trash displays the Trash window.

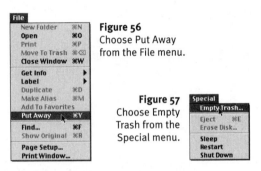

**Figure 56** Choose Put Away from the File menu.

**Figure 57** Choose Empty Trash from the Special menu.

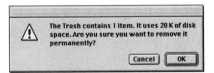

**Figure 58** The Trash warning dialog box asks you to confirm that you really do want to delete the items in the Trash.

**Figure 59** You can disable the Trash warning dialog box by turning off the Warn before emptying check box in the Trash Info window.

**Table 1**

| Terminology for Storage Media Capacity | | |
|---|---|---|
| TERM | ABBREVIATION | SIZE |
| byte | byte | 1 character |
| kilobyte | KB | 1,024 bytes |
| megabyte | MB | 1,024 KB |
| gigabyte | GB | 1,024 MB |

**Figure 60** The header in a disk window indicates how much space is available on the disk and whether the disk is write-protected or locked.

## ✔ Tips

- Don't confuse storage media with memory. The term *memory* usually refers to the amount of RAM in your computer, not disk space. I tell you about RAM in **Chapter 5**.

- At a minimum, all new Mac OS computers come with a hard disk and CD-ROM disc drives.

- Disk and other storage media drives can be internal (inside your computer) or external (attached to your computer by a cable).

- External storage devices must be properly connected and turned on *before* you start your computer or your computer may not recognize the device.

- Disk storage media capacity is specified in terms of bytes, kilobytes, megabytes, and gigabytes (**Table 1**).

# Disks & Other Storage Media

A Mac OS-compatible computer can read data from or write data to a wide range of storage media, including:

- **Hard disks**—high capacity magnetic media.

- **Floppy disks or diskettes**—low capacity, removable magnetic media.

- **CD-ROM, CD-R, and DVD discs**—high capacity, removable optical media.

- **Zip, Jaz, SyQuest, or other disks or cartridges**—high capacity, removable magnetic media.

To use storage media, it must be:

- **Mounted**—inserted, attached, or otherwise accessible to your computer.

- **Formatted** or **initialized**—specially prepared for use with your computer.

I tell you about all of these things on the following pages.

- You can tell how much space is available on a disk by checking the header in any of the disk's windows (**Figure 60**).

- If a disk is *write-protected* or *locked*, files cannot be saved or copied to it. To write protect a floppy disk, move the plastic tab on the back of the disk so it exposes the square hole beneath it. To unlock a disk, move the plastic tab on the back of the disk so it covers the square hole.

- All windows for a write-protected or locked disk display a padlock icon in the upper left corner (**Figure 60**).

- Unless you have a special CD-Recordable drive and recording software, you cannot write data to a CD-ROM disc.

# Mounting Disks

You *mount* a disk by inserting it in the disk drive so it appears on the Mac OS Desktop.

## ✔ Tips

- You must mount a disk to use it.

- I tell you more about mounting PC disks in **Chapter 9**.

- To learn how to mount disks that are not specifically covered in this book, consult the documentation that came with the disk drive.

- If you cannot successfully mount a CD-ROM disc or Zip disk by following these instructions, check to be sure the appropriate driver software has been installed and loaded. I tell you about driver software in **Chapter 13**.

## To mount a floppy disk

Insert the disk in the computer's floppy disk drive, label side up, metal side in. The disk's icon appears on the Desktop (**Figure 61**).

## To mount a CD-ROM disc

1. Follow the manufacturer's instructions to open the CD-ROM disc tray or eject the CD-ROM caddy.

2. Place the CD-ROM disc in the tray or caddy, label side up.

3. Gently push the tray or caddy into the CD-ROM drive. After a moment, the CD-ROM disc icon appears on the Desktop (**Figure 61**).

## To mount a Zip disk

Insert the disk in the Zip drive, label side up, metal side in. After a moment, the Zip disk icon appears on the Desktop (**Figure 61**).

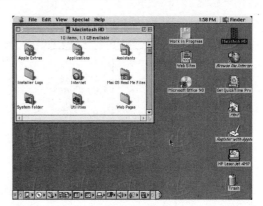

**Figure 61** Here's a Desktop with a hard disk, floppy disk, Zip disk, and CD-ROM disc mounted.

**Figure 62**
Select the disk, and then choose Eject from the Special menu...

**Figure 63**
...or drag the disk icon to the Trash.

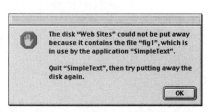

**Figure 64** A dialog box like this appears if you try to eject a disk that contains open files.

# Ejecting Disks

When you eject a disk, the disk is physically removed from the disk drive and its icon disappears from the Desktop.

## ✔ Tip

■ When the disk's icon disappears from the Desktop, it is said to be *unmounted*.

## To eject a disk

1. Click the disk's icon once to select it.
2. Choose Special > Eject (**Figure 62**) or press ⌘E.

   *or*

   Choose File > Put Away (**Figure 56**) or press ⌘Y.

*or*

1. Drag the disk's icon to the Trash.
2. When the mouse pointer moves over the Trash icon, it becomes highlighted (**Figure 63**). Release the mouse button.

## ✔ Tip

■ If you try to eject a disk that contains one or more files that are in use by your computer, a dialog box like the one in **Figure 64** appears. Click OK or press Return or Enter to dismiss the dialog box, then quit the open application. You should then be able to eject the disk. I tell you more about working with applications in **Chapter 5**.

# Formatting Disks

To use a floppy disk or other magnetic media, it must be *formatted* or *initialized* for the computer on which it will be used. A Mac OS computer can format disks for three different computer platforms:

◆ **Mac OS**—for Macintosh and Macintosh-compatible computers.

◆ **MS-DOS**—for Intel-based computer systems, including systems running Microsoft Windows and OS/2.

◆ **Pro-DOS**—for old Apple II computers.

## ✔ Tips

■ The terms *formatting* and *initializing* are sometimes used interchangeably. Although these two words don't mean exactly the same thing, they're close enough for our purposes.

■ Nowadays, most floppy disks come preformatted. If you buy preformatted disks, make sure they are formatted for Macintosh computers. Otherwise, you'll have to reformat them for use with your Mac OS system.

■ Formatting or initializing a disk erases all the information on the disk. If the disk is brand new, however, it probably doesn't have any information on it anyway.

■ High capacity magnetic media like hard disks, Zip and Jaz disks, and SyQuest cartridges must be formatted using special software that comes with the device drive. For example, you format an Apple hard disk with Drive Setup. For more information, consult the documentation that came with the drive. I tell you about Drive Setup in **Chapter 8**.

■ You cannot format a write-protected or locked disk.

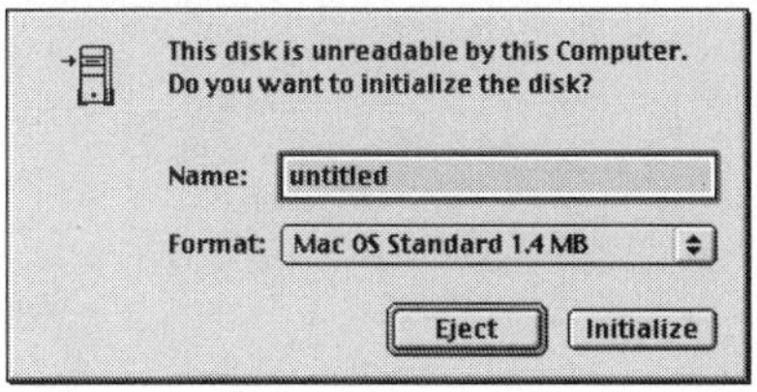

**Figure 65** When you insert a brand new unformatted disk, a dialog box like this appears.

**Figure 66** Enter a name for the disk in the Name edit box.

**Figure 67a & 67b** The options under the Format pop-up menu depend on the type of disk inserted: high density (top) or double-sided (bottom).

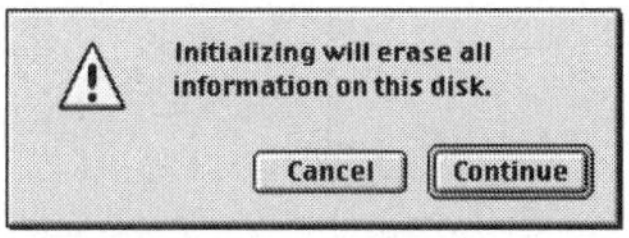

**Figure 68** A warning dialog box like this appears when you format a disk.

**Figure 69** Choose Erase Disk from the Special menu.

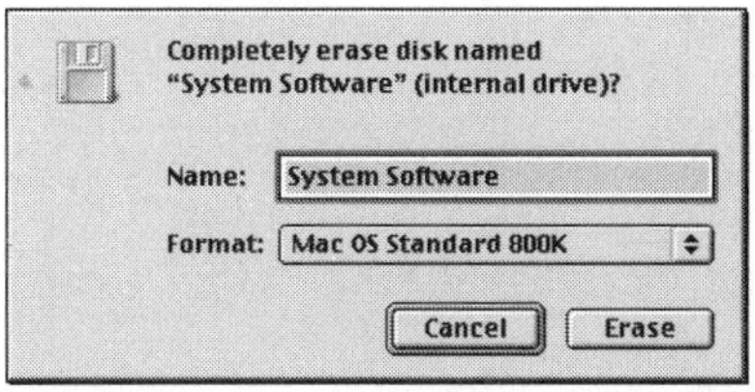

**Figure 70** This dialog box appears when you use the Erase Disk command to erase a selected disk.

## To format a disk for the first time

1. Insert the disk into the disk drive. A dialog box like the one in **Figure 65** appears.

2. Type a name for the disk in the Name edit box (**Figure 66**).

3. If desired, choose an option from the Format pop-up menu. As you can see in **Figures 67a** and **67b**, the options vary depending on the type of disk you inserted.

4. Click Initialize.

5. A warning dialog box like the one in **Figure 68** appears. If you're sure you want to initialize the disk, click Continue.

6. A status window appears while the disk is initialized and verified. Wait until it disappears. The icon for the formatted disk appears on the Desktop with the name you gave it.

## To erase a disk

1. Insert the disk into the disk drive. If the disk is readable, its icon appears on the Desktop.

2. If necessary, click the disk icon once to select it.

3. Choose Special > Erase Disk (**Figure 69**). A dialog box like the one in **Figure 70** appears.

4. If desired, type a new name for the disk in the Name edit box (**Figure 66**).

5. If desired, choose an option from the Format pop-up menu (**Figures 67a** and **67b**).

6. Click Erase.

7. A status window appears while the disk is erased and verified. Wait until it disappears. The icon for the disk appears on the Desktop with the name you gave it.

FORMATTING & ERASING DISKS

# ADVANCED FINDER TECHNIQUES

## Advanced Finder Techniques

In addition to the basic Finder and file management techniques covered in **Chapters 1** and **2**, Mac OS 8.6 offers more advanced techniques you can use to customize the Finder, work with windows, and manage files:

◆ Use the Preferences window to change the way the Finder looks and works.

◆ Use hierarchical outlines in list view windows.

◆ Use pop-up windows to keep frequently used windows handy but out of sight.

◆ Use spring-loaded folders to automatically open and then close multiple levels of folders while copying or moving items.

◆ Use aliases to make frequently used files easier to access without actually moving them.

◆ Use the Info window to learn more about an item or set options for it.

## ✔ Tips

■ If you're brand new to Mac OS, be sure to read the information in **Chapters 2** and **3** before working with this chapter. Those chapters contain information and instructions about techniques that are used throughout this chapter.

■ This chapter is especially useful for experienced Mac OS users since it goes beyond the basics with new or advanced Mac OS features.

# Finder Preferences

The Finder's Preferences window lets you customize many aspects of Finder appearance and operation. There are three categories of options:

◆ **General** (**Figure 3**) lets you set Simple Finder, Spring-loaded folder, and Grid Spacing options.

◆ **Views** (**Figure 7**) lets you set the standard view options for Icon, Button, and List view windows.

◆ **Labels** (**Figure 9**) lets you set the name and color of options on the Label submenu under the File menu.

## ✔ Tip

■ I tell you about more Mac OS 8.6 customization features in **Chapter 13**.

## To open the Preferences window

Choose Edit > Preferences (**Figure 1**). The Preferences window appears (**Figure 3**, **7**, or **9**).

## To close the Preferences window

Click the Preferences window's close box.

*or*

1. Activate the Preferences window.

2. Choose File > Close Window (**Figure 2**) or press ⌃ ⌘ W.

## ✔ Tip

■ Closing the Preferences window automatically saves all the settings within it.

**Figure 1**
Choose Preferences from the Edit menu.

**Figure 2**
Choose Close Window from the File menu.

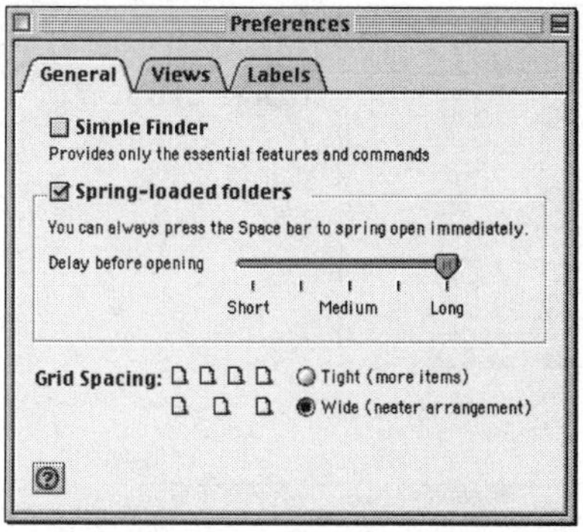

**Figure 3** The default settings in the General tab of the Preferences window.

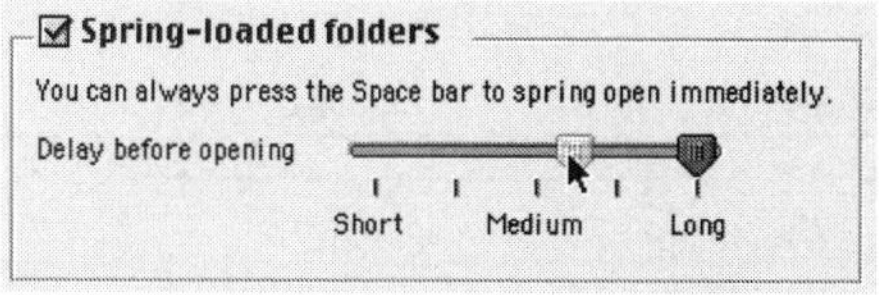

**Figure 4** Use the slider control to set the spring-loaded folder delay.

## To enable or disable Simple Finder

1. In the Preferences window, click the General tab to display its options (**Figure 3**).

2. To enable Simple Finder, turn on the Simple Finder check box.

   *or*

   To disable Simple Finder, turn off the Simple Finder check box.

## ✔ Tips

■ Simple Finder simplifies Finder menus by reducing the number of options.

■ The illustrations throughout this book were created with Simple Finder disabled.

■ **Appendix A** illustrates both standard Finder and Simple Finder menus.

## To set spring-loaded folder options

1. In the Preferences window, click the General tab to display its options (**Figure 3**).

2. To enable the spring-loaded folders feature, turn on the Spring-loaded folders check box. Then use the slider bar beside it (**Figure 4**) to set the delay from the time an item is dragged onto a folder to the time the folder opens.

   *or*

   To disable the spring-loaded folders feature, turn off the Spring-loaded folders check box.

## ✔ Tip

■ I tell you how to use spring-loaded folders later in this chapter.

## To set grid spacing

1. In the Preferences window, click the General tab to display its options (**Figure 3**).

2. For less space between icons or buttons in icon or button view windows (**Figure 5**), select the Tight radio button.

   *or*

   For more space between icons or buttons in icon or button view windows (**Figure 6**), select the Wide radio button.

## ✔ Tip

■ Wide grid spacing yields a neater arrangement because file names are less likely to overlap (**Figure 6**).

## To set standard view options

1. In the Preferences window, click the Views tab to display its options (**Figure 7**).

2. Select the type of view for which you want to set standard options from the pop-up menu (**Figure 8**).

3. Turn on check boxes for view options and select an Icon Size radio button as desired.

4. Repeat steps 2 and 3 for each type of view that you want to set.

## ✔ Tips

■ I tell you about the options for icon, button, and list views in **Chapter 3**.

■ The options you set in the Preferences window affect only those windows for which you did not set options in the View Options dialog box. I discuss the View Options dialog box in **Chapter 3**.

**Figure 5**
Tight spacing enables you to view more icons in less space.

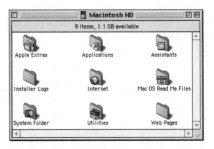

**Figure 6** Wide spacing offers a neater arrangement because names don't overlap.

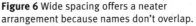

**Figure 7** The default settings in the Views tab of the Preferences window.

**Figure 8** Use this pop-up menu to select the type of view for which you want to set standard options.

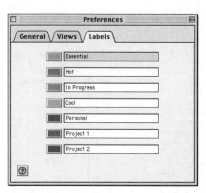

**Figure 9** The default settings in the Labels tab of the Preferences window.

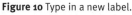

**Figure 10** Type in a new label.

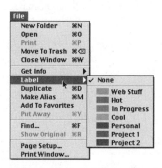

**Figure 11** The new label appears in the Label submenu under the File menu.

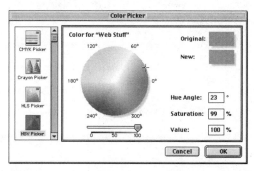

**Figure 12** The Color Picker dialog box lets you select a new color.

## To change the text of labels

1.  In the Preferences window, click the Labels tab to display its options (**Figure 9**).

2.  Drag the mouse pointer over the text in the edit box containing the label you want to change. This selects the text (**Figure 9**).

3.  Type the text you want to use as a label (**Figure 10**).

4.  Repeat steps 2 and 3 for each label that you want to change.

## ✔ Tip

- The changes you make are reflected in the Labels submenu under the File menu (**Figure 11**).

## To change the color of labels

1.  In the Preferences window, click the Labels tab to display its options (**Figure 9**).

2.  Click the color you want to change. The Color Picker dialog box appears (**Figure 12**).

3.  Click in the color wheel to select a new color. The color appears in the New sample area.

4.  If desired, use the slider near the bottom of the dialog box to change the brightness of the color.

5.  Click OK. The color you clicked in the Preferences window changes.

6.  Repeat steps 2 though 5 for each color that you want to change.

## ✔ Tip

- The changes you make are reflected in the Labels submenu under the File menu and in the color of the icons which have labels applied.

**SETTING LABEL PREFERENCES**

# Outlines in List View

Windows displayed in list view have a feature not found in icon or button views: They can display the contents of folders within the window as an outline (**Figure 13**).

## ✔ Tip

■ I tell you more about views in **Chapter 2**.

## To display a folder's contents

Click the right-pointing triangle beside the folder (**Figure 14**).

*or*

Click the folder once to select it, and press ⌃ ⌘ →.

The items within that folder are listed below it, slightly indented (**Figure 15**).

## ✔ Tip

■ As shown in **Figure 13**, you can use this technique to display multiple levels of folders in the same window.

## To hide a folder's contents

Click the down-pointing triangle beside the folder (**Figure 15**).

*or*

Click the folder once to select it, and press ⌃ ⌘ ←.

The outline collapses to hide the items in the folder (**Figure 14**).

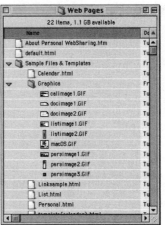

**Figure 13**
The outline feature lets you display the contents of folders within the same list view window.

*Click here to expand the outline*

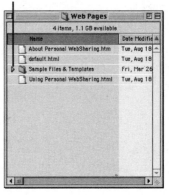

**Figure 14**
The contents of a folder can be hidden...

*Click here to collapse the outline*

**Figure 15**
...or displayed.

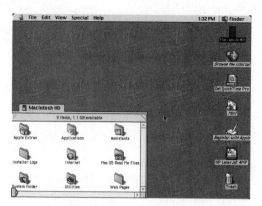

Figure 16 A pop-up window has a tab that you can click...

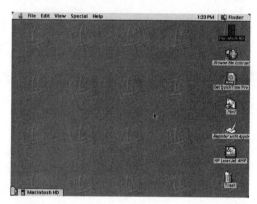

Figure 17 ...to hide the window at the bottom of the screen.

Figure 18
Choose as Pop-up
Window from the
View menu.

# Pop-up Windows

The pop-up windows feature changes the appearance and functionality of a window by adding a tab and hiding the window at the very bottom of the screen. Click the tab to display the window (**Figure 16**). Click either outside the window or on the tab to hide the window again (**Figure 17**).

## ✔ Tip

■ This feature makes it easy to keep frequently used windows handy without letting them clutter up the screen.

## To turn a window into a pop-up window

1. Activate the window that you want to turn into a pop-up window.

2. Choose View > as Pop-up Window (**Figure 18**). The window changes to a pop-up window (**Figure 16**).

   *or*

   Drag the window's title bar to the bottom of the screen. When a tab shape appears at the top of its gray outline (**Figure 19**), release the mouse button. The window changes into a pop-up window tab (**Figure 17**).

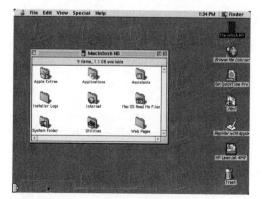

Figure 19 Drag the window's title bar until a tab appears on its outline.

## To activate or deactivate a pop-up window

Click the tab at the top of the window.

If the window is active (fully visible) when you click its tab, it disappears, displaying only a tab at the bottom of the screen (**Figure 17**).

If the window is inactive (displayed as a tab) when you click its tab, it appears (**Figure 16**).

## ✔ Tip

- You can also deactivate a pop-up window by clicking anywhere outside the window frame.

## To resize a pop-up window

1. Position the mouse pointer on one of the top corners of the active pop-up window (**Figure 20**).

2. Drag to make the window larger or smaller. As you drag, a dotted line border indicates the new edges of the window (**Figure 21**).

3. Release the mouse button. The window resizes (**Figure 22**).

## To turn a pop-up window into a standard window

1. Activate the pop-up window that you want to turn into a standard window.

2. Choose View > as Window (**Figure 23**). The window changes to a standard window.

   *or*

   Position the mouse pointer on the tab of the pop-up window and drag up until the tab disappears from the gray outline of the window (**Figure 24**). Release the mouse button. The window changes to a standard window.

**Figure 20** A pop-up window has size boxes on the two upper corners of the active window.

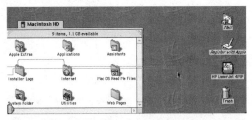

**Figure 21** As you drag a size box, a dotted-line border indicates the window's new borders.

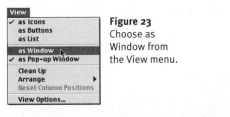

**Figure 22** When you release the mouse button, the window resizes.

**Figure 23** Choose as Window from the View menu.

**Figure 24** Drag a pop-up window's tab up until the tab disappears from the gray outline.

WORKING WITH POP-UP WINDOWS

**Figure 25** Drag an icon onto a folder icon and wait...

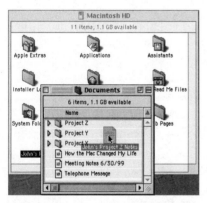

**Figure 26** ...until the folder opens.

# Spring-Loaded Folders

The spring-loaded folders feature lets you move or copy items into folders deep within the file structure of your disk—without manually opening a single folder. Instead, you simply drag icons onto folders (**Figures 25** and **27**) and wait as they're automatically opened (**Figures 26** and **28**). When you drop the icon into the final window, all windows except the source and destination windows automatically close (**Figure 29**).

## ✔ Tips

- The spring-loaded folders feature is sometimes referred to as *spring-open folders*.

- Using the spring-loaded folders feature requires a steady hand, good mouse skills, and knowledge of the location of folders on your disk.

- To use the spring-loaded folders feature, the Spring-loaded folders check box must be turned on in the General tab of the Preferences window (**Figure 3**). You can also set the spring-loaded folder delay length in the Preferences window (**Figure 4**). I tell you about Preferences at the beginning of this chapter.

- To use the spring-loaded folders feature to move or copy more than one item at a time, select the items first, then drag any one of them.

## To move an item using spring-loaded folders

1. Drag the item you want to move onto the folder in which you want to move it (**Figure 25**), but do not release the mouse button. After a moment, the folder blinks and opens (**Figure 26**).

2. Without releasing the mouse button, repeat step 1. The destination folder becomes selected (**Figure 27**), then blinks and opens (**Figure 28**). Do this until you reach the final destination.

3. Release the mouse button to place the item into the destination window (**Figure 29**).

### ✔ Tips

- In steps 1 and 2, to open a folder immediately, press [Spacebar] while dragging an item onto it.

- To close a folder's window so you can open a different folder in the same window, drag the item away from the open window. The window closes so you can drag the item onto a different folder and open it.

## To copy an item using spring-loaded folders

Hold down [Option] while following the above steps.

### ✔ Tip

- If the destination folder is on another disk, it is not necessary to hold down [Option] to copy items; they're automatically copied.

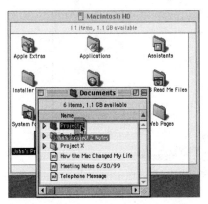

**Figure 27** Continue to drag the icon onto a folder in that window and wait...

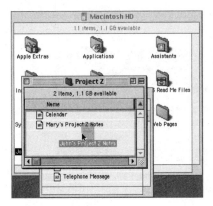

**Figure 28** ...until that folder opens.

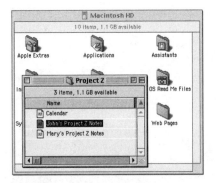

**Figure 29** The icon appears in the final destination window.

**Figure 30** Point to the folder you want to browse.

**Figure 31** When you click one and a half times on the folder, the mouse pointer turns into a magnifying glass...

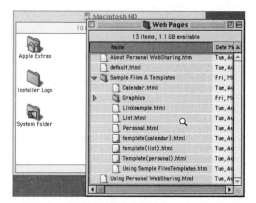

**Figure 32** ...and the folder opens.

## To browse folder or disk contents with "click and a half"

1. Position the mouse pointer on the folder or disk you want to browse (**Figure 30**).

2. Double-click the mouse button but do not release the mouse button during the second click. After a moment, the mouse pointer turns into a magnifying glass (**Figure 31**) and the folder or disk blinks and opens (**Figure 32**).

3. Without releasing the mouse button, drag the magnifying glass pointer over a folder you want to open within the open window. The folder becomes selected, then blinks and opens. Repeat as necessary to open other folders.

4. Release the mouse button to close all windows except the first and last ones that were open.

## ✔ Tips

- In steps 2 and 3, to open a folder immediately, press ⟨Spacebar⟩ while pointing to it.

- To close a folder's window so you can open a different folder in the same window, move the mouse pointer out of the open window. The window closes so you can move the mouse pointer onto a different folder and open it.

BROWSING FOLDERS WITH "CLICK AND A HALF"

# Aliases

An *alias* is a pointer to an item. You can make an alias of an item and place it anywhere on your computer. Then, when you need to open the item, just open its alias.

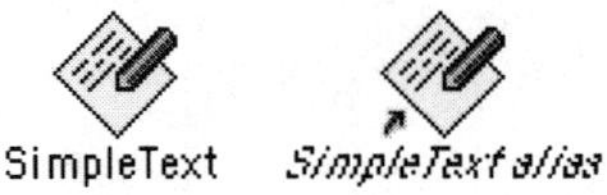

## ✔ Tips

- It's important to remember that an alias is not a copy of the item—it's a pointer. If you delete the original item, the alias will not open.

- You can use the Fix Alias dialog box (**Figure 49**) to reassign an original to an alias. I explain how later in this chapter.

- By putting aliases of frequently used items together where you can quickly access them—like on the Desktop or in a pop-up window—you make the items more accessible without actually moving them. I tell you about pop-up windows earlier in this chapter.

- The Favorites feature, automatically creates aliases and puts them in a folder accessible under the Apple menu. I tell you about Favorites in **Chapter 7**.

- You can make an alias for any item on your computer—including items accessible over a network. I tell you more about networking in **Chapter 11**.

- You can name an alias anything you like, as long as you follow the file naming guidelines I discuss in **Chapter 3**. An alias's name does not need to include the word *alias*.

- The icon for an alias looks very much like the icon for the original item but includes a tiny arrow (**Figure 33**). An alias's name appears in italic letters.

- You can move, copy, rename, open, and delete an alias just like any other file.

 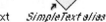

SimpleText      *SimpleText alias*

**Figure 33** The icon for an alias looks like the original item's icon but includes an arrow. An alias's name always appears in italic letters.

**Figure 34** To create an alias, begin by selecting the item for which you want to make an alias.

**Figure 35**
Choose Make Alias from the File menu.

**Figure 36**
The alias appears right beneath the original.

**Figure 37**
Select the alias's icon.

**Figure 38**
Choose Show Original from the File menu.

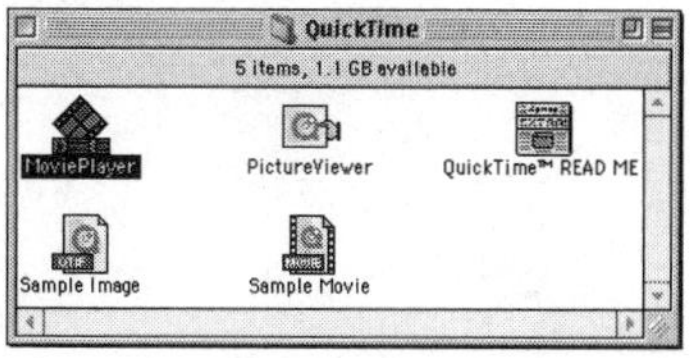

**Figure 39**
The original item appears selected in its window.

## To create an alias

1. Select the item for which you want to make an alias (**Figure 34**).

2. Choose Make Alias from the File menu (**Figure 35**) or press ⌘ ⌘ M.

   The alias appears right beneath the original item (**Figure 36**).

*or*

Hold down ⌘ ⌘ Option and drag the item for which you want to make an alias to a new location. The alias appears in the destination location.

## ✔ Tip

■ An alias's name is selected right after it is created (**Figure 36**). If desired, you can immediately type in a new name to replace the default name.

## To find an alias's original file

1. Select the alias's icon (**Figure 37**).

2. Choose File > Show Original (**Figure 38**) or press ⌘ ⌘ R.

   The original item appears selected in the window in which it resides on disk (**Figure 39**).

WORKING WITH ALIASES

# The Info Window

You can learn more about an item by opening its Info window (**Figures 40** through **43**). Depending on the type of icon (disk, folder, application, document, alias, Trash, etc.), the General Information in the Info window will provide some or all of the following information:

- **Icon** that appears in the Finder.
- **Name** of the item.
- **Kind** or type of item.
- **Format** of item (disks only).
- **Capacity** of item (disks only).
- **Available** space (disks only).
- **Used** space (disks only).
- **Size** of item or contents (folders and files only).
- **Where** or location of item.
- **Contents** (Trash only).
- **Created** date and time.
- **Modified** date and time.
- **Version** number or copyright date (files only).
- **Original** location on disk (aliases only).
- **Label** assigned to item.
- **Comments** entered by users (like you).
- **Locked** check box to prevent the file from being deleted or overwritten (files only).
- **Stationery** check box to convert the file into a stationery format file (documents only).
- **Warn before emptying** check box to toggle the Trash warning dialog box (Trash only).

## ✔ Tips

- I tell you about stationery pads in **Chapter 5**.
- I tell you about File Sharing and Memory information in the Info window in **Chapters 11** and **5** respectively.

**Figure 40**
The Info window for a hard disk.

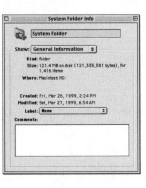

**Figure 41**
The Info window for a folder.

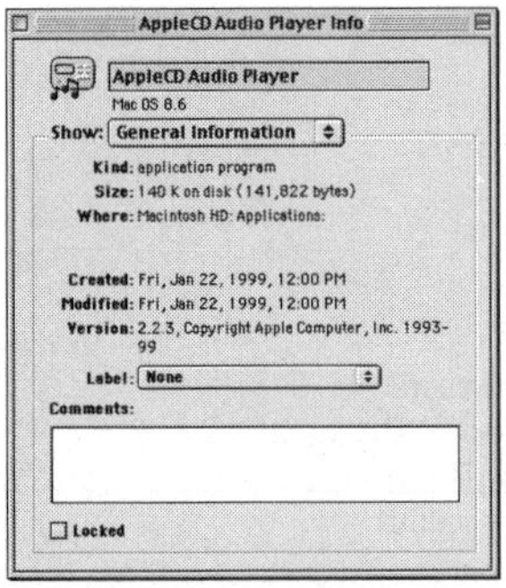

**Figure 42**
The Info window for an application.

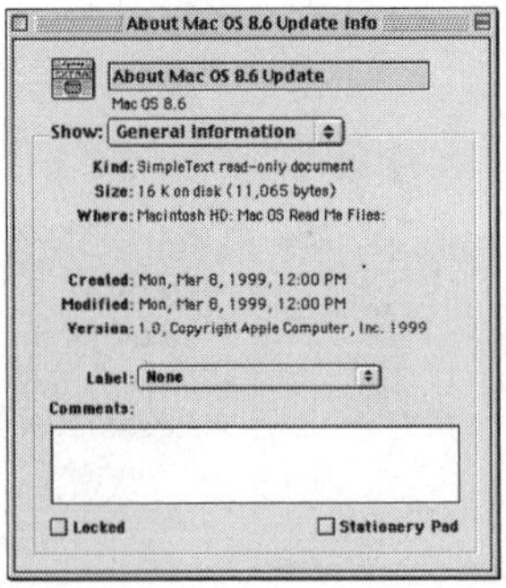

**Figure 43**
The Info window for a document.

**Figure 44**
Select the item for which you want to open the Info window.

**Figure 45** Choose General Information from the Get Info submenu under the File menu.

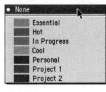

**Figure 46**
Choose a label from the Label pop-up menu.

## To open the Info window

1.  Select the item for which you want to open the Info window (**Figure 44**).

2.  Choose File > Get Info > General Information (**Figure 45**) or press ⌘ I.

    The Info window for that item appears (**Figure 41**).

## To close the Info window

Click the Info window's close box.

*or*

1.  Activate the Info window.

2.  Choose File > Close Window (**Figure 2**) or press ⌘ W.

## ✔ Tip

■ Closing the Info window saves all changes you made to its options.

## To change an item's name

1.  In the Info window, drag the mouse pointer over the item's name to select it.

2.  Type in the new name. What you type replaces the selected text.

## ✔ Tip

■ You can change the name of an item only if its name appears within an edit box (**Figures 41** through **43**). If there is no edit box around the item's name (**Figure 40**), you cannot rename it.

## To change an item's label

In the Info window, choose a label from the Label pop-up menu (**Figure 46**). The label is applied to the item.

## ✔ Tip

■ I tell you more about labels in **Chapter 3**.

## To enter comments in the Info window

1. Open the Info window for the item for which you want to enter comments.

2. Click in the Comments box to position the blinking insertion point there.

3. Type your comments (**Figure 47**).

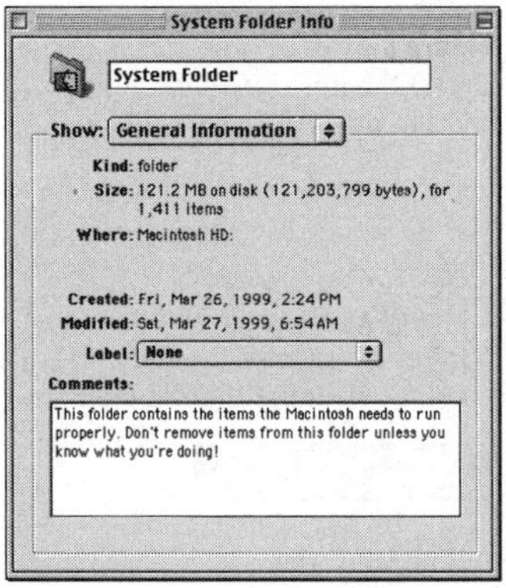

## To lock an application or document

1. Open the Info window for the item you want to lock (**Figure 42** or **43**).

2. Turn on the Locked check box.

## ✔ Tip

- Locked items cannot be deleted or overwritten. They can, however, be moved.

## To select a new original item for an alias

1. In the Info window for the alias (**Figure 48**), click the Select New Original button.

2. Use the Fix Alias dialog box that appears (**Figure 49**) to locate and select the item that you want to use as the original for the alias.

3. Click Choose. The item you selected is assigned to the alias.

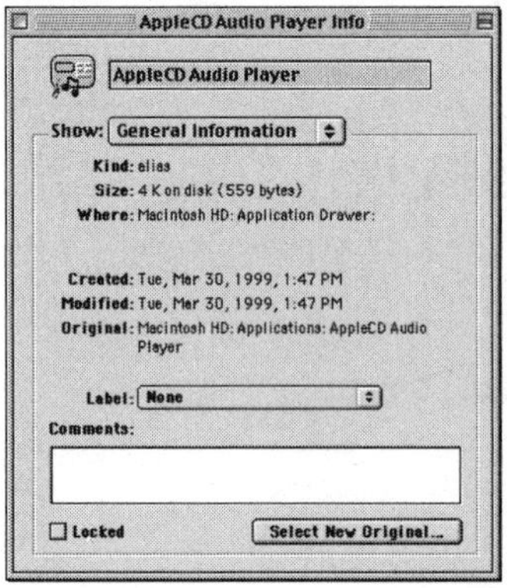

## ✔ Tip

- The Fix Alias dialog box takes advantage of the Navigation Services feature that first appeared in Mac OS 8.5. I explain how to use dialog boxes like this one in **Chapter 5**.

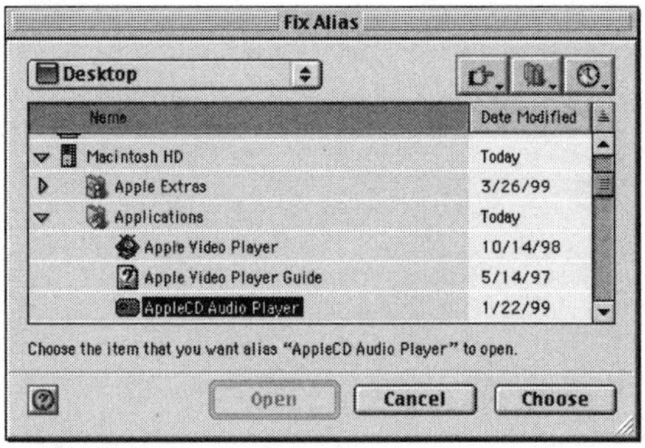

**Figure 47**
You can enter information about the item in the Comments box.

**Figure 48**
You can click the Select New Original button in the Info window for an alias to assign a new original to the alias.

**Figure 49** Use the Fix Alias dialog box to locate and choose a new original for an alias.

# USING APPLICATIONS

## Applications

*Applications*, which are also known as *programs*, are software packages you use to get work done. Here are some examples:

◆ **Word processors**, such as SimpleText and Microsoft Word, are used to write letters, reports, and other text-based documents.

◆ **Spreadsheets**, such as Microsoft Excel, have built-in calculation features that are useful for creating number-based documents like worksheets and charts.

◆ **Databases**, such as FileMaker Pro, are used to organize related information, like the names and addresses of customers or the artists and titles in a record collection.

◆ **Graphics** and **presentation** programs such as Adobe Photoshop, Macromedia Freehand, and Microsoft PowerPoint, are used to create illustrations, presentations, and animations.

◆ **Communications** programs, such as Apple Remote Access, Microsoft Internet Explorer, and America Online, are used to connect to other computers, including online services and the Internet.

◆ **Integrated** software, such as AppleWorks and Microsoft Works, combines "lite" versions of most other types of software into one cost-effective package.

◆ **Utility** software such as Disk First Aid, Drive Setup, and Norton Utilities, performs tasks to help manage computer files or keep your computer in good working order.

## ✔ Tips

■ Your Mac OS-compatible computer comes with some application software, most of which is discussed throughout this book.

■ Unless you have a DOS compatibility card, Virtual PC, or SoftWindows installed in your computer, you should make sure the software you buy is Mac OS-compatible. I tell you more about working with PCs in **Chapter 9**.

# Using Applications & Creating Documents

You use an application by opening, or *launching*, it. It loads into the computer's memory, or *RAM*. Its menu bar replaces the Finder's menu bar and offers commands that can be used only with that application. It may also display a document window and tools specific to that program.

Most applications create *documents*—files written in a format understood by the application. When you save documents, they remain on disk so you can open, edit, print, or just view them at a later date.

For example, you may use Microsoft Word to write a letter. When you save the letter, it becomes a Word document file that includes all the text and formatting you put into the letter, written in a format that Microsoft Word can understand.

Your computer keeps track of applications and documents. It automatically associates documents with the applications that created them. That's how your computer is able to open a document with the correct application when you open the document from the Finder.

## ✔ Tips

■ You can launch an application by opening a document that it created.

■ You can often tell which documents were created by a specific application just by looking at their icons. **Figure 1** shows some examples.

■ A document created by an application that is not installed on your computer is sometimes referred to as an *orphan* document since no *parent* application is available. An orphan document usually has a generic document icon (**Figure 2**).

Microsoft Word    Document

FrameMaker 5    Document

Claris Home Page    Document

Acrobat™ Reader    Document

**Figure 1** Application and document icons often share elements that make them appear as part of a matched set.

Ducati.jpg

**Figure 2**
An orphan document often has a generic document icon like this one.

**Figure 3**
Select the icon for the application that you want to open.

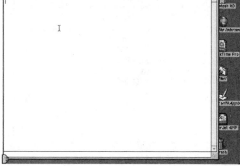

**Figure 4**
Choose Open from the File menu.

**Figure 5** When you launch SimpleText by opening its application icon, it displays an empty document window.

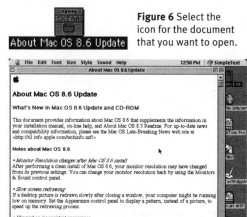

**Figure 6** Select the icon for the document that you want to open.

**Figure 7** When you launch SimpleText by opening one of its documents, it displays the document.

## To launch an application

Double-click the application's icon.

*or*

1. Select the application's icon (**Figure 3**).
2. Choose File > Open (**Figure 4**), or press ⌃⌘O.

The application opens (**Figure 5**).

## To launch an application & open a document at the same time

Double-click the icon for the document that you want to open.

*or*

1. Select the icon for the document that you want to open (**Figure 6**).
2. Choose File > Open (**Figure 4**), or press ⌃⌘O.

The application that created the document launches. The document appears in a window (**Figure 7**).

## ✔ Tips

- If the application that created the document is already open, it does not launch again. Instead, it becomes active and displays the document in a window.

- If you try to open an orphan document, a dialog box will either tell you it can't open the document (**Figure 10**) or offer to open it with an installed application (**Figure 9**). I tell you more about opening orphan documents on the next page.

**LAUNCHING APPLICATIONS**

## To open a document with drag & drop

1. Drag the icon for the document that you want to open onto the icon for the application with which you want to open it.

2. When the application icon becomes selected (**Figure 8**), release the mouse button. The application launches and displays the document (**Figure 7**).

## ✔ Tips

■ This is a good way to open a document with an application other than the one that created it.

■ Not all applications can read all documents. Dragging a document icon onto the icon for an application that can't open it either won't launch the application or will display an error message.

## To open an orphan document

Double-click the icon for the document that you want to open.

*or*

1. Select the icon for the document that you want to open.

2. Choose File > Open (**Figure 4**), or press ⌘ O.

3. If a dialog box like the one in **Figure 9** appears, click to select the name of the application with which you want to try to open the document. Then click Open. The application you selected launches and attempts to open the document.

*or*

If a dialog box like the one in **Figure 10** appears, you don't have an application that will open the file. Click OK.

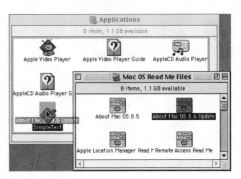

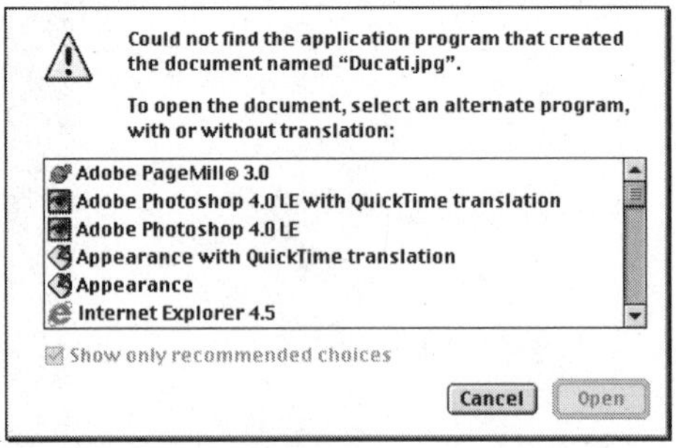

**Figure 8** Drag the document icon onto the application icon.

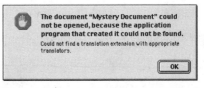

**Figure 9** A dialog box like this appears if you try to open an orphan document and have at least one program that can open it.

**Figure 10** If you don't have any programs that can open an orphan document, a dialog box like this appears.

## ✔ Tip

■ If you don't have a program that will open an orphan file, find someone who does, open it on his machine, and save it in a format you can open.

OPENING DOCUMENTS

**Figure 11**
The Application menu lists all open applications, identifies the active application, and lets you activate the application of your choice.

**1:33 PM**

**Figure 12** Clicking the vertical bar to the left of the application menu collapses it to display only the application's icon.

# Multitasking & the Application Menu

Mac OS uses a form of *multitasking* that makes it possible for more than one application to be open at the same time. Only one application, however, can be *active*. The active application is the one whose menu bar appears at the top of the screen and whose windows are at the top of the stack of windows on your screen.

The Application menu at the far right end of the menu bar (**Figure 11**) lets you do a number of things:

◆ Identify the active application. The name and icon for the active application appears at the top of the application menu. When you display the menu, the active application has a check mark to the left of its name (**Figure 11**).

◆ Activate a different open application.

◆ Hide the active application.

◆ Hide all applications except the active application.

◆ Show all open applications.

## ✔ Tips

■ One application that is always open is the Finder, which I cover in detail in **Chapters 2** through **4**.

■ The number of applications that can be opened at the same time depends on the amount of RAM in your computer. I tell you more about RAM later in this chapter.

■ Hiding an application removes all of its windows from the screen, thus reducing screen clutter.

■ If you click the vertical bar to the left of the application menu, it collapses to display only the icon for the active application (**Figure 12**). (This is how the application menu appeared prior to Mac OS 8.5.)

MULTITASKING & THE APPLICATION MENU

## To switch from one open application to another

From the Application menu, choose the application you want (**Figure 13**).

*or*

Click on a window of the application that you want (**Figure 14**). You may have to move windows that are blocking your view.

## To hide an application

1. If necessary, activate the application.

2. From the Application menu, choose Hide *Application* (**Figure 15**). Although the exact wording of this command changes depending on the name of the application, it's always the first option on the Application menu.

## ✔ Tips

■ You cannot hide the active application if it is the only application that is open or if all the other open applications are already hidden.

■ The icon for a hidden application appears faded on the Application menu (**Figure 17**).

## To hide all applications except the active one

1. If necessary, activate the application that you don't want to hide.

2. From the Application menu, choose Hide Others (**Figure 16**).

## To unhide all applications

From the Application menu, choose Show All (**Figure 17**).

## ✔ Tip

■ The Show All command is gray if all applications are already showing (**Figure 15**).

**Figure 13**
Choose the application that you want from the Application menu.

*Click here to activate this program.*

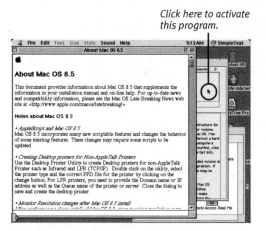

**Figure 14** In this example, SimpleText is the active application. Clicking on the Disk First Aid window sticking out behind it will activate Disk First Aid.

**Figure 15**
The first command under the Application menu hides the active application.

**Figure 16**
The Hide Others command hides all applications except the active one.

**Figure 17**
The Show All command shows all applications, including those that were hidden.

**SWITCHING & HIDING APPLICATIONS**

**Figure 18**
To display the Application Switcher, drag the Application menu down to "tear it off" the menu bar.

Close box  Zoom box  Collapse box

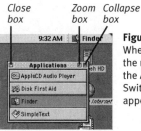

**Figure 19**
When you release the mouse button, the Application Switcher's window appears.

**Figure 20**
Clicking the Application Switcher's zoom box displays it as a column of icons without application names.

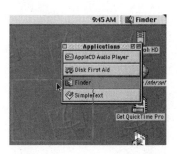

**Figure 21** You can move the Application Switcher like any other window—by dragging its title bar.

# Using the Application Switcher

The Application Switcher offers another way to switch from one open application to another. It displays a floating palette with a button for each open application. Simply click a button to activate its application.

## To display the Application Switcher

1. In the menu bar, position the mouse pointer on the name of the application that appears at the top of the Application menu.

2. Press the mouse button down and drag down. As you drag, the application menu appears. Then a gray rectangle appears to indicate that the menu is being "torn off" the menu bar (**Figure 18**).

3. Release the mouse button. The Application Switcher window appears (**Figure 19**).

## ✔ Tips

■ To display the Application Switcher as a column of icons (**Figure 20**), click its zoom box.

■ To display the Application Switcher with larger icons, hold down (Option) while clicking its zoom box. This works for the Application Switcher's standard icon and application name view as well as its icon only view.

## To move the Application Switcher

1. Position the mouse pointer on the Application Switcher's title bar.

2. Press the mouse button down and drag. As you drag, a gray border indicates where the Application Switcher will appear when you release the mouse button (**Figure 21**).

3. When the Application Switcher's border is in the desired position, release the mouse button. It moves.

## To switch from one open application to another

Click the Application Switcher button for the application you want.

### ✔ Tip

- The active application's button always appears "pushed in," or selected (**Figures 19** and **20**).

## To hide the active application while switching to another application

Hold down ⌥ Option while clicking the Application Switcher button for the application you want.

### ✔ Tips

- The icon for a hidden application appears faded in the Application Switcher window (**Figure 22**).

- This technique also works when activating an application by clicking its window or choosing its name from the Application menu as discussed earlier in this chapter.

## To hide the Application Switcher

Click the Application Switcher's close box (**Figure 19**). It disappears.

**Figure 22**
The icon for a hidden application appears faded in the Application Switcher window.

USING THE APPLICATION SWITCHER

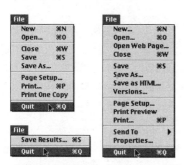

**Figures 23a, 23b, & 23c** The Quit command is always under the File menu. Here are three examples: SimpleText (top-left), Disk First Aid (bottom-left), and Microsoft Word (right).

**Figure 24** If there are unsaved documents, a dialog box like this one appears for each one, giving you a last chance to save them.

# Quitting an Application

When you're finished using an application, you should properly quit it. This completely clears the application out of RAM, freeing up RAM for other applications you may want to launch.

## ✔ Tip

- Closing all of an application's open windows is not the same as quitting. An application is still running—and still taking up RAM—until you quit it.

## To quit an application

1. If necessary, activate the application that you want to quit.

2. Choose File > Quit (**Figures 23a**, **23b**, and **23c**), or press ⌃ ⌘Q.

3. If unsaved documents are open, a dialog box like the one in **Figure 24** appears for each unsaved document.

   ▲ Click Save or press Return or Enter to save the document.

   ▲ Click Don't Save to quit without saving the document.

   ▲ Click Cancel or press Esc to return to the application without quitting.

   The application closes all windows, saves preference files (if applicable), and quits.

## ✔ Tip

- I tell you more about saving documents later in this chapter.

QUITTING APPLICATIONS

# Dialog Boxes

Mac OS-compatible applications use *dialog boxes* to tell you things (**Figure 25**) and get information from you (**Figures 26** through **29**). Think of it as the way your computer has a conversation—or dialog—with you.

Every application has its own set of dialog boxes, but there are some dialog boxes that are basically the same from one application to another:

◆ **Open** dialog box (**Figure 26**) lets you open a document from within an application (as opposed to opening it from the Finder).

◆ **Save As** dialog box (**Figure 27**) lets you save a document with the name and in the disk location you specify.

◆ **Page Setup** dialog box (**Figure 28**) lets you specify page and PostScript settings.

◆ **Print** dialog box (**Figure 29**) lets you specify print settings and print.

This part of the chapter explains how to use the standard parts of a dialog box—edit boxes, radio buttons, check boxes, scrolling lists, and push buttons—as well as how to use the Open and Save As dialog boxes.

## ✔ Tips

■ I tell you how to use the Page Setup and Print dialog boxes in **Chapter 10**.

■ It is often difficult to distinguish between windows and dialog boxes since Mac OS uses both to communicate with you. Throughout this book, a dialog box will refer to a window-like box that appears on screen and requires you to click a button to dismiss it. A window, on the other hand, can always be closed by clicking a close box or using the Close or Close Window command under the File menu.

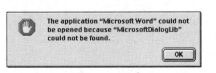

**Figure 25** This dialog box just gives you a message.

**Figure 26** Four SimpleText dialog boxes: the Open dialog box,...

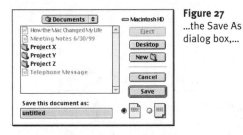

**Figure 27** ...the Save As dialog box,...

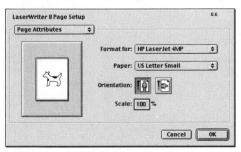

**Figure 28** ...the Page Setup dialog box,...

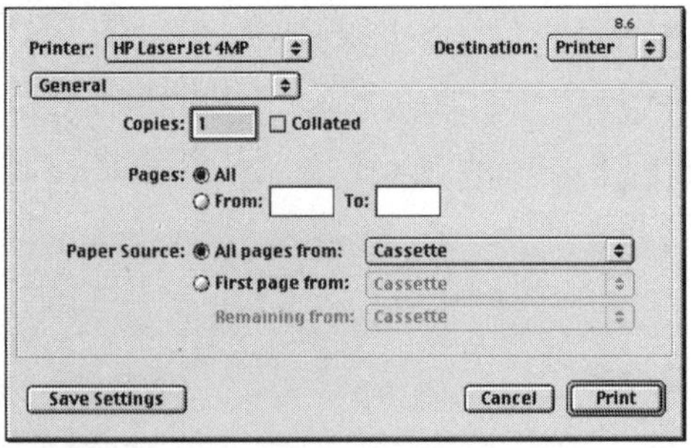

**Figure 29** ...and the Print dialog box.

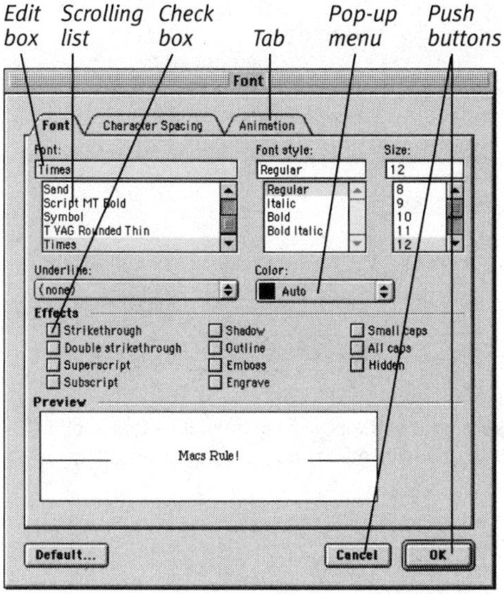

Edit Scrolling Check          Pop-up    Push
box  list     box     Tab     menu      buttons

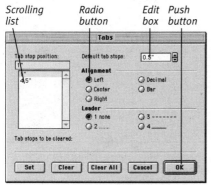

**Figure 30** One Microsoft Word dialog box illustrates most standard dialog box parts...

Scrolling      Radio        Edit   Push
list           button       box    button

**Figure 31** ...and another illustrates the rest.

# To use dialog box parts

◆ Enter text or numbers into edit boxes (**Figures 30** and **31**).

◆ Use scroll bars to view the contents of scrolling lists (**Figures 30** and **31**). Click once on a list item to select it.

◆ Click a check box (**Figure 30**) to turn it on or off.

◆ Click a tab (**Figure 30**) to view its options.

◆ Click a pop-up menu (**Figure 30**) to display its options. Drag through the menu to choose an option.

◆ Click a push button (**Figures 30** and **31**) to select it.

◆ Click a radio button (**Figure 31**) to select it.

## ✔ Tips

■ If an edit box has a pair of arrows or triangles beside it (**Figure 31**) you can click the triangles to increase or decrease a value already in the edit box.

■ The default push button is the one with the dark border around it (**Figures 30** and **31**). You can always select a default button by pressing ⟨Enter⟩ and often by pressing ⟨Return⟩.

■ You can usually select a Cancel button (**Figures 30** and **31**) by pressing ⟨Esc⟩ or ⟨⌘ .⟩.

■ One and only one radio button in a group must be selected (**Figure 31**). If you try to select a second button, the first button becomes deselected.

■ If you click the Cancel button in a dialog box (**Figures 30** and **31**), any options you set are lost.

## To use the Open dialog box

1. Choose File > Open (**Figure 32**) or press
   ⌃⌘O.

   A dialog box similar to the one in **Figure
   26** appears.

2. Use these two techniques to navigate to the
   file you want to open:

   ▲ To open an item in a scrolling list, click
   to select it and then click Open or
   double-click it.

   ▲ To back up out of the current folder to
   a previous folder in the file hierarchy,
   choose a folder from the pop-up menu
   above the scrolling list (**Figures 33** and
   **34**) or press ⌃⌘↑ to back up one
   folder level at a time.

3. Click to select the name of the file that you
   want to open and then click Open (**Figure
   35**) or press Return or Enter.

   *or*

   Double-click the name of the file that you
   want to open.

## ✔ Tips

■ To use this dialog box successfully, you must
   understand the file hierarchy. Remember
   that files reside in folders that are sometimes inside other folders.

■ To quickly view the items on the Desktop,
   click the Desktop button (**Figures 26** and
   **35**) or press ⌃⌘D. This enables you to
   open folders, files, and other disks on your
   Desktop.

■ Some Open dialog boxes offer pop-up
   menus that let you narrow down a file list
   by document or file type.

**Figure 32**
Choose Open from the
application's—in this case
SimpleText's—File menu.

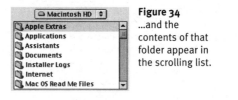

**Figure 33** Use the pop-up menu above the scrolling
list to choose a different folder in the hierarchy...

**Figure 34**
...and the
contents of that
folder appear in
the scrolling list.

**Figure 35** Select the file's name and click Open to
open it within the application.

File
New ⌘N
Open... ⌘O
Close ⌘W
Save ⌘S
Save As...
Page Setup...
Print... ⌘P
Print One Copy
Quit ⌘Q

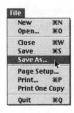

**Figure 36** Choose Save As from the application's—in this case, SimpleText's— File menu.

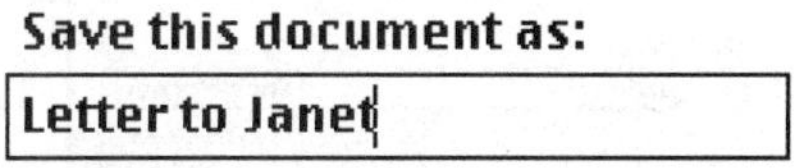

Save this document as:
Letter to Janet

**Figure 37** Enter a name for the document in the edit box.

Documents
7 items, 1.1 GB available
Name
How the Mac Changed My Life
Letter to Janet
Meeting Notes 6/30/99
Project X
Project Y
Project Z
Telephone Message

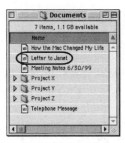

**Figure 38** An icon for the document you saved appears in the folder in which you saved it.

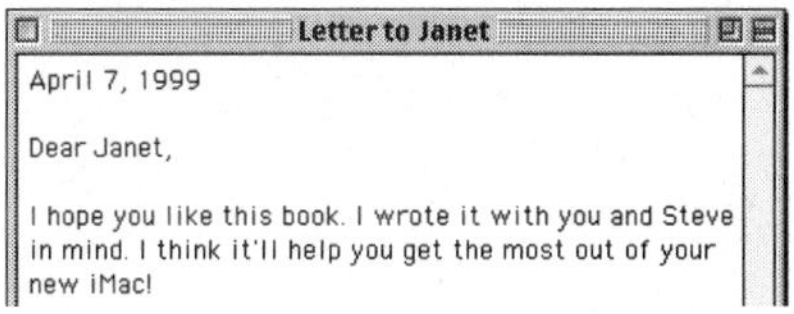

Letter to Janet
April 7, 1999
Dear Janet,
I hope you like this book. I wrote it with you and Steve in mind. I think it'll help you get the most out of your new iMac!

**Figure 39** The name of the document appears in the title bar of the document window.

## To use the Save As dialog box

1. Choose File > Save As (**Figure 36**). A dialog box similar to the one in **Figure 27** appears.
2. Use these two techniques to navigate to the folder in which you want to save the document:
   - ▲ To open an item in a scrolling list, click to select it and then click Open or double-click it.
   - ▲ To back up out of the current folder to a previous folder in the file hierarchy, choose a folder from the pop-up menu above the scrolling list (**Figure 33**) or press [⌘ ⌘][↑] to back up one folder level at a time.
3. In the edit box beneath the scrolling list, enter the name that you want to give the document (**Figure 37**).
4. Click Save, or press [Return] or [Enter].

The file is saved to disk in the destination you specified (**Figure 38**). The name you gave it appears in the title bar of the document window (**Figure 39**).

### ✔ Tips

- If you have never saved the document, you can also choose Save from the application's file menu or press [⌘ ⌘][S] to display the Save As dialog box.
- The folder navigation techniques in the Save As dialog box work just like those in the Open dialog box discussed on the previous page.
- To quickly view the items on the Desktop, click the Desktop button (**Figure 27**) or press [⌘ ⌘][D]. This enables you to open folders and other disks on your Desktop.
- Some Save As dialog boxes offer a pop-up menu you can use to save a file in a specific file format.

# Navigation Services

Navigation Services, which was added to Mac OS in version 8.5, changes the appearance and functionality of the Open (**Figure 40**) and Save As (**Figure 41**) dialog boxes, making them more flexible and convenient to use.

## ✔ Tips

- ■ Mac OS Help refers to the dialog boxes introduced with Navigation Services as the "new" Open and Save As dialog boxes.

- ■ This feature must be implemented within a program for the dialog boxes on this page to appear.

- ■ Within Mac OS 8.6, you can see this new feature at work in:

  - ▲ The Fix Alias dialog box, which I discuss in **Chapter 4**.

  - ▲ Network Browser, which I discuss in **Chapter 11**.

  - ▲ The Appearance control panel, which I discuss in **Chapter 13**.

- ■ As more software developers adopt the Navigation Services technology, the dialog boxes depicted on these pages will become more and more common.

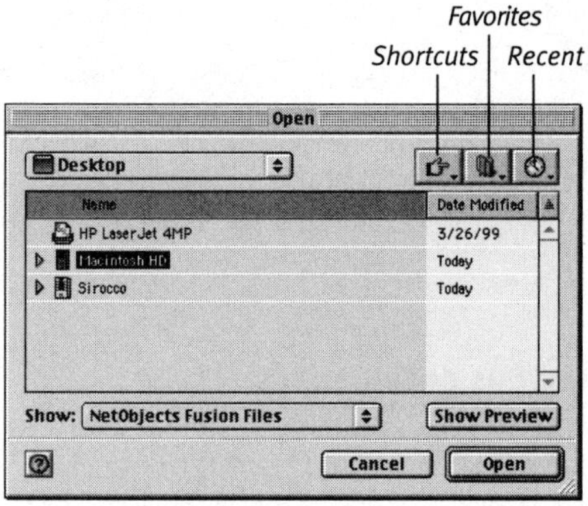

*Favorites*
*Shortcuts* | *Recent*

**Figure 40** The new Open dialog box...

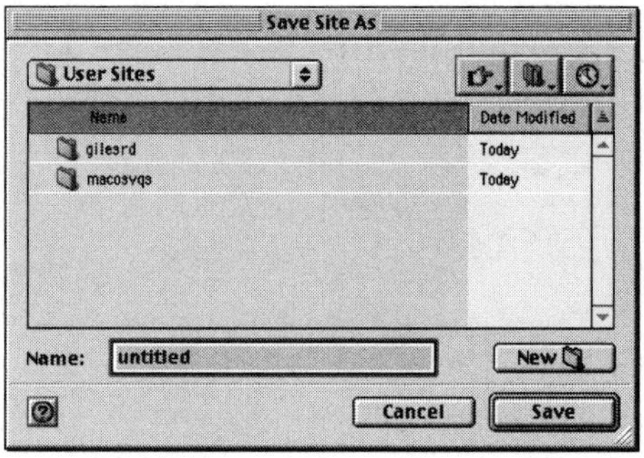

**Figure 41** ...and the new Save As dialog box.

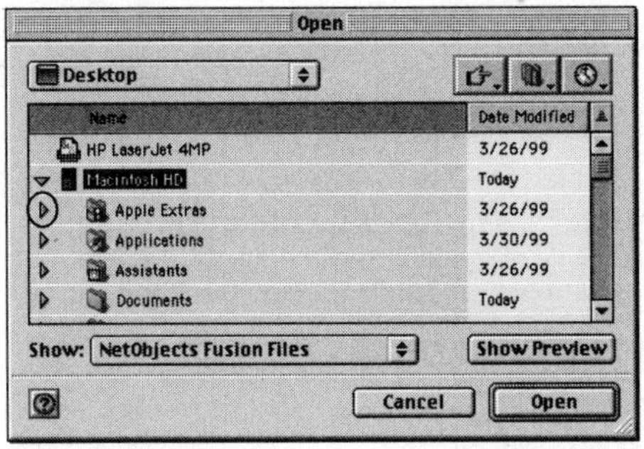

Figure 42 Click a triangle to display the items within its folder or disk.

**Figure 43**
The Shortcuts button displays the desktop, network connections, and other mounted disks.

**Figure 44**
The Favorites button displays your Favorites.

Figure 45 The Recent button displays items recently opened with that application.

## To use the new Open & Save As dialog boxes

All of the instructions on page 92 apply to the new Open dialog box (**Figure 40**).

*and*

All of the instructions on page 89 apply to the new Save As dialog box (**Figure 41**).

The following procedures also work with these dialog boxes:

◆ Click the triangle to the left of the name of a disk or folder that you want to open to display its contents along with the contents of other disks or folders (**Figure 42**). (This works with the Open dialog box only.)

◆ Open several files at once by holding down (Shift) while clicking the names of the files you want to open. (This works with the Open dialog box only.)

◆ Choose an option from the Shortcuts button menu (**Figure 43**) to quickly access the desktop, mounted disks, or disks available over the network or Internet.

◆ Choose an item from the Favorites button menu (**Figure 44**) to open a Favorite item.

◆ Choose an item from the Recent button's menu (**Figure 45**) to open an item you recently opened with that application.

## ✔ Tip

■ I cover networking in **Chapter 11**, the Internet in **Chapter 12**, and favorites in **Chapter 7**.

# Stationery Pads

A *stationery pad is* a document used as a form for creating similar documents. It's like a template—you open and modify it to suit your specific needs. When you save it, it automatically prompts you to give it a different name, making it very difficult to accidentally overwrite the original file.

## To turn an existing document into stationery

1. Select the icon for the document that you want to turn into stationery (**Figure 46**).

2. Choose File > Get Info > General Information (**Figure 47**), or press ⌃⌘ I . The Info window for the file appears.

3. Turn on the Stationery Pad check box (**Figure 48**).

4. Close the Info window.

## ✔ Tip

■ I tell you more about General Information options in the Info window in **Chapter 4**.

## To create stationery from scratch

1. In the application of your choice, create the document that you want to turn into stationery.

2. Choose File > Save As.

3. In the Save As dialog box, enter a name for the file, select a disk location, and choose a file type of Stationery or Stationery Pad (**Figures 49** and **50**).

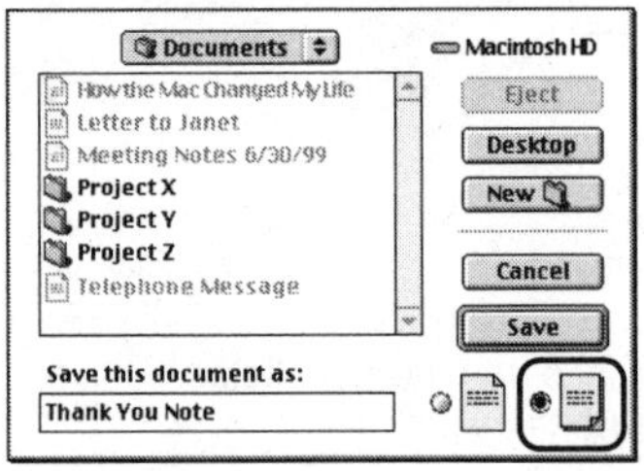

## ✔ Tip

■ Not all applications let you save files as stationery. If the application you want to use doesn't, save the file as a regular document and turn it into a stationery pad in the Finder as instructed above.

**Figure 46**
Select the icon for the file that you want to turn into a stationery pad.

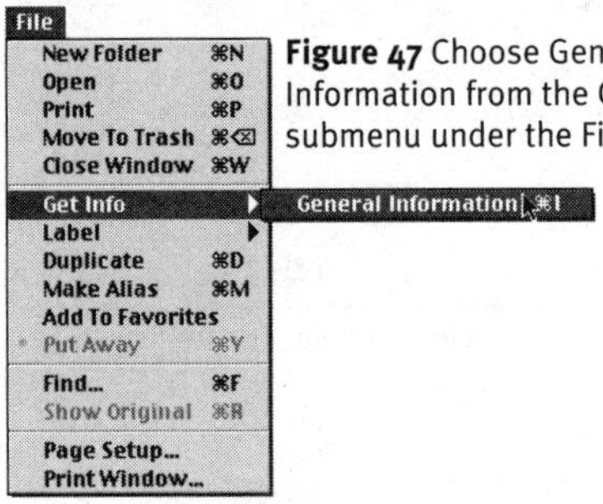

**Figure 47** Choose General Information from the Get Info submenu under the File menu.

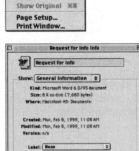

**Figure 48**
Turn on the Stationery Pad check box in the Info window.

**Figure 49**
SimpleText offers a radio button to choose stationery pad format.

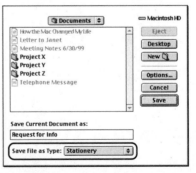

**Figure 50** Word offers a pop-up menu for file types, including stationery pad format.

WORKING WITH STATIONERY PADS

**Figure 51** Dragging a selection from a document window to the Finder creates a clipping file.

untitled clipping

---

| untitled clipping |
|---|
| Clipping contents: styled text |
| Drag this text |

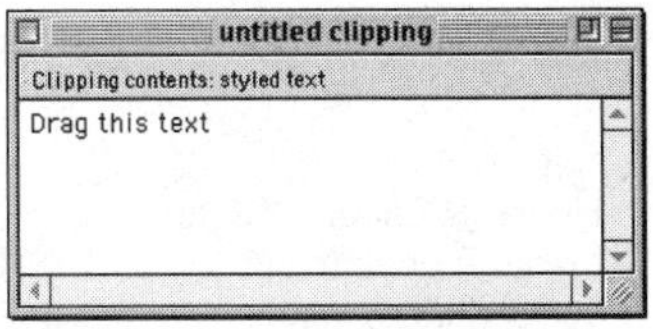

**Figure 52** Opening a clipping file displays its contents in a window.

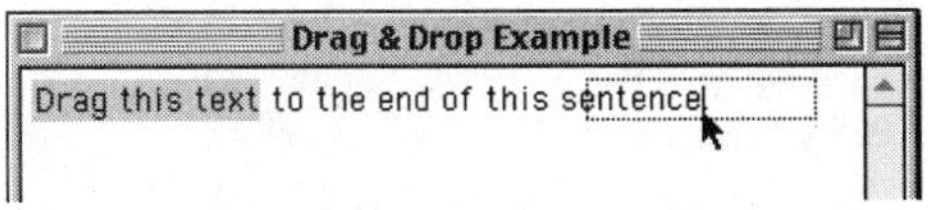

---

| Drag & Drop Example |
|---|
| Drag this text to the end of this sentence |

**Figure 53** Drag the selection to a new destination.

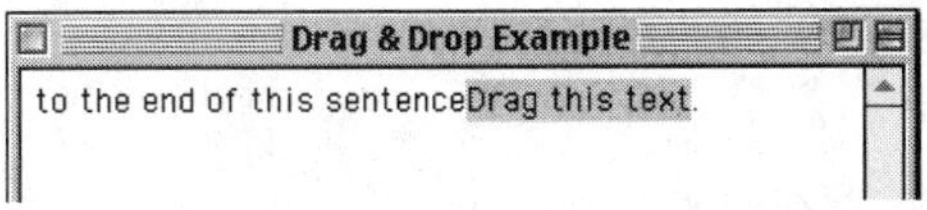

---

| Drag & Drop Example |
|---|
| to the end of this sentenceDrag this text. |

**Figure 54** When you release the mouse button, the selection moves.

# Macintosh Drag & Drop

Macintosh drag and drop enables you to copy or move information by dragging selections from one location to another:

◆ Dragging a selection from one location in a document window to another moves the selection.

◆ Dragging a selection from one document window to another in the same application copies the selection.

◆ Dragging a selection from one application's document window to another application's document window copies the selection.

◆ Holding down Option while dragging a selection copies the selection.

◆ Dragging a selection from a document window to the Finder creates a clipping file (**Figure 51**) containing the selection (**Figure 52**).

◆ Dragging a Finder icon into a document window copies the contents of that icon into the document.

## ✔ Tips

■ Not all applications support Macintosh drag and drop. Try it in your favorite applications to see if they do.

■ A selection can include text or graphics or sometimes a combination of the two.

## To use Macintosh drag & drop

1. Select the text or graphics that you want to move or copy.

2. Drag the selection to the new destination. Depending on what you drag, an insertion point might appear to indicate where the selection will be inserted (**Figure 53**).

3. When the selection is in the desired position, release the mouse button. The selection moves (**Figure 54**) or is copied.

# RAM

*RAM* (random access memory) is your computer's working memory. All the applications and documents you open are loaded into RAM so your computer's *CPU* (central processing unit) can access them quickly.

The amount of RAM an application needs to run is called its *RAM allocation*, or *application heap*. Although every application's RAM allocation is preset by the programmer, you can raise it to make the application run more smoothly or lower it so the application requires less RAM to run.

## ✔ Tips

- Don't confuse memory or RAM with hard disk space. I tell you about hard disks in **Chapter 3**.

- The more RAM your computer has, the more applications it can open at once.

- Programs that work with large graphics files, like Photoshop and Director, need lots of RAM to work efficiently.

- Lowering an application's RAM allocation isn't recommended because it can cause the application to behave erratically and unexpectedly crash.

## To change an application's RAM allocation

1. Select the icon for the application whose RAM allocation you want to change (**Figure 55**).

2. Choose File > Get Info > Memory (**Figure 56**). The Memory information of the Info window for the application appears (**Figure 57**).

3. Enter a value for the desired RAM allocation in the Preferred Size edit box (**Figure 58**).

4. Close the Info window.

**Figure 55** Select the icon for the application whose RAM allocation you want to change.

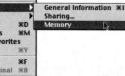

**Figure 56** Choose Memory from the Get Info submenu under the File menu.

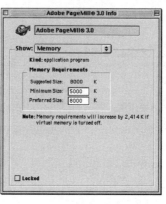

**Figure 57** Use the Info window to change an application's RAM allocation.

**Figure 58** Enter the desired RAM allocation value in the Preferred Size edit box.

# USING SIMPLETEXT

SimpleText

**Figure 1**
The SimpleText
application icon.

About Mac OS 8.6

**Figure 2**
A SimpleText read-only
document's icon.

Letter to Janet

**Figure 3**
A standard SimpleText
document's icon.

## ✔ Tips

- MoviePlayer, which also comes with Mac OS, offers more features than SimpleText for working with QuickTime movies. I tell you about QuickTime and MoviePlayer in **Chapter 8**.

- SimpleText read-only documents, like those that come with Mac OS 8.6, cannot be edited. You can identify a SimpleText read only document by its icon, which looks like a newspaper (**Figure 2**). A regular SimpleText document icon looks like a piece of paper with its corner folded down (**Figure 3**).

## SimpleText

*SimpleText* (**Figure 1**) is a basic text editing application that comes with Mac OS. Simple-Text lets you:

- ◆ Create, open, edit, and print text documents, including the "Read Me" files that come with many applications.

- ◆ Open and print PICT, GIF, and other graphic format documents and QuickTime movies.

In this chapter, I tell you how to use Simple-Text to create, edit, format, open, and save documents.

- Although SimpleText offers many of the basic features found in a word processing application, it falls far short of the feature list of word processors such as Microsoft Word and the word processing components of integrated software such as AppleWorks.

- If you're new to Mac OS, don't skip this chapter. Not only does it explain how to use SimpleText but it provides instructions for basic text editing skills—like text entry and the Copy, Cut, and Paste commands—that you'll use in all Mac OS-compatible applications.

# Launching & Quitting SimpleText

Like any other application, you must launch SimpleText before you can use it. This loads it into RAM so your computer can work with it. Likewise, when you're finished using Simple-Text, its important to quit it to clear it from RAM.

## To launch SimpleText

Double-click the SimpleText application icon.

*or*

1. Select the SimpleText application icon (**Figure 1**).

2. Choose File > Open (**Figure 4**), or press [⌘][O].

SimpleText launches. An untitled document window appears (**Figure 5**).

## ✔ Tip

■ As illustrated in **Figure 5**, the SimpleText document window has the same standard window parts found in Finder windows. I tell you how to use Finder windows in **Chapter 2**; SimpleText and other application windows work the same way.

## To quit SimpleText

1. Choose File > Quit (**Figure 6**), or press [⌘][Q].

2. If unsaved documents are open, a dialog box like the one in **Figure 7** appears for each unsaved document.

   ▲ Click Save or press [Return] or [Enter] to save the document.

   ▲ Click Don't Save to quit without saving the document.

   ▲ Click Cancel or press [Esc] to return to the application without quitting.

   SimpleText closes all windows and quits.

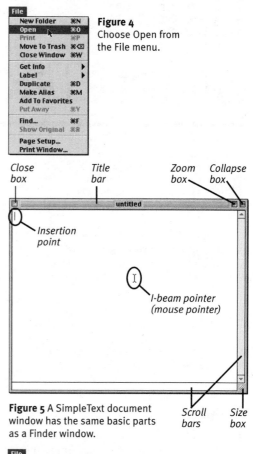

**Figure 4**
Choose Open from the File menu.

*Close box*    *Title bar*    *Zoom box*   *Collapse box*

*Insertion point*

*I-beam pointer (mouse pointer)*

**Figure 5** A SimpleText document window has the same basic parts as a Finder window.

*Scroll bars*    *Size box*

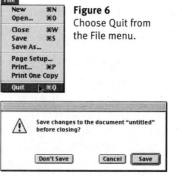

**Figure 6**
Choose Quit from the File menu.

Save changes to the document "untitled" before closing?

Don't Save    Cancel    Save

**Figure 7** A dialog box like this appears when you quit SimpleText and unsaved documents are open.

## ✔ Tip

■ I tell you more about saving SimpleText documents later in this chapter.

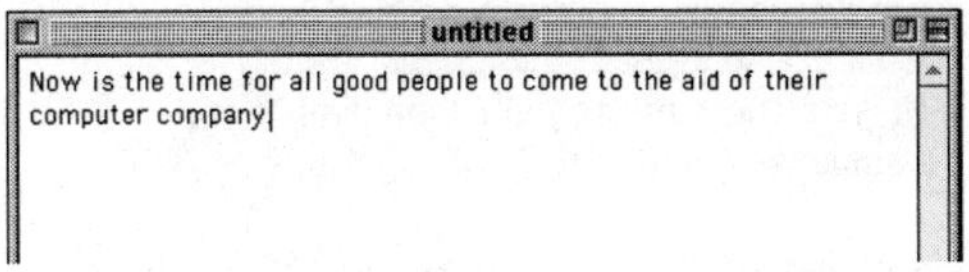

```
┌──────────────────────────────────────────┐
│ ▣   ▥▥▥▥▥▥ untitled ▥▥▥▥▥▥  ▣ ▤ │
│ Now is the time for all good people to come to the aid of their │
│ computer company| │
│                                              │
│                                              │
└──────────────────────────────────────────┘
```

**Figure 8** The text you type appears at the blinking insertion point.

# Entering & Editing Text

You enter text into a SimpleText document by typing it in. Don't worry about making mistakes; you can fix them as you type or when you're finished. This section tells you how.

## ✔ Tip

- The text entry and editing techniques covered in this section work exactly the same in most word processors, as well as many other Mac OS applications.

## To enter text

Type the text you want to enter. It appears at the blinking insertion point (**Figure 8**).

## ✔ Tips

- It is not necessary to press [Return] at the end of a line. When the text you type reaches the end of the line, it automatically begins a new line. This is called *word wrap* and is a feature of all word processors.

- The insertion point moves as you type.

- To correct an error as you type, press [Delete]. This key deletes the character to the left of the insertion point.

ENTERING TEXT

## To move the insertion point

Press ←, →, ↑, or ↓ to move the insertion point left, right, down, or up one character or line at a time.

*or*

1. Position the mouse pointer, which looks like an I-beam pointer, where you want the insertion point to appear (**Figure 9**).

2. Click the mouse button once. The insertion point appears at the mouse pointer (**Figure 10**).

## ✔ Tips

■ Since the text you type appears at the insertion point, it's a good idea to know where the insertion point is *before* you start typing.

■ When moving the insertion point with the mouse, you must click to complete the move. If you simply point with the I-beam pointer, the insertion point will stay right where it is (**Figure 9**).

## To insert text

1. Position the insertion point where you want the text to appear (**Figure 11**).

2. Type the text that you want to insert. The text is inserted at the insertion point (**Figure 12**).

## ✔ Tip

■ Word wrap changes automatically to accommodate inserted text.

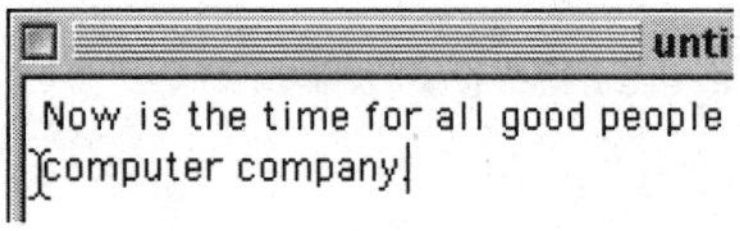

**Figure 9** Position the mouse pointer...

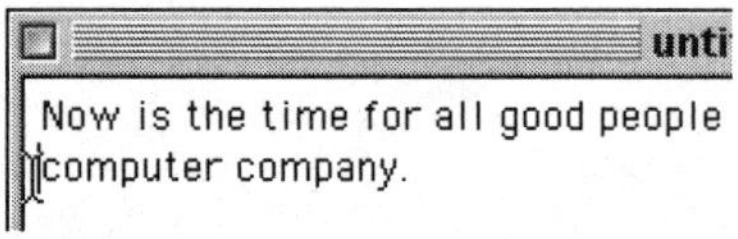

**Figure 10** ...and click to move the insertion point.

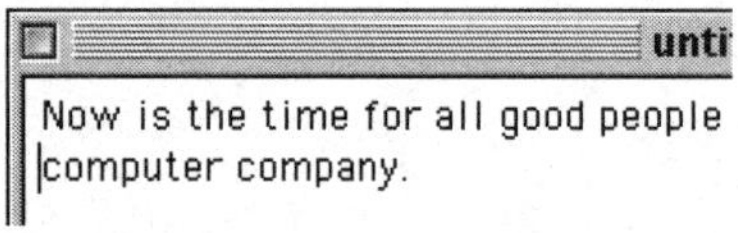

**Figure 11** Position the insertion point...

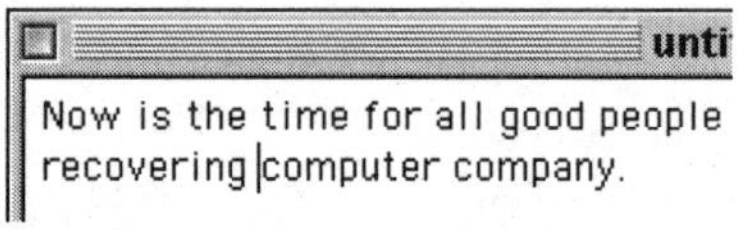

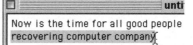

**Figure 12** ...and type in the text that you want to appear.

**Figure 13** Drag the mouse pointer over the text that you want to select.

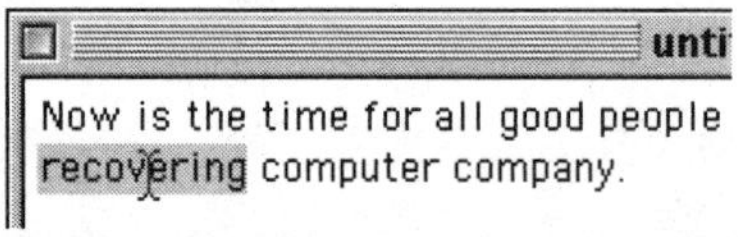

**Figure 14** Double-click the word that you want to select.

MOVING THE INSERTION POINT, INSERTING TEXT

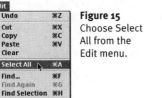

**Figure 15**
Choose Select All from the Edit menu.

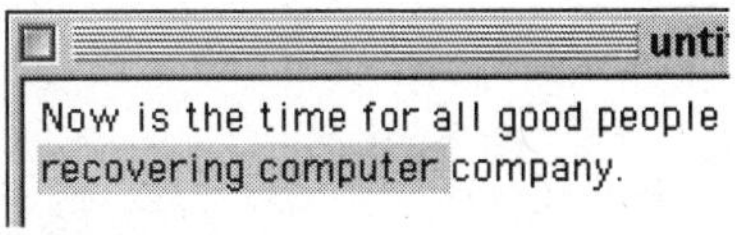

**Figure 16** Select the text that you want to delete.

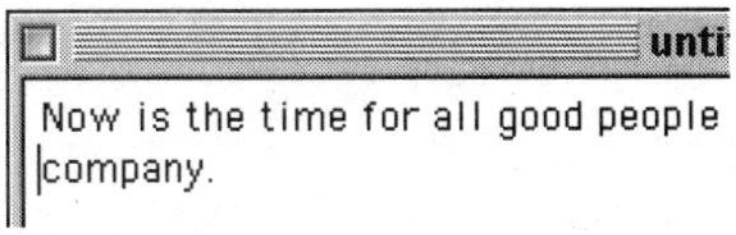

**Figure 17** When you press [Delete], the selected text disappears.

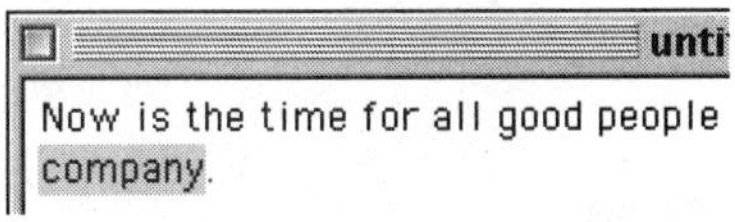

**Figure 18** Select the text that you want to replace.

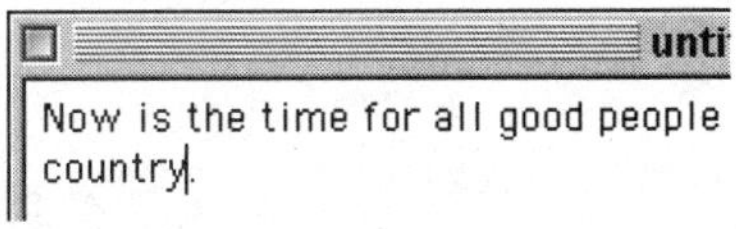

**Figure 19** The text you type replaces the selected text.

## To select text

To select any amount of text, drag the I-beam pointer over the text (**Figure 13**).

*or*

To select a single word, double-click the word (**Figure 14**).

*or*

To select the entire document, choose Edit > Select All (**Figure 15**) or press [⌃ ⌘ A].

The text you select becomes highlighted (**Figures 13** and **14**).

## ✔ Tips

- There are other selection techniques in SimpleText and other applications. These are the basic techniques and they work in every application.

- In some applications, double-clicking a word also selects the space after the word.

## To delete text

1. Select the text that you want to delete (**Figure 16**).

2. Press [Delete] or [Del]. The selected text disappears (**Figure 17**).

## ✔ Tip

- You can delete a character to the left of the insertion point by pressing [Delete]. You can delete a character to the right of the insertion point by pressing [Del].

## To replace text

1. Select the text that you want to replace (**Figure 18**).

2. Type the new text. The selected text is replaced by what you type (**Figure 19**).

# Formatting Text

SimpleText also offers some basic formatting features that you can use to change the appearance of text.

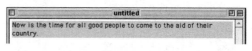

**Figure 20** Select the text to which you want to apply a different font.

## To apply a different font to text

1. Select the text to which you want to apply a different font (**Figure 20**).

2. Choose a font from the Font menu (**Figure 21**). The font you chose is applied to the selected text (**Figure 22**).

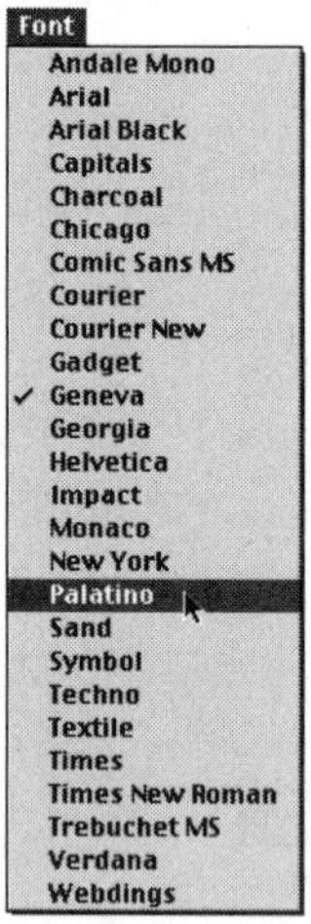

### ✔ Tips

■ Generally speaking, a *font* is style of typeface.

■ The Font menu displays all fonts that are properly installed in your System. Your Font menu may differ from the one illustrated in **Figure 21**.

■ A check mark appears on the Font menu beside the font currently applied to the selected text (**Figure 21**).

■ I tell you more about fonts in **Chapter 13**.

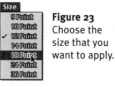

**Figure 21**
Choose the font that you want to apply.

## To change the size of text characters

1. Select the text that you want to resize (**Figure 22**).

2. Choose a size from the Size menu (**Figure 23**). The size you chose is applied to the selected text (**Figure 24**).

### ✔ Tips

■ The larger the text size, the less text appears on screen or on a printed page.

■ A check mark appears on the Size menu beside the size currently applied to the selected text (**Figure 23**).

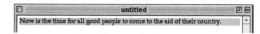

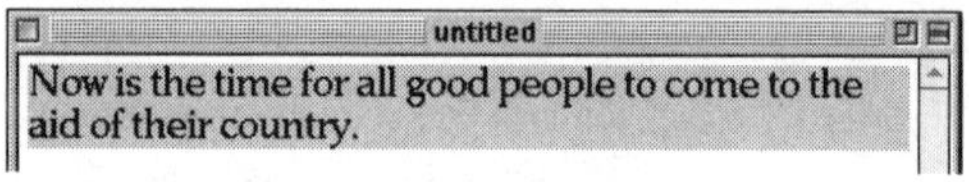

**Figure 22** The font you chose is applied.

**Figure 23**
Choose the size that you want to apply.

Now is the time for all good people to come to the aid of their country.

**Figure 24** The size you chose is applied.

APPLYING FONTS, CHANGING TEXT SIZE

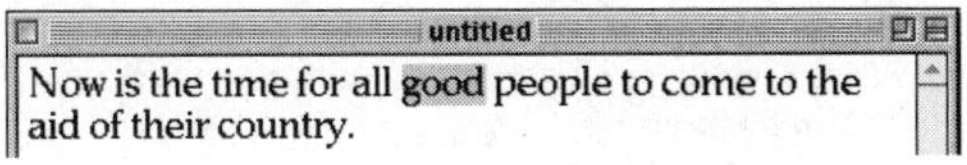

> **untitled**
>
> Now is the time for all **good** people to come to the aid of their country.

**Figure 25** Select the text to which you want to apply a style.

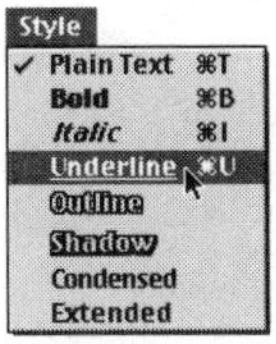

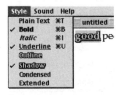

**Figure 26** Choose the style that you want to apply.

> **untitled**
>
> Now is the time for all **good** people to come to the aid of their country.

**Figure 27** The style you chose is applied.

**Figure 28** A check mark appears beside the name of each style applied to selected text.

**Figure 29** Choose Undo from the Edit menu.

## To apply a different style to text

1. Select the text to which you want to apply a different style (**Figure 25**).

2. Choose a style from the Style menu (**Figure 26**). The style you chose is applied to the selected text (**Figure 27**).

## ✔ Tips

- You can apply more than one style to text (**Figure 28**). Simply select each style you want to apply.

- A check mark appears on the Style menu beside each style applied to a selection (**Figure 28**).

- The Plain Text style removes all other styles from text.

- To remove an applied style (except Plain Text), choose it from the Style menu again.

- Some text styles can be applied with keyboard commands: ⌃ ⌘ T for Plain Text, ⌃ ⌘ B for Bold, ⌃ ⌘ I for Italic, and ⌃ ⌘ U for Underline.

# Undoing Actions

The Undo command enables you to reverse your last action, thus offering an easy way to fix errors immediately after you make them.

## To undo the last action

Choose Undo from the Edit menu (**Figure 29**) or press ⌃ ⌘ Z. The last thing you did is undone.

## ✔ Tips

- The Undo command is available in most applications and can always be found at the top of the Edit menu.

- Although some programs, like Microsoft Word 98 and Adobe Photoshop 5, offer multiple levels of undo, most programs let you undo only the very last thing you did.

# Copy, Cut, & Paste

The Copy, Cut, and Paste commands enable you to duplicate or move document contents. Text that is copied or cut is placed on the Clipboard, where it can be viewed if desired.

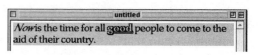

**Figure 30** Select the text you want to copy or cut.

## ✔ Tip

- Almost all Mac OS applications include the Copy, Cut, and Paste commands on the Edit menu. These commands work very much the same in all applications that support them.

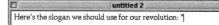

**Figure 31**
The Copy, Cut, and Paste commands are all on the Edit menu.

## To copy text

1. Select the text that you want to copy (**Figure 30**).

2. Choose Edit > Copy (**Figure 31**), or press ⌃ ⌘ C.

    The text is copied to the Clipboard so it can be pasted elsewhere. The original remains in the document.

## To cut text

1. Select the text that you want to cut (**Figure 30**).

2. Choose Edit > Cut (**Figure 31**), or press ⌃ ⌘ X.

    The text is copied to the Clipboard so it can be pasted elsewhere. The original is removed from the document.

**Figure 32** Position the insertion point where you want the contents of the Clipboard to appear.

## To paste Clipboard contents

1. Position the insertion point where you want the Clipboard contents to appear (**Figure 32**).

2. Choose Edit > Paste (**Figure 31**), or press ⌃ ⌘ V.

    The Clipboard's contents are pasted into the document (**Figure 33**).

**Figure 33** The contents of the Clipboard are pasted into the document.

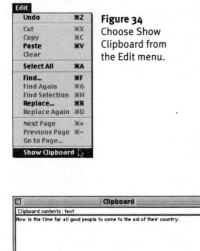

**Figure 34**
Choose Show
Clipboard from
the Edit menu.

**Figure 35** The Clipboard window displays the
contents of the Clipboard.

**Figure 36**
Choose Hide
Clipboard
from the Edit
menu...

**Figure 37**
...or choose
Close from the
File menu.

## To view the Clipboard

Choose Edit > Show Clipboard (**Figure 34**).

## ✔ Tips

■ The Clipboard window (**Figure 35**) displays
the last thing you copied or cut.

■ The Clipboard is shared by all applications.
This makes it possible to copy something
created in one document or application
and paste it in another.

■ Items remain on the Clipboard until you
use the Cut or Copy commands again or
shut off your computer.

## To close the Clipboard

Click the Clipboard window's close box
(**Figure 35**).

*or*

Choose Edit > Hide Clipboard (**Figure 36**).

*or*

1. If necessary, activate the Clipboard window.

2. Choose File > Close (**Figure 37**), or press
   ⌃ ⌘ W.

VIEWING THE CLIPBOARD

# Find & Replace

SimpleText's Find and Replace commands enable you to quickly locate or replace occurrences of text strings in your document.

## ✔ Tip

- Most word processing and page layout applications include find and replace features. Although these features are somewhat limited in SimpleText, full-featured applications such as Microsoft Word and PageMaker enable you to search for text, formatting, and other document elements as well as plain text.

## To find text

1. Choose Edit > Find (**Figure 38**), or press ⌃ ⌘ F. The Find dialog box appears (**Figure 39**).

2. Enter the text that you want to find in the Find what edit box.

3. Click Find. The Find what text is highlighted in the document.

## To replace text

1. Choose Edit > Replace (**Figure 38**), or press ⌃ ⌘ R. The Replace dialog box appears (**Figure 40**).

2. Enter the text that you want to find in the top edit box.

3. Enter the text that you want to replace it with in the bottom edit box.

4. To replace just the next occurrence of the text, click Replace. The text is replaced.

   *or*

   To replace all occurrences of the text, click Replace All. Every occurrence of the text from the insertion point to the end of the document is replaced.

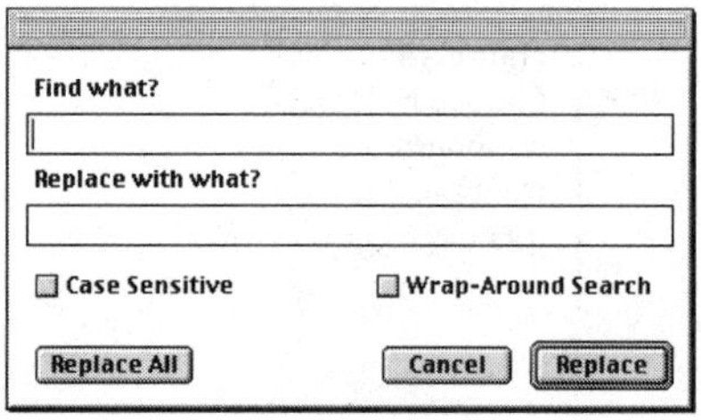

**Figure 38**
You'll find the Find and Replace commands on the Edit menu.

**Figure 39** Use the Find dialog box to enter the text that you want to find.

**Figure 40** Use the Replace dialog box to enter the text that you want to find and the text that you want to replace it with.

FINDING & REPLACING TEXT

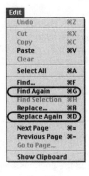

**Figure 41**
Once you've entered information in the Find or Replace dialog box, you can use the Find Again or Replace Again commands.

## ✔ Find & Replace Tips

■ Once you've conducted a search, you can use the Find Again (⌘G) or Replace Again (⌘D) commands under the Edit menu (**Figure 41**) to repeat the Find or Replace procedure with the same settings.

■ To find only text that matches the capitalization of the Find what text, turn on the Case Sensitive check box (**Figures 39** and **40**).

■ To continue the search at the beginning of the document, turn on the Wrap-Around Search check box (**Figures 39** and **40**). Otherwise, the search begins at the insertion point and ends at the end of the document.

# Speech & Sound

Mac OS includes Text-to-Speech software that makes it possible for your Mac to read the contents of text documents. In addition, if your Mac has a microphone (either built-in or external), you can record sounds. SimpleText supports both of these features.

### ✔ Tip

■ I explain how to set speech and sound options in **Chapter 13**.

## To speak text

1. Select the text you want to hear.

2. Choose Sound > Speak Selection (**Figure 42**), or press ⌘ ⌘ J.

*or*

1. Make sure no text is selected.

2. Choose Sound > Speak All (**Figure 43**), or press ⌘ ⌘ J.

### ✔ Tips

■ You can stop text from being spoken by choosing Sound > Stop Speaking (**Figure 44**), or pressing ⌘ ⌘ . .

■ You can change the voice with which text is spoken by choosing a voice from the Voices submenu under the Sound menu (**Figure 45**).

■ I tell you more about speaking text and alerts in **Chapter 13**.

**Figure 42**
Choose the Speak Selection command to have your computer read selected text...

**Figure 43**
...or choose the Speak All command to have your computer read all the text in the document.

**Figure 44**
Choose Stop Speaking to shut your computer up.

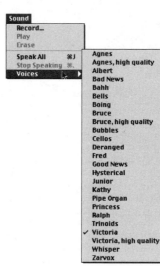

**Figure 45**
The Voices submenu offers a variety of male and female voices.

SPEAKING TEXT

**Figure 46**
Choose Record from the Sound menu.

**Figure 47** Use the Recording dialog box to record and save a sound.

**Figure 48**
Once you've recorded a sound, you can use the Play and Erase commands.

## To record & play a sounds

1. Choose Sound > Record (**Figure 46**).

2. Use the Recording dialog box that appears (**Figure 47**) to record a sound.

3. Click the Save button to save the sound in the SimpleText file.

4. Choose Sound > Play (**Figure 48**) to play back the sound.

## ✔ Tips

■ Your computer must have a microphone (either built-in or external) to record sounds.

■ I explain how to use the Recording dialog box in **Chapter 7**.

■ You can only record one sound per SimpleText document.

■ To erase the sound, choose Sound > Erase (**Figure 87**).

RECORDING & PLAYING SOUNDS

# Saving & Opening Files

When you're finished working with a Simple-Text document, you may want to save it. You can then open it another time to review, edit, or print it.

## To save a document for the first time

1. Choose File > Save (**Figure 49**), or press [⌘][⌘][S].

   *or*

   Choose File > Save As (**Figure 49**).

2. Use the Save As dialog box that appears (**Figure 50**) to enter a name and select a location for the file.

3. Click Save, or press [Return] or [Enter].

The document is saved with the name you entered in the location you specified. The name of the document appears on the document's title bar.

## ✔ Tips

- I explain how to use the Save As dialog box in **Chapter 5**.

- There's only one difference between the Save and Save As commands:

  - ▲ The Save command opens the Save As dialog box only if the document has never been saved.

  - ▲ The Save As command always opens the Save As dialog box.

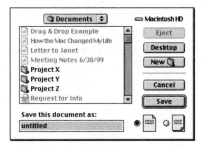

**Figure 49**
Use the Save and Save As commands to save the active document.

**Figure 50** Use the Save As dialog box to set options for saving a file.

## To save changes to an existing document

Choose File > Save (**Figure 49**), or press
⌃ ⌘ S.

The document is saved. No dialog box appears.

## ✔ Tip

■ It's a good idea to save changes to a document frequently as you work with it. This helps prevent loss of data in the event of a system crash or power outage.

## To save an existing document with a new name or in a new location

1. Choose File > Save As (**Figure 49**).

2. Use the Save As dialog box that appears (**Figure 50**) to enter a different name or select a different location (or both) for the file.

3. Click Save, or press Return or Enter.

A copy of the document is saved with the name you entered in the location you specified. The new document name appears in the document's title bar. The original document remains untouched.

## ✔ Tip

■ You can use the Save As command to create a new document based on an existing document—without overwriting the original document with your changes.

**SAVING DOCUMENTS**

## To open a document

1. Choose File > Open (**Figure 51**).

   *or*

   Press ⌃ ⌘ O.

2. Use the Open dialog box that appears
   (**Figure 52**) to locate and select the document that you want to open.

3. Click Open, or press ⌐Return⌐ or ⌐Enter⌐.

## ✔ Tip

■ I explain how to use the Open dialog box in
  **Chapter 5**.

**Figure 51**
Choose Open from
the File menu.

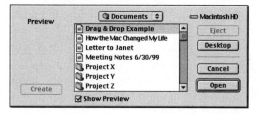

**Figure 52** Use the Open dialog box to locate and open
a file.

# APPLE MENU ITEMS

7

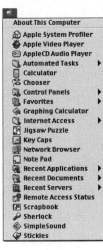

**Figure 1**
The Apple menu offers quick and easy access to just about anything you want. These are the Apple menu items that were automatically installed on my Power Macintosh 8500/180.

## The Apple Menu

The Apple menu (**Figure 1**) offers easy access to whatever applications, documents, folders, or other items you want to put there. It also automatically keeps track of recently used documents, applications, and network servers.

In this chapter, I tell you:

◆ How to open items on the Apple menu.

◆ How to customize the appearance and functionality of the Apple menu.

◆ How to add items to the Apple menu.

◆ How to use many of the items on the Apple menu.

### ✔ Tips

■ The Mac OS Installer installs the Apple menu items that are compatible with your computer. Because of this, your Apple menu may include more or fewer items than what you see in **Figure 1**. If you do not have a video-in port, for example, Apple Video Player will not be installed. This book covers the most common options.

■ There are a few Apple menu items that I don't discuss in this chapter: Chooser (**Chapters 10** and **11**), control panels (**Chapter 13** and throughout this book), Internet Access and Remote Access Status (**Chapter 14**), Network Browser (**Chapter 11**), and Sherlock (**Chapter 8**).

### Operating System Trivia

Back in the days before System 7, when the average Macintosh had only 1 MB of RAM, the Apple menu offered users access to little programs called desk accessories that could be opened and used at any time—even when another program was running. Although it doesn't sound impressive now, back then it was a very big deal.

## To open an Apple menu item

Choose the item from the Apple menu (**Figure 2**).

*or*

Choose the item from a submenu under the Apple menu (**Figure 3**).

## ✔ Tips

- An item with a submenu is a folder. Mac OS automatically creates a submenu that lists the contents of the folder (**Figures 3** and **6**).

- I explain how to use menus, including submenus, in **Chapter 2**.

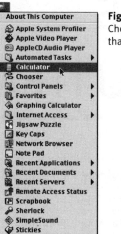

**Figure 2**
Choose the item that you want.

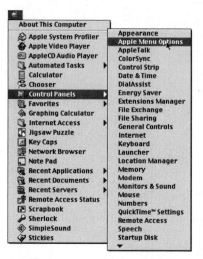

**Figure 3** If the item that you want is on a submenu, display the submenu and then choose the item.

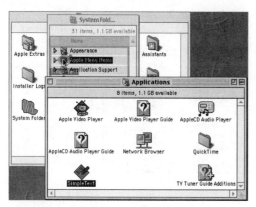

**Figure 4** Drag the item that you want to add to the Apple menu into the Apple Menu Items folder in your System Folder.

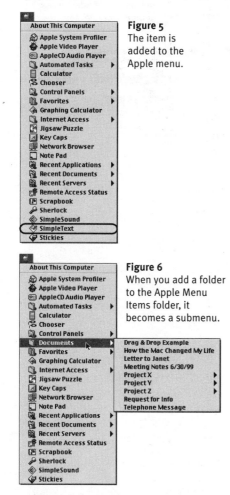

**Figure 5** The item is added to the Apple menu.

**Figure 6** When you add a folder to the Apple Menu Items folder, it becomes a submenu.

## To add items to the Apple menu

1. Open the icon for your computer's startup disk.

2. Locate and open the icon for the System Folder.

3. Drag the item that you want to add to the Apple menu into the Apple Menu Items folder in your System Folder (**Figure 4**). The item is added to the Apple menu (**Figure 5**).

## ✔ Tips

- Adding items to the Apple menu is a great way to make them quick and easy to access.

- Your computer's startup disk is normally its internal hard disk.

- It's a good idea to add an alias of an item to the Apple Menu Items folder rather than the original item. This makes it easy to keep applications and documents where they belong so they're easy to find and back up. I tell you about aliases in **Chapter 4**.

- The Favorites feature of Mac OS enables you to add aliases of items to the Favorites folder, which appears under the Apple menu. I tell you about Favorites later in this chapter.

- When you add a folder or an alias to a folder to the Apple Menu Items folder, a submenu with the folder's contents is automatically created (**Figure 6**).

ADDING ITEMS TO THE APPLE MENU

117

## To set Apple menu options

1. Choose Apple menu > Control Panels > Apple Menu Options (**Figure 3**). The Apple Menu Options control panel appears (**Figure 7**).

2. To display the contents of folders on the Apple menu as submenus, select the On radio button under Submenus.

   *or*

   To display the folders on the Apple menu as items without submenus, select the Off radio button under Submenus.

3. To have Mac OS automatically track recently used items, make sure the Remember recently used items check box is turned on. Then enter values in the three edit boxes to specify the number of recent items Mac OS should track.

4. Close the Apple Menu Options control panel window to save your settings.

## ✔ Tips

- I tell you about recently used items later in this chapter.

- The submenus feature, which is often referred to as *hierarchical folders*, can display up to five levels of folders (**Figure 8**).

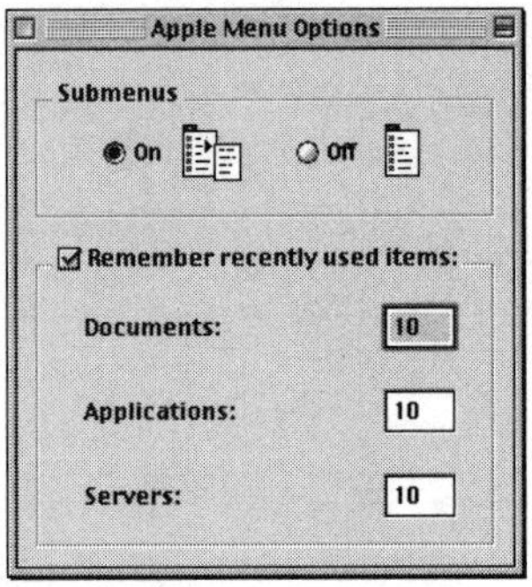

**Figure 7**
The Apple Menu Options control panel gives you some control over the way the Apple menu works.

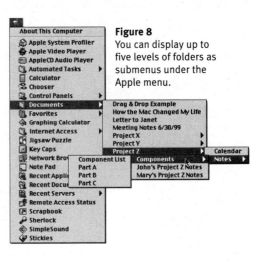

**Figure 8**
You can display up to five levels of folders as submenus under the Apple menu.

SETTING APPLE MENU OPTIONS

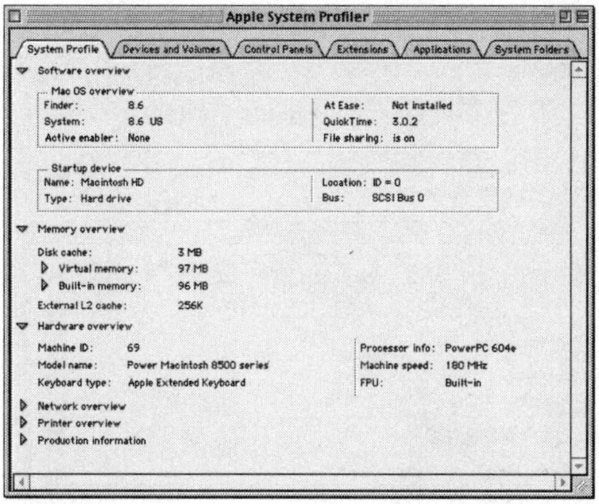

**Figure 9** The Apple System Profiler's System Profile tab provides information about your computer's hardware, Mac OS version, printer, and network connections.

# Apple System Profiler

Apple System Profiler (**Figure 9**) is an application that can provide information about your computer, its software, and its network and Internet connections. Each tab on its window displays different information:

◆ **System Profile** (**Figure 9**) provides information about your computer's hardware, Mac OS version, printer, and network connections.

◆ **Devices and Volumes** provides information about devices attached to your computer and lists all accessible storage media.

◆ **Control Panels** provides information about all installed control panels.

◆ **Extensions** provides information about all installed extensions.

◆ **Applications** provides information about all installed applications on the startup disk.

◆ **System Folders** provides information about all System Folders on your startup disk (there should be only one).

## ✔ Tips

■ The information available from Apple System Profiler is especially useful when you need technical support to solve a problem.

■ I cover networking in **Chapter 11**, connecting to the Internet in **Chapter 12**, control panels and extensions in **Chapter 13**, and applications in **Chapter 5**.

APPLE SYSTEM PROFILER

## To get system information with Apple System Profiler

1. Choose Apple menu > Apple System Profiler (**Figure 1**). The Apple System Profiler window appears (**Figure 9**).

2. Click the tab for the type of information you want to view.

### ✔ Tips

- You can click the triangle to the left of an item to expand (**Figure 10**) or collapse the item.

- You can click an item in a list to learn more about it (**Figure 11**).

## To create a report of system information

1. Choose File > New Report, or press ⌃ ⌘ N.

2. In the New Report dialog box that appears (**Figure 12**), turn on the check boxes for the information you want to include in the report.

3. Click OK.

   A system report window appears on screen (**Figure 13**).

### ✔ Tip

- You can use the File menu's Save and Print commands to save and print reports you create. I tell you about saving documents in **Chapter 5** and about printing in **Chapter 10**.

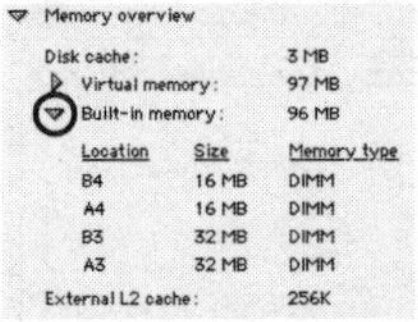

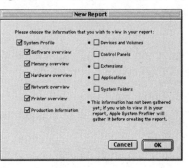

**Figure 10**
When you click a right-pointing triangle, you expand the item to see its details.

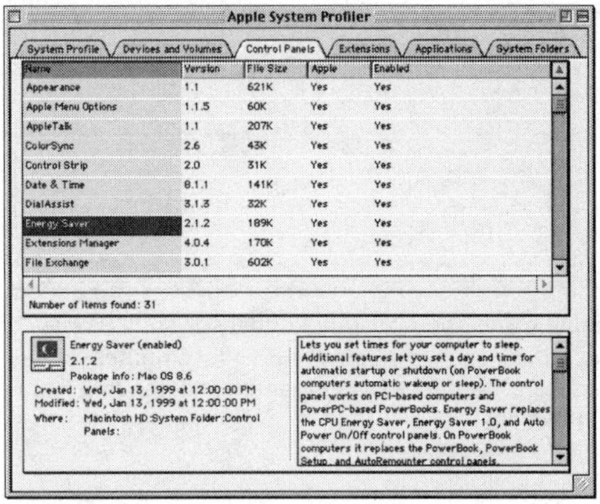

**Figure 11** Click an item in a list to learn more about it.

**Figure 12** Use this dialog box to select the items that you want to include in a report.

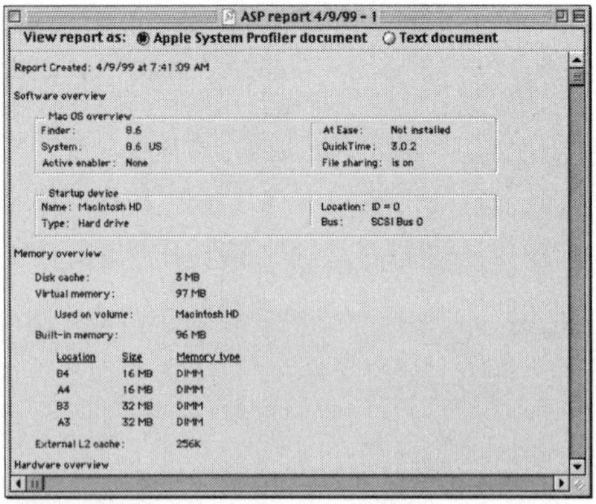

**Figure 13** Here's a report for one of my Macs.

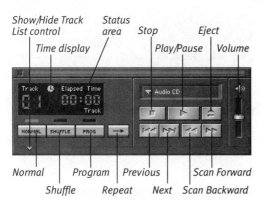

Show/Hide Track List control — Status area — Stop — Eject — Time display — Play/Pause — Volume

Normal — Program — Previous — Scan Forward — Shuffle — Repeat — Next — Scan Backward

**Figure 14** The controls on AppleCD Audio Player look a lot like the ones you'd find on a regular CD player.

AppleCD Audio Player

**Figure 15**
Another way to launch AppleCD Audio Player is to open its icon.

**Figure 16** AppleCD Audio Player's window expanded to show the play list.

**Figure 17** If you enter CD and track information, it will automatically appear the next time you play the CD.

# AppleCD Audio Player

AppleCD Audio Player enables you to play audio compact discs on your internal CD-ROM drive.

## ✔ Tip

■ You insert an audio CD disc just like you insert a CD-ROM disc. I tell you how in **Chapter 3**.

## To open AppleCD Audio Player

Choose Apple menu > AppleCD Audio Player (**Figure 1**). The AppleCD Audio Player window appears (**Figure 14**).

## ✔ Tips

■ You can also launch AppleCD Audio Player by opening its icon (**Figure 15**), which you can find in the Applications folder on your hard disk.

■ The AppleCD Audio Player window's status area is blank when no audio CD is in the CD-ROM drive.

## To show the play list

Click the Show/Hide Track List control button (**Figure 14**). The window expands to show the play list (**Figure 16**).

## ✔ Tip

■ If desired, you can enter the name of the CD and each CD track in the edit boxes of AppleCD Audio Player. Click a box to select it, then type in the appropriate information. **Figure 17** shows an example. The information you enter is saved to a preferences file so it appears automatically when you play the CD.

## To control audio CD play

Click the control buttons (**Figure 14**) to control the play of an audio CD:

◆ **Normal** plays CD tracks in order.

◆ **Shuffle** plays CD tracks in random order.

◆ **Program** plays CD tracks in the order you specify in the Playlist (see below).

◆ **Repeat** plays the CD until you stop it.

◆ **Stop** stops play.

◆ **Play/Pause** starts play or, if the CD is already playing, pauses play.

◆ **Previous** plays the previous track.

◆ **Next** plays the next track.

◆ **Scan Backward** quickly reverses the CD.

◆ **Scan Forward** fast forwards the CD.

◆ **Eject** ejects the CD.

◆ **Volume** control changes play volume; drag the slider up or down.

## To program CD play

1. If necessary, display the play list (**Figures 16** and **17**).

2. Click the Program button (**Figure 14**). The Playlist area changes to display Tracks and Playlist (**Figure 18**).

3. Drag a track from the Tracks side to the Playlist side (**Figure 19**). When you release the mouse button, the track appears on the Playlist side (**Figure 20**).

4. Repeat step 3 for each track that you want to include in the program.

## To customize AppleCD Audio Player appearance & sound

Under the Options menu, choose customization commands from the Window Color (**Figure 21**), Indicator Color (**Figure 22**), and Sound (**Figure 23**) submenus.

**Figure 18** Click the Program button to program CD play.

**Figure 19** Drag a track from the list on the left to the list on the right.

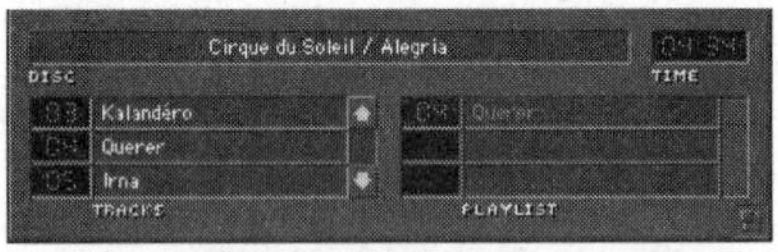

**Figure 20** When you release the mouse button, the track appears in the list on the right side.

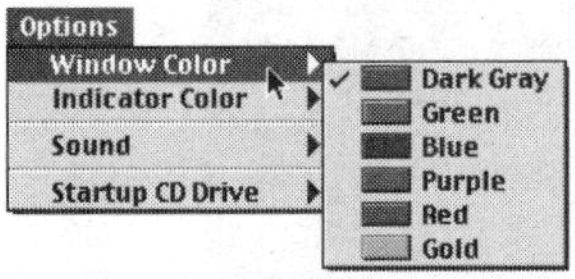

**Figure 21** The Window Color submenu lets you change the color of the window.

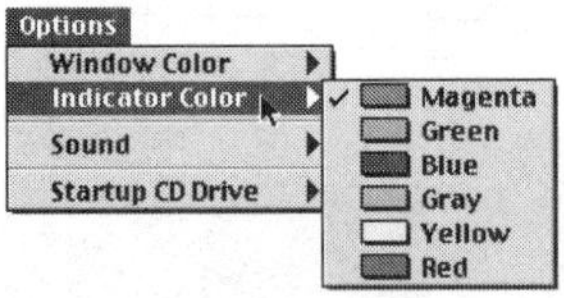

**Figure 22** The Indicator Color submenu lets you change the color of the numbers and track names.

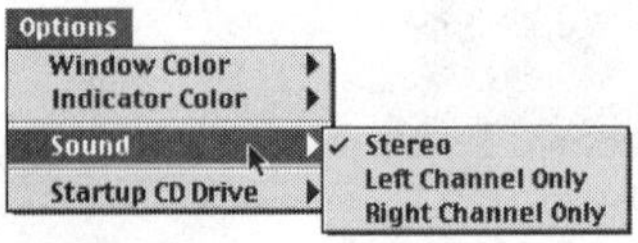

**Figure 23** The Sound submenu lets you change the way stereo sound is played.

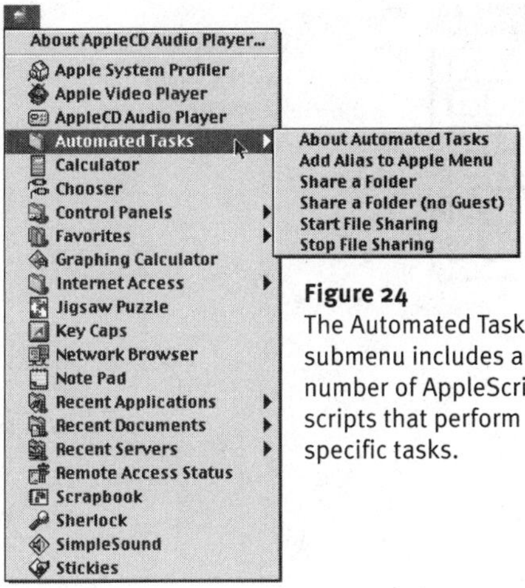

**About AppleCD Audio Player...**
Apple System Profiler
Apple Video Player
AppleCD Audio Player
**Automated Tasks**
Calculator
Chooser
Control Panels
Favorites
Graphing Calculator
Internet Access
Jigsaw Puzzle
Key Caps
Network Browser
Note Pad
Recent Applications
Recent Documents
Recent Servers
Remote Access Status
Scrapbook
Sherlock
SimpleSound
Stickies

**About Automated Tasks**
Add Alias to Apple Menu
Share a Folder
Share a Folder (no Guest)
Start File Sharing
Stop File Sharing

**Figure 24**
The Automated Tasks
submenu includes a
number of AppleScript
scripts that perform
specific tasks.

# Automated Tasks

Automated Tasks are AppleScript scripts you
can use to perform a variety of tasks:

◆ **Add Alias to Apple Menu** creates an alias
of a selected icon and moves it to the Apple
Menu Items folder, thus adding it to the
Apple menu.

◆ **Share a Folder** turns on file sharing and
sets access privileges for a folder named
*Shared Folder* on your hard disk. If the
folder does not exist, it is created.

◆ **Share a Folder (no Guest)** does the same
as Share a Folder but allows access only to
registered network users.

◆ **Start File Sharing** turns on file sharing.

◆ **Stop File Sharing** turns off file sharing.

## ✔ Tips

■ The first option on the Automated Tasks
submenu (**Figure 24**) is not a script; it's a
SimpleText document. Choose it to learn
more about automated tasks.

■ I tell you about AppleScript in **Chapter 8**
and about file sharing in **Chapter 11**.

■ You can add an item to the Automated
Tasks submenu (**Figure 24**) by dragging an
AppleScript script icon to the Automated
Tasks folder in the Apple Menu Items
folder.

## To use an automated task

1. To use the Add Alias to Apple Menu task,
begin by selecting the icons for items you
want to add to the Apple menu.

   *or*

   To use one of the Share a Folder tasks, begin
   by selecting the folder you want to share.

2. Choose the task that you want to use from
the Automated Tasks submenu under the
Apple menu (**Figure 24**).

# Calculators

The Apple menu includes two calculators:

**Figure 25**
The Calculator desk accessory has the same functionality as a $5 pocket calculator.

◆ **Calculator** (**Figure 25**) is a simple calculator that can perform addition, subtraction, multiplication, and division.

◆ **Graphing Calculator** is a charting tool that can create static and dynamic 2-D and 3-D graphs based on formulas.

## To use the Calculator

1. Choose Apple menu > Calculator (**Figure 1**). The Calculator window appears (**Figure 25**).

2. Use your mouse to click buttons for numbers and operators.

   *or*

   Press keyboard keys corresponding to numbers and operators.

   The numbers you enter and the results of your calculations appear at the top of the Calculator window.

## ✔ Tip

■ You can use the Cut, Copy, and Paste commands to copy the results of calculations into documents. I tell you about cutting and copying in **Chapter 6**.

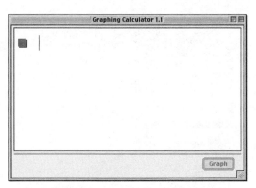

Figure 26 The Graphing Calculator window before you enter a formula.

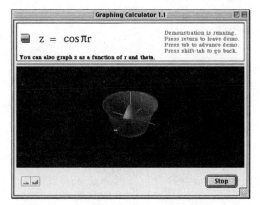

Figure 27 The Graphing Calculator can even create animated, three-dimensional graphs.

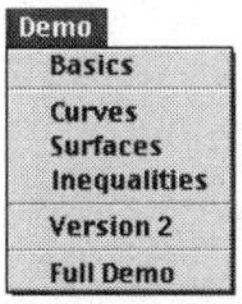

Figure 28
Use the Demo menu to view a variety of Graphing Calculator demos.

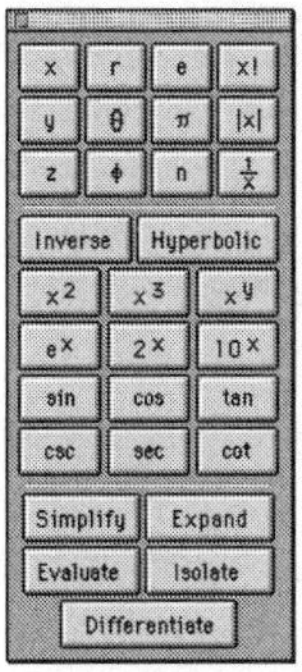

Figure 29
Graphing Calculator's keypad makes it easy to enter complex functions.

## To use the Graphing Calculator

1. Choose Apple menu > Graphing Calculator (**Figure 1**). The Graphing Calculator window appears (**Figure 26**).

2. In the window, enter the formula that you want to graph.

3. Click Graph to create the graph (**Figure 27**).

## ✔ Tips

■ If a formula is already in the Graphing Calculator when you open it, it appears as a split window (**Figure 27**). You can enter a new formula in the top half of the window to create a different graph.

■ If the graph you create is three-dimensional (**Figure 27**), it rotates.

■ You can use commands under the Demo menu (**Figure 28**) to view Graphing Calculator demonstrations.

■ To display a clickable keypad of functions that you can include in your formulas (**Figure 29**), choose Equation > Show Keypad.

■ You can use the Copy Graph command under the Edit menu to copy the graph for inclusion in other documents.

USING THE GRAPHING CALCULATOR

125

# Favorites

Favorites enables you to add frequently used documents, applications, network servers and volumes, and Internet locations to a submenu on the Apple menu. This makes them quick and easy to access.

**Figure 30**
Select the item that you want to add as a favorite item.

## ✔ Tips

■ Favorites also appear in the Network Browser and the new Open and Save As dialog boxes. I discuss the Network Browser in **Chapter 11** and the new Open and Save As dialog boxes in **Chapter 5**.

■ The favorites feature works with aliases, which I discuss in **Chapter 4**.

■ I tell you more about network servers and volumes in **Chapter 11** and Internet locations in **Chapter 12**.

**Figure 31**
Choose Add To Favorites from the File menu.

## To add a favorite item

1. In the Finder, select the icon for the item that you want to add as a favorite item (**Figure 30**).

2. Choose File > Add To Favorites (**Figure 31**).

   The item is added to the Favorites submenu under the Apple menu (**Figure 32**).

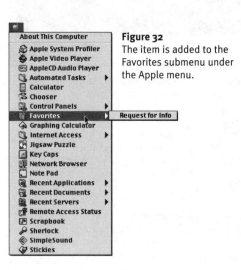

**Figure 32**
The item is added to the Favorites submenu under the Apple menu.

## ✔ Tip

■ You can also add an item to the Favorites folder by making an alias of the item and dragging the alias into the Favorites folder inside the System Folder.

**Figure 33** As you add Favorites, the Favorites folder can get cluttered with items.

**Figure 34** You can use folders to organize the contents of the Favorites folder.

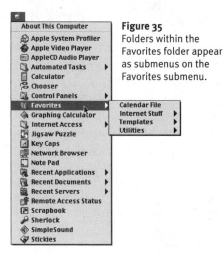

**Figure 35**
Folders within the Favorites folder appear as submenus on the Favorites submenu.

## To organize favorites

1. Choose Apple menu > Favorites (**Figure 32**) to open the Favorites folder window (**Figure 33**).

2. Create and name folders for different groups of items. Store the appropriate items in each folder (**Figure 34**).

3. Close the Favorites folder window.

   The Favorites submenu displays each folder within it as a submenu (**Figure 35**).

## To use a favorite item

From the Favorites submenu under the Apple menu (**Figures 32** and **35**), choose the item you want to open.

## To remove a favorite

1. Choose Apple menu > Favorites (**Figure 32**) to open the Favorites folder window (**Figures 33** or **34**).

2. Drag the item that you want to remove out of the window.

3. Close the Favorites folder window.

   The item is removed from the Favorites submenu.

ORGANIZING, USING, & REMOVING FAVORITES

# Jigsaw Puzzle

The Jigsaw Puzzle is an electronic puzzle. You work on the puzzle by scattering the pieces and then dragging them into position inside the frame.

## To use the Jigsaw Puzzle

1. Choose Apple menu > Jigsaw Puzzle (**Figure 1**). The Jigsaw Puzzle window appears (**Figure 36**).

2. Choose Options > Start New Puzzle (**Figure 37**).

3. In the dialog box that appears (**Figure 38**), select the radio button for the size of the pieces you want. Then click OK. The picture breaks up into puzzle pieces that are scattered in the window (**Figure 39**).

4. Drag the pieces into their proper position in the puzzle window. When in the correct position, they "snap" into place with a sound.

## ✔ Tips

■ The smaller the pieces you select in step 3, the more difficult the puzzle will be.

■ To have the puzzle solved automatically for you, choose Options > Solve Puzzle.

■ To change the picture in the puzzle, use SimpleText or your favorite graphics application to open a picture that you like. Use the Edit menu's Copy command to copy the picture to the Clipboard. Then switch back to Jigsaw Puzzle and use the Edit menu's Paste command to paste the picture in (**Figure 40**).

**Figure 36** The Jigsaw Puzzle window.

**Figure 37** Choose Start New Puzzle from the Options menu.

**Figure 38** Select the size that you want for the puzzle pieces.

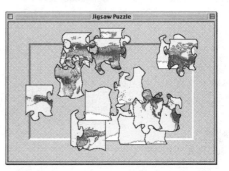

**Figure 39** The puzzle pieces are scattered in the window.

**Figure 40** Turn a picture into a puzzle by pasting it in. This is my friend Janet, who will be very surprised to see her picture in this book.

USING THE JIGSAW PUZZLE

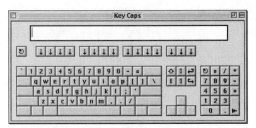

**Figure 41** The Key Caps window displaying some characters of the Charcoal font.

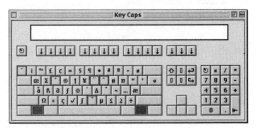

**Figure 42** In this example, holding down ⟨Option⟩ displays additional characters in the Charcoal font.

**Figure 43** Choose the font whose characters you want to view from the Fonts menu...

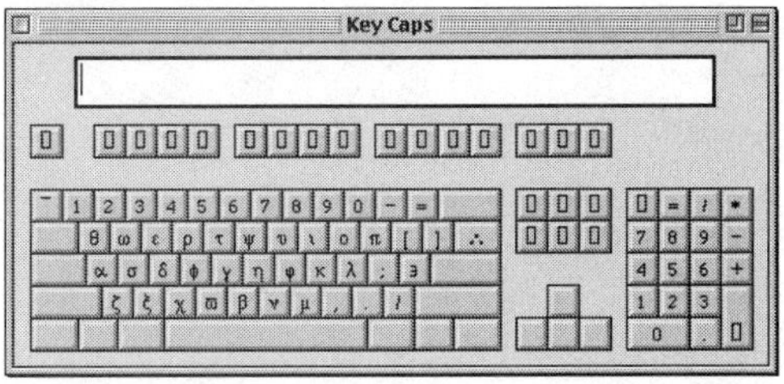

**Figure 44** ...and they appear in the Key Caps window.

# Key Caps

Key Caps enables you to see what the characters in your fonts are and where they are located on your keyboard.

## To use Key Caps

1. Choose Apple menu > Key Caps (**Figure 1**). The Key Caps window appears (**Figure 41**).

2. To see what characters look like with various modifier keys pressed (like ⟨Shift⟩, ⟨Option⟩, or ⟨Ctrl⟩), press the modifier key. The Key Caps characters change (**Figure 42**).

3. To see what the characters of a different font look like, choose the font name from the Fonts menu (**Figure 43**). The Key Caps characters change (**Figure 44**).

## ✔ Tips

- You can type in the Key Caps window to see what a string of text looks like.

- Key Caps offers a great way to learn where special characters are hidden away in a font. For example, hold down ⟨Option⟩ while looking at the Key Caps window (**Figure 42**) to see a bullet (•), trademark symbol (™), registered trademark symbol (®), and copyright symbol (©). To type one of these characters in a document, hold down ⟨Option⟩ while pressing the appropriate keyboard key: ⟨Option⟩⟨8⟩ for •, ⟨Option⟩⟨2⟩ for ™, ⟨Option⟩⟨R⟩ for ®, ⟨Option⟩⟨G⟩ for ©.

- Some special characters, like accented characters (for example, é, á, and ü) require two keystrokes to type. First type the keystroke for the accent that you want, then type the character that you want the accent to appear over. For example, to type á, press ⟨Option⟩⟨E⟩ and then ⟨A⟩. The two-stroke characters appear in Key Caps with a gray box around them (**Figure 42**).

# The Note Pad & Scrapbook

The Note Pad and Scrapbook are two little programs you can use to store information for reference to use in other documents.

◆ **Note Pad** offers several "pages" where you can enter text. It's a good place to jot down notes such as phone numbers, lists of things to do, or plain text you use over and over in documents.

◆ **Scrapbook** offers an unlimited number of entries for storing formatted text, sounds, graphics, and movies. The Scrapbook is best used to store things that you use over and over in documents, like a company logo, formatted text, or your signature.

## To use the Note Pad

1. Choose Apple menu > Note Pad (**Figure 1**). The Note Pad window appears (**Figure 45**).

2. Type or paste in the text you want to store in the Note Pad (**Figure 46**).

## ✔ Tips

■ To turn the page, click the "folded up" corner of the page (**Figure 45**).

■ The Note Pad starts with eight notes. You can add or remove notes using the File menu's New Note and Delete Note commands (**Figure 47**).

■ You can print notes using the File Menu's Print Current Note or Print One commands (**Figure 47**). I tell you more about printing in **Chapter 10**.

■ The contents of the Note Pad are automatically saved when you close it.

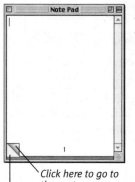

**Figure 45**
The Note Pad window.

*Click here to go to the next page*
*Click here to go to the previous page*

**Figure 46**
Type in the text you want to store in the Note Pad.

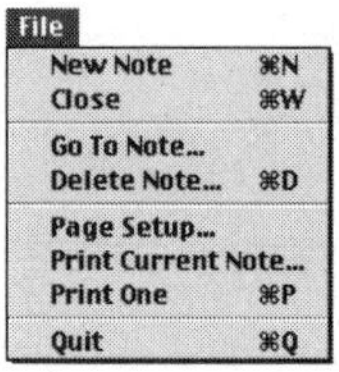

**Figure 47**
The File menu offers commands for creating, deleting, and printing notes.

**Figure 48** The Scrapbook window.

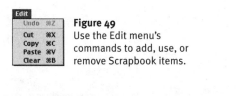

**Figure 49**
Use the Edit menu's commands to add, use, or remove Scrapbook items.

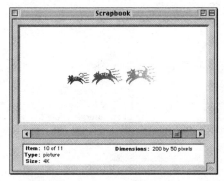

**Figure 50** Choosing the Paste command pastes the contents of the Clipboard into the Scrapbook.

## To use the Scrapbook

1. Choose Apple menu > Scrapbook (**Figure 1**). The Scrapbook window appears (**Figure 48**).

2. Click the scroll bar arrows to view the entries in the Scrapbook file.

3. Use Edit menu commands (**Figure 49**) to work with Scrapbook items:

   ▲ To add an item to the Scrapbook, open and select it in the application in which it was created, choose Edit > Copy to copy it to the Clipboard, switch to the Scrapbook, and choose Edit > Paste (**Figure 49**) to paste it into the Scrapbook (**Figure 50**).

   ▲ To use a Scrapbook item in another document, display the item you want to use, choose Edit > Copy (**Figure 49**) to copy it to the Clipboard, switch to the document in which you want to paste the item, and choose Edit > Paste to paste it into the document.

   ▲ To remove an item from the Scrapbook, display the item you want to remove and choose Edit > Cut (**Figure 49**).

## ✔ Tips

■ You can use the Scrapbook to store frequently used formatted text, graphics, movies, and sounds.

■ I tell you about the Copy, Cut, and Paste commands in **Chapter 6**.

■ The contents of the Scrapbook are automatically saved when you close it.

**USING THE SCRAPBOOK**

# SimpleSound

SimpleSound is an application you can use to select an alert sound or add sounds to your System.

## ✔ Tip

- To record sounds with your Macintosh, you must have a microphone.

## To select an alert sound

1. Choose Apple menu > SimpleSound (**Figure 1**). The Alert Sounds window appears (**Figure 51**).

2. Click to select the name of the sound that you want. It plays back so you can hear it.

3. Close the Alert Sounds window to save your selection.

## To add an alert sound

1. Choose Apple menu > SimpleSound (**Figure 1**). The Alert Sounds window appears (**Figure 51**).

2. Click Add to display the Recording dialog box (**Figure 52**).

3. Click Record, and record a sound with your microphone.

4. When you are finished recording the sound, click Stop.

5. To play back the sound, click Play.

6. To save the sound, click Save.

7. A dialog box like the one in **Figure 53** appears. Enter a name for the sound, and click OK.

   The sound you recorded appears in the Alert Sounds window (**Figure 54**).

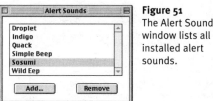

**Figure 51**
The Alert Sounds window lists all installed alert sounds.

**Figure 52** Use the Recording dialog box to record, play, and save a sound.

**Figure 53**
You'll see this dialog box when you save an alert sound.

**Figure 54**
The Alert Sounds window also lists the sounds you add.

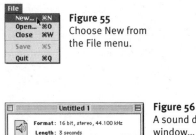

**Figure 55**
Choose New from
the File menu.

**Figure 56**
A sound document
window...

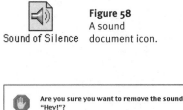

**Figure 57** ...and a Save As dialog box
appear when you save a sound file.

Sound of Silence

**Figure 58**
A sound
document icon.

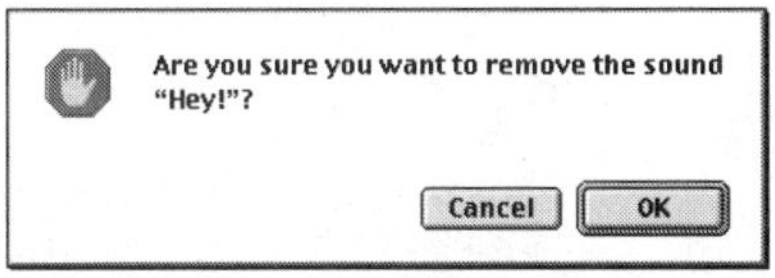

Are you sure you want to remove the sound
"Hey!"?

Cancel    OK

**Figure 59** This confirmation window
appears when you try to delete a sound.

## To create a sound file

1. Choose Apple menu > SimpleSound
   (**Figure 1**). The Alert Sounds window
   appears (**Figure 51**).

2. Choose File > New (**Figure 55**) or press
   ⌃⌘N to display the Recording dialog box
   (**Figure 52**).

3. Click Record, and record a sound with your
   microphone.

4. When you are finished recording the
   sound, click Stop.

5. To play back the sound, click Play.

6. To save the sound, click Save.

7. A sound document window (**Figure 56**)
   and a Save As dialog box (**Figure 57**)
   appear. Use the Save As dialog box to save
   the file to disk.

   A sound document icon (**Figure 58**)
   appears in the Finder in the location in
   which you saved the sound file.

## ✔ Tips

■ I tell you how to use the Save As dialog box
  in **Chapter 5**.

■ You can play a sound file by double-clicking
  its icon.

## To delete an alert sound

1. Choose Apple menu > SimpleSound
   (**Figure 1**). The Alert Sounds window
   appears (**Figure 51**).

2. Select the sound that you want to delete,
   and click Remove.

3. A confirmation dialog box appears (**Figure
   59**). Click OK.

   The alert sound is removed from the list.

# Stickies

Stickies are computerized sticky notes that you can use to place reminders on your screen.

## To use Stickies

1. Choose Apple menu > Stickies (**Figure 1**). A Stickies note window should appear (**Figure 60**); if one doesn't appear, choose File > New Note or press ⌃ ⌘ N.

2. Type the text that you want to include in the note (**Figure 61**).

3. To change the style of note text, choose Note > Text Style (**Figure 62**) or press ⌃ ⌘ T. Select font, size, and style options in the Text Style dialog box that appears (**Figure 63**). Then click OK. All the text in the note changes.

4. To change the color of the note, choose a color from the Color menu (**Figure 64**).

## ✔ Tips

- You can use options under the File menu (**Figure 65**) to create a new note, save all notes, or print notes.

- If you close a Stickies note, a dialog box like the one in **Figure 66** tells you it will be deleted from the Desktop and offers to save its contents to a text file. If you click Save, use the Save As dialog box that appears to save the note as text.

- Stickies notes remain on the Desktop until you quit Stickies.

- When you quit Stickies, all notes are automatically saved to disk.

- The first time you quit Stickies, a dialog box like the one in **Figure 67** lets you specify whether you want Stickies to automatically appear on your Desktop when you restart your computer.

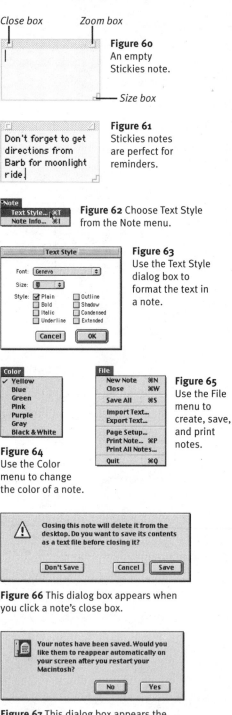

*Close box* *Zoom box*

**Figure 60**
An empty
Stickies note.

— *Size box*

**Figure 61**
Stickies notes
are perfect for
reminders.

Don't forget to get directions from Barb for moonlight ride.

**Figure 62** Choose Text Style from the Note menu.

**Figure 63**
Use the Text Style dialog box to format the text in a note.

**Figure 65**
Use the File menu to create, save, and print notes.

**Figure 64**
Use the Color menu to change the color of a note.

Closing this note will delete it from the desktop. Do you want to save its contents as a text file before closing it?

Don't Save    Cancel    Save

**Figure 66** This dialog box appears when you click a note's close box.

Your notes have been saved. Would you like them to reappear automatically on your screen after you restart your Macintosh?

No    Yes

**Figure 67** This dialog box appears the first time you quit Stickies.

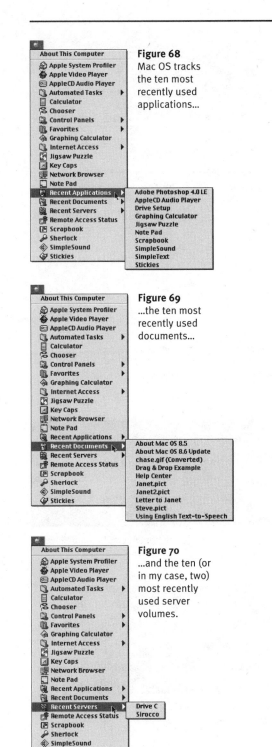

**Figure 68**
Mac OS tracks the ten most recently used applications...

**Figure 69**
...the ten most recently used documents...

**Figure 70**
...and the ten (or in my case, two) most recently used server volumes.

# Recent Items

Recent items are recently opened applications, documents, and servers. Mac OS automatically tracks the things you open and creates submenus of the ten most recently opened items in each category, making it quick and easy to open them again.

## To open recent items

To open a recently used application, choose its name from the Recent Applications submenu under the Apple menu (**Figure 68**).

*or*

To open a recently used document, choose its name from the Recent Document submenu under the Apple menu (**Figure 69**).

*or*

To open a recently used server, choose its name from the Recent Servers submenu under the Apple menu (**Figure 70**).

## ✔ Tips

- You can change the number of tracked items in the Apple Menu Options control panel (**Figure 7**).

- If your computer is not connected to a network, or you have never connected to a network server, there will be no Recent Servers submenu.

- When you select a server from the Recent Servers submenu, you may be prompted to log on to the server machine by providing a User Name and Password.

- I tell you about applications and documents in **Chapter 5** and about servers in **Chapter 11**.

OPENING RECENT ITEMS

# The About Window

The very first option on the Apple menu opens the About window. Its name varies based on the current application:

◆ When the Finder is active, choose About This Computer to display a window like the one in **Figure 71**. This window provides information about the version of System software running on your computer as well as the installed and available RAM and open applications.

◆ When an application is active, choose About *Application Name* to display a window like the ones in **Figures 72** and **73**.

## ✔ Tip

■ An *Easter egg* is an undocumented program feature included in a program by its programmers. Mac OS is known for its Easter eggs. Here's one for you to find: With the Finder active, hold down (Option) while choosing Apple menu > About The Finder. A window with a colorful mountain scene appears. Wait a moment, and the names of the Finder programming team will scroll past in the window (**Figure 74**). (Want more Easter eggs? Be sure to visit the companion Web site for this book: *http://www.gilesrd.com/macosvqs/.*)

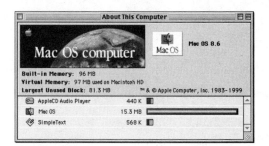

**Figure 71** The About This Computer window provides information about your computer's System software and memory.

**Figure 72** Most About windows display version and programmer information, like this one from SimpleText...

**Figure 73** ...and this one from AppleCD Audio Player.

**Figure 74** This About The Finder window is an example of an Easter egg.

THE ABOUT WINDOW

# USING MAC OS UTILITIES

## Mac OS 8.6 Utilities

In addition to SimpleText, which I discuss in **Chapter 6**, and the Apple menu items, which I discuss in **Chapter 7**, Mac OS 8.6 includes a number of applications and utilities that are automatically installed when you complete a standard installation:

- ◆ **QuickTime**, **MoviePlayer**, and **Picture-Viewer**, which enable you to work with QuickTime and other graphic format files.

- ◆ **Sherlock**, which enables you to locate files on local or networked disks, based on a variety of search criteria.

- ◆ **Disk First Aid**, which enables you to diagnose and repair disk problems.

- ◆ **Drive Setup**, which enables you to initialize hard disks and install or update hard disk drivers.

- ◆ **AppleScript**, which enable you to create scripts for automatically performing tasks.

I tell you about all of these programs in this chapter.

### ✔ Tip

- ■ I tell you about Mac OS 8.6 components in the **Introduction** and about installing Mac OS in **Chapter 1**.

# QuickTime, MoviePlayer, & PictureViewer

QuickTime is a video and audio technology developed by Apple Computer, Inc. Mac OS uses the QuickTime System extension to understand files in QuickTime format.

MoviePlayer and PictureViewer (**Figure 1**) are applications you can use to work with QuickTime and graphics files. You can find these programs in the QuickTime folder inside the Applications folder on your hard disk. Mac OS 8.6 also includes QuickTime plug-in files for your Web browser so you can view QuickTime files on the Web.

On the next few pages, I tell you how to use MoviePlayer and PictureViewer, as well as how to upgrade to QuickTime Pro.

## ✔ Tips

- QuickTime version 3, which is included with Mac OS 8.6, has fewer features than the Pro version, which also enables you to edit and save QuickTime files.

- I tell you more about System extensions in **Chapter 13** and about the Web in **Chapter 14**.

## To open a QuickTime movie

Double-click the QuickTime movie's icon.

*or*

1. Select the icon for the movie that you want to open (**Figure 2**).

2. Choose File > Open, or press ⌘O.

MoviePlayer launches. The movie's first frame appears in a window (**Figure 3**).

## ✔ Tip

- You can also open a QuickTime movie by using the Open command on MoviePlayer's File menu (**Figure 4**). I tell you how to use the Open dialog box in **Chapter 5**.

MoviePlayer          PictureViewer

**Figure 1** MoviePlayer lets you play QuickTime movies; PictureViewer lets you view graphics files using QuickTime's built-in translators.

**Figure 2**
Select the icon for the QuickTime movie that you want to open.

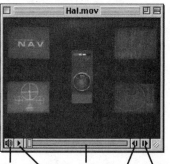

**Figure 3**
The first frame of the QuickTime movie appears in a MoviePlayer window.

Volume    Play/    Play    Step       Step
control   Stop     bar     backward   forward

**Figure 4**
MoviePlayer's File menu.

**Figure 5**
Click the Volume control to display a slider. Then drag the slider up or down to change the movie's volume.

**Figure 6**
Options under the Movie menu let you change the viewing size of a QuickTime movie.

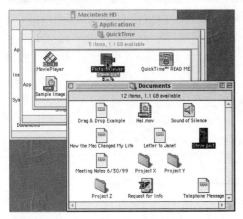

**Figure 7** Drag a graphic file's icon onto the PictureViewer icon to open it with PictureViewer.

**Figure 8**
The graphic file opens in a window like this. (This is Steve on his tractor.)

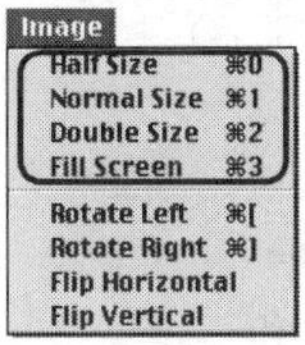

**Figure 9** PictureViewer's Image menu offers a number of size options for viewing the graphic files you open.

## To control movie play

Click the control buttons (**Figure 3**) to control the play of a QuickTime movie file:

◆ **Volume control** changes movie volume; click the icon to display a slider that you can drag up or down (**Figure 5**).

◆ **Play/Stop** starts play or, if the movie is already playing, stops play.

◆ **Step Backward** moves backward through the movie, one frame at a time.

◆ **Step Forward** moves forward through the movie, one frame at a time.

◆ **Play bar** tracks movie progress. By dragging the slider, you can scroll through the movie without sound.

## To specify movie size

Select a size option from the Movie menu (**Figure 6**). The size of the movie's window changes accordingly.

## To open a graphic file

Drag the icon for the graphic file onto the icon for the PictureViewer application (**Figure 7**). PictureViewer launches and displays the graphic file (**Figure 8**).

## ✔ Tip

■ You can also open a graphic file by using the Open command on PictureViewer's File menu, which is identical to MoviePlayer's File menu (**Figure 4**). I tell you how to use the Open dialog box in **Chapter 5**.

## To specify picture size

Select a size option from the Image menu (**Figure 9**). The size of the graphic's window changes accordingly.

## To upgrade to QuickTime Pro

1. If you have Internet access, double-click the Get QuickTime Pro icon on the Desktop (**Figure 10**). In the Upgrade to QuickTime Pro window that appears (**Figure 11**), click the Now button. Then wait while your computer connects to the Internet. Follow the instructions that appear in your Web browser window to obtain a QuickTime Pro access key. You can then disconnect from the Internet and quit your Web browser software.

   *or*

   If you do not have Internet Access, call *1-888-295-0648* to obtain an access key.

2. Choose Apple menu > Control Panels > QuickTime. The QuickTime Settings window appears (**Figure 12**).

3. Choose Registration from the pop-up menu (**Figure 13**) to display Registration options (**Figure 14**).

4. Click the Enter Registration button to display the Registration window (**Figure 15**).

5. Enter your Name, Organization, and the Registration Number provided by Apple in the appropriate edit boxes.

6. Click OK. The information you entered appears in the QuickTime Settings window, along with the words *QuickTime: Pro Player Edition*.

7. Close the window.

## ✔ Tips

■ To learn more about QuickTime Pro, use your Web browser to visit *http://www.apple.com/quicktime/upgrade/*.

■ QuickTime Pro costs $29.99. You must provide credit card information when requesting an access code.

Get QuickTime Pro

**Figure 10** To obtain the QuickTime Pro access key from the Internet, double-click this icon on the Desktop.

**Figure 11** Click the Now button in this window.

**Figure 12** The QuickTime Settings control panel window.

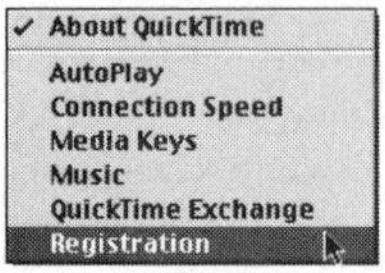

**Figure 13** Choose Registration from the pop-up menu.

**Figure 14** The Registration options in the QuickTime Settings control panel window.

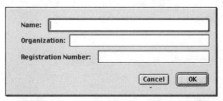

**Figure 15** Enter your Name, Organization, and the Registration Number provided by Apple.

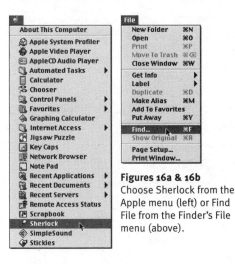

Criteria area

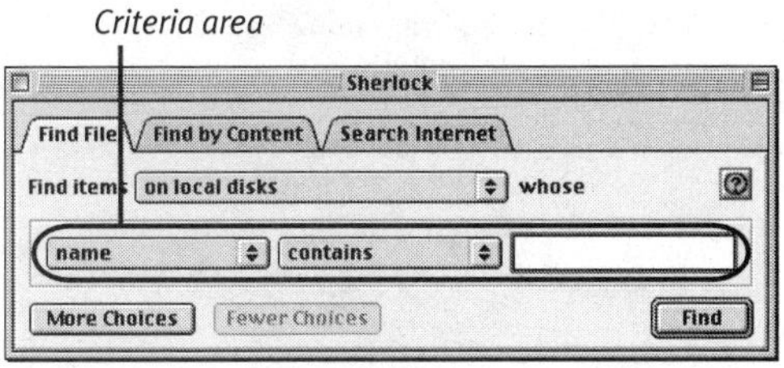

**Figure 17** The Find File tab of the Sherlock window lets you set up search criteria.

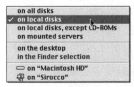

**Figure 18**
Choose a location to search from the pop-up menu near the top of the Find File tab of the Sherlock window.

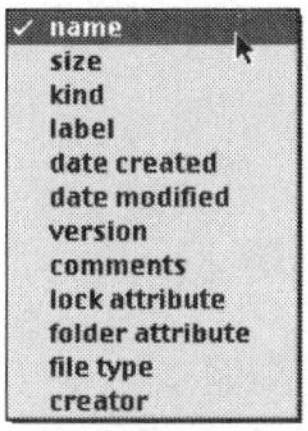

**Figure 19**
Choose a criteria type from the first pop-up menu in the middle of the Find File tab of the Sherlock window.

# Sherlock

Sherlock is an application you can use to locate files on your hard disk or other disks accessible over a network.

## ✔ Tips

- You can also use Sherlock to search the Internet. I explain how in **Chapter 12**.

- I tell you more about networked hard disks in **Chapter 11**.

## To find files by attribute

1. Choose Apple menu > Sherlock (**Figure 16a**).

   or

   With the Finder active, choose File > Find (**Figure 16b**) or press ⌃ ⌘ F.

2. The Sherlock window appears. If necessary, click the Find File tab to display its options (**Figure 17**).

3. Choose a search location from the Find Items pop-up menu (**Figure 18**).

4. Use the first pop-up menu in the criteria area to choose a criteria type (**Figure 19**):

   ▲ **Name** is the name of the item.

   ▲ **Size** is the size of the file, in kilobytes.

   ▲ **Kind** is the type of item.

   ▲ **Label** is the item's Finder label.

   ▲ **Date created** is the date the item was created.

   ▲ **Date modified** is the date the item was changed.

   ▲ **Version** is the item's version number.

   ▲ **Comments** is the text entered into the Comments field of the item's Info window.

   ▲ **Lock attribute** is whether the item is locked or unlocked.

*Continued on next page...*

FINDING FILES BY ATTRIBUTE

*Continued from previous page.*

▲ **Folder attribute** is whether the item is or isn't a folder.

▲ **File type** is the four-character, case-sensitive type code assigned to the item.

▲ **Creator** is the four-character, case-sensitive creator code assigned to the item.

5. Use the other options in the criteria area (**Figure 20**) to complete the search criteria. The options vary depending on the criteria type you chose in step 4.

6. Click Find. The Items Found window appears (**Figure 21**).

7. To open a found item, double-click its name in the top half of the Items Found window.

*or*

To view the location of a found item, click it once and look at the folder hierarchy in the bottom half of the Items Found window (**Figure 21**).

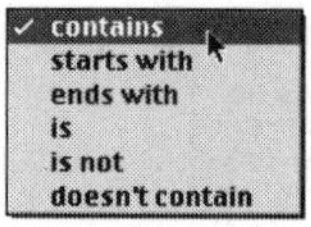

## ✔ Tips

■ To search a specific folder, select the folder before opening the Sherlock window. Then choose in the Finder selection from the Find Items pop-up menu (**Figure 18**).

■ To enter a date, select each part of the date individually and click the up or down triangles beside it to change the value (**Figure 22**).

■ To include additional search criteria, click the More Choices button in the Find File tab of the Sherlock window. The window expands to add another line of criteria (**Figure 23**). When performing the search, Mac OS matches all criteria.

■ Hold down Option while displaying the criteria type pop-up menu in step 4 to see additional options (**Figure 24**).

**Figure 20** The match options that appear on the middle pop-up menu when Name is chosen on the left pop-up menu.

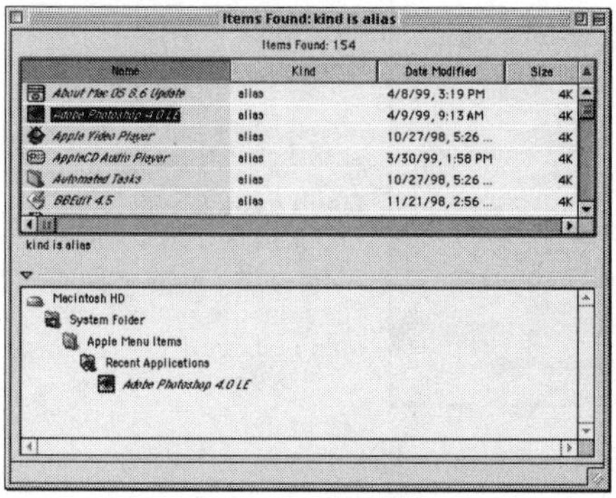

**Figure 21** The items found window lists all items that match the search criteria.

**Figure 22** Click the triangles beside the date to change digits.

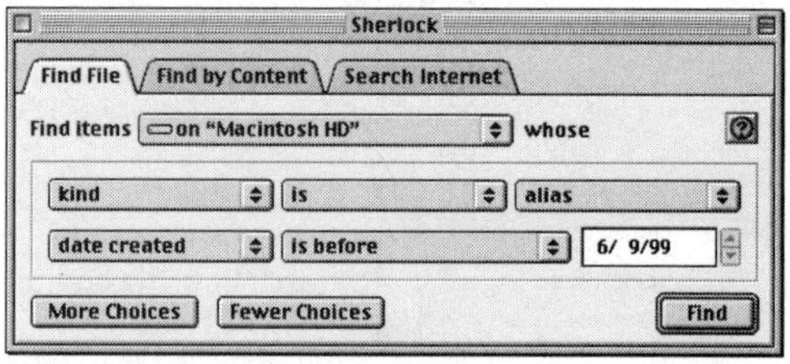

**Figure 23** Clicking the More Choices button expands the Find File tab of the Sherlock window.

**Figure 24** Holding down Option expands the list of criteria types.

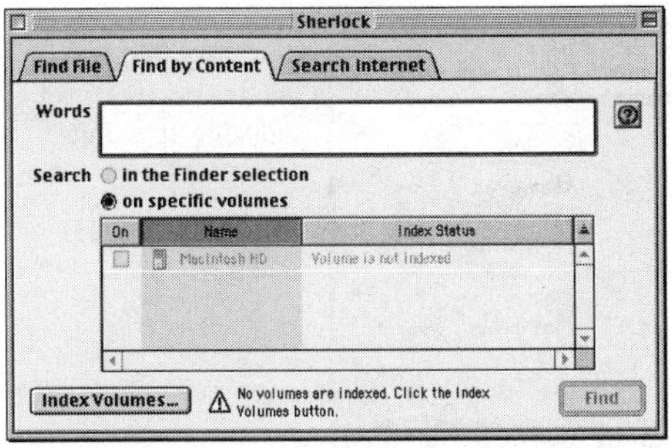

**Figure 25** The Find by Content tab of the Sherlock window.

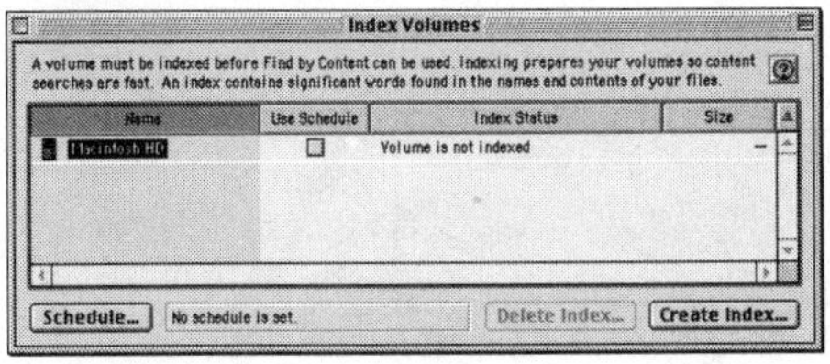

**Figure 26** Use the Index Volumes window to select the disks you want to index.

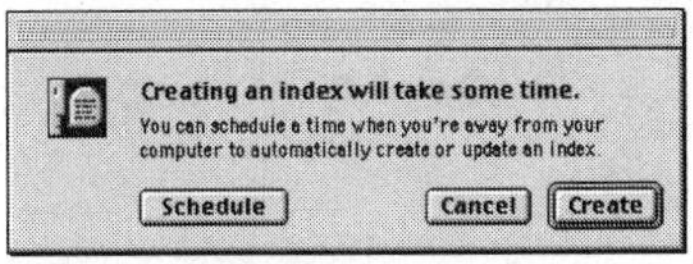

**Figure 27** This dialog box warns you that creating an index can take some time.

**Figure 28** A dialog box like this appears while your computer creates the index.

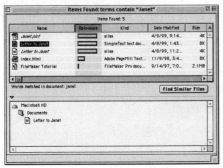

**Figure 29** The items found window lists the items that match the search criteria.

## To find files by content

1. Choose Apple menu > Sherlock (**Figure 16a**).

   *or*

   With the Finder active, choose File > Find (**Figure 16b**) or press ⌃ ⌘ F.

2. The Sherlock window appears. If necessary, click the Find by Content tab to display its options (**Figure 25**).

3. If the disk has been recently indexed, skip ahead to step 8. Otherwise, click the Index Volumes button.

4. In the Index Volumes window that appears (**Figure 26**), select the disks you want to index, and click the Create Index button.

5. A dialog box like the one in **Figure 27** appears. Click the Create button.

6. Wait while the disks are indexed. The Indexing Progress dialog box appears while it works (**Figure 28**). When it disappears, the indexing is finished.

7. Close the Index Volumes window to return to the Sherlock window.

8. In theWords edit box, enter the text you want to search for.

9. Select a Search option:

   ▲ **in the Finder selection** searches only the disk or folder that is selected in the Finder.

   ▲ **on specific volumes** enables you to select the disks you want to search. If you select this option, turn on the check box beside each disk you want to search.

10. Click the Find button. After a moment, the Items Found window appears (**Figure 29**).

*Continued on next page...*

## Chapter 8

*Continued from previous page.*

11. To open a found item, double-click its name in the top half of the Items Found window.

    *or*

    To view the location of a found item, click it once and look at the folder hierarchy in the bottom half of the Items Found window (**Figure 29**).

## ✔ Tips

■ The Find by Content feature searches the index, not the actual files. Therefore, it cannot find files that match criteria if the files were created or modified after the index was last updated.

■ You can automatically index your hard disk using a predetermined schedule. In the Index Volumes window (**Figure 26**), click the Schedule button. Use the Schedule window that appears (**Figure 30**) to create an indexing schedule, and click OK. Then turn on the check box for each volume in the Index Volumes window that you want to automatically index, and close the window.

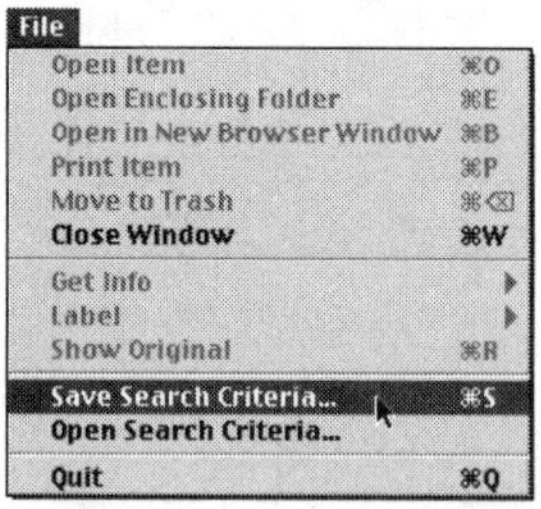

## To save search criteria

1. Choose File >Save Search Criteria (**Figure 31**).

2. Use the Save As dialog box that appears (**Figure 32**) to create and save a file containing the search criteria.

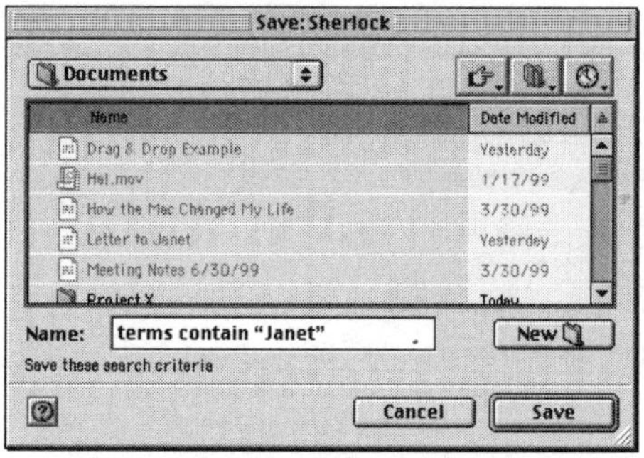

## To use saved search criteria

Double-click the icon for the saved search criteria (**Figure 33**).

*or*

Select the icon for the saved search criteria, and choose File > Open.

Sherlock launches and automatically performs the search.

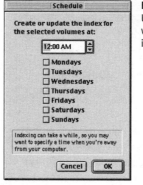

**Figure 30**
Use the Schedule window to create an indexing schedule.

**Figure 31**
Choose Save Search Criteria from the File menu.

**Figure 32** Use this Save As dialog box to save the search criteria as a document.

terms contain "Janet"

**Figure 33** The icon for a saved search criteria document looks like this.

**Figure 34**
Launch Disk First Aid
by opening its icon.

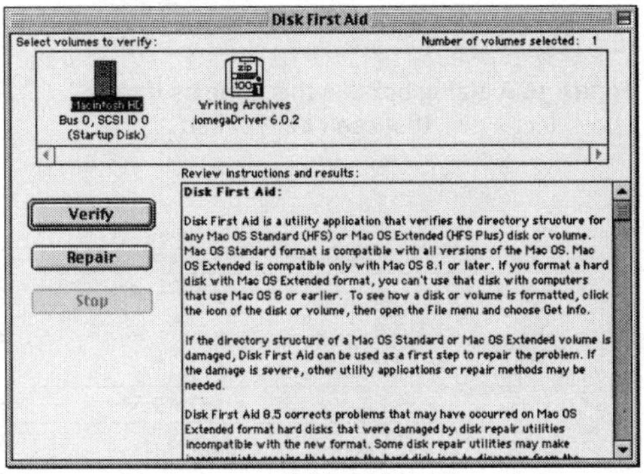

Disk First Aid

---

**Figure 35** The Disk First Aid window.

# Disk First Aid

Disk First Aid is a utility application that enables you to check for and repair minor directory damage on your hard disk caused by bad media, crashes, improper shutdowns, and other problems.

## ✔ Tips

- Disk First Aid is similar in function to Norton Utilities for Macintosh, a utility by Symantec Corporation.

- It's a good idea to use Disk First Aid to verify all your important disks on a regular basis—at least once a month.

## To launch Disk First Aid

Open the Disk First Aid icon (**Figure 34**), which can be found in the Utilities folder on your hard disk.

The Disk First Aid window appears (**Figure 35**). It displays all disks mounted on the Desktop and provides information about how it works and what it does.

## ✔ Tips

- I tell you about mounting disks in **Chapter 3**.

- You cannot verify or repair a disk if file sharing is turned on. Before launching Disk First Aid, turn off file sharing. I explain how in **Chapter 11**.

LAUNCHING DISK FIRST AID

## To verify or repair a disk

**1.** Select the disks that you want to verify or repair.

**2.** If you select a disk with open files or a write-protected disk, a dialog box like the one in **Figure 36** appears, telling you that certain disks cannot be repaired. Click OK to dismiss it.

**3.** To verify the selected disks, click Verify or press [Return] or [Enter].

*or*

To repair the selected disks, click Repair.

**4.** Wait while Disk First Aid checks or checks and repairs the selected disks. You can monitor its progress in the bottom half of the Disk First Aid window (**Figure 37**). When Disk First Aid is finished, the condition of the disk appears in bold in the window (**Figure 38**).

## ✔ Tips

■ To select more than one disk, hold down [Shift] while clicking each disk.

■ The Repair button will be gray if you selected a disk that cannot be repaired.

■ You can use the File menu's Save Results command to save a report of Disk First Aid's results.

■ You can use the Option menu's Erase Disk command to erase a selected disk. Just be sure to select the correct disk!

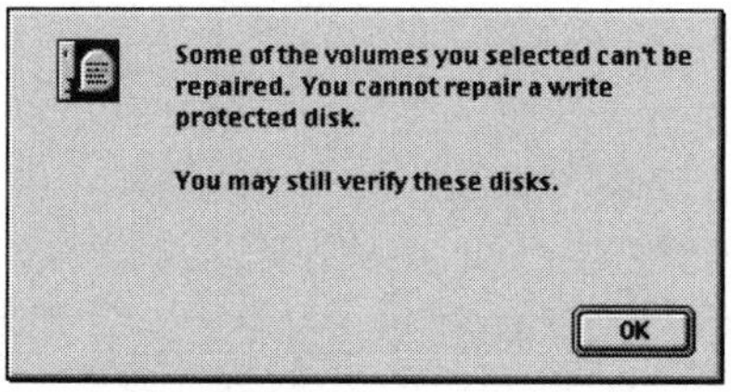

**Figure 36** A dialog box like this appears if you select a disk that can't be repaired.

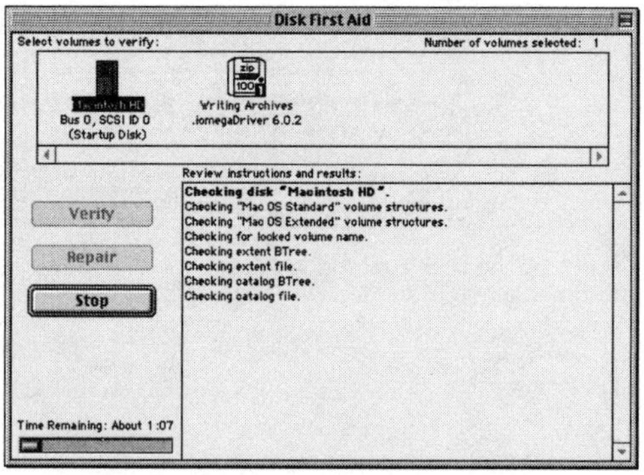

**Figure 37** You can monitor Disk First Aid's progress in the bottom of its window.

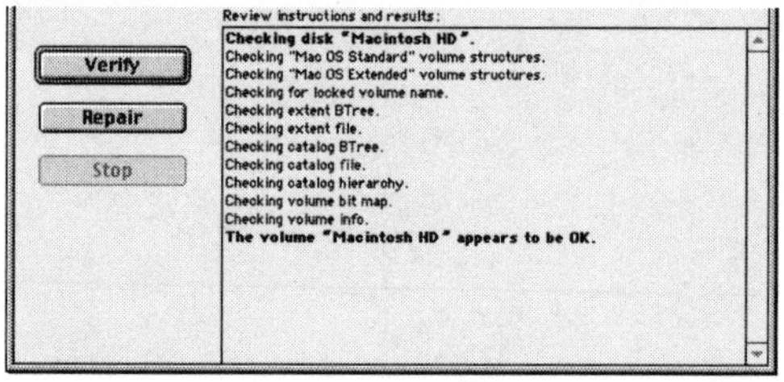

**Figure 38** Disk First Aid's diagnosis appears in bold in the Disk First Aid window.

**Figure 39**
Open the Drive
Drive Setup    Setup icon.

**Drive Setup**

**List of Drives**

| Volume Name(s) | Type | Bus ID LUN |
|---|---|---|
| Macintosh HD | SCSI | 0  0  0 |
| Veronica | SCSI | 0  3  0 |
| Zip 100 | SCSI | 0  5  0 |

Select a drive and then a function.

Initialize...

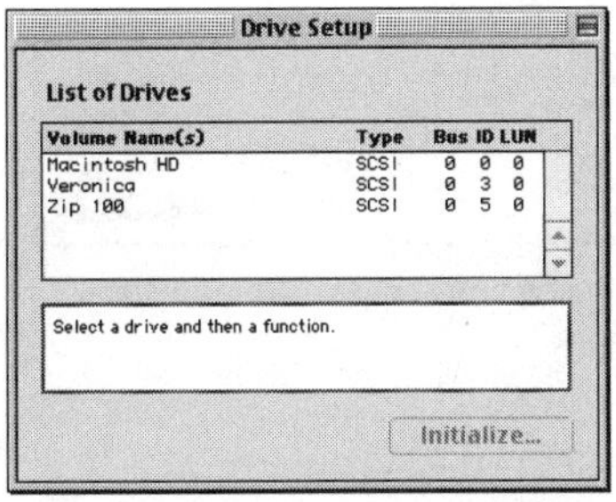

**Figure 40** In this example, Drive Setup has found my internal hard disk, CD-ROM drive, and Zip drive (which is set up as the startup disk).

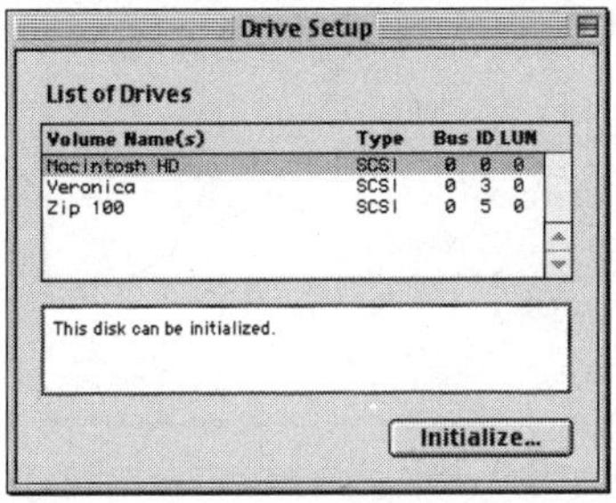

**Drive Setup**

**List of Drives**

| Volume Name(s) | Type | Bus ID LUN |
|---|---|---|
| Macintosh HD | SCSI | 0  0  0 |
| Veronica | SCSI | 0  3  0 |
| Zip 100 | SCSI | 0  5  0 |

This disk can be initialized.

Initialize...

**Figure 41** When you select a disk, a window at the bottom of the Drive Setup window tells you whether you can initialize it.

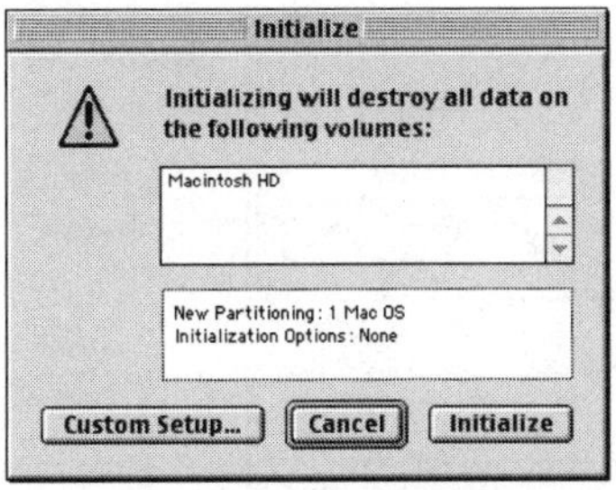

**Initialize**

⚠  **Initializing will destroy all data on the following volumes:**

Macintosh HD

New Partitioning: 1 Mac OS
Initialization Options: None

Custom Setup...    Cancel    Initialize

**Figure 42** Click Initialize in the Initialize dialog box only if you're sure you want to erase the disk.

# Drive Setup

Drive Setup is a utility that enables you to initialize a hard disk, install or update a disk driver, and test a disk.

## ✔ Tips

- Drive Setup is not compatible with all hard disks. It should, however, work with the hard disk inside your Macintosh.

- You should use the disk utility software that came with your external hard disk, Zip or Jaz disk, or other storage device to prepare that device's media for use.

## To launch Drive Setup

Open the Drive Setup icon (**Figure 39**), which can be found in the Utilities folder on your hard disk. The Drive Setup window appears. It searches for and displays all storage devices connected to your computer (**Figure 40**).

## To initialize a disk

1. Select the disk that you want to initialize by clicking its name in the Drive Setup window (**Figure 41**).

2. Click Initialize. The Initialize dialog box appears (**Figure 42**).

3. If you are absolutely sure you want to erase the disk, click Initialize.

4. Wait while Drive Setup initializes the disk. This can take a while, depending on the size of the disk.

## ✔ Tips

- Initializing a disk completely erases it. If a disk contains important files, back them up *before* initializing the disk!

- You cannot initialize a disk if file sharing is turned on. I tell you about file sharing in **Chapter 11**.

- You cannot initialize the startup disk.

LAUNCHING DRIVE SETUP, INITIALIZING DISKS

## To update a disk's driver

1. In the Drive Setup window (**Figure 41**), select the disk whose driver you want to update by clicking its name.

2. Choose Functions > Update Driver (**Figure 43**).

3. Wait a moment while Drive Setup updates the driver on the disk. When it is finished, a dialog box like the one in **Figure 44** appears. Click OK.

4. Restart your computer to automatically load the updated driver.

## ✔ Tips

■ Every hard disk or other high-capacity magnetic storage media has a driver written to the disk. The driver tells the computer how to read the disk.

■ You should update the driver on your hard disk whenever you install a new version of Mac OS.

## To test a disk

1. Select the disk that you want to test by clicking its name in the Drive Setup window (**Figure 41**).

2. Choose Functions > Test Disk (**Figure 45**).

3. A dialog box like the one in **Figure 46** appears. It explains what the test does. Click Start to dismiss the dialog box and begin the test.

4. Wait while the test is conducted. You can monitor its progress in the Drive Setup window (**Figure 47**). When the test is finished, its results appear in the bottom of the Drive Setup window (**Figure 48**).

## ✔ Tip

■ A bad block is a portion of the disk that is badly corrupted and can no longer be used.

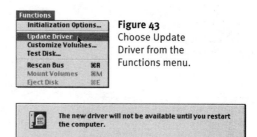

**Figure 43** Choose Update Driver from the Functions menu.

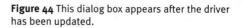

**Figure 44** This dialog box appears after the driver has been updated.

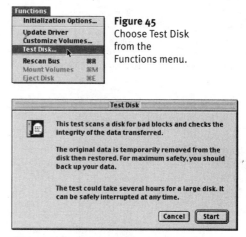

**Figure 45** Choose Test Disk from the Functions menu.

**Figure 46** The Test Disk dialog box explains what the test is for.

**Figure 47** You can monitor the test progress in the Drive Setup window.

**Figure 48** Test results appear in the bottom of the Drive Setup window.

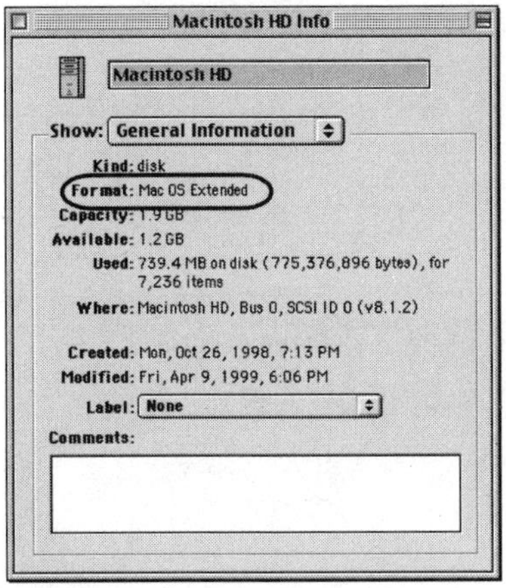

**Figure 49** The Info window for a disk displays the disk's format.

# Mac OS Extended Format (or HFS Plus)

With Mac OS 8.1, Apple introduced *Mac OS Extended Format*, or *HFS Plus*. Designed for high-capacity hard disks, HFS Plus decreases the minimum size of an allocation block, thus decreasing the amount of disk space that small files require. The net effect: you can store more information on disk.

## ✔ Tips

- To use HFS Plus, the computer to which the hard disk is directly connected must have Mac OS 8.1 or later installed.

- Do not use HFS Plus to format removable media (Zip, Jaz, etc.) that is shared with computers running Mac OS versions prior to 8.1. Those computers will not be able to read individual files on HFS Plus disks.

- HFS Plus works best with hard disks that are 1 GB or larger in capacity.

- The "old" format for hard disks that works with all versions of the System software is now called *Mac OS Standard Format* (or just plain *HFS*).

- You can identify a disk's format by checking its Info window (**Figure 49**). I tell you about the Info window in **Chapter 5**.

- In case you're wondering, HFS stands for *Hierarchical Filing System*.

**Mac OS Extended Format (or HFS Plus)**

## To format a disk with HFS Plus

1. Back up all data on the hard disk you plan to format as HFS Plus. ***Do not skip this step!***

2. In the Finder, select the icon for the disk you plan to format as HFS Plus.

3. Choose Special > Erase Disk (**Figure 50**).

4. The Erase Disk dialog box appears (**Figure 51**). Choose Mac OS Extended from the Format pop-up menu (**Figure 52**).

5. **Stop!** Did you complete step 1? If not, click Cancel and start over again. If your data is backed up, click the Erase button. The selected disk is erased and formatted as HFS Plus.

6. Restore the backed up files to the erased hard disk.

## ✔ Tips

- If you fail to back up the data on a disk you format as HFS Plus, all the data on the disk will be lost forever.

- To format a startup disk as HFS Plus, you must start your computer with another disk, preferably the Mac OS 8.6 CD-ROM disc. I tell you how to select a startup disk in **Chapter 13**.

- You may also be able to use Drive Setup to format a hard disk with HFS Plus formatting. Follow the instructions on page 137 to initialize the disk, but click Custom Setup in the Initialize dialog box (**Figure 42**) to display the Custom Setup dialog box (**Figure 53**). Choose Mac OS Extended from the Type pop-up menu (**Figure 54**), and click OK. Then complete the initialization process.

**Figure 50** Choose Erase Disk from the Special menu.

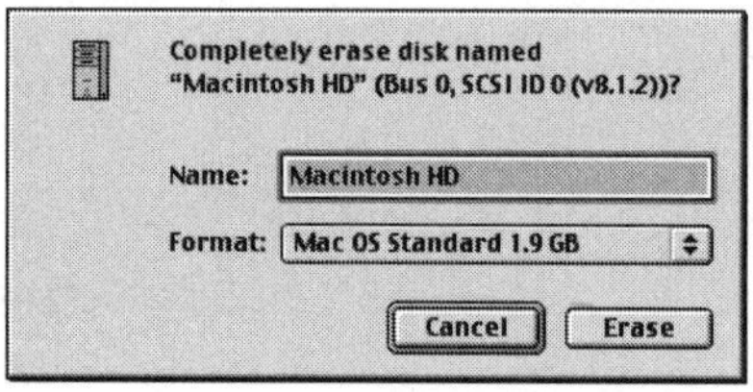

**Figure 51** The Erase Disk dialog box.

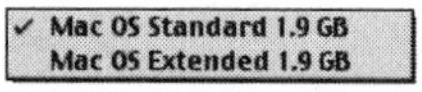

**Figure 52** The two options on the Format pop-up menu.

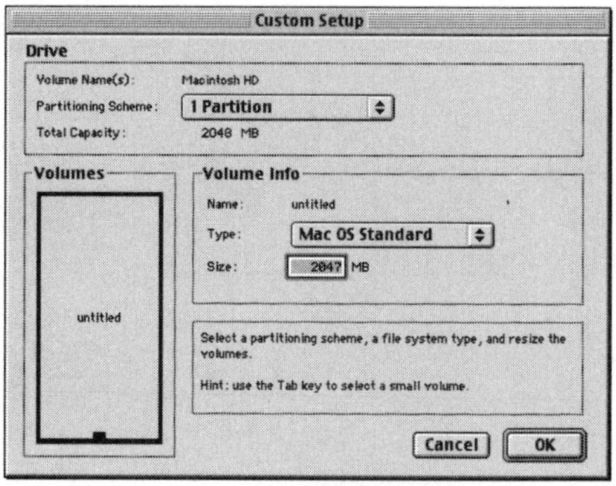

**Figure 53** Drive Setup's Custom Setup dialog box.

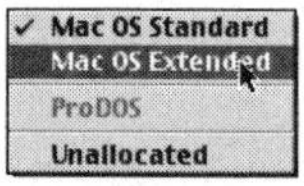

**Figure 54** Choose Mac OS Extended from the Type pop-up menu.

**Figure 55**
The Script
Editor icon.

**Figure 56**
A Script Editor
document
window.

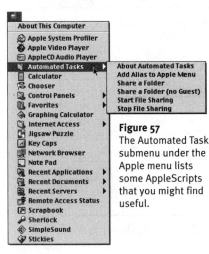

**Figure 57**
The Automated Task
submenu under the
Apple menu lists
some AppleScripts
that you might find
useful.

# AppleScript

AppleScript is a scripting language that's part of Mac OS. You can use it to program your computer to automatically perform a series of tasks called a *script*.

You create scripts with a program called Script Editor (**Figure 55**), which is included with Mac OS 8.6. Script Editor works with the Finder and with *scriptable applications*—applications that support AppleScript commands.

There are two ways to create a script with Script Editor:

◆ Use the Script Editor's recording feature to record script steps as you perform them. This is probably the best way to get started with AppleScript, although it does limit what you can do with it.

◆ Use the Script Editor window (**Figure 56**) to write the script. To do this, you must know the AppleScript scripting language.

As you can imagine, AppleScript is an advanced and powerful feature of Mac OS—one that is far beyond the scope of this book. But to get you started, I'll tell you how to record, run, and save a simple script.

## ✔ Tip

■ The Automated Tasks submenu under the Apple menu (**Figure 57**) lists a number of AppleScripts that come with Mac OS 8.6. I tell you how to use Automated Tasks in **Chapter 8**.

## To launch Script Editor

Open the Script Editor icon (**Figure 55**). You can find it in the AppleScript folder inside the Apple Extras folder on your hard disk.

An untitled Script Editor window appears (**Figure 56**).

APPLESCRIPT, LAUNCHING SCRIPT EDITOR

## To record a script

1. In the Script Editor window (**Figure 56**), click Record. A recording icon blinks at the far-left end of the menu (**Figure 58**).

2. Perform all of the following steps, in order, for a test script:

   1. Double-click the hard disk icon to open it.

   2. Hold down [Option] and double-click the Applications folder to open it and close the hard disk window.

   3. Hold down [Option] and double-click the SimpleText icon to open it and close the Applications window.

3. Choose Script Editor from the Application menu at the far right end of the menu bar to activate Script Editor. The Script Editor window appears. It now has a series of script steps (**Figure 59**).

4. Click Stop.

## To run a script

In the Script Editor window (**Figure 59**), click Run. The script should play back all the steps you just recorded.

## To save a script as an application

1. Choose File > Save, or press [Ctrl] [⌘] [S]. A Save As dialog box appears (**Figure 60**).

2. Enter a name for the script, and select a disk location.

3. Choose Application from the Kind pop-up menu (**Figure 61**).

4. Click Save.

## ✔ Tip

- Once a script has been saved as an application, you can simply open its icon (**Figure 62**) to run it.

**Figure 58** An icon like this blinks over the Apple menu when Script Editor is recording.

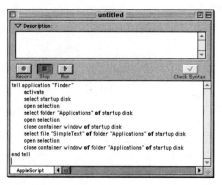

**Figure 59** Script Editor automatically writes the script steps for you.

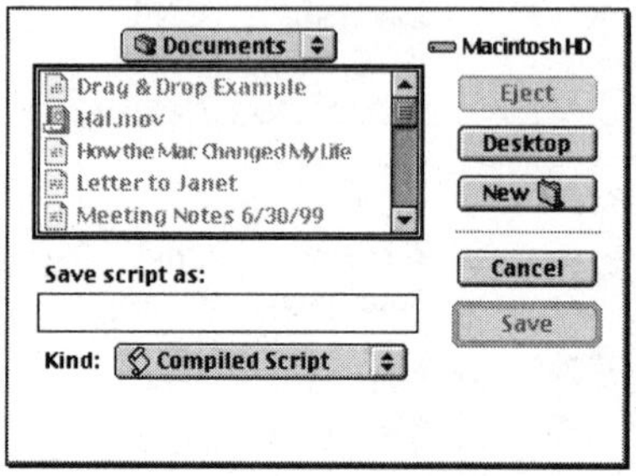

**Figure 60** Use a Save As dialog box to save your script.

**Figure 61** Choose Application from the Kind pop-up menu.

**Figure 62** Here's the icon for an application written in AppleScript.

# WORKING WITH PC FILES

## Working with PC Files

Documents created on a DOS- or Windows-compatible computer aren't the same as those created on a Mac OS-compatible computer. Some differences include:

◆ Disk formats vary based on the operating system that formatted the disk.

◆ Document formats vary based on characters and special codes recognized or required by each operating system.

◆ Document formats also vary based on application codes and formats.

Mac OS 8.6 comes with File Exchange, a software tool that helps you work with PC files by performing three functions:

◆ Reads PC-formatted disks on your Mac OS computer.

◆ Maps DOS and Windows extensions to Mac OS applications.

◆ Displays a list of the applications that can open a document you double-click if the creator application is not installed on your computer.

I tell you about all these things in this chapter.

## ✔ Tip

■ If you're interested in running DOS or Windows software on your computer, here are two options:

　▲ A DOS compatibility card puts PC chips and circuitry inside your Mac. Orange Micro offers these cards.

　▲ Software emulation "fools" PC software into thinking it's running on a PC. Connectix's Virtual PC and Insignia Solutions' SoftWindows are two examples.

# Reading PC Disks

File Exchange makes it possible for your Mac OS computer to read PC-formatted disks. It does this automatically without any additional effort on your part. File Exchange, which is automatically installed as part of a standard Mac OS 8.6 installation, is preconfigured to do this job so there's nothing to set up.

**Figure 1**
When you insert a PC-formatted disk, its icon appears on the Desktop like any other disk.

### ✔ Tip

- File Exchange works with all kinds of PC disks, including floppy disks, Zip and Jaz disks, and hard disks connected directly to your computer with a SCSI, USB, or FireWire cable.

**Figure 2** When you double-click the disk, its files appear as icons in the disk window just like any Mac disk.

## To read a PC-formatted disk

1. Insert the PC disk in your disk drive. After a moment, the disk's icon appears on your Desktop (**Figure 1**).

2. Double-click the disk icon to open a window displaying its contents (**Figure 2**).

### ✔ Tips

- If you look carefully, you can see the letters *PC* on a PC disk icon (**Figure 1**).

- You can work with a PC-formatted disk just like any other disk. I tell you about working with files and disks in **Chapter 3**.

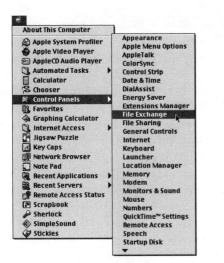

**Figure 3** Choose File Exchange from the Control Panels submenu under the Apple menu.

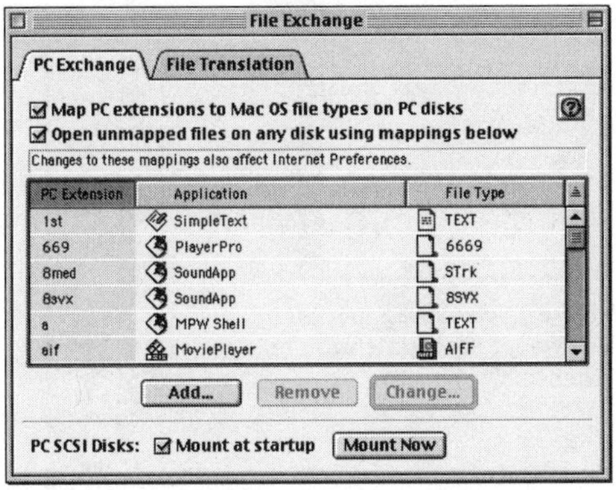

**Figure 4** The default settings in the PC Exchange exchange tab of the File Exchange control panel.

# PC Exchange

PC Exchange is the part of File Exchange that enables you to *map*, or match, PC file extensions, or suffixes, to Mac OS applications. This does two things:

◆ It enables your Mac to display the correct icons for PC files (**Figure 2**).

◆ It enables you to open a PC file with a specific application by simply double-clicking it.

PC Exchange is preconfigured with many common extension mappings, but you can add, remove, or modify mappings as desired.

## ✔ Tip

■ Mapping an extension to an application doesn't guarantee that the application can successfully open the document.

## To set file mapping options

1. Choose Apple menu > Control Panels > File Exchange (**Figure 3**).

2. If necessary, click the PC Exchange tab in the File Exchange window to display its options (**Figure 4**).

3. Toggle the check boxes near the top of the window as desired:

   ▲ **Map PC extensions for Mac OS file types on PC disks** enables extension mapping. With this option turned off, PC files are treated as text files.

   ▲ **Open unmapped files on any disk using mappings below** uses the PC Exchange extension mappings to open files types that are not mapped in the File Translation tab of the File Exchange control panel.

4. Close File Exchange to save your settings.

## To change an extension mapping

1.  Choose Apple menu > Control Panels > File Exchange (**Figure 3**).

2.  If necessary, click the PC Exchange tab in the File Exchange window to display its options (**Figure 4**).

3.  In the scrolling list of mappings, click to select the Extension for which you want to change the mapping (**Figure 5**).

4.  Click Change to display the Change Mapping dialog box (**Figure 6**).

5.  In the Application list, select the program you want to associate with the extension (**Figure 7**).

6.  If necessary, choose a document type from the File Type pop-up menu (**Figure 8**).

7.  Click Change. The revised mapping appears in the PC Exchange tab of the File Exchange window (**Figure 9**).

8.  Close File Exchange to save your change.

## ✔ Tips

-   The File Type pop-up menu (**Figure 8**) displays only the file types supported by the currently selected application.

-   When you change a mapping, the icon for files using that mapping may also change (**Figure 10**).

-   Clicking the Show Advanced Options button expands the dialog box to display options of interest to advanced users (**Figure 11**). Coverage of these options are beyond the scope of this book.

| PC Extension | Application | File Type |
| --- | --- | --- |
| jpe | PictureViewer | JPEG |
| jpeg | PictureViewer | JPEG |
| jpg | PictureViewer | JPEG |
| latex | OzTex | TEXT |
| lbm | GraphicConverter | ILBM |
| lha | MacLHA | LHA |

**Figure 5** Select the mapping you want to change.

**Figure 6**
The Change Mapping dialog box.

| Application |
| --- |
| Address Book Export |
| Adobe PhotoDeluxe™ |
| Apple Video Player |
| Disk Copy |
| DropStuff™ |
| FileMaker Help Viewer |
| FileMaker Pro |

**Figure 7** Select the application you want to associate with the extension.

8BPF
PHUT
PICT
SCRN
TIFF
GIFf
rsrc
BMP
8BXM
8BAM
G8im
BWim
8BFM
G8tc
8BIM
PNGf
FPX
PCX
8BMC
8BVM
8BPS
8BM1
8BM2
8BIF
JPEG

**Figure 8**
If necessary,
select the type of
file from the File
Type pop-up list.

| PC Extension | Application | File Type |
| --- | --- | --- |
| jfx | JFax Communicator | TIFF |
| jpe | PictureViewer | JPEG |
| jpeg | PictureViewer | JPEG |
| jpg | Adobe PhotoDeluxe™ | JPEG |
| latex | OzTex | TEXT |
| lbm | GraphicConverter | ILBM |

**Figure 9** The mapping change appears in the PC Exchange tab of the File Exchange window.

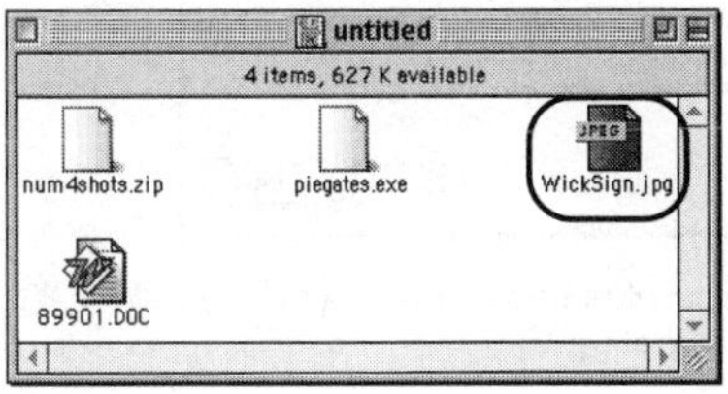

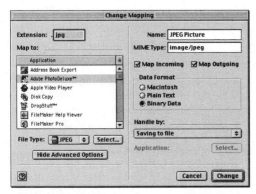

**Figure 10** Changing a mapping can change a file's icon.

**Figure 11** When you click the Show Advanced Options button, the Change Mapping dialog box expands to show additional options for advanced users.

**Figure 12**
The Add Mapping dialog box.

## To add an extension mapping

1. Choose Apple menu > Control Panels > File Exchange (**Figure 3**).

2. If necessary, click the PC Exchange tab in the File Exchange window to display its options (**Figure 4**).

3. Click Add to display the Add Mapping dialog box (**Figure 12**).

4. In the Extension edit box, enter the three-character extension for a type of DOS file. Do not include the period (or "dot") before the extension.

5. In the Application list, select the progam you want to associate with the extension.

6. If necessary, choose a document type from the File Type pop-up menu.

7. Click Add. The new mapping appears.

8. Close File Exchange to save your change.

## ✔ Tip

- PC Exchange's mapping list is extensive. Before adding an extension, scroll through the list to make sure a mapping does not already exist for the extension you want to add.

## To remove an extension mapping

1. Choose Apple menu > Control Panels > File Exchange (**Figure 3**).

2. If necessary, click the PC Exchange tab in the File Exchange window to display its options (**Figure 4**).

3. In the scrolling list of mappings, select the Extension you want to remove.

4. Click Remove.

5. In the confirmation dialog box that appears (**Figure 13**), click OK. The mapping is removed.

6. Close File Exchange to save your change.

## ✔ Tip

■ If you remove a mapping, Mac OS will no longer associate the extension with an application.

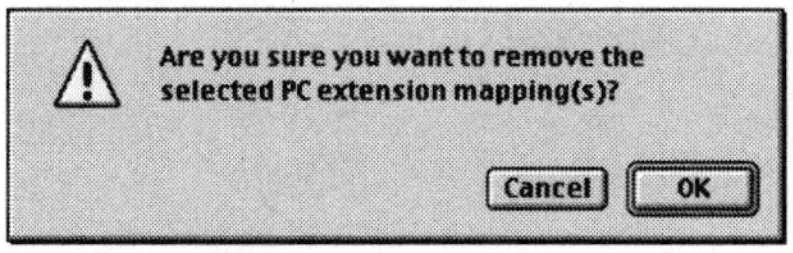

**Figure 13** Click OK in this dialog box to remove the mapping.

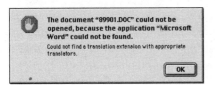

**Figure 14** A dialog box like this appears when you double-click the icon for a document that cannot be opened by any of your installed applications.

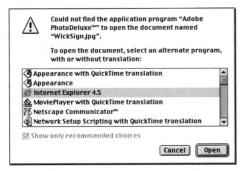

**Figure 15** This file translation window enables you to select an application to open a document—but only if the application that created the document is not installed on your computer.

**Figure 16** In this example, Internet Explorer is displaying a JPEG file created with Adobe PhotoDeluxe. (Now you know where Wickenburg is.)

# File Translation

File Translation is the part of File Exchange that enables you to open documents that were created by applications that are not installed on your computer. This feature works with PC and Mac OS files, using mappings in the PC Exchange tab and translation preferences in the File Translation tab of the File Exchange window.

## To use file translation

1. Double-click an icon for a file created by an application not installed on your computer.

2. One of two things happens:

   ▲ If the file cannot be opened by any program on your computer, a dialog box like the one in **Figure 14** appears. Click OK and skip the rest of these steps— you'll have to install a program that can open the file or take the file to someone else's computer and open it there.

   ▲ If the file can be opened by a program on your computer, a dialog box like the one in **Figure 15** appears. Continue to step 3.

3. Select an application to open the file.

4. Click OK. The file opens (**Figure 16**).

## ✔ Tips

■ Not every program listed in the translation window (**Figure 15**) will always be able to successfully open the file.

■ The choices you make in the translation dialog box (**Figure 15**) are automatically saved as preferences in the File Translation tab of the File Exchange control panel (**Figure 17**).

## To set file translation options

1.  Choose Apple menu > Control Panels > File Exchange (**Figure 3**).

2.  If necessary, click the File Translation tab in the File Exchange window to display its options (**Figure 17**).

3.  Toggle the check boxes near the top of the window as desired:

    ▲ **Translate documents automatically** enables file translation. This option must be turned on to select either of the first two options beneath it.

    ▲ **Always show choices when translating files** displays the translation dialog box (**Figure 15**) each time your computer needs to translate a file. If this option is turned off, the dialog box only appears if a translation preference does not already exist for the file you want to open. This option must be turned on to select the first option beneath it.

    ▲ **Don't show choices if there's only one** does not display the translation dialog box (**Figure 15**) if there's only one translation option. Instead, it automatically opens the file using the only option.

    ▲ **Include applications on servers in translation choices** checks all mounted hard disks, including server volumes, for possible translation applications and includes them in the translation dialog box (**Figure 15**).

4.  Close the File Exchange window to save your settings.

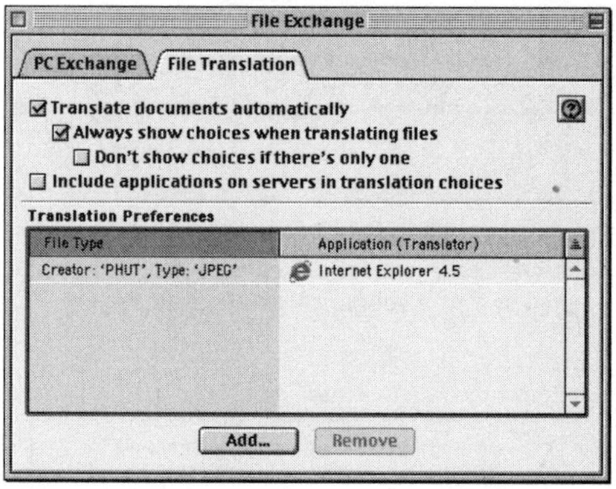

**Figure 17** The File Translation tab of the File Exchange control panel.

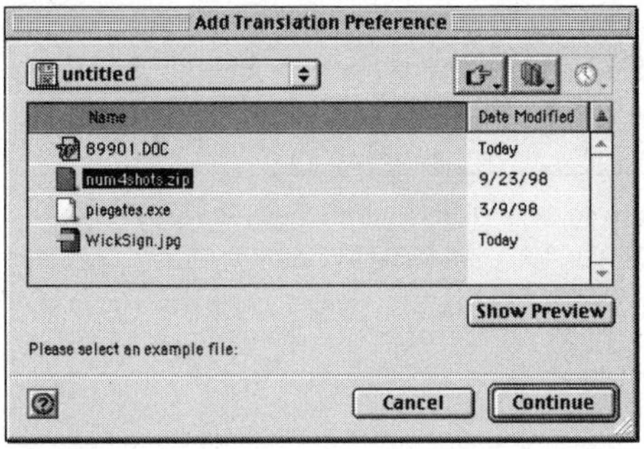

**Figure 18** Use an Open dialog box like this one to locate and select a document like the one for which you want to set a translation preference.

## To add a translation preference

1. Choose Apple menu > Control Panels > File Exchange (**Figure 3**).

2. If necessary, click the File Translation tab in the File Exchange window to display its options (**Figure 17**).

3. Click the Add button.

4. Use the Add Translation Preference dialog box that appears (**Figure 18**) to locate and select a document file like the one for which you want to set a translation preference.

5. Click Continue.

6. In the translation dialog box that appears (**Figure 15**), select the application with which you want to open the document.

7. Click OK. The preference is added to the File Translation tab of the File Exchange control panel window.

8. Close the File Exchange window to save your changes.

## ✔ Tips

■ Translation preferences are automatically added or updated each time you use the translation dialog box (**Figure 15**).

■ You cannot add a preference for a type of file for which a preference already exists. You must first remove the existing preference, as instructed on the next page.

ADDING TRANSLATION PREFERENCES

## To remove a translation preference

1. Choose Apple menu > Control Panels > File Exchange (**Figure 3**).

2. If necessary, click the File Translation tab in the File Exchange window to display its options (**Figure 17**).

3. Click to select the translation preference you want to remove.

4. Click the Remove button.

5. In the confirmation dialog box that appears (**Figure 19**), Click OK. The preference is removed from the File Translation tab of the File Exchange control panel window.

6. Close the File Exchange window to save your changes.

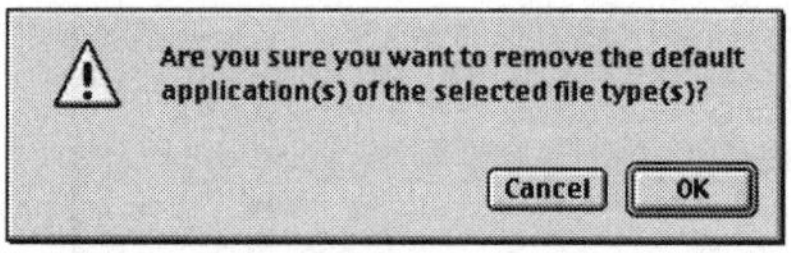

**Figure 19** Click OK to confirm that you really do want to remove the translation preference.

# PRINTING

## Printing

On a Mac OS system, printing is handled by the operating system rather than the individual applications. You choose the Print command in the application that created the document you want to print. Mac OS steps in, displaying the Print dialog box and telling the application how to send information to the printer. There are two main benefits to this:

◆ If you can print documents created with one application, you can probably print documents created with any application on your computer.

◆ The Page Setup and Print dialog boxes, which are generated by Mac OS, look very much the same in every application.

This chapter covers most aspects of printing on a computer running Mac OS 8.6.

### To print (an overview)

1. If necessary, select a printer.
2. Open the window or document that you want to print.
3. If desired, set options in the Page Setup dialog box and click OK.
4. Set options in the Print dialog box and click Print.

*or*

1. Drag the icon for the document you want to print onto a desktop printer icon.
2. Set options in the Print dialog box and click Print.

## To print the Finder Desktop

1. If necessary, activate the Finder by choosing Finder from the Application menu.

2. Click on the Desktop to activate it rather than any open windows.

3. Choose File > Print Desktop (**Figure 1**).

4. Use the Print dialog box that appears to set print options.

5. Click Print.

**Figure 1**
To print the Finder Desktop, choose Print Desktop from the File menu.

### ✔ Tip

■ I explain how to set options in the Print dialog box later in this chapter.

## To print a Finder window

1. If necessary, activate the Finder by choosing Finder from the Application menu.

2. Activate the window that you want to print by clicking it.

3. Choose File > Print Window (**Figure 2**).

4. Use the Print dialog box that appears to set print options.

5. Click Print.

**Figure 2**
To print a Finder window, choose Print Window from the File menu.

### ✔ Tip

■ I explain how to set options in the Print dialog box later in this chapter.

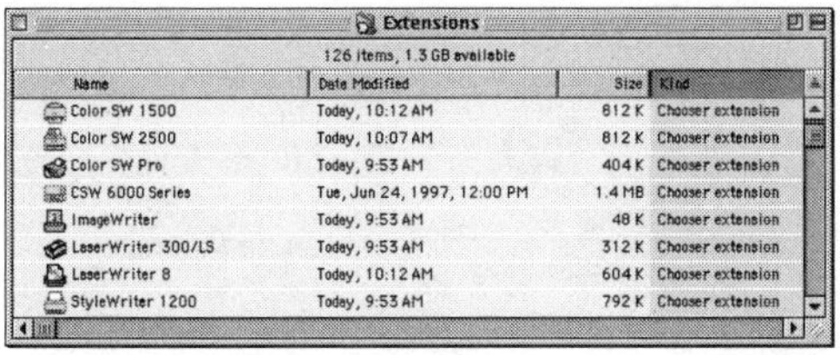

**Figure 3** The printer drivers installed as part of a Mac OS 8.6 standard installation.

# Printer Drivers

A *printer driver*, which is a type of *Chooser extension*, is a software file that Mac OS uses to communicate with a specific kind of printer. It contains information about the printer and instructions for using it. You can't open and read a printer driver, but your computer can.

There are basically two kinds of printers:

◆ A **PostScript** printer uses PostScript technology developed by Adobe Systems. Inside the printer is a *PostScript interpreter*, which can process PostScript language commands to print high-quality text and graphics. Examples of PostScript printers include most Apple LaserWriter printers and Hewlett-Packard LaserJet printers.

◆ A **QuickDraw** printer relies on the computer to send it all of the instructions it needs for printing text and graphics. It cannot process PostScript commands. Examples of Quick-Draw printers include Apple ImageWriters and StyleWriters, Hewlett-Packard DeskJet printers, and most Epson Stylus printers.

Mac OS comes with printer drivers for a variety of Apple branded PostScript and QuickDraw printers, including LaserWriters, StyleWriters, and ImageWriters. Mac OS-compatible printers by other manufacturers, such as Hewlett-Packard and Epson, come with the printer drivers you need to use them with your computer.

## ✔ Tips

■ If you do not have an appropriate printer driver for your printer, you may not be able to print.

■ Printer drivers are stored in the Extensions folder. **Figure 3** shows the printer drivers automatically installed as part of a basic installation of Mac OS 8.6.

## To install a printer driver

1. Insert the disk containing the printer driver that you want to install.

2. If necessary, double-click the disk to open it and view its contents (**Figures 4** and **5**).

3. If the disk includes an installer (**Figure 4**), double-click the installer to open it. Then follow the on-screen instructions to install the printer software. You may have to restart your computer when the installation is complete.

   *or*

   If the disk does not include an installer (**Figure 5**), drag the printer driver file icon onto the closed System Folder icon on your hard disk (**Figure 6**). When you release the mouse button, a dialog box like the one in **Figure 7** appears. Click OK, and wait while the printer driver is properly installed in the Extensions folder.

## ✔ Tip

- If you need to, you can use the Mac OS 8.6 installer to reinstall just the printer drivers. Do a custom installation of Mac OS 8.6 and select just the printing software. I tell you about installing Mac OS 8.6 and doing custom installations in **Chapter 1**.

## To uninstall a printer driver

1. Open the Extensions folder inside the System Folder on your hard disk.

2. Locate the icon for the printer driver that you want to uninstall.

3. Drag the printer driver out of the Extensions folder (**Figure 8**). You can leave it on the Desktop or in another window if you want to keep it, or you can drag it to the Trash if you want to delete it.

**Figure 4** This disk contains printer driver software and an installer...

**Figure 5** ...and this disk contains printer driver software without an installer.

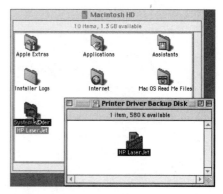
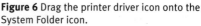

**Figure 6** Drag the printer driver icon onto the System Folder icon.

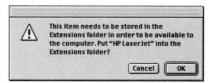

**Figure 7** When you drag a Chooser extension to the System Folder, a dialog box like this appears.

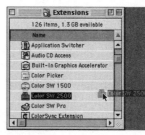

**Figure 8** To uninstall a printer driver, simply drag it out of the Extensions folder.

INSTALLING & UNINSTALLING PRINTER DRIVERS

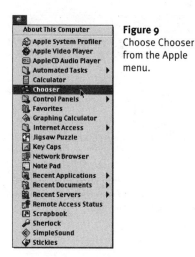

**Figure 9**
Choose Chooser
from the Apple
menu.

# The Chooser

The Chooser is a desk accessory that lets you select printers, file servers, and some other devices connected to your computer.

## ✔ Tips

- The Mac OS Setup Assistant, which I discuss in **Chapter 1**, sets the printer in the Chooser for you.

- I tell you about file servers in **Chapter 11**.

## To open the Chooser

Choose Apple menu > Chooser (**Figure 9**).

The Chooser window appears (**Figure 10**). It displays icons for printer drivers and other Chooser files, such as AppleShare, in the left side of the window.

## To select a network printer

1. Make sure the printer that you want to use is turned on and warmed up.

2. In the Chooser window, select the icon for the printer driver that you want to use (**Figure 11**).

3. If your computer is on a network with multiple zones, select the name of the zone in which the printer you want to use resides.

4. In the list of printers, select the name of the printer that you want to use (**Figure 11**).

## ✔ Tips

- The LaserWriter 8 printer driver works for most PostScript laser printers.

- If you're not sure which zone to select in a multiple-zone network, ask your system administrator.

- When selecting a network printer, make sure the Active radio button beside Apple-Talk is selected (**Figure 11**).

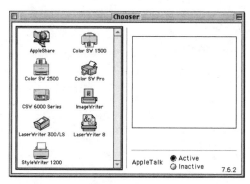

**Figure 10** The Chooser window. If you're on a network with multiple zones, the Chooser window will look a little different on your computer.

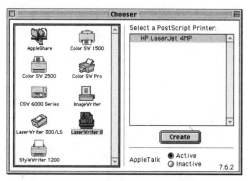

**Figure 11** Select the printer driver, the zone (if applicable; not shown here), and the printer.

## To select a directly connected printer

1. Make sure the printer that you want to use is turned on and warmed up.

2. In the Chooser window, select the icon for the printer driver that you want to use (**Figure 12**).

3. In the Connect to list, select the name or icon for the port to which the printer is connected (**Figure 12**).

### ✔ Tips

- If you're not sure which port the printer is connected to, check to see where the printer cable is connected to the back of your computer.

- You cannot directly connect a printer to the printer port if your computer is on a LocalTalk network. Instead, connect the printer to the modem port or, if possible, to the network.

## To set background printing options

After selecting a printer in the Chooser window, select the Background Printing area's On or Off radio button (**Figure 12**) to set your preference.

### ✔ Tips

- Background printing, when turned on, enables your computer to print while you continue working on other things.

- The Background Printing option is not available for all printer drivers or printers. Consult the documentation that came with your printer for more information about this option.

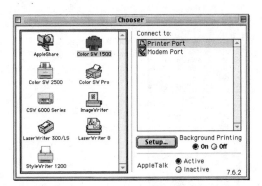

**Figure 12** Select the printer driver and the appropriate port for a directly connected printer.

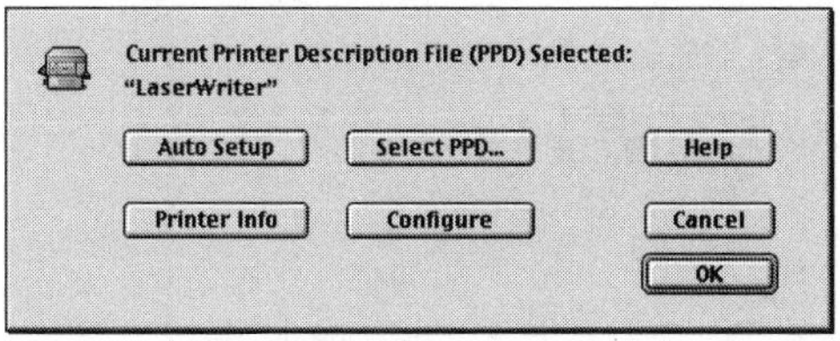

**Figure 13** Click the Auto Setup button in this dialog box to have Mac OS automatically set up your printer.

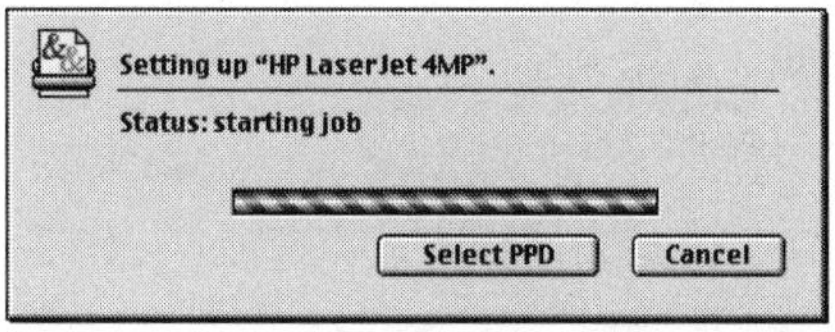

**Figure 14** When this dialog box appears, wait while Mac OS gets setup information from your printer.

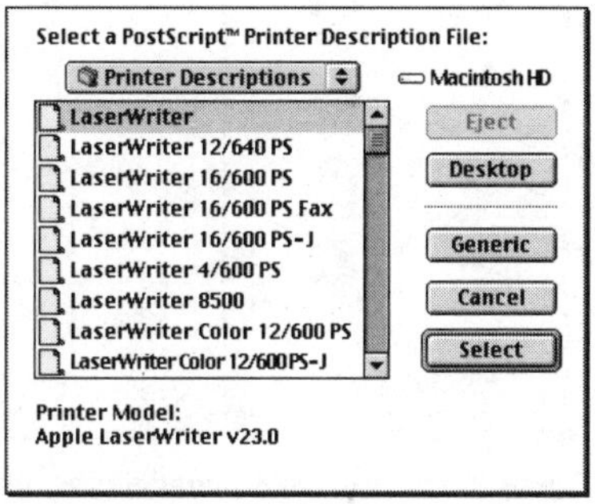

**Figure 15** Select a PPD file for your printer, or click the Generic button.

## To create or set up a PostScript printer

1. After selecting a printer in the Chooser window, click Create (**Figure 11**) or Setup.

2. If you clicked a Setup button in step 1, a Setup dialog box like the one in **Figure 13** appears. Click Auto Setup.

3. A dialog box like the one in **Figure 14** appears. After a moment, a dialog box like the one in **Figure 15** may appear. Use it to locate and select a PPD file for your printer. If there's no PPD file listed for your specific printer, click Generic.

4. Wait while your computer creates a desktop printer.

5. If you clicked a Setup button in step 1, the Setup dialog box (**Figure 13**) reappears. Click OK to dismiss it.

## ✔ Tips

- The name of the button in step 1 depends on which printer driver is selected and whether the printer has been used before.

- PPD (or *PostScript printer description*) files, which usually come with printer drivers, should be installed in the Printer Descriptions folder inside the Extensions folder in the System Folder on your hard disk.

- I tell you about desktop printers later in this chapter.

CREATING/SETTING UP POSTSCRIPT PRINTERS

## To set sharing setup options for a directly connected printer

1. After selecting a printer in the Chooser window, click Setup (**Figure 12**). A Sharing Setup dialog box appears (**Figure 16**).

2. To share the printer with other network users, turn on the Share this Printer check box. Then enter a printer name and, if desired, password (**Figure 17**).

3. To automatically create a log of printer use, turn on the Keep Log of Printer Usage check box.

4. Click OK to save your settings.

### ✔ Tips

■ Not all directly connected printers can be shared.

■ When you name a directly connected printer, its name appears in the Chooser window (**Figure 18**).

## To close the Chooser

1. Click the Chooser's close box (**Figure 18**).

   *or*

   Choose File > Close (**Figure 19**), or press ⌃ ⌘ W.

2. If you selected a different printer than what was originally selected, a dialog box like the one in **Figure 20** appears, telling you to check the options in the Page Setup dialog box of open applications. Click OK to dismiss it.

### ✔ Tips

■ I tell you about the Page Setup dialog box next.

■ If a desktop printer does not already exist for the printer you selected, one is created. I tell you about desktop printers later in this chapter.

**Figure 16** The Sharing Setup dialog box lets you share a directly connected printer with other users on your network.

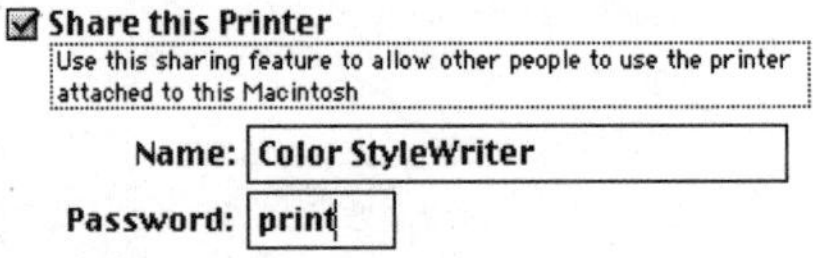

**☑ Share this Printer**
Use this sharing feature to allow other people to use the printer attached to this Macintosh

Name: **Color StyleWriter**

Password: **print**

**Figure 17** Once you turn on the Share this Printer check box, you can enter a name and password for the printer.

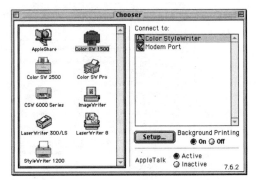

**Figure 18** The name of a shared printer appears in the Chooser window.

**Figure 19** Choose Close from the Chooser's File menu.

⚠ **You have changed your current printer. Please choose "Page Setup..." in all of the open applications.**

OK

**Figure 20** When you change your printer, a dialog box like this appears.

**Figure 21** A Color StyleWriter 1500 offers only a few Page Setup options.

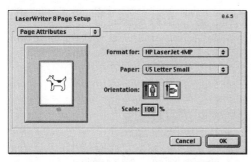

**Figure 22** A LaserWriter offers two categories of Page Setup options: Page Attributes...

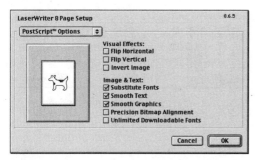

**Figure 23** ...and PostScript™ Options.

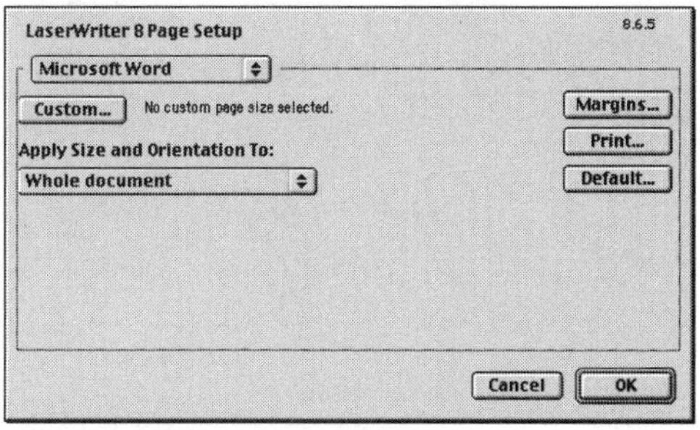

# The Page Setup Dialog Box

The Page Setup dialog box lets you set page options prior to printing. Although it is a standard dialog box, two things can cause its appearance and options to vary:

◆ Page Setup options vary depending on the selected printer driver (**Figures 21**, **22**, and **23**).

◆ Additional options may be offered by specific applications (**Figures 24** and **25**).

In this section, I tell you how to set the basic options—those options available for most printers and most applications—in the Page Setup dialog box.

## ✔ Tips

■ For information about using Page Setup options specific to an application, consult the documentation that came with the application.

■ Because Page Setup options can change when you change printers, it's a good idea to check Page Setup options after changing your printer. That's what the dialog box in **Figure 20** is all about.

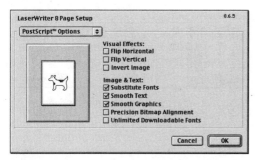

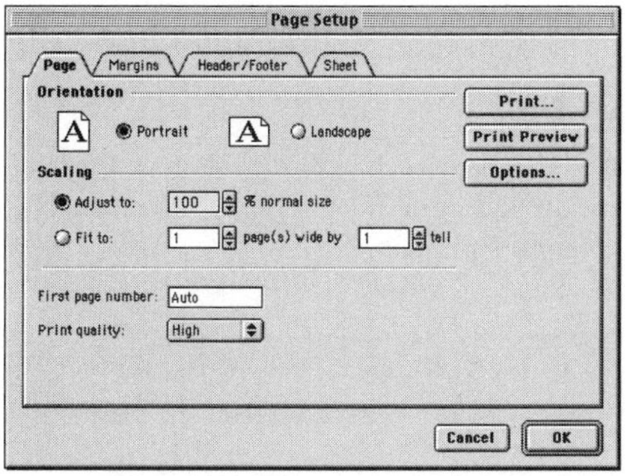

**Figure 24** Some applications offer more Page Setup options. These are options for Microsoft Word ...

**Figure 25** ...and these are options for Microsoft Excel.

**THE PAGE SETUP DIALOG BOX**

## To open the Page Setup dialog box

Choose File > Page Setup (**Figures 26a**, **26b**, and **26c**).

## To set Page Attributes

1. Open the Page Setup dialog box (**Figures 21** and **22**).

2. In the Page Setup dialog box for a PostScript printer, select Page Attributes from the top pop-up menu (**Figure 27**).

3. If necessary, select the correct printer from the Format for pop-up menu (**Figure 22**).

4. Select the correct paper size from the Paper or Page Size pop-up menu (**Figures 21** and **22**).

5. To print more than one document page on each sheet of paper, choose a Layout option (**Figure 21**). If you select an option other than 1 Up, you can also turn on the Borders check box to put a border around each document page (**Figure 28**).

6. Enter a scaling percentage in the Scaling (%) or Scale edit box (**Figures 21** and **22**). You may also be able to select a percentage from a pop-up menu beside the Scaling (%) edit box (**Figure 29**).

7. Select an Orientation option by clicking it (**Figures 21** and **22**).

8. Click OK to save your settings and dismiss the Page Setup dialog box.

## ✔ Tip

■ Options in each of the above steps vary depending on the printer driver selected for the printer.

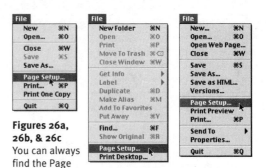

**Figures 26a, 26b, & 26c**
You can always find the Page Setup command under the File menu. Illustrated here are the File menus for SimpleText (left), the Finder (middle), and Microsoft Word (right).

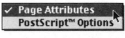

**Figure 27** In the Page Setup dialog box for a PostScript printer, select Page Attributes.

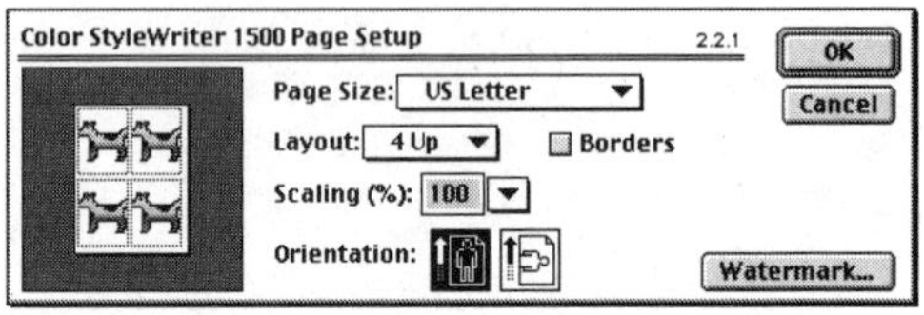

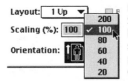

**Figure 28** Layout options enable you to print more than one document page on each sheet of paper.

**Figure 29**
Some Page Setup dialog boxes let you select a scaling percentage from a pop-up menu like this one.

*SETTING PAGE ATTRIBUTES*

**Figure 30** Choose PostScript™ Options from the pop-up menu at the top of the Page Setup dialog box for a PostScript printer.

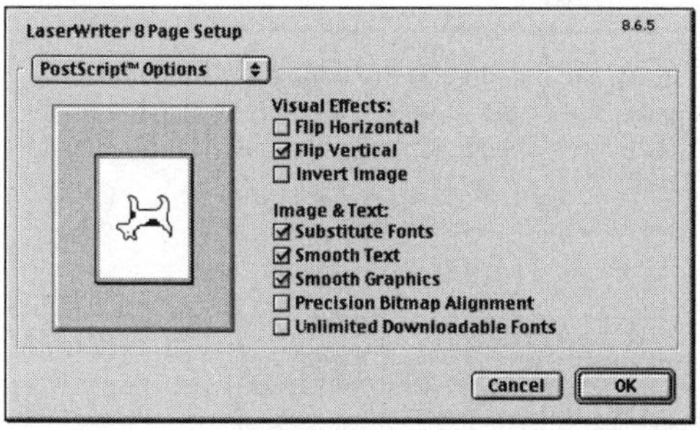

**Figure 31** Changing check box settings changes the dogcow in the sample image.

## To set PostScript options

1. Open the Page Setup dialog box for your PostScript printer (**Figure 22**).

2. Select PostScript™ Options from the top pop-up menu (**Figure 30**).

3. Click check boxes (**Figure 23**) to turn the following PostScript features on or off:

   ▲ **Flip Horizontal** makes a mirror image of the page.

   ▲ **Flip Vertical** turns the page upside down.

   ▲ **Invert Image** turns black to white and white to black.

   ▲ **Substitute Fonts** uses Times, Helvetica, and Courier PostScript fonts instead of New York, Geneva, and Monaco True-Type fonts.

   ▲ **Smooth Text** prints bitmapped fonts more clearly.

   ▲ **Smooth Graphics** prints graphics more clearly by smoothing jagged edges.

   ▲ **Precision Bitmap Alignment** reduces the document to correct for possible distortions in bitmap graphic images.

   ▲ **Unlimited Downloadable Fonts** lets you use as many fonts as you like in a document. This could, however, slow printing.

4. Click OK to save your settings and dismiss the Page Setup dialog box.

## ✔ Tips

■ Many of the changes you make in the check boxes are reflected in the sample image to the left of the check boxes in the Page Setup dialog box (**Figure 31**).

■ Another piece of Mac OS trivia: the animal that appears in the Page Setup dialog box is called a *dogcow*. Its name is Clarus (*not* Claris) and it says "Moof!"

SETTING POSTSCRIPT OPTIONS

## To set application-specific options

1. Open the Page Setup dialog box (**Figures 22** and **32**).

2. In the Page Setup dialog box for a Post-Script printer, select the name of the application from the top pop-up menu (**Figure 33**). That application's additional options appear (**Figure 24**).

3. Set options as desired.

4. Click OK to save your settings and dismiss the Page Setup dialog box.

## ✔ Tips

■ Some applications automatically display their own custom Page Setup dialog boxes when you choose Page Setup from their File menus. Microsoft Excel (**Figure 25**) is an example.

■ To learn more about the Page Setup options available in your favorite application, check the documentation that came with the application.

■ If the name of the application does not appear in the pop-up menu at the top of a PostScript printer's Page Setup dialog box (**Figures 27** and **30**), there are no application-specific options to set.

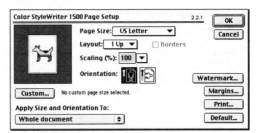

**Figure 32.** The Page Setup dialog box for a non-PostScript printer displays all options—including application-specific options like these for Microsoft Word.

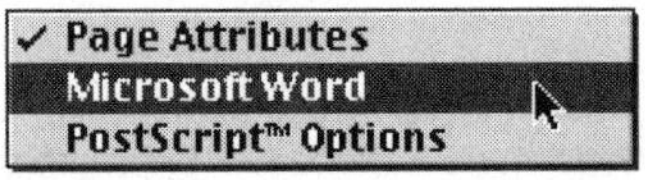

**Figure 33.** For a PostScript printer, choose the name of the application from the pop-up menu at the top of the Page Setup dialog box.

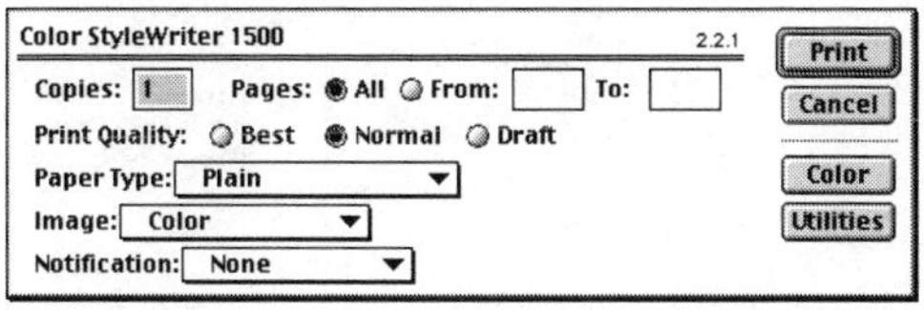

**Figure 34** The Print options for a Color StyleWriter 1500.

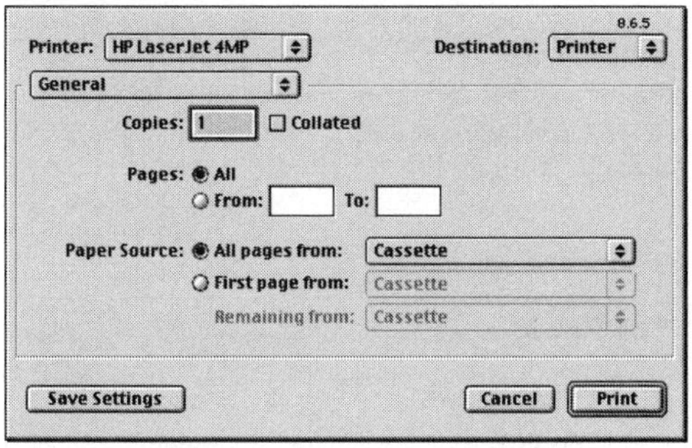

**Figure 35** The General options of the Print dialog box for a LaserWriter printer.

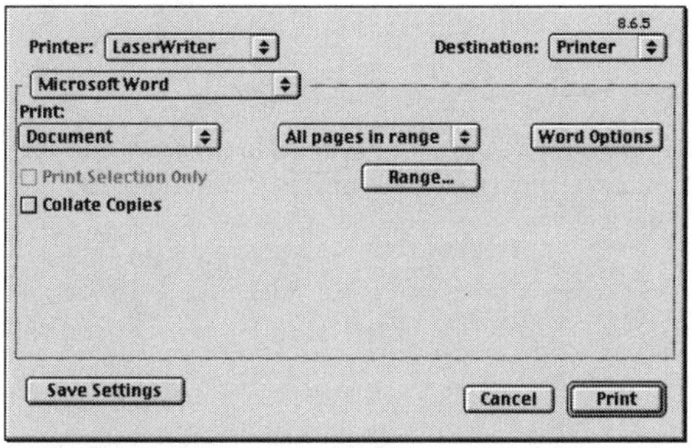

**Figure 36** Application-specific Print dialog box options for Microsoft Word...

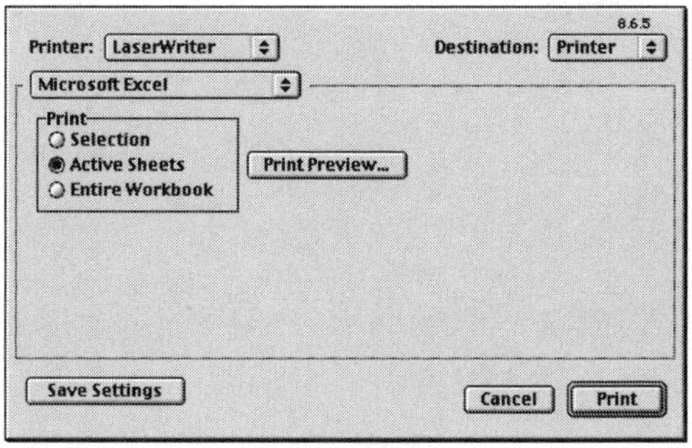

**Figure 37** ...and for Microsoft Excel.

# The Print Dialog Box

The Print dialog box lets you set printing options and send the print job to the printer. Like the Page Setup dialog box, the Print dialog box is a standard dialog box, but two things can cause its appearance and options to vary:

◆ Print options vary depending on the selected printer driver (**Figures 34**, **35**, and **39**).

◆ Additional options may be offered by specific applications (**Figures 36** and **37**).

In this section, I tell you how to set the basic options—those options available for most printers and most applications—in the Print dialog box.

## ✔ Tip

■ For information about using Print options specific to an application, consult the documentation that came with the application.

## To open the Print dialog box

Choose File > Print (**Figures 38a**, **38b**, and **38c**).

*or*

Press Ⅎ ⌘ P.

### ✔ Tip

■ To use the Finder's Print command, you must first select the icon for the document that you want to print.

## To set QuickDraw printer Print options

1. Open the Print dialog box (**Figures 34** and **39**).

2. In the Copies edit box, enter the number of copies of the document to print.

3. In the Page Range area, select either the All radio button to print all pages or enter values in the From and To edit boxes (**Figure 40**) to print specific pages.

4. Select a Quality radio button. Some of the options you might see include:

   ▲ **Best** is the best quality. It takes longer to print and uses more ink.

   ▲ **Normal** or **Faster** is standard quality; you'll use it most often.

   ▲ **Draft** prints only the text of the document, in one font and size. It's the quickest print option, but what you get on paper may not match what you see on screen.

5. Select other options specific to your printer, including Paper Type (**Figure 34**), Paper Feed (**Figure 39**), Image (**Figure 34**), and Notification (**Figure 34**). These options are self-explanatory; if you need more information, consult the documentation that came with your printer.

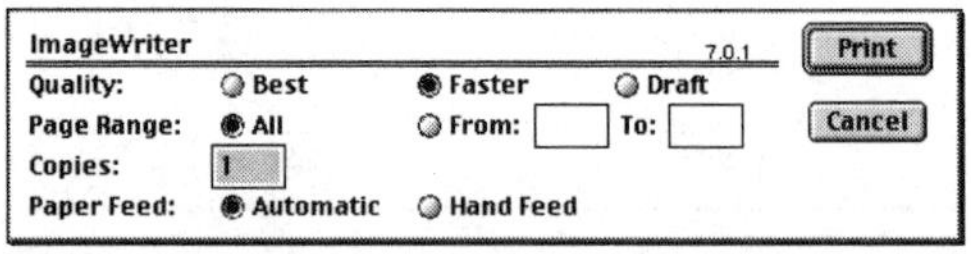

**Figure 38a, 38b, & 38c**
You can always find the Print command under the File menu. Here are the File menus for SimpleText (left), the Finder (middle), and Microsoft Word (right).

**Figure 39** The Print dialog box for an ImageWriter printer.

**Figure 40** When you enter values in the From and To edit boxes the From radio button is automatically selected.

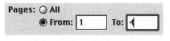

✓ General
  Background Printing
  Color Matching
  Cover Page
  Font Settings
  Job Logging
  Layout
  Save as File

**Figure 41**
Use the pop-up menu beneath the Printer pop-up menu to select a category of printing options.

Pages: ○ All
      ● From: 1    To: 4

**Figure 42** Use the Pages area to specify which pages to print.

Paper Source: ○ All pages from:  Cassette
              ● First page from:  Manual Feed
              Remaining from:  Cassette

**Figure 43** The Paper Source options make it possible to print the first page of a document on letterhead you manually feed and the rest of the pages on plain paper from the paper cassette.

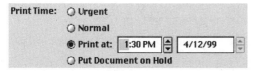

**Figure 44** The Background Printing options in the Print dialog box for a PostScript printer.

Print Time:  ○ Urgent
            ○ Normal
            ● Print at:  1:30 PM   4/12/99
            ○ Put Document on Hold

**Figure 45** When you select the Print at radio button, you can enter a date and time to print the document.

## To set PostScript printer General options

1. In the Print dialog box, choose General from the pop-up menu beneath the Printer pop-up menu (**Figure 41**) to display General options (**Figure 35**).

2. In the Copies edit box, enter the number of copies of the document to print.

3. To collate multiple copies, turn on the Collated check box.

4. In the Pages area, select either the All radio button to print all pages or enter values in the From and To edit boxes to print specific pages (**Figure 42**).

5. Select a Paper Source radio button. If you select First page, you can specify different paper sources for the first page and remaining pages (**Figure 43**).

## To set PostScript printer Background Printing options

1. In the Print dialog box, choose Background Printing from the pop-up menu beneath the Printer pop-up menu (**Figure 41**) to display Background Printing options (**Figure 44**).

2. To print while you wait, select the Foreground (no spool file) radio button.

   *or*

   To print while you continue to work with your computer, select the Background radio button.

3. Select a Print Time radio button:

   ▲ **Urgent** puts the job in the print queue before jobs marked Normal.

   ▲ **Normal** puts the job in the print queue in the order it was received.

   ▲ **Print at** lets you specify a date and time to print the job (**Figure 45**).

   ▲ **Put Document on Hold** puts the job in the print queue but does not schedule it for printing.

## To set PostScript printer Color Matching options

1. In the Print dialog box, choose Color Matching from the pop-up menu beneath the Printer pop-up menu (**Figure 41**) to display Color Matching options (**Figure 46**).

2. Choose an option from the Print Color pop-up menu (**Figure 47**):
   - ▲ **Black and White** prints in black and white.
   - ▲ **Grayscale** prints in shades of gray.
   - ▲ **Color/Grayscale** prints in color on a color printer or in shades of gray on a monochrome printer.
   - ▲ **ColorSync Color Matching** or **PostScript Color Matching** prints in color using characteristics of a specific printer. If you choose either of these options, you must also choose options from the Intent and Printer Profile pop-up menus.

### ✔ Tip

- ■ Color matching technology is beyond the scope of this book. If you have a color PostScript printer (lucky you!), consult the documentation that came with it for more information.

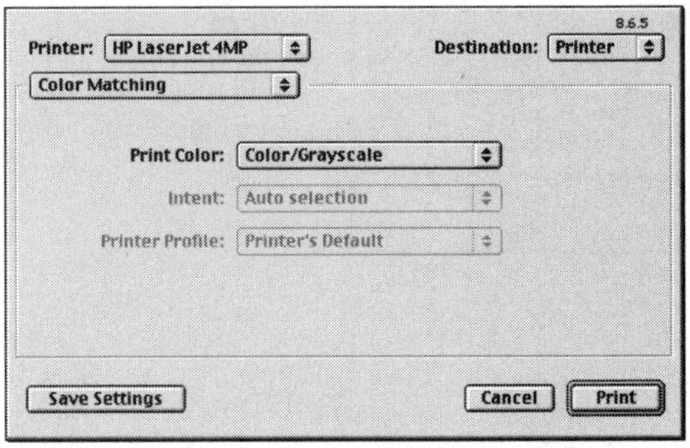

## To set PostScript printer Cover Page options

1. In the Print dialog box, choose Cover Page from the pop-up menu beneath the Printer pop-up menu (**Figure 41**) to display Cover Page options (**Figure 48**).

2. To print a cover page before or after the document, select either the Before Document or After Document radio button. Then use the Cover Page Paper Source pop-up menu (**Figure 49**) to specify the cover page source.

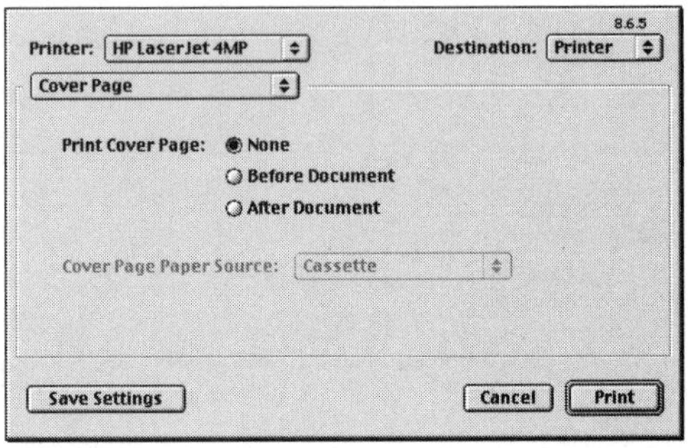

### ✔ Tips

- ■ A cover page is a sheet of paper that identifies the source of the print job.

**Figure 46** The Color Matching options in the Print dialog box for a PostScript printer.

**Figure 47** There are five options on the Print Color pop-up menu.

**Figure 48** The Cover Page options in the Print dialog box for a PostScript printer.

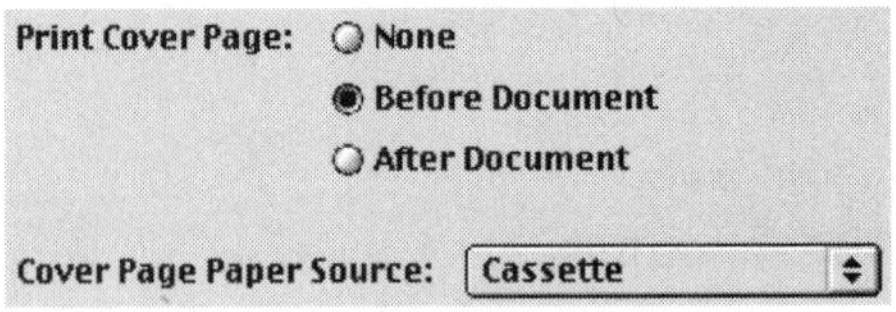

**Figure 49** If you decide to print a cover page, you can select a paper source for it.

- ■ Cover pages waste paper. Unless you're on a network and need to separate your print job from others, don't print a cover page.

SETTING POSTSCRIPT PRINTER OPTIONS

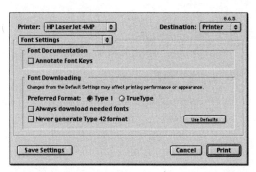

**Figure 50** The Font Settings options in the Print dialog box for a PostScript printer.

## To set PostScript printer Font Settings options

1. In the Print dialog box, choose Font Settings from the pop-up menu beneath the Printer pop-up menu (**Figure 41**) to display Font Settings options (**Figure 50**).

2. Turn on check boxes for desired options:

   ▲ **Annotate Font Keys** includes information about font keys in PostScript output.

   ▲ **Preferred Format** enables you to select the font format you prefer for printing when you have both the PostScript Type 1 and TrueType version of a font.

   ▲ **Always download needed fonts** instructs your computer to download PostScript fonts even when the font already resides on the printer.

   ▲ **Never generate Type 42 format** prevents your computer from generating Type 42 format fonts based on TrueType format fonts.

## ✔ Tips

■ The Always download needed fonts option helps ensure consistency from one printout to another when a document is printed on a variety of printers.

■ To restore settings to their default values, click the Use Defaults button.

■ I tell you more about fonts in **Chapter 13**.

## To set PostScript printer Job Logging options

1. In the Print dialog box, choose Job Logging from the pop-up menu beneath the Printer pop-up menu (**Figure 41**) to display Job Logging options (**Figure 51**).

2. Select one of the radio buttons in the If there is a PostScript™ error area:

   ▲ **No special reporting** does not report PostScript errors.

   ▲ **Summarize on screen** displays Post-Script errors on screen as they occur.

   ▲ **Print detailed report** prints a report of PostScript errors after they occur.

3. Turn on check boxes for desired Job Documentation options:

   ▲ **Generate Job Copy** creates a copy of the job in PostScript format. (This file can later be sent to a PostScript printer to reprint the job without opening the original application.)

   ▲ **Generate Job Log** creates a log that provides information about the print job and printer.

4. To specify the folder in which job documentation should be saved, click the Change button beneath the Job Documentation Folder scrolling window. Then use the dialog box that appears (**Figure 52**) to locate and choose a folder. When you click Choose, the folder you selected appears in the Job Documentation Folder scrolling window (**Figure 53**).

## ✔ Tips

■ I explain how to use Navigation Services dialog boxes like the one in **Figure 52** in **Chapter 5**.

■ The PostScript files generated by turning on the Generate Job Copy check box can be very large.

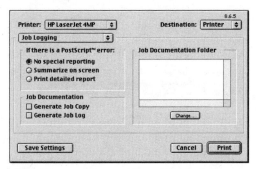

**Figure 51** The Job Logging options in the Print dialog box for a PostScript printer.

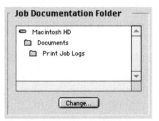

**Figure 52** Use a dialog box like this one to locate and choose a folder to store job documentation.

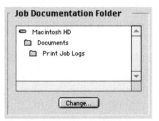

**Figure 53** The folder you choose (or create and choose as illustrated here) appears in the Job Documentation Folder scrolling window.

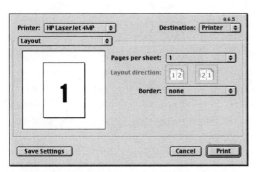

Figure 54 The Layout options in the Print dialog box for a PostScript printer.

**Figure 55**
Choose the number of document pages that you want to appear on each printed page.

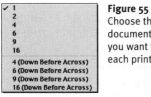

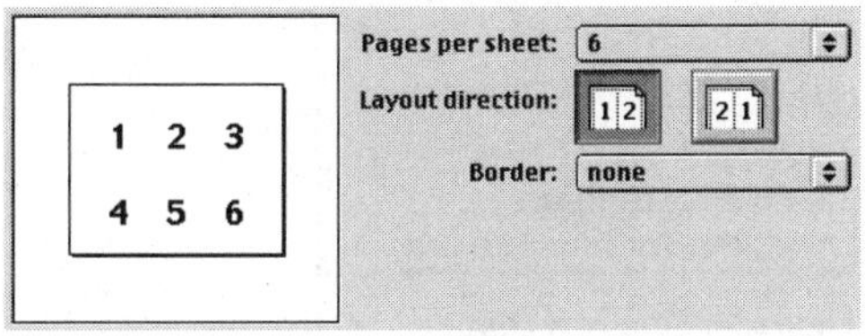

Figure 56 The Print dialog box displays a sample layout for the number of pages you selected.

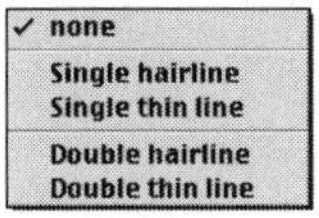

**Figure 57**
Choose an option from the Border pop-up menu to remove or add a border around document pages.

## To set PostScript printer Layout options

1. In the Print dialog box, choose Layout from the pop-up menu beneath the Printer pop-up menu (**Figure 41**) to display Layout options (**Figure 54**).

2. Choose the number of document pages that you want to print on each sheet of paper from the Pages per Sheet pop-up menu (**Figure 55**).

3. If you select a value higher than 1 in step 3, click a Layout Direction button (**Figure 56**) to specify the order in which document pages should appear on the printed pages.

4. To add a border around each document page, choose an option from the Border pop-up menu (**Figure 57**).

## ✔ Tip

■ Select 2 or 4 from the Pages per Sheet pop-up menu (**Figure 55**) to print legible page proofs with less paper.

## To set PostScript printer Save as File options

1. In the Print dialog box, choose Save as File from the pop-up menu beneath the Printer pop-up menu (**Figure 41**) to display Save as File options (**Figure 58**).

2. Choose File from the Destination pop-up menu (**Figure 58**).

3. Choose an option from the Format pop-up menu (**Figure 59**):

   ▲ **PostScript Job** saves the document as a standard PostScript file.

   ▲ **EPS Mac Standard Preview** saves the document as an encapsulated Post-Script file with a bitmap preview.

   ▲ **EPS Mac Enhanced Preview** saves the document as an encapsulated Post-Script file with a PICT preview.

   ▲ **EPS No Preview** saves the document as an encapsulated PostScript file without a preview.

   ▲ **Acrobat PDF** saves the document as an Adobe Acrobat PDF file. This option is only available if you have the full version of Adobe Acrobat (not just Acrobat Reader) installed on your computer.

4. Select a PostScript Level radio button.

5. Select a Data Format radio button.

6. Choose an option from the Font Inclusion pop-up menu (**Figure 60**):

   ▲ **None** does not save any fonts with the file.

   ▲ **All** saves all the fonts with the file.

   ▲ **All But Standard 13** saves all the fonts with the file except the 13 fonts found on most PostScript printers.

   ▲ **All But Fonts in PPD file** saves all the fonts with the file except the fonts listed in printer's PPD file.

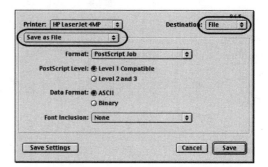

**Figure 58** The Save as File options in the Print dialog box for a PostScript printer.

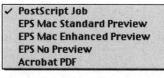

**Figure 59** Choose an option from the Format pop-up menu to specify a PostScript file format.

**Figure 60** Choose an option from the Font Inclusion pop-up menu to specify which fonts should be included with the file.

## ✔ Tips

■ If you're not sure how to set these options, leave all of them set to their default values except Font Inclusion, which you should set to All. This produces the most compatible PostScript files.

■ Details about PostScript options are beyond the scope of this book.

SETTING POSTSCRIPT PRINTER OPTIONS

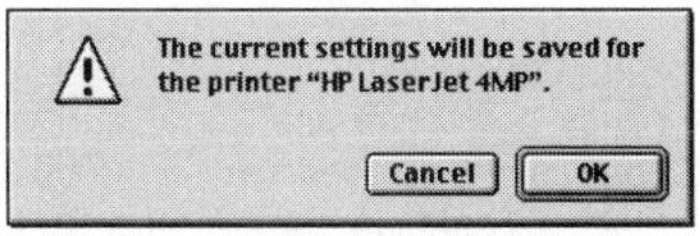

**Figure 61** The dialog box confirms that you really do want to save settings for your printer.

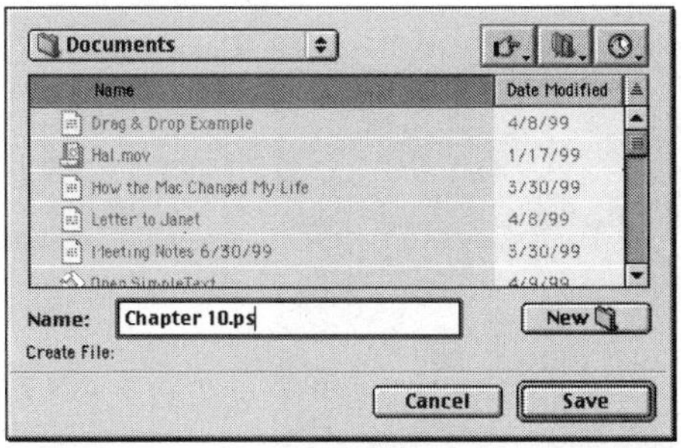

**Figure 62** Use this Save As dialog box to enter a name, select a location, and Save a document as a PostScript file.

## ✔ Tips

- You can normally cancel a print job as it is being spooled to the print queue or printer by pressing ⌘ . . Any pages spooled *before* you press ⌘ . , however, may be printed anyway.

- I tell you how to cancel a print job that has already been spooled to a print queue later in this chapter.

- I tell you how to use the Save As dialog box in **Chapter 5**.

## To save PostScript printer Print options

1. Click the Save Settings button at the bottom of the Print dialog box (**Figures 35, 44, 46, 48, 50, 54**, and **58**).

2. A dialog box like the one in **Figure 61** appears. Click OK to save the current settings for the printer.

## ✔ Tip

- Saving the settings for your printer displays the options you selected as the default options for the printer each time you use the Print dialog box.

## To process the print job

1. Click the Print button in the Print dialog box (**Figures 35, 44, 46, 48, 50**, and **54**).

   or

   Click the Save button in the Print dialog box (**Figure 58**).

2. If background printing is turned on, the print job is sent to the print queue, where it waits for its turn to be printed. You can continue working as soon as the spooling window disappears.

   or

   If background printing is turned off, the print job is sent to the printer and printed. You'll have to wait until it's completely spooled to the printer before you can continue working with your computer.

   or

   If you saved the document as a PostScript file, a Save As dialog box appears (**Figure 62**). Use it to enter a name, select a disk location, and save the file.

# The Print One Command

Some applications include a Print One or Print One Copy command under the File menu (**Figure 63**). This command sends a single copy of the active document to the printer using the current Page Setup and Print options. The print dialog box does not appear.

## ✔ Tip

■ The Print One command is a quick way to print one copy of a document, avoiding the Print dialog box.

# Desktop Printers

When you use the Chooser to select and set up a printer, Mac OS automatically creates a desktop printer for it. As the name suggests, it appears on the desktop as a printer driver icon (**Figure 64**).

Desktop printers can be used for a number of things:

◆ Identify and change the default printer.

◆ Print documents using drag and drop.

◆ Check or change items in a print queue.

◆ Stop or start a print queue.

I tell you about these things on the following pages.

## To identify the default printer

If you have only one desktop printer icon, it represents the default printer.

*or*

If you have multiple desktop printer icons, the one with the dark border around it represents the default printer (**Figure 64**).

## ✔ Tip

■ The default printer is the currently selected printer.

**Figure 63**
SimpleText's Print One Copy command does just that—it prints one copy of the active document without displaying the Print dialog box.

**Figure 64**
Desktop printer icons. In this illustration, the one on the top is the default printer.

**Figures 65a & 65b**
The commands on the Printing menu vary depending on what desktop printer icon is selected. These Printing menus are for a Color StyleWriter 1500 (left) and a LaserWriter, which is set up as the default printer (right).

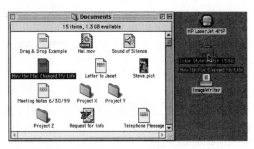

**Figure 66** Drag the icon for the document that you want to print onto the desktop printer icon for the printer on which you want to print it.

**Figure 67**
A page icon appears on a desktop printer that has at least one print job queued.

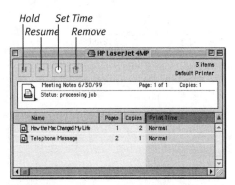

Hold   Set Time
Resume   Remove

**Figure 68** Opening a desktop printer displays its print queue.

## To change the default printer

1. Select the desktop printer icon for the printer that you want to set as the default printer.

2. Choose Set Default Printer from the Printing menu (**Figures 65a** and **65b**), or press ⌘ L.

## To print a document with drag & drop

1. Drag the icon for the document that you want to print onto the desktop printer icon for the printer on which you want to print it (**Figure 66**). If the application that created the document is not already running, Mac OS launches it.

2. Set options in the Print dialog box that appears.

3. Click Print.

## ✔ Tips

■ Drag and drop printing is a great way to print documents on any printer—without changing the default printer.

■ When a desktop printer contains one or more documents to be printed, a page icon appears on it (**Figure 67**).

■ I tell you about the Print dialog box earlier in this chapter.

## To open a desktop printer

Double-click the desktop printer icon.

*or*

Select the desktop printer icon and choose File > Open or press ⌘ O.

The desktop printer's window opens. If any print jobs are waiting to be printed, they appear in a list (**Figure 68**).

## To change the order of items in a print queue

1. Open the desktop printer for the print queue that you want to change (**Figure 68**).

2. Drag the item that you want to move into a higher (**Figure 69**) or lower position on the list of files to be printed. When you release the mouse button, the item moves (**Figure 70**).

## To set print time for a job

1. Open the desktop printer for the print queue that you want to change (**Figure 68**).

2. Select the icon for the print job that you want to schedule (**Figure 70**).

3. Click the Set Time (clock) button. The Set Print time dialog box appears (**Figure 71**).

4. Select the radio button for the time option that you want:

   ▲ **Urgent** puts the job in the print queue before jobs marked Normal.

   ▲ **Normal** puts the job in the print queue in the order it was received.

   ▲ **At Time** lets you specify a date and time to print the job (**Figure 72**).

5. Click OK. The date and time you set appears in the Print Time column of the desktop printer window (**Figure 73**).

## To remove a job from a print queue

1. Open the desktop printer for the print queue that you want to change (**Figure 66**).

2. Select the icon for the print job that you want to cancel (**Figure 73**).

3. Click the Remove (trash can) button. The selected print job disappears.

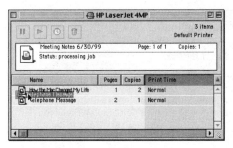

**Figure 69** Drag the item that you want to move into a new position in the print queue.

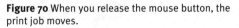

**Figure 70** When you release the mouse button, the print job moves.

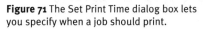

**Figure 71** The Set Print Time dialog box lets you specify when a job should print.

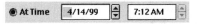

**Figure 72** Select the At Time radio button to enter the date and time for a job to print.

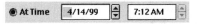

**Figure 73** The print time column of the desktop printer window displays the date and time a job is scheduled to print.

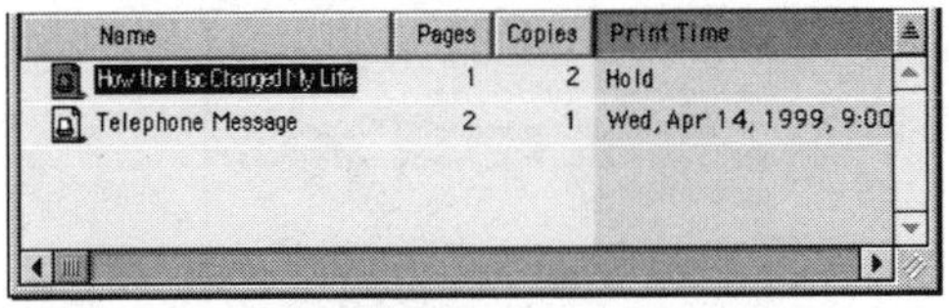

Figure 74 When you put a print job on hold, the word *Hold* appears in the Print Time column.

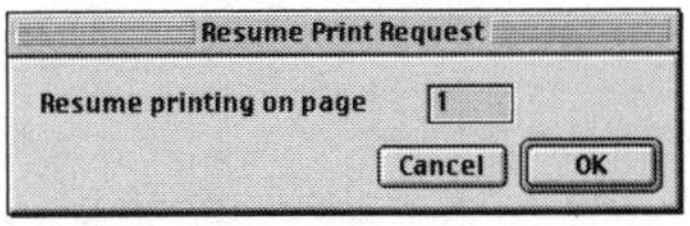

Figure 75 The Resume Print Request dialog box lets you specify the page from which to resume printing.

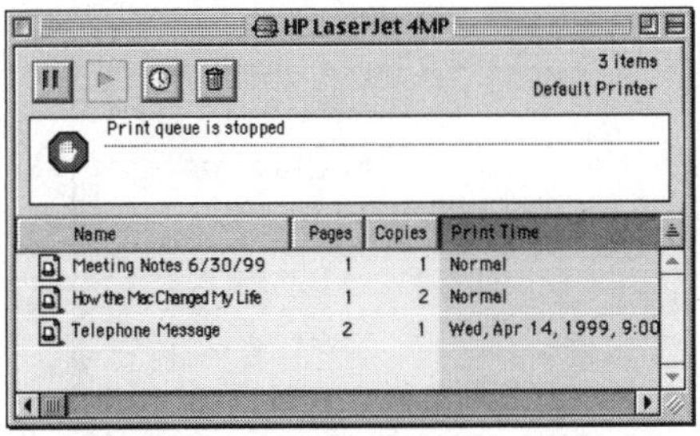

Figure 76 When you stop a print queue, a stop sign appears in the print queue window...

Figure 77
...and on the desktop printer icon.

## To put a print job on hold

1. Open the desktop printer for the print queue that you want to change (**Figure 68**).

2. Select the icon for the print job that you want to put on hold (**Figure 73**).

3. Click the Hold (double red bar) button. The word *Hold* appears in the Print Time column of the window (F**igure 74**).

## ✔ Tip

- A print job on hold will remain on hold until you resume it.

## To resume a job

1. Open the desktop printer for the print queue that you want to change (**Figure 68**).

2. Select the icon for a print job on hold that you want to resume (**Figure 73**).

3. Click the Resume (green triangle) button.

4. The Resume Print Request dialog box appears (**Figure 75**). Enter the number of the page on which you want to resume printing, and click OK. The word *Normal* appears in the Print Time column of the window (F**igure 68**).

## To stop a print queue

Choose Stop Print Queue from the Printing menu (**Figures 65a** and **65b**). A stop sign icon appears in the print queue window (**Figure 76**) and on the desktop printer icon (**Figure 77**).

## ✔ Tip

- A stopped print queue will remain stopped until you restart it.

## To restart a print queue

Choose Start Print Queue from the Printing menu (**Figures 65a** and **65b**). The stop sign icons disappear.

HOLDING PRINT JOBS, STOPPING PRINT QUEUES

# Troubleshooting Printing Problems

When a printing problem occurs, Mac OS can often give you hints to help you figure out why. Here are some examples:

◆ A dialog box like the one in **Figure 78** appears when your computer can't find the selected printer. Check to make sure the printer is properly connected and turned on.

◆ A dialog box like the one in **Figure 79** appears when your printer is out of paper. Add paper!

◆ The desktop printer's print queue window can often provide information about the printer's status. In **Figure 80**, the printer is off line; touching a button on the printer solves the problem.

## ✔ Tip

■ If you have printing problems that Mac OS can't help you identify, check the trouble-shooting section of the documentation that came with your printer.

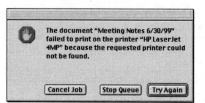

**Figure 78** This dialog box appeared when my printer wasn't turned on.

**Figure 79** This dialog box appeared when my printer ran out of paper.

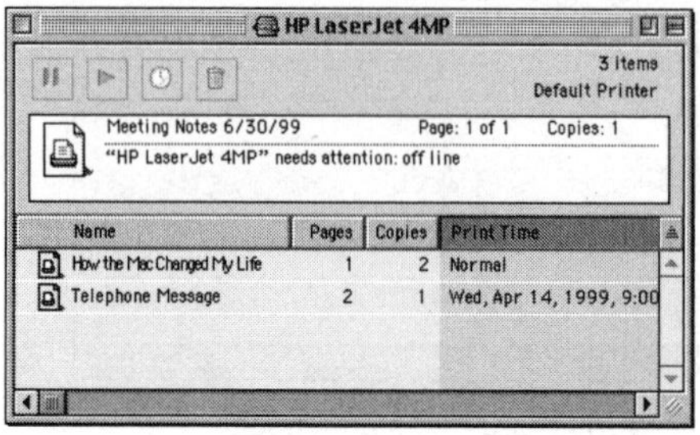

**Figure 80** This desktop printer window notes that my printer is off line.

# NETWORKING & TELECOMM

## Networking & Telecommunications

Mac OS computers offer two ways to connect to other computers:

- ◆ **Networking** uses direct connections and network protocols to connect your computer to others on a network. Once connected, you can share files, access e-mail, and run special network applications on server computers.

- ◆ **Telecommunications** uses a modem, telephone line, and communications software to connect your computer to another computer. Once connected, you can exchange files, access e-mail, and work with other features offered by the host computer.

## ✔ Tips

- ■ If you use your computer at work, you may be connected to a companywide network; if so, you'll find the networking part of this chapter very helpful. But if you use your computer at home and have only one computer, you won't have much need for the networking information here.

- ■ Online services, such as America Online, are huge computer systems offering a wealth of information and entertainment for a fee. You can access these systems via modem or Internet connection.

- ■ You can access the Internet with a network or modem connection. I tell you about connecting to the Internet in **Chapter 12**.

# Open Transport & Network Connections

Mac OS 8.6 includes *Open Transport*, system software that enables a Mac OS computer to connect to virtually any kind of network.

Most networks use one of the following two types of cables and connectors:

◆ **LocalTalk** connectors and standard telephone cables connect to the serial ports of computers and network printers. Devices are *daisy-chained*—linked one after another in a chain. LocalTalk is cheap and easy networking, but it is very slow.

◆ **Ethernet** cables connect to the Ethernet ports or Ethernet network interface cards of computers and network printers. Depending on the type of port and size of the network, additional hardware such as *transceivers* and *hubs* may be needed. Ethernet is faster than LocalTalk and is widely used for company and corporate networks.

## ✔ Tips

■ Details on network configurations are far beyond the scope of this book. The information here is provided primarily to give you an idea of how network connections work and introduce some of the network terms you might encounter when working with your computer and other documentation.

■ If your computer is on a large network, consult the system administrator before changing any network configuration options.

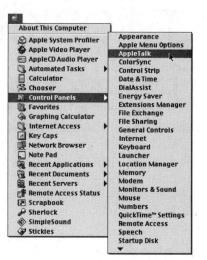

**Figure 1** Choose AppleTalk from the Control Panels submenu under the Apple menu.

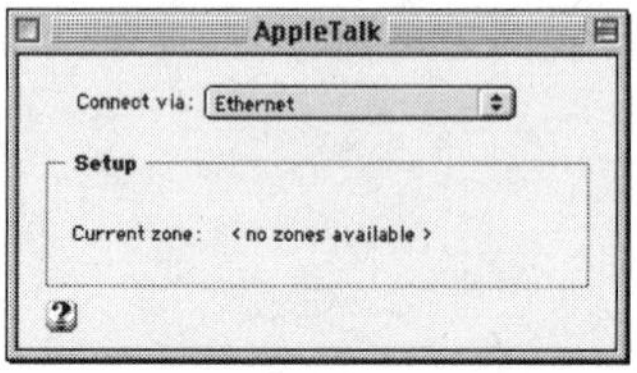

**Figure 2** The AppleTalk control panel lets you select the network connection port.

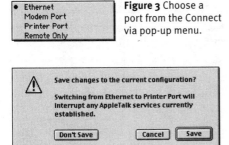

**Figure 3** Choose a port from the Connect via pop-up menu.

**Figure 4** Click Save in this dialog box if you're sure that you've selected the correct port.

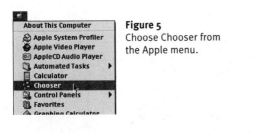

**Figure 5** Choose Chooser from the Apple menu.

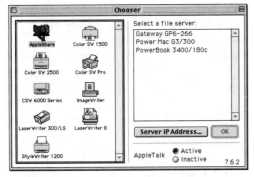

**Figure 6** The Chooser window with the AppleShare icon selected. The Chooser window may look different if you're on a multiple-zone network.

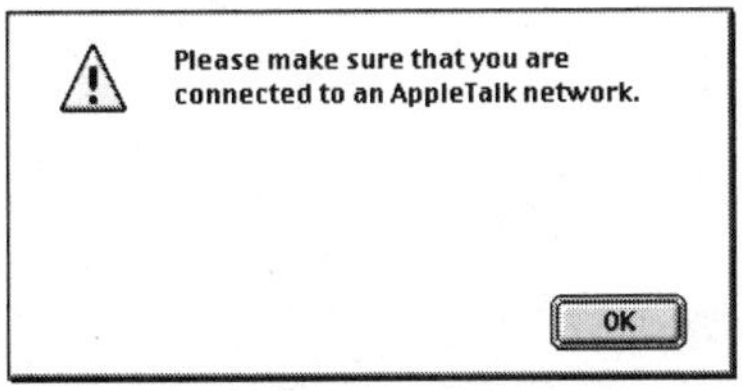

**Figure 7** If you have to turn AppleTalk on, a dialog box like this reminds you to make sure you're connected to a network.

## To select the network connection port

1. Choose Apple menu > Control Panels > AppleTalk (**Figure 1**).

2. In the AppleTalk control panel that appears (**Figure 2**), use the Connect via pop-up menu (**Figure 3**) to select the port to which the network is connected to your computer.

3. Close the AppleTalk control panel.

4. If you changed the configuration, a dialog box like the one in **Figure 4** appears. Click Save.

### ✔ Tips

- The Mac OS Setup Assistant should automatically configure the network connection for you—if you are connected to the network when you run it. I tell you about the Mac OS Setup Assistant in **Chapter 1**.

- If you select the wrong port in step 2, your network connection will not work.

- I tell you more about control panels in **Chapter 13**.

## To turn on AppleTalk

1. Choose Apple menu > Chooser (**Figure 5**) to display the Chooser window (**Figure 6**).

2. Select the Active radio button at the bottom of the Chooser window. A dialog box like the one in **Figure 7** appears. Click OK.

3. Close the Chooser to save your settings.

### ✔ Tip

- As the dialog box in **Figure 7** reminds you, you must be connected to an AppleTalk network to activate AppleTalk.

# Connecting to Another Computer

Mac OS 8.6 offers two tools to establish a connection to another computer via network:

◆ The **Chooser** (**Figure 8**) is the traditional way of accessing network volumes on a Mac OS computer.

◆ The **Network Browser** (**Figures 15** and **16**) enables you access network volumes using an interface similar to the new Open dialog box.

Both tools enable you to select and connect to a computer on the network, then mount one or more network volumes. Once you mount a volume, you can use the Finder to browse and work with its contents.

## ✔ Tips

■ You can only connect to computers that recognize you as a user or allow guest connections.

■ Although the Chooser and Network Browser refer to other computers as *file servers*, you can connect to any computer on the network that allows connections—not just dedicated file servers.

■ Network volumes are usually disks, but a folder can also be a network volume, depending on how file sharing is set up on the networked computer. I tell you about setting up file sharing later in this chapter.

■ I explain how to use the new Open dialog box in **Chapter 5**.

■ You can use Mac OS's alias or Favorites feature to create an alias or Favorite for a frequently mounted network volume. You can then open that volume by opening its alias or choosing it from the Favorites submenu under the Apple menu. I explain how to use aliases in **Chapter 4** and Favorites in **Chapter 5**.

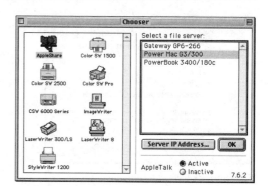

**Figure 8** Select the computer to which you want to connect.

**Figure 9** Use this dialog box to log onto the computer.

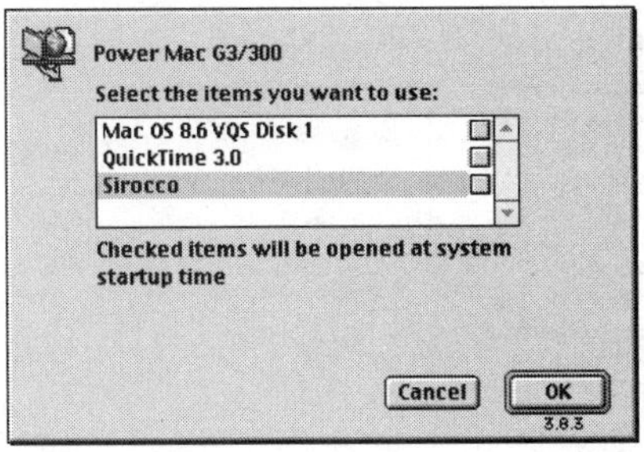

Power Mac G3/300

Select the items you want to use:

Mac OS 8.6 VQS Disk 1
QuickTime 3.0
Sirocco

Checked items will be opened at system startup time

Cancel   OK
3.8.3

**Figure 10** Select the volume or folder to which you want to connect.

**Figure 11**
The icon for the item to which you are connected appears on the Desktop.

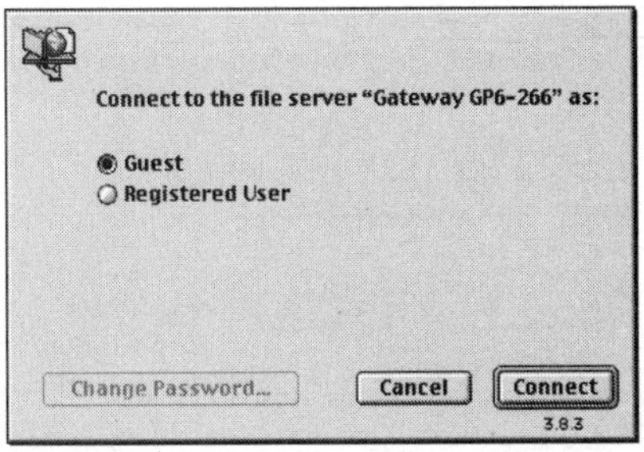

Connect to the file server "Gateway GP6-266" as:

◉ Guest
○ Registered User

Change Password...   Cancel   Connect
3.8.3

**Figure 12** Some computers allow guest connections. If so, the Guest radio button will be available in the connection dialog box.

Enter the Server Address:

⚠ Aliases made of this Server will fail if TCP/IP is not available.

Cancel   Connect

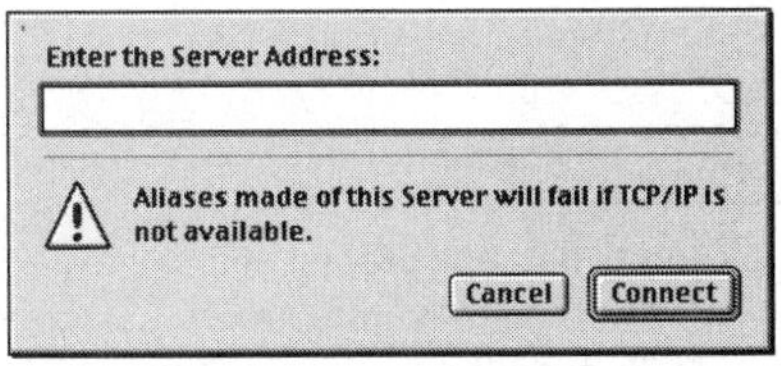

**Figure 13** Enter a server's IP address in this dialog box.

## To mount a network volume with the Chooser

1. Choose Apple menu > Chooser (**Figure 5**).

2. Select the AppleShare icon on the left side of the Chooser window (**Figure 6**).

3. If you're on a multiple-zone network, select the name of the zone in which the computer you want to connect to resides.

4. Select the name of the computer to which you want to connect (**Figure 8**).

5. Click OK.

6. A dialog box like the one in **Figure 9** appears. Enter your name and password in the Name and Password edit boxes.

7. Click OK.

8. In the list of volumes that appears (**Figure 10**), select the one that you want to open.

9. Click OK. The icon for the item appears on your desktop (**Figure 11**).

10. Close the Chooser window.

## ✔ Tips

■ If you're not sure which zone to select in step 3, ask your system administrator.

■ To select more than one volume in step 8, hold down (Shift) while clicking each one.

■ To automatically connect to a volume when you start your computer, turn on the check box beside the volume name (**Figure 10**).

■ To connect to another computer as a guest, select the Guest radio button in the connection dialog box (**Figure 12**), and click Connect.

■ To connect to a server using its IP address, click the Server IP Address button in the Chooser window (**Figure 8**). Then enter the server's IP address in the dialog box that appears (**Figure 13**), and click Connect. I tell you about TCP/IP in **Chapter 12**.

USING THE CHOOSER

193

## To mount a network volume with the Network Browser

1. Choose Apple menu > Network Browser (**Figure 14**) to display the Network Browser.

2. If necessary, double-click the name of the AppleTalk zone in which the computer you want to connect to resides.

3. Double-click the name of the computer you want to connect to (**Figure 15**).

4. A dialog box like the one in **Figure 9** appears. Enter your name and password in the Name and Password edit boxes.

5. Click OK.

6. In the list of volumes that appears (**Figure 16**), double-click the one you want to mount. The icon for the item appears on your desktop (**Figure 11**), and its window opens.

7. Close the Network Browser window.

### ✔ Tips

■ To connect to another computer as a guest, select the Guest radio button in the connection dialog box (**Figure 12**), and click Connect.

■ To connect to a server using its IP address, choose Connect to Server from the Shortcut button's menu in the Network Browser window (**Figure 17**). Then enter the server's IP address in the dialog box that appears (**Figure 18**), and click Connect.

## To unmount a network volume

Drag the icon for the volume you want to unmount to the Trash.

### ✔ Tips

■ Dragging a server item to the Trash does not delete that item.

■ To completely disconnect from a computer, unmount all of its volumes.

**Figure 14**
Choose Network Browser from the Apple menu.

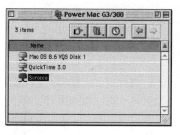

**Figure 15**
The Network window lists the networked computers.

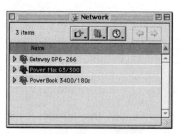

**Figure 16**
The window for a specific computer lists all of its volumes.

**Figure 17** The shortcuts menu enables you to view different Network Browser windows or connect to a server by entering its IP address.

**Figure 18**
Use this dialog box to enter the IP address for the server you want to connect to.

**USING THE NETWORK BROWSER**

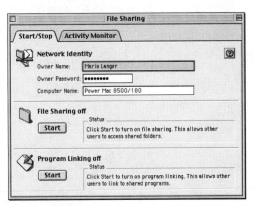

Figure 19 The Start/Stop options for the File Sharing control panel.

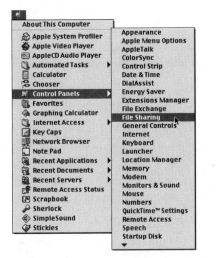

Figure 20 Choose File Sharing from the Control Panels submenu under the Apple menu.

# Sharing Files with Others

You can share files on your computer with other network users. To do this, you must do three things:

1. Use the File Sharing control panel to set a network identity and turn on file sharing.

2. Create user and group accounts for the individuals who you want to access your computer.

3. Set privileges for the items that you want to share.

I explain how to do all of these things on the next few pages.

# The File Sharing Control Panel

The File Sharing control panel (**Figures 19** and **27**) enables you to do the following:

◆ Set the network identity for your computer, including the owner name, owner password, and computer name.

◆ Turn file sharing and program linking on or off.

◆ See who is connected to your computer and what items are being shared.

## To open the File Sharing control panel

Choose Apple menu > Control Panels > File Sharing (**Figure 20**).

SHARING FILES WITH OTHERS

## To set or change your computer's network identity

1. Open the File Sharing control panel.

2. If necessary, click the Start/Stop tab to display its options (**Figure 19**).

3. Enter your name in the Owner Name edit box.

4. Enter a password to protect your computer in the Owner Password edit box. The characters you type turn to bullet characters when you advance to another edit box.

5. Enter a name for your computer in the Computer Name edit box.

6. Close the File Sharing control panel to save your settings.

## ✔ Tips

■ If you used the Mac OS Setup Assistant to configure your computer after installing Mac OS 8.6, your computer's network identity will already be set. I tell you about the Mac OS Setup Assistant in **Chapter 1**.

■ You can name your computer anything you like. I use model names on my personal network, but you may want to name your computer after yourself so that other network users know it's yours.

■ The Computer Name is what identifies your computer in the Chooser and Network Browser windows of other computers on the network.

■ Although you can leave the Owner Password edit box blank, doing so enables other users to connect to your computer without a password.

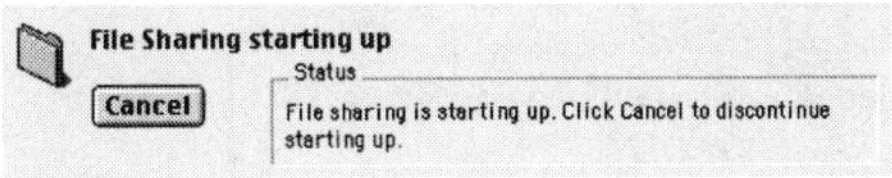

**Figure 21** The status area tells you that file sharing is starting up.

**Figure 22** The status area also tells you when file sharing is turned on.

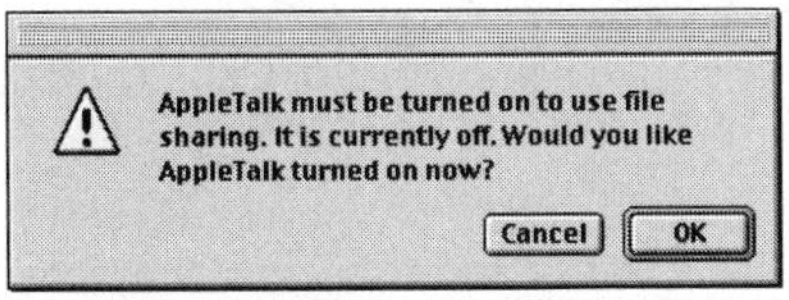

**Figure 23** As this dialog box points out, AppleTalk must be turned on before you can turn on file sharing.

## To turn file sharing on

1. Open the File Sharing control panel.

2. If necessary, click the Start/Stop tab to display its options (**Figure 19**).

3. Click the Start button in the File Sharing area. The status area indicates that sharing is starting up (**Figure 21**). After a moment, it indicates that file sharing is on (**Figure 22**).

4. Close the File Sharing control panel.

## ✔ Tips

■ File sharing enables other users to access files and folders on your hard disk as specified by users and groups settings and access privileges.

■ If there is a Stop button instead of a Start button in the File Sharing area of the File Sharing control panel, file sharing is already turned on (**Figure 22**).

■ If AppleTalk is not turned on when you attempt to start file sharing, a dialog box like the one in **Figure 23** appears. Click OK to dismiss the dialog box and turn Apple-Talk on. I explain how to turn AppleTalk on earlier in this chapter.

## To turn program linking on

1. Open the File Sharing control panel.

2. If necessary, click the Start/Stop tab to display its options (**Figure 19**).

3. Click the Start button in the Program Linking area. After a moment, the status area indicates that program linking is on.

4. Close the File Sharing control panel.

## ✔ Tip

■ Program linking enables other users to link to shared programs on your computer. If you're not sure if an application can be linked, check its documentation.

## To turn file sharing or program linking off

1. Open the File Sharing control panel.

2. If necessary, click the Start/Stop tab to display its options (**Figure 19**).

3. Click the Stop button in the File Sharing area (**Figure 23**) or Program Linking area.

4. If you turned off file sharing, a dialog box like the one in **Figure 24** appears. Enter the number of minutes before users are disconnected, and click OK.

5. Close the File Sharing control panel.

## ✔ Tips

■ When you turn off file sharing, connected users see dialog boxes like the ones in **Figures 25** and **26**.

■ When file sharing is turned off, all users are automatically disconnected.

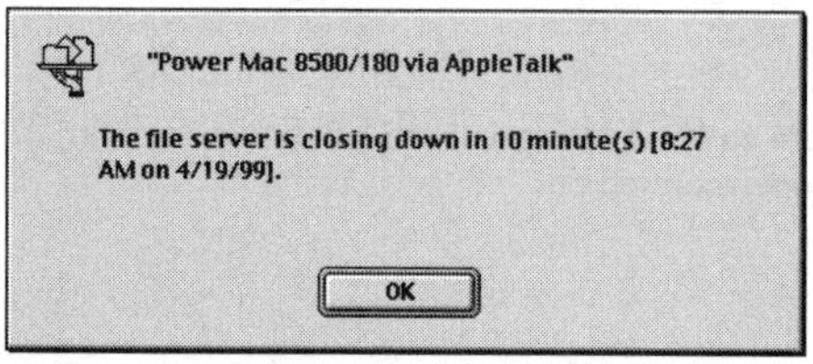

## To monitor file sharing activity

1. Open the File Sharing control panel.

2. If necessary, click the Activity Monitor tab. It displays connected users and shared items as well as an activity meter (**Figure 27**).

## ✔ Tips

■ You can disconnect a specific user by selecting his name in the Connected Users list and clicking the Disconnect button (**Figure 27**). A dialog box like the one in **Figure 24** lets you enter the number of minutes before the user is disconnected.

■ You can check privileges for shared items by selecting the item name in the Shared Items list and clicking the Privileges button (**Figure 27**). I tell you more about privileges later in this chapter.

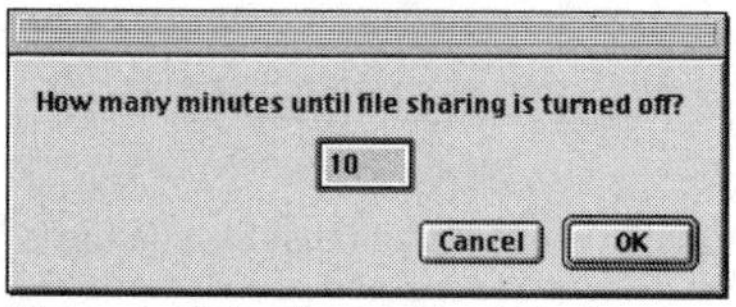

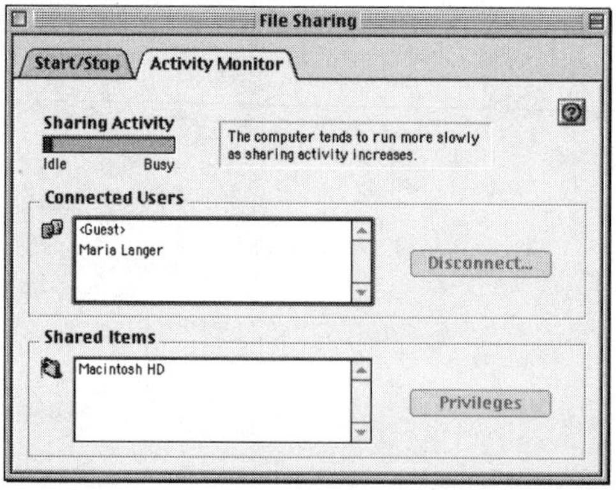

**Figure 24** Enter the number of minutes before users are disconnected.

**Figure 25** When you stop file sharing, connected users see one or more warning messages like this one...

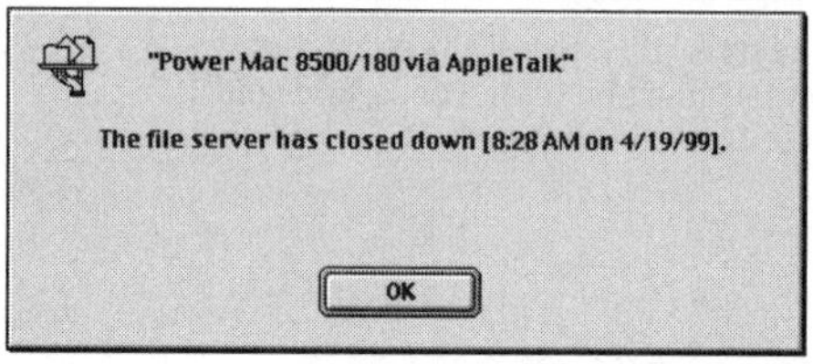

**Figure 26** ...before they're disconnected and see a message like this one.

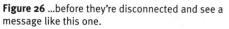

**Figure 27** The Activity Monitor tab of the File Sharing control panels lets you see who's connected.

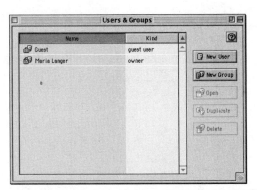

**Figure 28** The Users & Groups control panel enables you to maintain accounts for the people who access files on your computer.

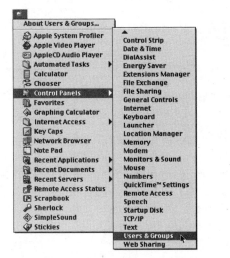

**Figure 29** Choose Users & Groups from the Control Panels submenu under the Apple menu.

# Users & Groups

File sharing is allowed on an individual or group basis set by users and groups:

◆ A *user* is an individual account consisting of a user name and password.

◆ A *group* is a number of users with the same privileges.

Users and groups are set up and modified with the Users & Groups control panel (**Figure 28**).

## ✔ Tip

■ You should set up a user account for each network user with whom you expect to share files.

## To open the Users & Groups control panel

Choose Apple menu > Control Panels > Users & Groups (**Figure 29**). The Users & Groups control panel appears (**Figure 28**). It lists all the users and groups set up for your computer.

## ✔ Tip

■ By default, your computer is set up with two users: the owner (you) and a guest user (Guest).

## To create a new user

1. Open the Users & Groups control panel (**Figure 28**).

2. Click the New User button. A New User window appears (**Figure 30**).

3. Enter the user's name in the Name edit box. The name appears in the title bar for the window when you advance to the next edit box.

4. Enter the user's password in the Password edit box. The characters you type change to bullets when you advance to another edit box (**Figure 31**).

5. To allow the user to change his password, make sure the Allow user to change password check box is turned on.

6. Select Sharing from the Show pop-up menu near the top of the window (**Figure 32**). The sharing options appear (**Figure 33**).

7. To enable file sharing for the user, make sure the Allow user to connect to this computer check box is turned on.

8. To enable program linking for the user, make sure the Allow user to link to programs on this computer check box is turned on.

9. Click the window's close box to save your settings. The user's name appears in the list of users and groups (**Figure 34**).

## ✔ Tip

■ I explain file sharing and program linking earlier in this chapter.

CREATING NEW USERS

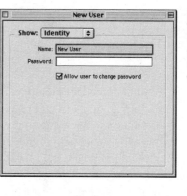

**Figure 30**
You create users with the New User window.

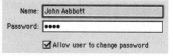

**Figure 31**
Enter a user's name and password.

**Figure 32** Choose Sharing from the Show pop-up menu.

**Figure 33**
Set sharing options in this window.

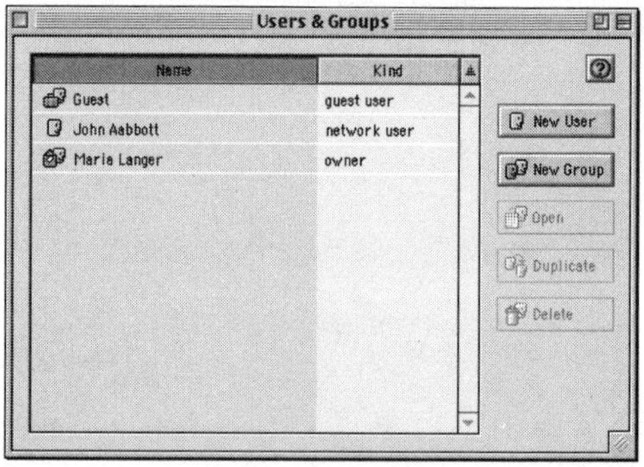

**Figure 34** The new user appears in the Users & Groups control panel window.

**Figure 35** Use the New Group window to name a group and add users to it.

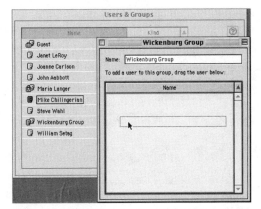

**Figure 36** Drag a user name from the Users & Groups control panel to the group window.

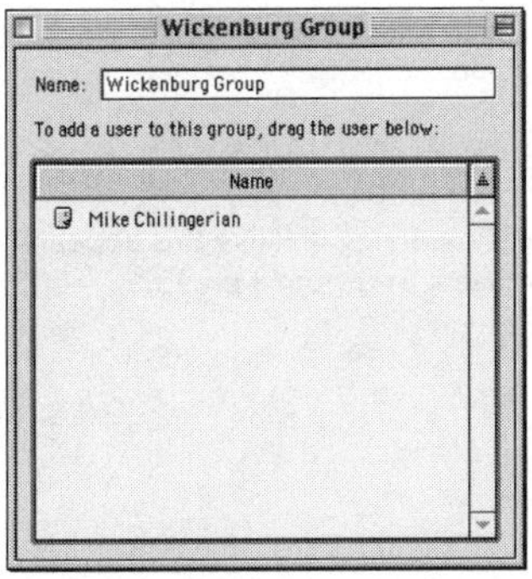

## To create a group

1. Open the Users & Groups control panel (**Figure 28**).

2. Click the New Group button. A New Group window appears (**Figure 35**).

3. Enter the group's name in the Name edit box. The name appears in the title bar for the window when you click outside the edit box.

4. Drag the icon for a user that you want to include in the group from the Users & Groups control panel window to the group window (**Figure 36**). When you release the mouse button, the user appears in the window (**Figure 37**).

5. Repeat step 4 for each user that you want to include in the group.

6. Click the group window's close box to close it. The group name appears in the Users & Groups control panel window (**Figure 38**).

## ✔ Tips

- You must create a user before you can add it to a group. I tell you how to create users on the previous page.

- You can add each user to as many groups as you like.

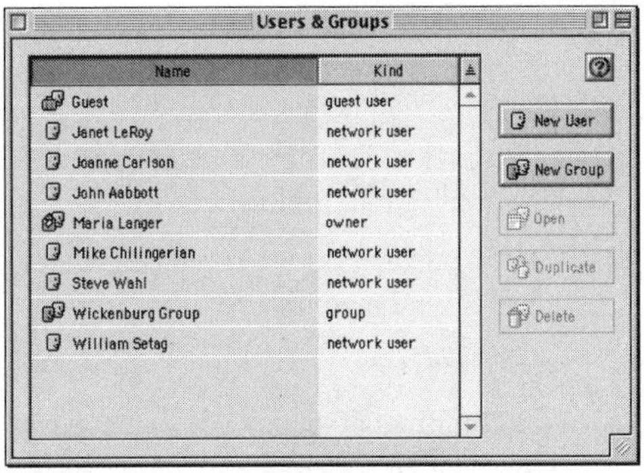

---

**Figure 37** When you release the mouse button, the user's name appears in the group window.

**Figure 38** The group name appears in the Users & Groups control panel window.

CREATING NEW GROUPS

## To modify a user or group

1. Open the Users & Groups control panel.

2. Select the name of the user or group that you want to modify (**Figure 39**), and click Open.

   *or*

   Double-click the name of the user or group that you want to modify.

3. Make changes in the user or group window (**Figures 30**, **33**, and **37**) as desired.

4. Click the window's close box to save your changes.

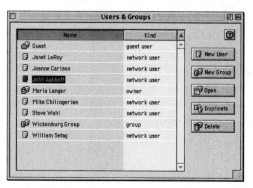

**Figure 39** Select the name of the user or group that you want to modify.

## To remove a user from a group

1. Open the Users & Groups control panel.

2. Double-click the name of the user that you want to remove from a group.

3. Choose Sharing from the pop-up menu at the top of the user window (**Figure 32**).

4. Click the name of the group from which you want to remove the user (**Figure 40**).

5. Press [Delete].

6. In the confirmation dialog box that appears (**Figure 41**), click Remove. The user's name disappears from the list.

7. Click the window's close box to save your changes.

   *or*

1. Open the Users & Groups control panel.

2. Double-click the name of the group from which you want to remove a user.

3. Click the name of the user that you want to remove from the group.

4. Press [Delete].

5. In the confirmation dialog box that appears (**Figure 41**), click Remove.

6. Click the window's close box to save your changes.

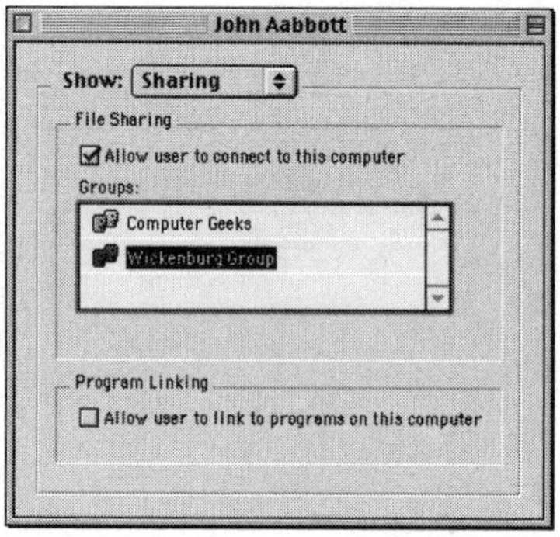

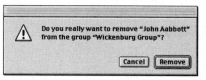

**Figure 40** The sharing settings in the user window list the groups to which the user belongs.

**Figure 41** A confirmation dialog box like this appears when you try to remove a user from a group.

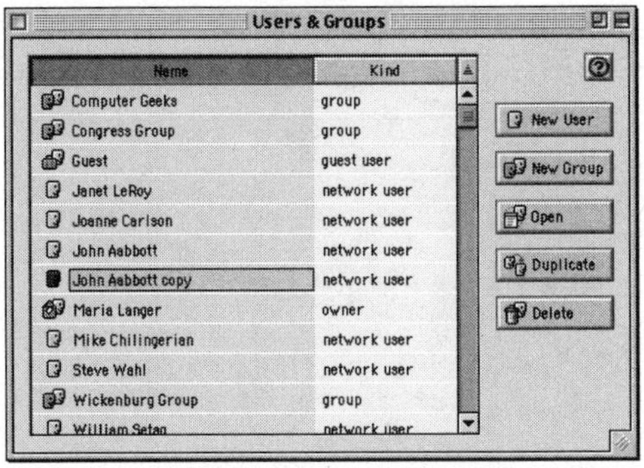

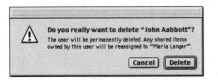

**Figure 42** When you duplicate a user or group, the copy appears beneath the original in the list.

Do you really want to delete "John Aabbott"?

The user will be permanently deleted. Any shared items owned by this user will be reassigned to "Maria Langer".

Cancel    Delete

**Figure 43** A confirmation dialog box like this one appears when you try to delete a user or group.

## To duplicate a user or group

1. Open the Users & Groups control panel.

2. Select the name of the user or group that you want to duplicate (**Figure 39**).

3. Click Duplicate. A copy of the item appears beneath the original (**Figure 42**).

## ✔ Tips

■ Duplicating a user or group is a quick way to create a new user or group with most of the same settings as an existing user or group.

■ Once you duplicate a user or group, you can open its window to modify it. I tell you about modifying users and groups on the previous page.

## To delete a user or group

1. Open the Users & Groups control panel.

2. Select the name of the user or group that you want to delete (**Figure 39**).

3. Click Delete.

4. A confirmation dialog box like the one in **Figure 43** appears. Click Delete.

## ✔ Tip

■ If you delete a user of group that owns items on your computer, those items are automatically reassigned to the computer's owner (you).

DUPLICATING & DELETING USERS & GROUPS

# Setting Privileges

The final step to sharing items is to specify which items will be shared and how users can access them. A user's access to an item is referred to as his *privileges*.

There are four types of privileges:

- **Read & write** privileges allow the user to open and save files.

- **Read only** privileges allow the user to open files, but not save files.

- **Write only** privileges allow the user to save files but not open them.

- **None** means the user can neither open nor save files.

Privileges can be set for three categories of users:

- **Owner** is the user or group who can set access privileges for the item. You will probably be the owner for most, if not all, of the folders on your computer.

- **User/Group** is the user or group that has access to the item. This can be set to None if only the owner should have access.

- **Everyone** is everyone else on the network.

You set privileges in the sharing information area of the Info window for a specific folder (**Figure 44**) or disk (**Figure 45**).

## ✔ Tips

- A disk or folder with write only privileges is sometimes referred to as a *drop box* because users can drag and drop files into it but cannot see its contents.

- It's vital that you set privileges correctly if there are confidential files on your computer. Otherwise those files could be accessible by other users on your network.

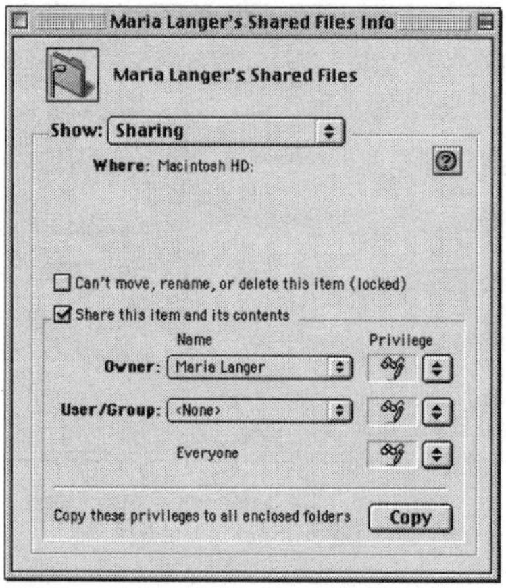

**Figure 44** The sharing information in the Info window for the Shared Files folder created by the Mac OS Setup Assistant...

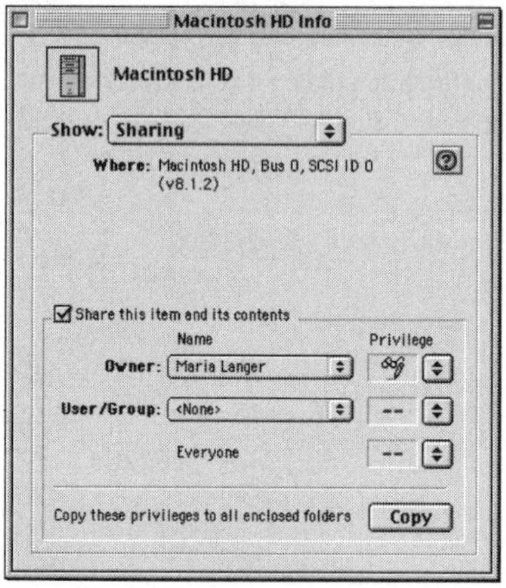

**Figure 45** ...and for a disk.

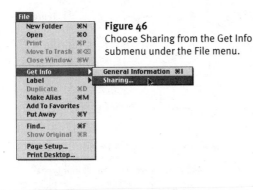

**Figure 46**
Choose Sharing from the Get Info submenu under the File menu.

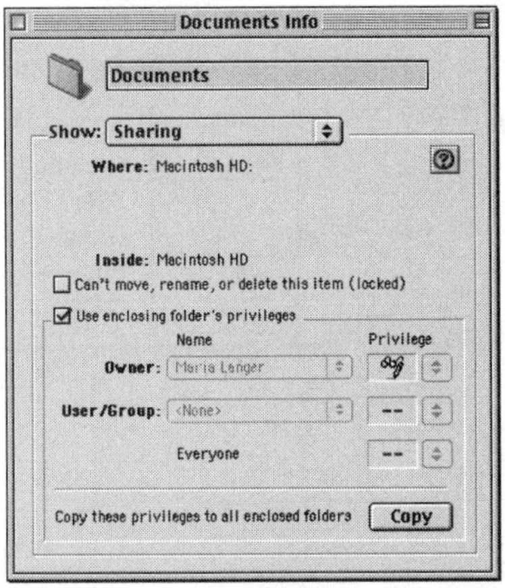

Documents Info

**Figure 47** If a folder resides inside a shared folder or disk, there will be no Share this item and its contents check box.

## To open the Sharing Info window

1. Select the folder or disk for which you want to open the sharing window.

2. Choose File > Get Info > Sharing (**Figure 46**). The sharing information of the Info window appears (**Figures 44** and **45**).

### ✔ Tip

- You cannot open a sharing window for an individual file.

## To turn on sharing

1. Open the Sharing Info window for the folder or disk (**Figures 44** and **45**).

2. Turn on the Share this item and its contents check box. The icon for the item may change (**Figure 44**).

3. Close the Sharing Info window.

### ✔ Tip

- If the folder is inside a shared folder or disk, the Sharing Info window will look like the one in **Figure 47**. If desired, you can turn on the Use enclosing folder's privileges check box to automatically assume the privileges of the folder or disk in which the folder resides—even if it is moved.

## To prevent a shared folder from being moved, renamed, or deleted

1. Open the Sharing Info window for the folder (**Figures 44** and **47**).

2. Turn on the Can't move, rename, or delete this item check box.

3. Close the Sharing Info window.

### ✔ Tip

- It's a good idea to enable this option if you're concerned about users modifying folders on your hard disk.

SETTING PRIVILEGES

## To set privileges

1. Open the sharing window for the folder or disk (**Figures 44**, **45**, and **47**).

2. Choose a user or group name from the Owner pop-up menu (**Figure 48**). Then choose a privilege from the Privilege pop-up menu on the same line (**Figure 49**).

3. If desired, choose a user or group name from the User/Group pop-up menu (**Figure 50**). Then choose a privilege from the Privilege pop-up menu on the same line (**Figure 49**).

4. If desired, choose a privilege from the Privilege pop-up menu on the Everyone line (**Figure 49**).

5. To assign the same privileges to every folder within the folder or disk, click the Copy button. A confirmation dialog box like the one in **Figure 51** appears. Click Copy to copy the privileges.

6. Close the sharing window.

## ✔ Tips

■ The Owner and User/Group pop-up menus include all users and groups in the Users & Groups control panel. I tell you about users and groups earlier in this chapter.

■ Confused? These two examples may help you understand how users and groups work.

  ▲ In **Figure 52a**, the item is owned by Maria Langer, who can open and save files. The primary group is Wickenburg Group, whose members can only save files. No one else can access the item.

  ▲ In **Figure 52b**, the item is owned by Maria Langer, who can open and save files. The primary user is John Aabbott, who can also open and save files. Everyone else can only save files.

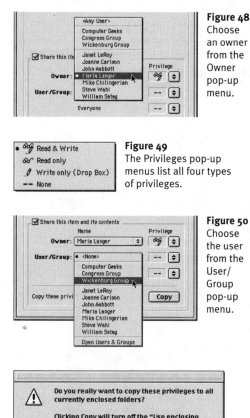

**Figure 48** Choose an owner from the Owner pop-up menu.

**Figure 49** The Privileges pop-up menus list all four types of privileges.

**Figure 50** Choose the user from the User/Group pop-up menu.

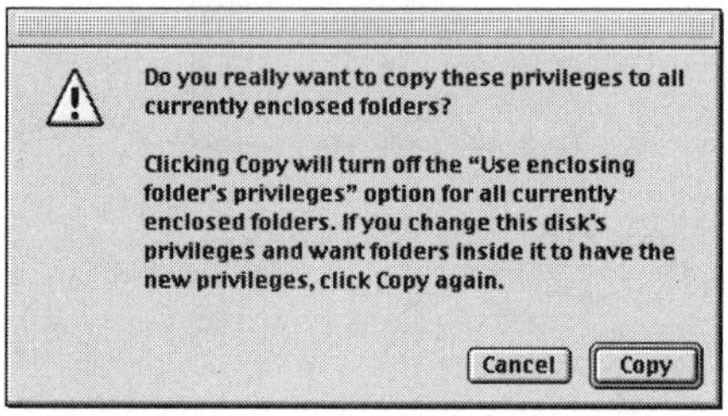

**Figure 51** When you click the Copy button, a confirmation dialog box like this one appears.

**Figures 52a & 52b** Two examples of how privileges can be set.

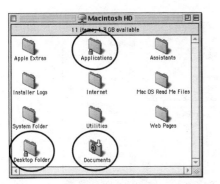

Figure 53 Folder icons indicate file-sharing privileges. (The Desktop folder is always a locked folder.)

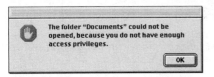

Figure 54 When you try to open a folder you're not allowed to open, a dialog box like this appears.

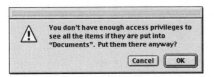

Figure 55 When you use a drop box, a dialog box like this appears.

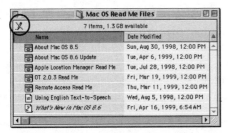

Figure 56 A tiny icon on the left side of the header indicates that this is a read-only folder.

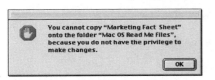

Figure 57 When you try to copy a file to a folder with read-only privileges, a dialog box like this appears.

# Icons & Windows of Shared Items

The appearance of a shared item provides visual clues to its privilege settings.

◆ Folders that cannot be opened have buckles around them (**Figure 53**). If you try to open of these folders, a dialog box like the one in **Figure 54** tells you why you can't.

◆ A drop-box folder has a down-pointing arrow above it (**Figure 53**). When you drop an item into one of these folders, a dialog box like the one in **Figure 55** reminds you that you won't be able to see it once it's gone.

◆ Folders that cannot be renamed, moved, or deleted display a padlock icon beside them (**Figure 53**).

◆ The window for a read-only folder displays a tiny pencil with a slash icon on the left side of the header (**Figure 56**). When you try to drag an item into it, a dialog box like the one in **Figure 57** tells you why you can't.

ICONS & WINDOWS OF SHARED ITEMS

# Modem Connections

You can also use a modem and a standard telephone line to connect to other computers. A *modem* is a hardware device that is either inside your computer (an *internal* modem) or connected to one of your computer's serial ports (an *external* modem). You configure a modem connection with the Modem control panel.

Having a modem isn't enough to connect to another computer. You also need telecommunications software. The software you use depends on the type of system you are connecting to. For example, to connect to a friend's computer, you could use a general-purpose program like ZTerm; to connect to an online service like America Online, you would use the freely distributable America Online client software. Modems usually come with one or more kinds of telecommunications software.

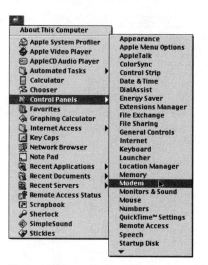

**Figure 58** Choose Modem from the Control Panels submenu under the Apple menu.

## ✔ Tips

- Although Mac OS 8.6 does not include any general purpose telecommunications software, it does include Remote Access, which can be used to connect to the Internet or an Apple Remote Access server. I discuss Internet connections in **Chapter 12** and an Apple Remote Access server connection at the end of this chapter.

- Most of today's modems can also send and receive faxes. Software to utilize this modem feature normally comes with the modem.

- There are many modem makes and models that will work with Mac OS computers— far too many to discuss in detail here. Read the documentation that came with your modem to learn more about using it and its features.

**Figure 59**
The Modem control panel.

## To set modem options with the Modem control panel

1. Choose Apple menu > Control Panels > Modem (**Figure 58**). The Modem control panel appears (**Figure 59**).

2. Choose an option from the Connect via pop-up menu (**Figure 60**). The options offered in the menu will vary depending on your computer model.

3. Select a modem make and model from the Modem pop-up menu (**Figure 61**).

4. Select one of the Sound radio buttons to turn the modem speaker On or Off.

5. Select one of the Dialing radio buttons to specify whether you have Tone or Pulse dialing.

6. To instruct the modem to dial no matter what the dial tone sounds like, turn on the Ignore dial tone check box.

7. Click the Modem control panel's close box.

8. In the confirmation dialog box that appears (**Figure 62**), click Save.

**Figure 60**
Choose the port to which your modem is connected from the Connect Via pop-up menu.

**Figure 61**
Choose your modem make and model from the Modem pop-up menu.

## ✔ Tips

- If you cannot find your modem make and model in the Modem pop-up menu (**Figure 61**), try another modem with the same brand name or one of the Hayes modems.

- Turn on the Ignore dial tone check box in step 6 if you have a telephone answering system that changes the sound of a dial tone when messages are waiting.

- The telecommunications software you use with your modem may have other settings. Check the documentation that came with the software for configuration information.

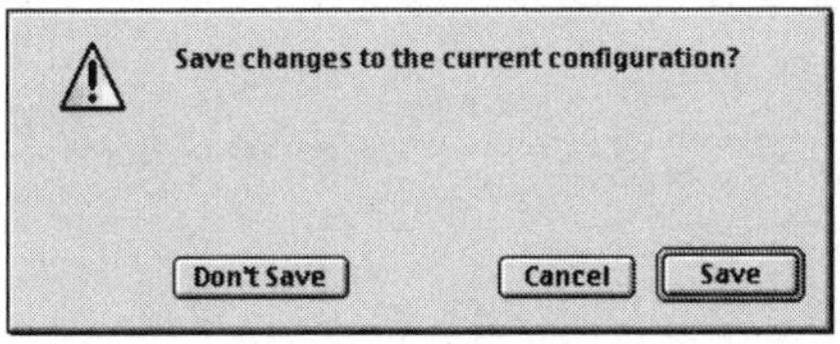

**Figure 62** Click Save to save your settings.

USING THE MODEM CONTROL PANEL

# Remote Access

Remote Access is telecommunications software that's part of Mac OS 8.6. It has two main functions:

◆ Use it to connect to Apple Remote Access (ARA) servers to access network volumes. I tell you how on the following pages.

◆ Use it to connect to an Internet Service Provider (ISP) via PPP. I tell you how in **Chapter 12**.

## ✔ Tips

■ Apple Remote Access server software does not come with Mac OS 8.6, so its installation and configuration is not discussed in this book.

■ The Remote Access control panel replaces the PPP control panel found in versions of Mac OS prior to 8.5.

## To create a Remote Access configuration for connecting to an ARA server

1. Choose Apple menu > Control Panels > Remote Access (**Figure 63**).

2. The Remote Access control panel window appears (**Figure 64**). If the edit boxes are empty, skip ahead to step 7.

3. Choose File > Configurations (**Figure 65**), or press ⌘ ⌘ K.

4. In the Configurations dialog box that appears (**Figure 66**), select Default and then click Duplicate.

5. In the Duplicate Configuration dialog box that appears (**Figure 67**), enter a name for the new configuration and click OK.

**Figure 63** Choose Remote Access from the Control Panels submenu under the Apple menu

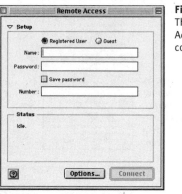

**Figure 64** The Remote Access control panel.

**Figure 65** Choose Configurations from the File menu.

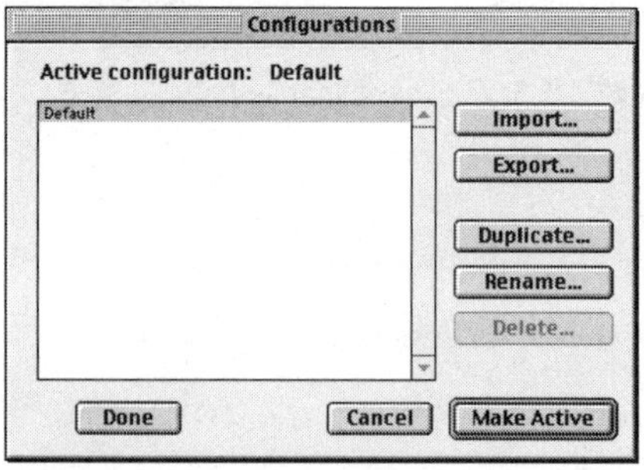

**Figure 66** The Configurations dialog box lists all Remote Access configurations, including those for Internet connections.

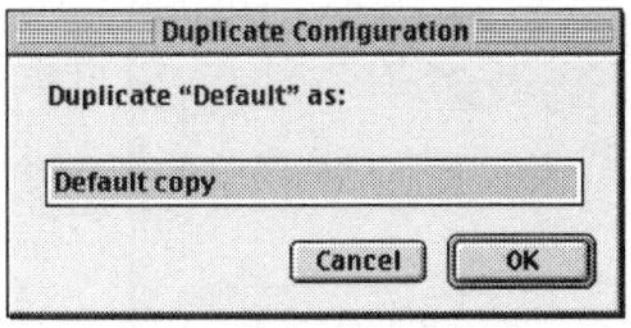

**Figure 67**
Use this dialog box to rename a duplicate configuration.

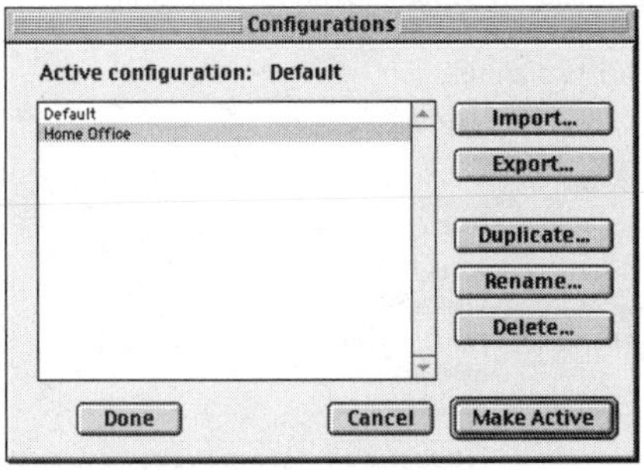

**Figure 68** Select the configuration you created and click Make Active.

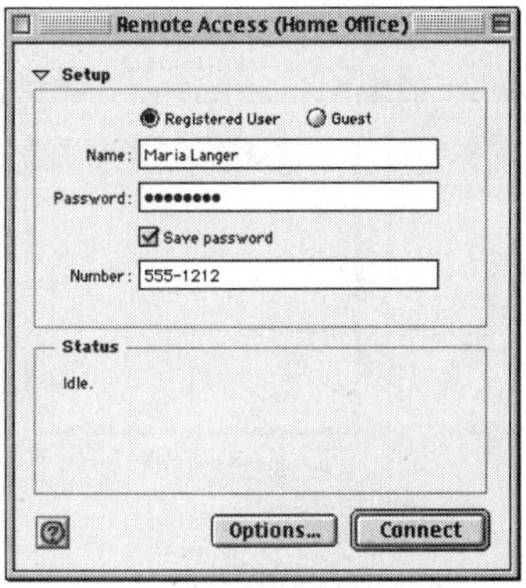

**Figure 69**
Here's what the connection information might look like in the Remote Access control panel window.

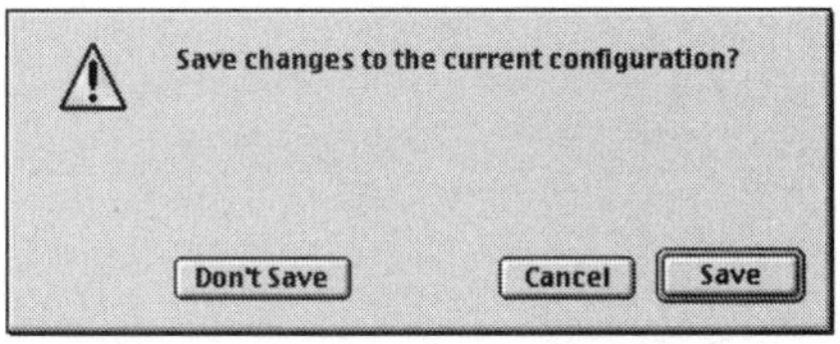

**Figure 70** If you close the Remote Access control panel or switch configurations after making changes to the active configuration, a dialog box like this one appears.

6. Back in the Configurations dialog box (**Figure 68**), make sure the configuration you just named is selected and click the Make Active button to return to the Remote Access control panel window.

7. Enter your user name on the remote system in the Name edit box.

8. Enter your password on the remote system in the Password edit box. The password you enter appears as bullet characters (**Figure 69**).

9. To instruct Remote Access to save your password so you don't have to enter it each time you connect, turn on the Save password check box.

10. Enter the telephone number for the remote system in the Number edit box. Be sure to include all numbers that must be dialed, such as long-distance prefixes or codes to disable call waiting.

11. To connect, follow the instructions on the next page.

   *or*

   To close the Remote Access control panel without connecting, click its close box. If a dialog box like the one in **Figure 70** appears, click Save.

## ✔ Tips

- You can create a separate configuration for each network to which you connect.

- If the edit boxes in the Remote Access control panel window are not empty, overwrite their contents with correct information. Since the configuration is a duplicate, you don't have to worry about losing information that may have been in the original configuration file.

# To connect to a Remote Access server

1. Choose Apple menu > Control Panels > Remote Access (**Figure 69**).

2. If necessary, choose File > Configurations (**Figure 65**) to open the Configurations dialog box (**Figure 68**). Select the configuration you want to use, and click the Make Active button.

3. Click Connect. The Status area of the window indicates that Remote Access is dialing (**Figure 71**). When you have successfully connected, the Status area shows Send and Receive bars as well as the time connected (**Figure 72**).

4. Follow the instructions in the section titled "Connecting to another computer" near the beginning of this chapter to connect to a computer on the network.

## ✔ Tips

- The Chooser looks and works the same when connecting via Remote Access (**Figure 73**) as it does when connecting from a computer on the network (**Figure 6**).

- Once connected, you can share files and applications and even print just as you would if you were on the network. Access speed, however, will be quite a bit slower.

# To disconnect from a Remote Access Server

1. Drag the icons for shared disks to the trash.

2. Click Disconnect in the Remote Access control panel window (**Figure 72**).

3. Wait while Remote Access disconnects.

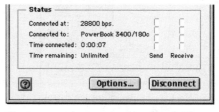

**Figure 71** The status area provides connection status information, from the moment Remote Access starts dialing...

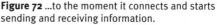

**Figure 72** ...to the moment it connects and starts sending and receiving information.

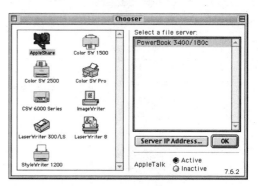

**Figure 73** Once connected, you can use the Chooser to connect to a network computer and access its volumes.

# CONNECTING TO THE INTERNET 12

## Connecting to the Internet

The *Internet* is a vast, worldwide network of computers that offers information, communication, online shopping, and entertainment for the whole family.

There are two ways to connect to the Internet:

◆ In a *direct* or *LAN connection*, your computer has a live network connection to the Internet all the time. This is costly for individuals, but if your computer is on a companywide network, you may have Internet access through the network.

◆ In a *modem* or *dial-up connection*, your computer uses its modem to dial in to a server at an *Internet Service Provider* (*ISP*), which gives it access to the Internet. This is a cheaper way to connect, but your access speed is limited by the speed of your modem.

In this chapter, I tell you how to configure your system for an Internet connection, connect to the Internet, and use the Internet applications and utilities included with Mac OS 8.6.

## ✔ Tips

■ An ISP is an organization that provides access to the Internet for a fee.

■ The *World Wide Web* is part of the Internet. I tell you about the Web and the *Web browser* software you use to access it later in this chapter.

■ I tell you more about modems in **Chapter 11**.

# The Internet Setup Assistant

The Internet Setup Assistant is an application that steps you through the process of configuring your computer to connect to the Internet. It has two parts that are launched automatically as you need them:

◆ **ISP Referral Assistant** helps you open an account with an Internet Service Provider (ISP). This is the part you'll use if you don't have an account with an ISP and want to open one.

◆ **Internet Editor Assistant** helps you add or modify existing Internet configuration settings. This is the part you'll use if you already have an account with an ISP or a direct connection to the Internet.

## To start the Internet Setup Assistant

1. Double-click the Internet Setup Assistant icon in the Assistants folder on your hard disk (**Figure 1**). The Internet Setup Assistant's main window appears (**Figure 2**).

2. Click the Yes button to display the second window of the Internet Setup Assistant (**Figure 3**).

## ✔ Tip

■ The Internet Setup Assistant is automatically launched when you click the Continue button at the end of a Mac OS 8.6 installation. I tell you about installing Mac OS 8.6 in **Chapter 1**.

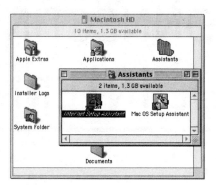

**Figure 1** Double-click the Internet Setup Assistant icon in the Assistants folder.

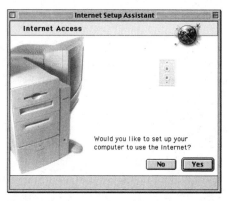

**Figure 2** The main window of the Internet Setup Assistant.

**Figure 3** The second window of the Internet Setup Assistant asks if you already have an Internet connection.

**Figure 4** The Introduction window tells you what the assistant does.

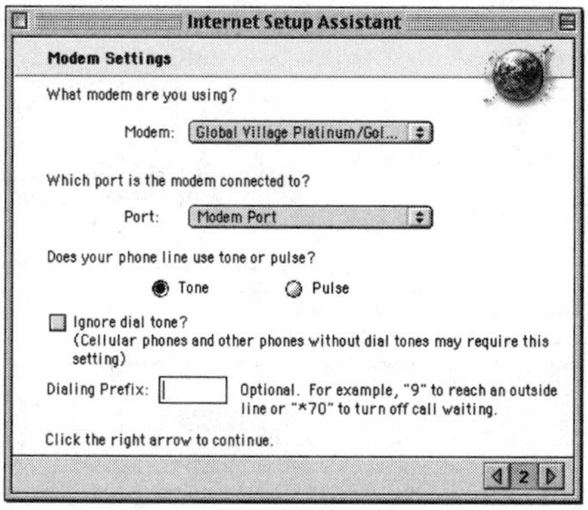

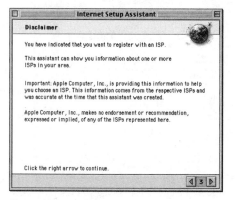

**Figure 5** The Modem Settings window lets you configure your modem.

**Figure 6** The Disclaimer window was obviously inserted by an Apple lawyer.

## To register with an ISP

1. In the second window of the Internet Setup Assistant (**Figure 3**), click No.

2. Read the information in the Introduction window that appears (**Figure 4**). Then click the right arrow at the bottom of the window.

3. The Modem Settings window appears next (**Figure 5**). Select the make and model of your modem from the Modem pop-up menu. Use the Port pop-up menu to select the port to which your modem is connected. Select the radio button for either Tone or Pulse dialing. To instruct your computer to dial whether or not it detects a dial tone, turn on the Ignore dial tone check box. To dial certain digits before each call, enter the digits in the Dialing Prefix edit box. Then click the right arrow.

4. The Disclaimer window appears next (**Figure 6**). Read its contents and click the right arrow.

5. Next, the Country and Area Code window appears (**Figure 7**). Choose your Country from the Country pop-up menu. Enter your area code in the Area Code edit box and the first three digits of your phone number in the Phone Prefix edit box. Then click Register.

*Continued on next page...*

**Figure 7** Enter your country, area code, and first three numbers of your phone number.

*Continued from previous page.*

6. Wait while your computer uses your modem to retrieve a list of ISPs in your area. (It dials a toll-free number.)

7. The Conclusion window appears next (**Figure 8**). Read the information it contains, and click the Go Ahead button.

8. The Connection Status window appears while your modem connects to Apple's ISP server. When you successfully connect, Internet Explorer launches.

9. Wait while the Internet Account Server Web page loads. When it's finished, it'll look something like **Figure 9**.

10. Follow the instructions that appear on screen to choose a service and fill out forms. The information you'll have to provide includes:

    ▲ Your service preferences (if the ISP offers multiple levels of service).

    ▲ Your user ID and password.

    ▲ Billing and payment information.

    During this process, you'll also select the phone number that your modem will dial to connect to the Internet.

11. Wait while the information you entered is processed.

12. An Internet Setup Assistant window like the one in **Figure 10** appears. It contains information about your new account. Click Done.

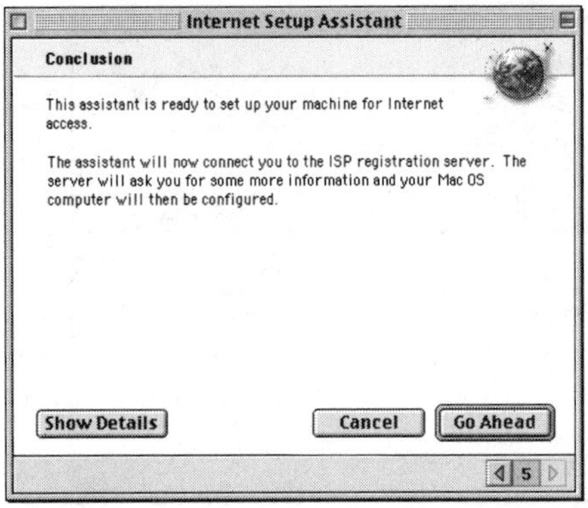

**Figure 8** The Conclusion window tells you what will happen next.

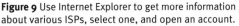

**Figure 9** Use Internet Explorer to get more information about various ISPs, select one, and open an account.

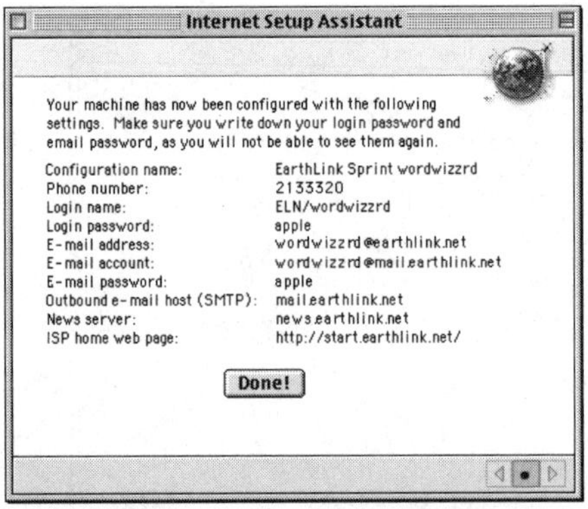

**Figure 10** At the end of the ISP registration process, the Internet Setup Assistant summarizes your account information.

**Figure 11** A dialog box like this may appear when you submit information entered in a Web page form.

## ✔ Tips

- If your modem's make and model are not listed in the Modem pop-up menu in step 3, try a similar model from the same manufacturer or one of the Hayes models. I tell you more about modems in **Chapter 11**.

- If you click the Show Details button in step 10, you'll see a summary of the information you entered in the previous steps.

- If a security warning dialog box like the one in **Figure 11** appears during step 10, click Send to go on.

- While comparing Internet deals in step 10 (if multiple deals are offered for your area), note the toll-free numbers for the ISPs. You can call any ISP directly if you have more questions.

- If you live in an out-of-the-way place (like Wickenburg, AZ), the ISPs in step 10 may not have an access number that is local to you. Although you may be able to access an ISP using a toll-free number for an additional hourly charge, this may be costly if you plan to spend a lot of time online. If you can't find a local provider using the Internet Setup Assistant, do some research with the phone book to find the best ISP for you. (I called a local computer consultant; she gave me the name and number of the only local ISP.) Then use the Internet Setup Assistant to set up an Internet connection for an existing ISP account, as discussed on the next few pages.

- In step 12, write down your ISP account log on information and put it in a safe place. Although this information is automatically entered in your system, it's a good idea to have it written down in case you ever need to enter it manually.

## To add a dialup configuration

1.  In the second window of the Internet Setup Assistant (**Figure 3**), click Yes.

2.  Read the information in the Introduction window that appears (**Figure 12**). Then click the right arrow at the bottom of the window.

3.  The Configuration name and connection type window appears (**Figure 13**). Enter a name for the connection in the edit box. Then select the Modem radio button and click the right arrow button.

4.  The Modem Settings window appears next (**Figure 5**). Select the make and model of your modem from the Modem pop-up menu. Use the Port pop-up menu to select the port to which your modem is connected. Select the radio button for either Tone or Pulse dialing. To instruct your computer to dial whether or not it detects a dial tone, turn on the Ignore dial tone check box. To dial certain digits before each call, enter the digits in the Dialing Prefix edit box. Then click the right arrow.

5.  In the Configuration information window that appears next (**Figure 14**), enter the local access number for your ISP in the top

**Figure 12** The Introduction window explains what the Internet Setup Assistant does and what information you'll need to use it.

**Figure 13** Use the Configuration Name and Connection Type window to provide a name and specify a type of configuration.

**Figure 14** In the Configuration Information window, enter the local access number and log on information for your ISP.

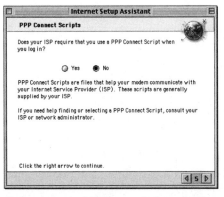

**Figure 15** Use the PPP Connect Scripts window to indicate whether your ISP requires a PPP connect script.

Figure 16 Choose a script from the Script pop-up menu.

Figure 17 Use this IP Address window to specify whether you have your own IP address.

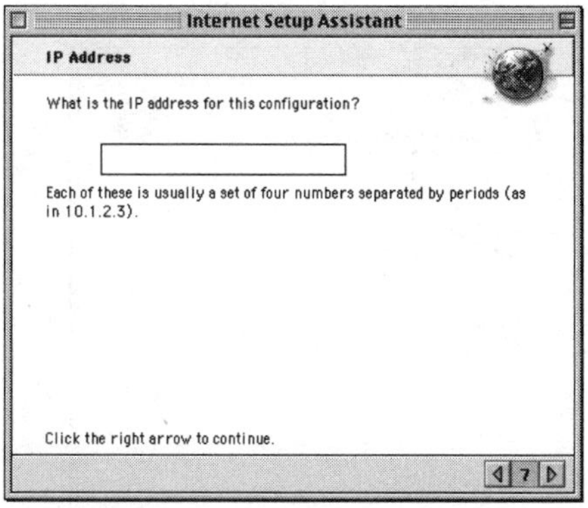

Figure 18 Use this IP Address window to enter your IP address if you selected Yes in the previous window.

edit box, your user ID in the middle edit box, and your password in the bottom edit box. Then click the right arrow.

6. The PPP Connect Scripts window appears next (**Figure 15**). Select a radio button to indicate whether your ISP requires a PPP connect script. Click the right arrow.

7. If you selected Yes in step 6, a second PPP Connect Scripts window appears (**Figure 16**). Choose a connect script from the Script pop-up menu, and click the right arrow.

8. The IP Address window appears next (**Figure 17**). Select a radio button to indicate whether your have been assigned your own IP address. Then click the right arrow.

9. If you selected Yes in step 8, another IP Address window appears (**Figure 18**). Enter the IP address in the edit box, and click the right arrow.

10. The Domain Name Servers window appears next (**Figure 19**). Enter the DNS address or addresses in the top edit box. If there is more than one, make sure you press [Return] between each one. Then enter the domain name in the bottom edit box. Click the right arrow.

Continued on next page...

Figure 19 Use the Domain Name Servers window to enter the DNS addresses and domain name for your ISP.

ADDING A DIALUP CONFIGURATION

*Continued from previous page.*

11. In the E-mail Address and Password window (**Figure 20**), enter your e-mail address in the top edit box and your e-mail password in the bottom edit box. Then click the right arrow.

12. In the E-mail Account and Host Computer window (**Figure 21**), enter the POP account in the top edit box and the SMTP host in the bottom edit box. Click the right arrow.

13. In the Newsgroup Host Computer window (**Figure 22**), enter the NNTP host. Then click the right arrow.

14. The Proxies window that appears next (**Figure 23**) asks if you use a proxy server for Internet connections. Select the appropriate radio button, and click the right arrow.

15. If you selected Yes in step 14, the Proxies window appears (**Figure 24**). Turn on the check boxes for the types of proxies you use, then enter proxy information in the corresponding edit boxes. When you're finished, click the right arrow.

16. The Conclusion window finally appears (**Figure 25**). To connect to the ISP when the settings have been entered, make sure the Connect when finished check box is turned on. Then click Go Ahead.

17. The Internet Setup Assistant window indicates the progress of your configuration. Once completed, if you turned on the Connect when finished check box in step 15, the software attempts to connect to the ISP. Otherwise, it quits.

**Figure 20** In the E-mail Address and Password window, enter your e-mail address and password.

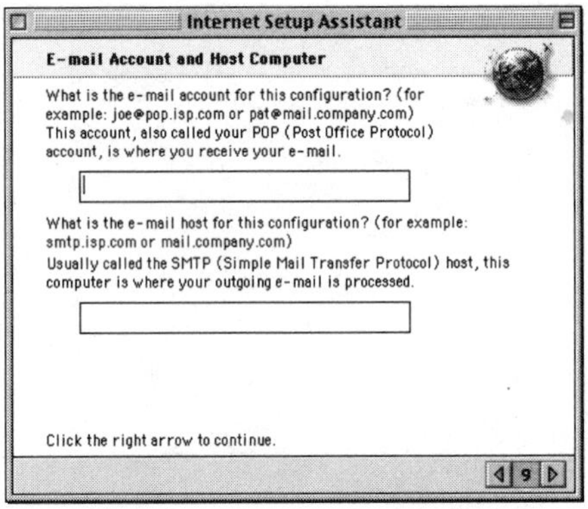

**Figure 21** In the E-mail Account and Host Computer window, enter the POP account and SMTP host provided by your ISP.

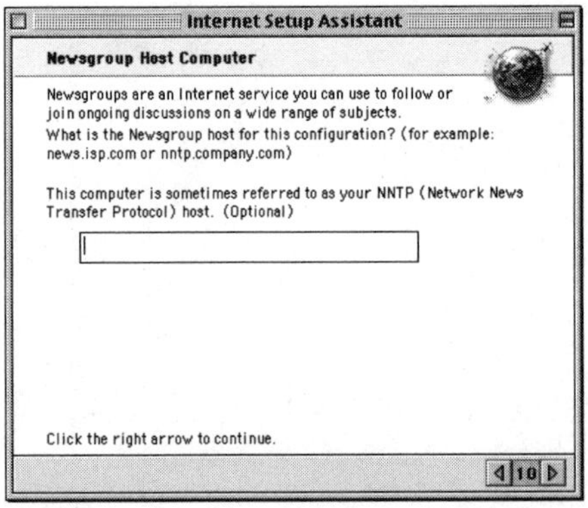

**Figure 22** Enter the NNTP host provided by your ISP in the Newsgroup Host Computer window.

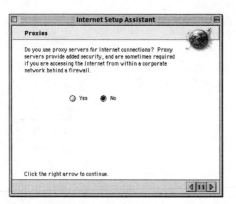

**Figure 23** This Proxies window asks whether you connect to the Internet through a proxy server.

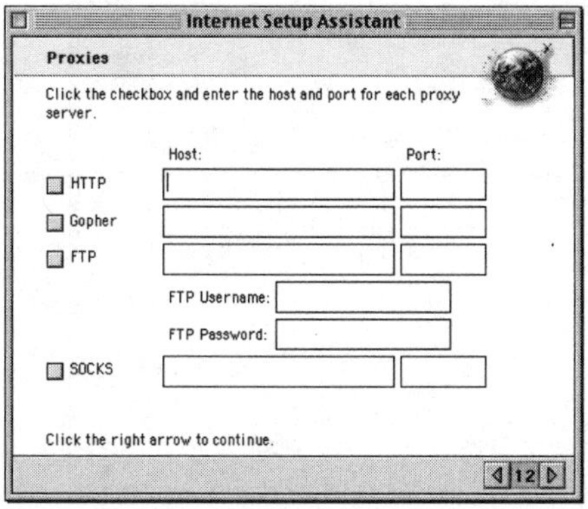

**Figure 24** You can enter your proxy server information in this Proxies window.

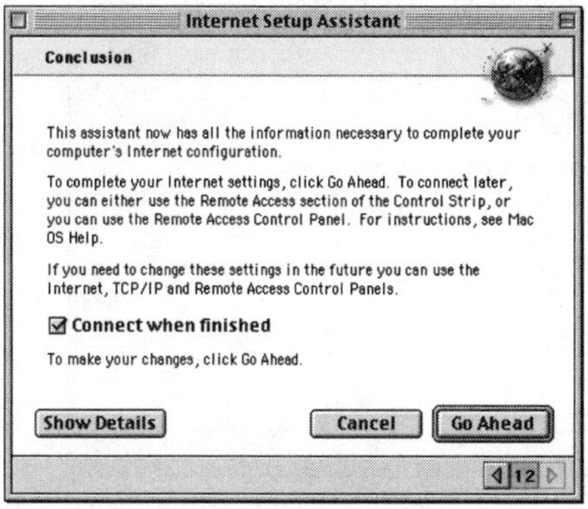

**Figure 25** The Conclusion window lets you know you're done entering information.

## ✔ Tips

- If your modem's make and model are not listed in the Modem pop-up menu in step 4, try a similar model from the same manufacturer or one of the Hayes models. I tell you more about modems in **Chapter 11**.

- If your ISP provided a PPP Connect Script, copy it to the PPP Connect Scripts folder inside the Extensions folder in your System Folder before using the Internet Setup Assistant to set up for Internet access. Doing so will automatically display the script in the Scripts pop-up menu in step 4.

- You can get most of the configuration information you need from your ISP or system administrator.

- It is not necessary to enter your password in steps 5 and 11. If you omit it, you'll have to enter it when connecting to your ISP or checking your e-mail.

- If you click the Show Details button in step 17, you'll see a summary of all the information you entered.

**ADDING A DIALUP CONFIGURATION**

## To add a LAN configuration

1. In the second window of the Internet Setup Assistant (**Figure 3**), click Yes.

2. Read the information in the Introduction window (**Figure 12**). Then click the right arrow at the bottom of the window.

3. The Configuration name and connection type window appears (**Figure 13**). Enter a name for the connection in the edit box. Then select the Network radio button, and click the right arrow button.

4. The Apple Remote Access window appears next (**Figure 26**). It asks if you want to connect to the Internet by dialing in to your local area network.

   ▲ If you do, select the Yes radio button. Then, if necessary, connect to the network, and switch back to the Internet Setup Assistant. Click the right arrow, and skip ahead to step 9.

   ▲ If you don't, select the No radio button, and click the right arrow.

5. The IP Address window appears next (**Figure 17**). If you have been assigned your own IP address, select the Yes radio button. If not, select the No radio button. Click the right arrow.

6. If you selected Yes in step 5, another IP Address window appears (**Figure 18**). Enter the IP address in the edit box, and click the right arrow.

7. If you selected Yes in step 5, the Subnet Mask and Router Address window appears (**Figure 27**). Enter the subnet mask in the top edit box and router address in the bottom edit box. Then click the right arrow, and skip to step 10.

8. If you selected No in step 5, the Dynamic Configuration window appears (**Figure 28**). Select the radio button for the appropriate protocol: MacIP or Other. Then click the right arrow.

**Figure 26** Use the Apple Remote Access window to indicate whether you want to connect to the Internet through a remote connection to your network.

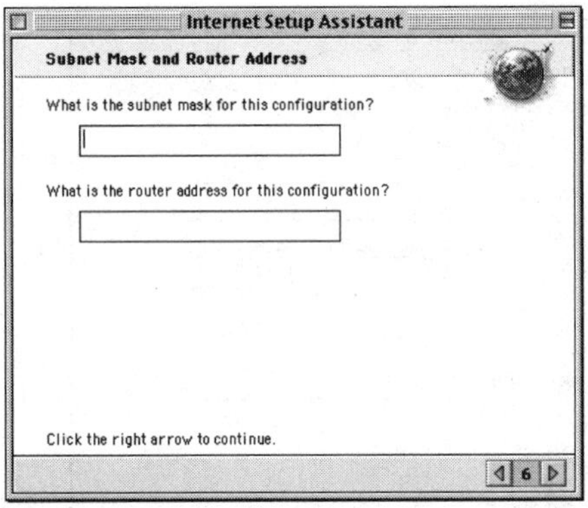

**Figure 27** Use the Subnet Mask and Router Address window to enter additional information if you have your own IP address on the LAN.

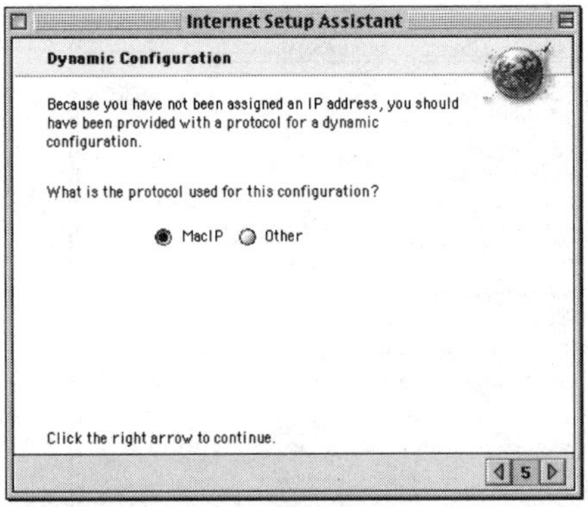

**Figure 28** Use the Dynamic Configuration window to specify the protocol for the dynamic configuration.

**Figure 29** When you're finished, the Conclusion window tells you.

## ✔ Tips

- You can get most of the configuration information you need from your LAN administrator.

- It is not necessary to enter your password in step 11. If you omit it, you can enter it when checking your e-mail.

- If you click the Show Details button in step 16, you'll see a summary of all the information you entered.

**9.** If you selected Yes in step 4 or MacIP in step 8, the MacIP Zone window appears next. Use it to select a MacIP zone, and click the right arrow.

**10.** The Domain Name Servers window appears next (**Figure 19**). Enter the DNS address or addresses in the top edit box. If there is more than one, make sure you press (Return) between each one. Then enter the domain name in the bottom edit box. Click the right arrow.

**11.** In the E-mail Address and Password window (**Figure 20**), enter your e-mail address in the top edit box and your e-mail password in the bottom edit box. Then click the right arrow.

**12.** In the E-mail Account and Host Computer window (**Figure 21**), enter the POP account in the top edit box and the SMTP host in the bottom edit box. Click the right arrow.

**13.** In the Newsgroup Host Computer window (**Figure 22**), enter the NNTP host. Then click the right arrow.

**14.** The Proxies window, which appears next (**Figure 23**), asks if you use a proxy server for Internet connections. Select the appropriate radio button, and click the right arrow.

**15.** If you selected Yes in step 14, the Proxies window appears (**Figure 24**). Turn on the check boxes for the types of proxies you use, then enter proxy information in the corresponding edit boxes. When you're finished, click the right arrow.

**16.** The Conclusion window finally appears (**Figure 29**). Click Go Ahead.

**17.** The Internet Setup Assistant window indicates the progress of your configuration. When it's finished, it quits.

# TCP/IP, PPP, & Remote Access

Your computer accesses the Internet through via a TCP/IP network connection. *TCP/IP* is a standard Internet protocol, or set of rules, for exchanging information.

A TCP/IP connection works like a pipeline. Once established, Internet applications—like your Web browser and e-mail program—reach through the TCP/IP pipeline to get the information they need. When the information has been sent or received, it stops flowing through the pipeline. But the pipeline is not disconnected.

If you have a direct or network connection to the Internet, the Internet is accessible all the time. But if you have to connect via modem, you need to use *Remote Access*. This software, which comes with Mac OS, uses PPP to connect to TCP/IP networks via modem. *PPP* is a standard protocol for connecting to networks.

When you connect via modem using Remote Access, you set up a temporary TCP/IP pipeline. Internet applications are smart enough to automatically use Remote Access to connect to the Internet when necessary. When you're finished accessing Internet services you should tell Remote Access to disconnect.

## ✔ Tip

- Remote Access is also used to connect to an Apple Remote Access server. I tell you more about that in **Chapter 11**.

# Setting Internet Configuration Options

Mac OS 8.6 includes three control panels you can use to manually set up an Internet configuration:

◆ **TCP/IP** enables you to set server IP address and domain name information.

◆ **Remote Access** enables you to set dial-up connection options.

◆ **Internet** enables you to set a wide variety of configuration options, including personal, e-mail, Web, and news information.

Many of these options are configured when you use the Internet Setup Assistant, so you shouldn't have to use these control panels to configure your Internet connection. In this section, however, I show you the configuration options in all three control panels in case you ever need or want to modify settings.

## ✔ Tips

■ The Remote Access control panel replaces the PPP control panel found in versions of Mac OS prior to 8.5.

■ If your Internet configuration is working fine, don't change it! Internet connections follow one of the golden rules of computing: *If it ain't broke, don't fix it.*

**SETTING INTERNET CONFIGURATION OPTIONS**

## To set options in the TCP/IP control panel

1. Choose Apple menu > Control Panels > TCP/IP (**Figure 30**). The TCP/IP control panel appears (**Figure 31**). The name of the active configuration appears in the title bar.

2. To select a different configuration, choose File > Configurations. In the Configurations window that appears (**Figure 32**), select the configuration that you want to use and click Make Active.

3. If desired, make changes in the TCP/IP control panel window (**Figure 31**).

4. Close the TCP/IP control panel window.

5. If you made changes to the configuration, a dialog box like the one in **Figure 33** appears. Click Save.

### ✔ Tips

- Do not change settings in the TCP/IP control panel unless you have to. Changes that are incorrect could prevent your Internet connection from functioning properly.

- If you're not sure what to select or enter in the TCP/IP control panel, use the Internet Setup Assistant to create a new Internet connection with the desired settings. Although it may take longer to work with its interface, it's easier to use and understand.

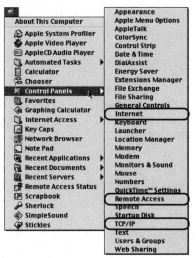

**Figure 30** TCP/IP, Remote Access, and Internet can be found under the Control Panels submenu under the Apple menu.

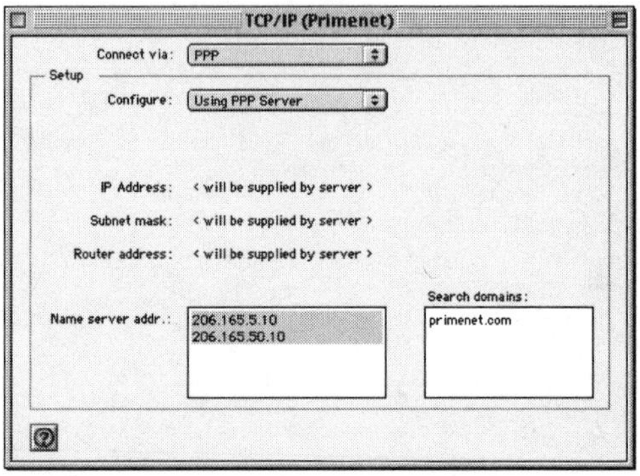

**Figure 31** The TCP/IP control panel.

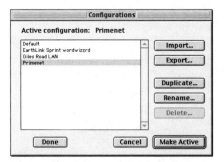

**Figure 32** Select the configuration that you want, and click Make Active. This dialog box looks the same for TCP/IP and Remote Access.

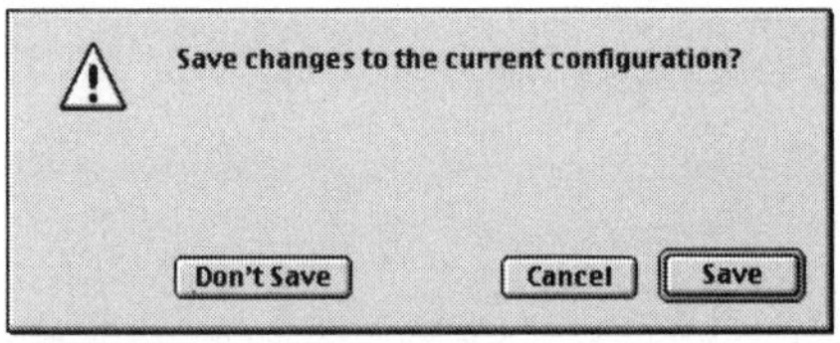

**Figure 33** Click Save to save your changes.

**SETTING TCP/IP OPTIONS**

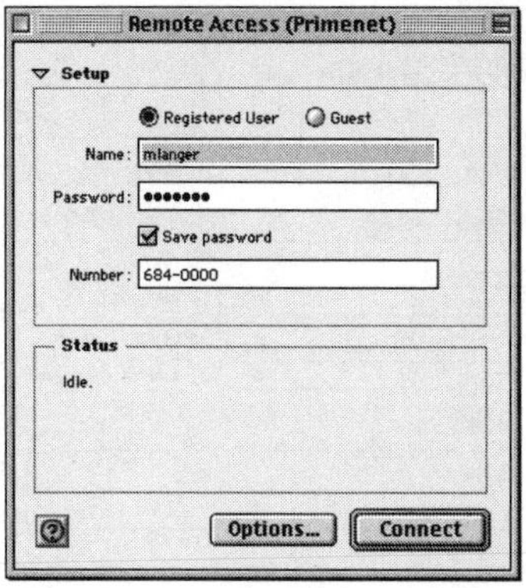

**Figure 34**
The Remote Access control panel.

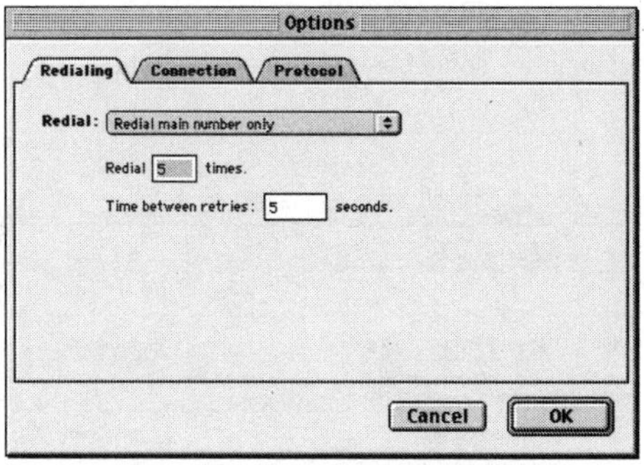

**Figure 35** Use the Options dialog box to change redialing, connection, and protocol options.

## ✔ Tips

■ If you have a direct or LAN connection to the Internet, you do not need to set up or modify Remote Access configurations.

■ You can also use the Remote Access control panel to establish a connection to the Internet. I tell you more about connecting to the Internet later in this chapter.

## To set options in the Remote Access control panel

1. Choose Apple menu > Control Panels > Remote Access (**Figure 30**). The Remote Access control panel appears (**Figure 34**). It includes the name of the active configuration file in the title bar.

2. To select a different configuration, choose Configurations from the File menu. In the Configurations window that appears (**Figure 32**), select the configuration that you want to use and click Make Active.

3. If desired, make changes in the Remote Access control panel window (**Figure 34**).

4. If desired, click Options to display the Options dialog box (**Figure 35**). Click tabs to display and change redialing, connection, and protocol options. When you are finished, click OK.

5. Close the Remote Access control panel window.

6. If you made changes to the configuration, a dialog box like the one in **Figure 33** appears. Click Save.

■ Do not change settings in the Remote Access control panel unless you have to. Changes that are incorrect could prevent you from successfully connecting to your ISP.

■ If you're not sure what to select or enter in the Remote Access control panel, use the Internet Setup Assistant to create a new configuration for your dial-up connection. Although it may take longer to work with its interface, it's easier to use and understand.

**SETTING REMOTE ACCESS OPTIONS**

227

## To set options in the Internet control panel

1. Choose Apple menu > Control Panels > Internet (**Figure 30**). The Internet control panel appears (**Figure 36**).

2. To make a different set of options active, choose its name from the Active Set pop-up menu.

3. To edit a set of options, choose its name from the Edit Set pop-up menu.

4. If desired, make changes in the various tabs of the Internet control panel window to modify the set of options displayed in the Edit Set pop-up menu:

   ▲ **Personal** (**Figure 36**) includes your name, e-mail address, and organization (or, in my case, title). You can also enter additional information and an e-mail signature that can appear at the bottom of every e-mail message you send.

   ▲ **E-mail** (**Figure 37**) includes your e-mail configuration information as well as notification options for incoming e-mail and your default e-mail application.

   ▲ **Web** (**Figure 38**) includes the URLs for your default home and search pages as well as the folder for downloaded files, colors to use for Web page links and backgrounds, and your default Web browser application.

   ▲ **News** (**Figure 39**) includes your Internet news configuration information and your default newsreader application.

5. Close the Remote Access control panel window.

6. If you made changes to a set, a confirmation dialog box appears. Click Save to save the changes.

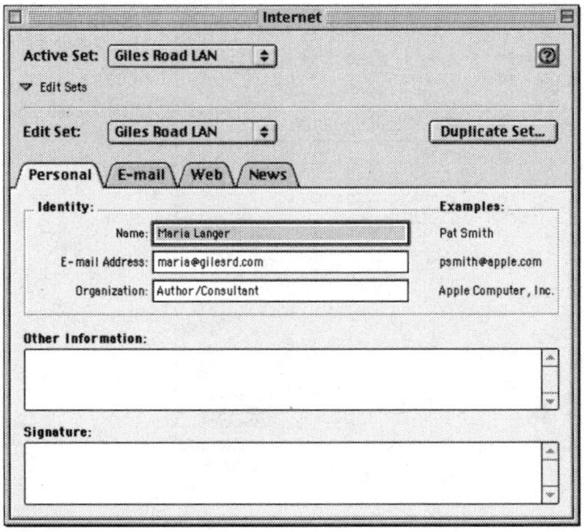

**Figure 36** The Personal tab of the Internet control panel includes some basic information about you.

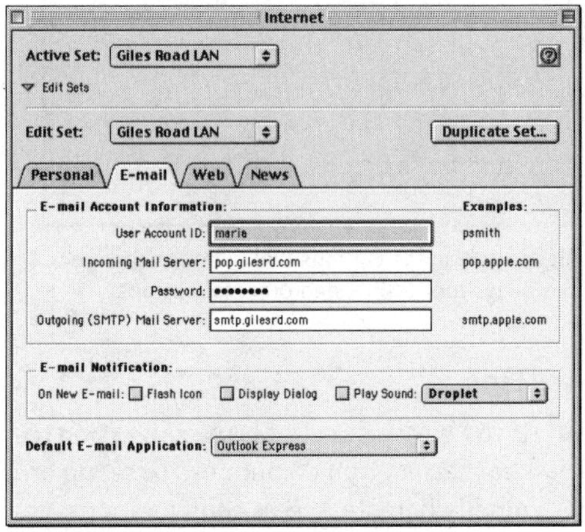

**Figure 37** The E-mail tab of the Internet control panel includes a variety of e-mail configuration information.

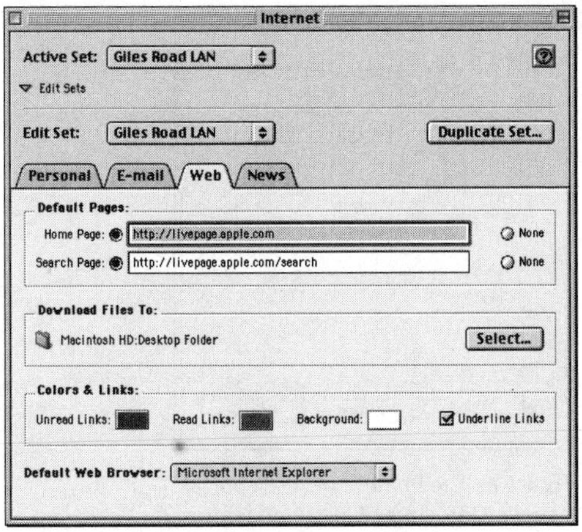

**Figure 38** The Web tab of the Internet control panel includes Web-related configuration options.

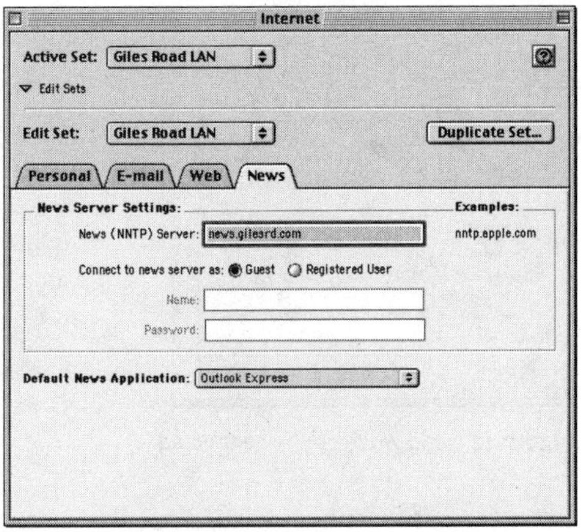

**Figure 39** The News tab of the Internet control panel has configuration options for accessing Internet news.

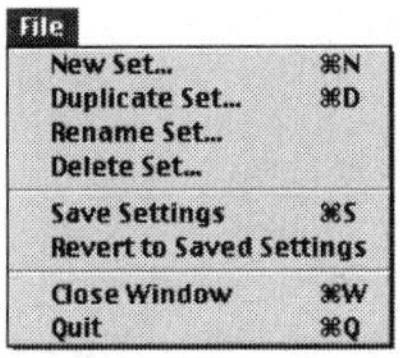

**Figure 40**
Use the Internet control panel's File menu to work with sets of options.

## ✔ Tips

- The Internet control panel replaces the Internet Config application found in versions of Mac OS prior to 8.5.

- In step 4, you can change a link or background color in the Web tab by clicking a colored box, then using the color picker dialog box that appears to select a new color. I tell you about the color picker in **Chapter 3**.

- Microsoft Outlook and Microsoft Internet Explorer are the e-mail program and Web browser that are bundled with Mac OS 8.6. You can use the pop-up menus in the E-mail, Web, and News tabs to locate and choose other applications you may have installed on your computer for Internet access.

- You can also use options under the Internet control panel's File menu (**Figure 40**) to create, duplicate, and rename a set of options.

# Connecting to an ISP

There are two ways to establish a PPP connection to your ISP:

◆ Use the Remote Access control panel or Remote Access Status Monitor application to dial in whenever you want.

◆ Launch an application that requires an Internet connection (like Microsoft Internet Explorer); a PPP connection is automatically established.

## ✔ Tip

■ If you have a direct or LAN connection to the Internet, you don't have to worry about establishing a connection—it's always there.

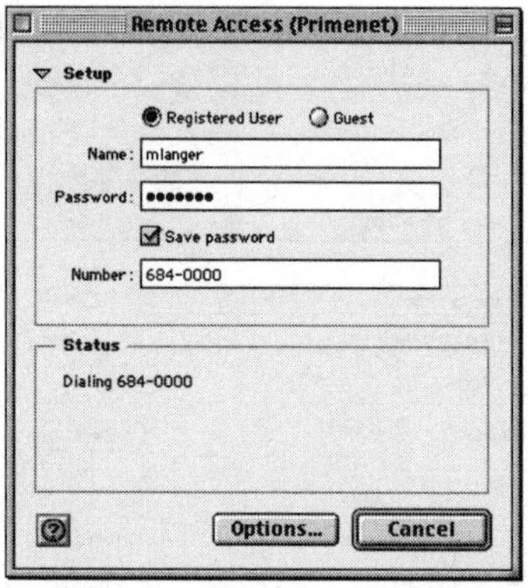

## To connect to an ISP with the Remote Access control panel

1. Choose Apple menu > Control Panels > Remote Access (**Figure 30**) to display the Remote Access control panel (**Figure 34**).

2. If necessary, switch to the configuration with which you want to connect.

3. Click the Connect button. Remote Access initializes your modem and dials. It displays the connection status in its status area (**Figure 41**).

   When Remote Access has successfully connected, the Connect button turns into a Disconnect button and the Status area fills with connection information. You can see all this in **Figure 42**.

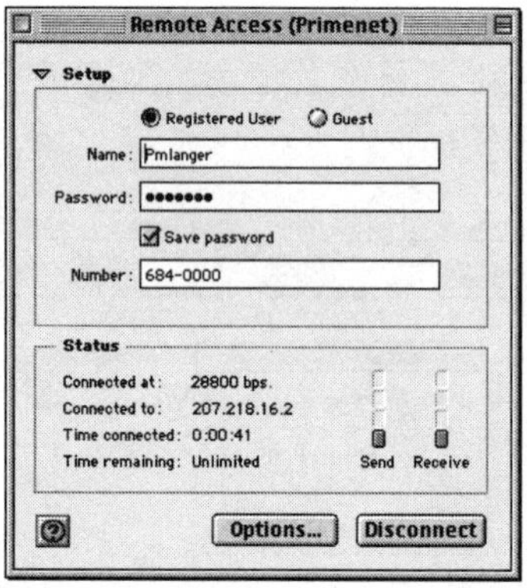

## ✔ Tip

■ The Remote Access control panel does not have to be open while you are connected to the Internet.

**Figure 41** The Remote Access control panel's Status area keeps you informed about a connection as you connect...

**Figure 42** ...and while you're connected.

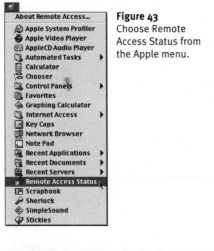

**Figure 43**
Choose Remote Access Status from the Apple menu.

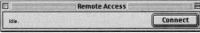

**Figure 44** The tiny Remote Access Status Monitor window.

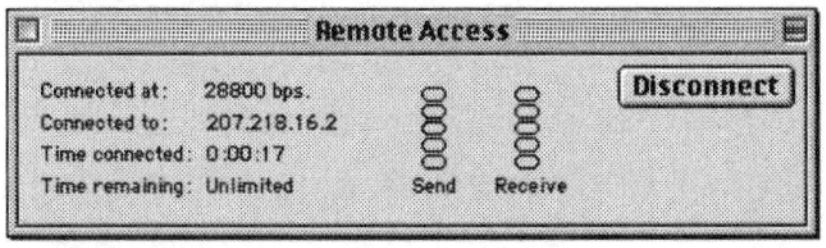

**Figure 45** The Remote Access Status window expands to show connection status.

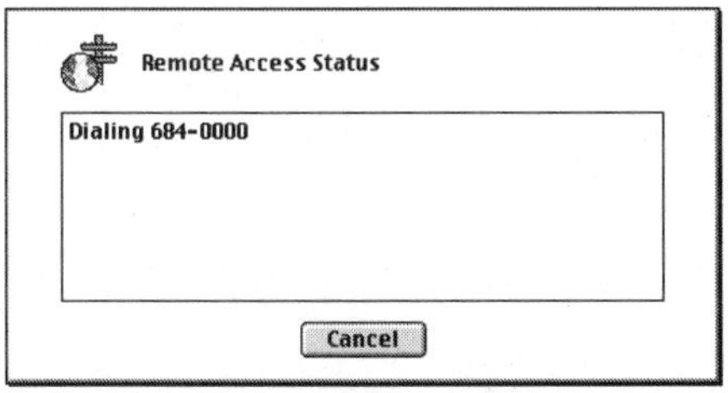

**Figure 46** The Remote Access Status dialog box appears when you launch a program that requires an Internet connection but you are not connected to the Internet.

**Figure 47** An icon like this blinks over the Apple menu while you are connected to the Internet — no matter how you connected.

## To connect to an ISP with the Remote Access Status Monitor

1. Choose Apple menu > Control Panels > Remote Access Status (**Figure 43**) to display the Remote Access Status window (**Figure 44**).

2. Click the Connect button. Remote Access Status initializes your modem and dials. It displays the connection status.

   When Remote Access Status has successfully connected, the Connect button turns into a Disconnect button and the status area fills with connection information. You can see all this in **Figure 45**.

## ✔ Tip

- The Remote Access Status Monitor application does not have to be open while you are connected to the Internet.

## To automatically connect to an ISP

Launch any program that requires an Internet connection. After the program's splash screen appears, a dialog box like the one in **Figure 46** appears to show connection status. When the PPP connection is established, the dialog box disappears.

## To disconnect from an ISP

1. Open or switch to Remote Access or Remote Access Status (**Figure 42** or **45**).

2. Click the Disconnect button. The connection is terminated.

## ✔ Tip

- You can always tell if you're connected to the Internet by looking at the Apple menu icon. If it blinks with an icon like the one in **Figure 47**, you are connected to the Internet.

CONNECTING TO AN ISP

231

# Internet Applications

Mac OS 8.6 includes two full-featured applications for accessing the Internet:

◆ **Outlook Express** is a Microsoft program that enables you to send and receive e-mail and participate in Internet newsgroups.

◆ **Internet Explorer** is a Microsoft program that enables you to browse Web sites and download files from FTP sites.

In this section, I provide brief instructions for using these two programs. You can explore the other features of these programs on your own.

## ✔ Tips

■ Outlook Express and Internet Explorer are set as the default e-mail, newsgroup, and Web browser programs. If you prefer to use other applications, be sure to change the appropriate settings in the Internet control panel, which I discuss earlier in this chapter.

■ Mac OS 8.6 also comes with Netscape Communicator, another Web browser. Communicator works very much like Internet Explorer does; consult the instructions for using Internet Explorer to learn the same basics that apply to Communicator.

**Figure 48**
You can open your e-mail and Web browser applications by double-clicking icons on the Desktop.

**Figure 49**
You can access Internet features with commands on the Internet Access submenu.

**Figure 50** You can also launch Microsoft Outlook Express or Microsoft Internet Explorer by double-clicking icons in the Internet window.

# Launching Internet Applications

There are three main ways to launch an Internet application in Mac OS 8.6:

◆ Double-click a Desktop icon (**Figure 48**).

◆ Choose a command from the Internet Access submenu (**Figure 49**).

◆ Double-click an icon in the Internet folder (**Figure 50**).

## To open Outlook Express

Use one of the following techniques:

◆ Double-click the Mail icon on your Desktop (**Figure 48**).

◆ Choose Apple menu > Internet Access > Mail (**Figure 49**).

◆ Double-click the Microsoft Outlook Express icon in the Internet folder on your hard disk (**Figure 50**).

## ✔ Tip

■ Mail launches the default e-mail application set in the Internet control panel (**Figure 37**).

## To open Internet Explorer

Use one of the following techniques:

◆ Double-click the Browse the Internet icon on your Desktop (**Figure 48**).

◆ Choose Apple menu > Internet Access > Browse the Internet (**Figure 49**).

◆ Double-click the Microsoft Internet Explorer icon in the Internet folder on your hard disk (**Figure 50**).

## ✔ Tip

■ Browse the Internet launches the default Web browser application set in the Internet control panel (**Figure 38**).

LAUNCHING INTERNET APPLICATIONS

# Outlook Express

Outlook Express (**Figure 51**) is an e-mail application from Microsoft Corporation. It enables you to send and receive e-mail messages using your Internet account.

In this section, I tell you enough about Outlook Express to get you started sending and receiving e-mail.

## ✔ Tips

- I explain how to launch Outlook Express on the previous page.

- The first time you launch Outlook Express, a Welcome dialog box like the one in **Figure 52** appears. Click OK to dismiss it.

- The first time you launch Outlook Express, the Preferences dialog box appears (**Figure 53**). All the options for your e-mail setup should already be entered by the Internet Setup Assistant, but you can change them if you need to. Click OK to accept the settings.

- You can reopen the Preferences dialog box (**Figure 53**) by choosing Edit > Preferences.

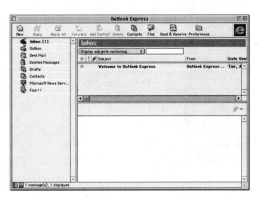

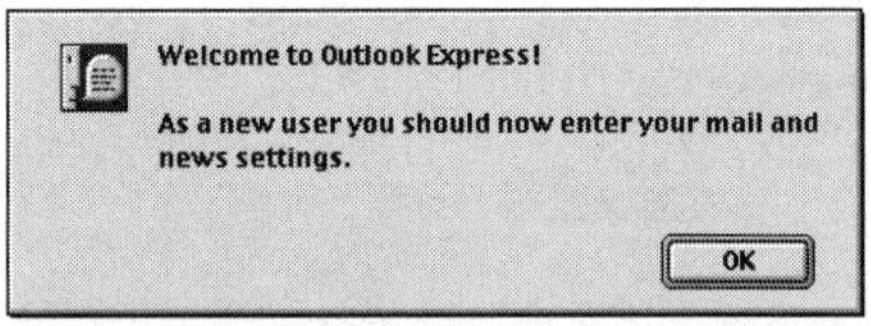

**Figure 51** The Outlook Express main window with the Inbox displayed.

**Welcome to Outlook Express!**

**As a new user you should now enter your mail and news settings.**

OK

**Figure 52** Outlook Express displays this dialog box the first time you launch it.

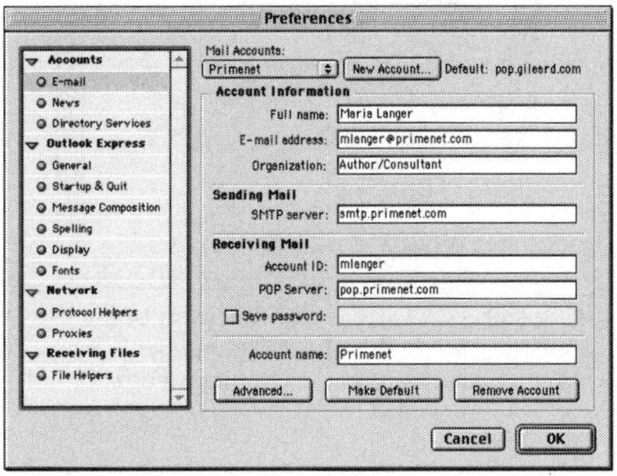

**Preferences**

Mail Accounts: Primenet | New Account... | Default: pop.gileard.com

**Account Information**
Full name: Marie Langer
E-mail address: mlanger@primenet.com
Organization: Author/Consultant

**Sending Mail**
SMTP server: smtp.primenet.com

**Receiving Mail**
Account ID: mlanger
POP Server: pop.primenet.com
☐ Save password:

Account name: Primenet

Advanced... | Make Default | Remove Account

Cancel | OK

**Figure 53** The Outlook Express Preferences dialog box offers many options.

OUTLOOK EXPRESS

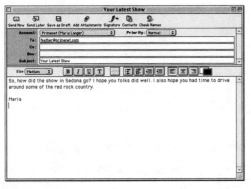

**Figure 54** Clicking the New button opens an untitled message window like this one.

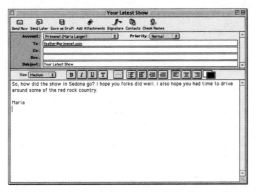

**Figure 55** Here's a short message ready to be sent.

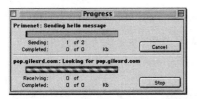

**Figure 56** Outlook Express displays a Progress dialog box like this one when it sends or retrieves messages.

## To create & send a message

1. Click the New button at the top of the Outlook Express main window (**Figure 51**). An untitled message window appears (**Figure 54**).

2. Enter the e-mail address of the message recipient in the To edit box.

3. Enter a subject for the message in the Subject edit box.

4. Type your message into the large edit box at the bottom of the window. When you are finished, the window might look like the one in **Figure 55**.

5. Click the Send button near the top of the window. Outlook Express sends the message. It displays a Progress dialog box as it works (**Figure 56**). When it disappears, the message has been sent.

## ✔ Tips

- You can use Outlook Express's contacts feature to maintain a directory of the people you write to.

- You can click buttons in the area above the message text area to format selected text. Keep in mind, however, that your formatting may not be visible to the recipient.

- In step 5, if you are not connected to the Internet, Outlook Express initiates a connection before sending the message.

- If you prefer to compose e-mail messages while *offline* (not connected to the Internet), click the Send Later button in step 5. Your messages will be stored in the Outbox until you send them. When you're ready to send all messages (and receive new ones), click the Send & Receive button in the main window (**Figure 51**) to connect to the Internet and exchange mail.

## To retrieve e-mail messages

1. Click the Send & Receive button at the top of the main window (**Figure 51**).

2. Outlook Express connects to your e-mail server and downloads messages waiting for you. It displays a Progress dialog box as it works (**Figure 56**). When the dialog box disappears, any incoming messages appear in bold in the Inbox area of the main window (**Figure 57**).

## ✔ Tips

- The Send & Receive button tells Outlook Express to retrieve all e-mail items waiting on the mail server and send any e-mail items in the Outbox.

- You can view the contents of the Inbox or Outbox by clicking the appropriate icon in the left side of the main Outlook Express window (**Figure 51**).

## To read an incoming message

1. In the Inbox window, click the message that you want to read. It appears in the bottom half of the main Outlook Express window (**Figure 58**).

2. Read the message.

## ✔ Tips

- You can also double-click a message in the Inbox to display it in its own message window (**Figure 59**).

- To reply to the message, click Reply. A preaddressed message window with the entire message quoted appears (**Figure 60**). Type your reply and click Send.

- To forward the message to another e-mail address, click Forward. A message window containing a copy of the message appears. Enter the e-mail address for the recipient in the To edit box, and click Send.

**Figure 57** New incoming messages appear in bold in the Inbox.

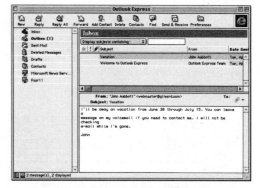

**Figure 58** Click a message to display its contents in the bottom half of the Outlook Express window.

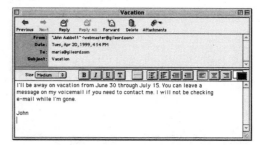

**Figure 59** Double-click a message to open it in its own window.

**Figure 60** When you click the Reply button, a preaddressed message window appears.

RETRIEVING & READING E-MAIL MESSAGES

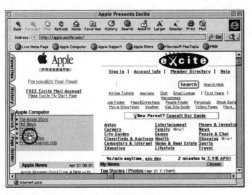

**Figure 61** When you launch Internet Explorer, it connects to the Internet and displays the default home page—in this case, Apple's "Live Page."

**Figure 62** Clicking the link in **Figure 61** displays this page.

# Internet Explorer

Internet Explorer is a popular Web browser application from Microsoft. It enables you to view, or *browse*, pages on the World Wide Web.

A Web *page* is a window full of formatted text and graphics (**Figures 61**). You move from page to page by clicking text or graphic links or by opening *URLs* (*uniform resource locators*) for specific Web pages. These two methods of navigating the World Wide Web can open a whole world of useful or interesting information.

## ✔ Tips

- I explain how to launch Internet Explorer earlier in this chapter. If you are not connected to the Internet when you launch Internet Explorer, it automatically connects for you.

- The version of Internet Explorer included with Mac OS has been customized to start with a specific home page and offer buttons with links to Apple and Microsoft pages.

- You can easily identify a link by pointing to it; the mouse pointer turns into a pointing finger (**Figure 61**).

## To follow a link

1. Position the mouse pointer on a text or graphic link. The mouse pointer turns into a pointing finger (**Figure 61**).

2. Click. After a moment, the page or other location for the link you clicked will appear (**Figure 62**).

INTERNET EXPLORER, FOLLOWING A LINK

## To view a specific URL

1. Choose File > Open Location (**Figure 63**), or press ⌃ ⌘ L.

2. Enter the URL in the Open Internet Address dialog box (**Figure 64**), and click Open.

*or*

1. Choose Apple menu > Internet Access > Connect To (**Figure 49**).

2. Enter the URL in the dialog box that appears (**Figure 65**), and click Connect.

*or*

Enter the URL in the edit box near the top of the Internet Explorer window (**Figure 66**), and press Return or Enter.

## To return to the home page

Click the Home button at the top of the Internet Explorer window (**Figure 61**).

## ✔ Tip

- You can change the default home page by specifying a different page's URL in the Web tab of the Internet control panel. The page you specify will load each time you launch Internet Explorer. I tell you about the Internet control panel earlier in this chapter.

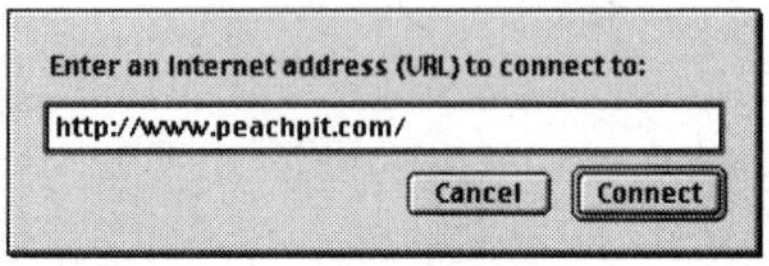

**Figure 63**
Choose Open Location from the File menu.

**Figure 64** Then enter the URL in the Open Internet Address dialog box, and click Open.

**Figure 65** Or enter the URL in the dialog box that appears when you choose Connect To from the Internet Access submenu under the Apple menu.

**Figure 66** Or enter the URL in the edit box at the top of the Internet Explorer window, and press Enter.

NAVIGATING THE WEB

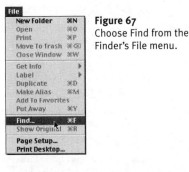

**Figure 67**
Choose Find from the Finder's File menu.

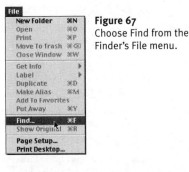

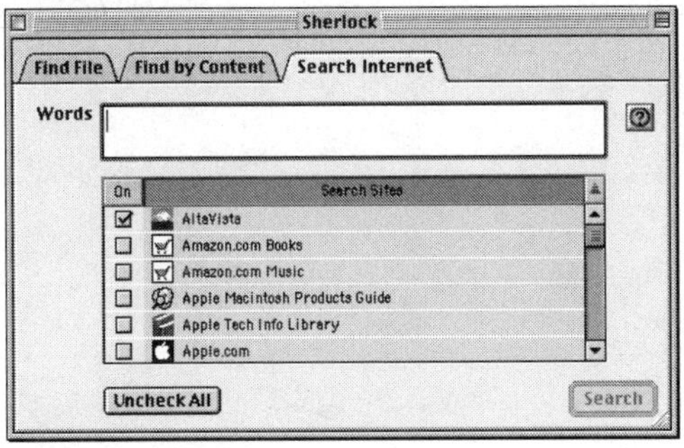

**Figure 68** The Search Internet tab of the Sherlock window.

**Figure 69** Enter one or more search words in the Words box at the top of the Sherlock window.

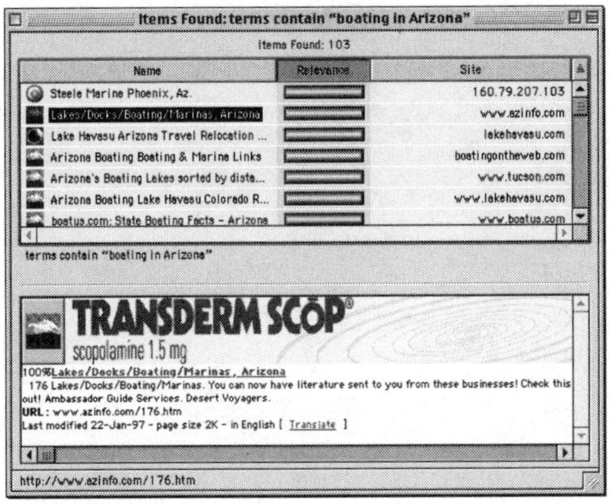

**Figure 70** Click an item in the list of found items to view a short description with a link to the actual page.

# Searching the Internet

Sherlock, Mac OS 8.6's searching program, can also search the Internet for information. You enter search words in the Sherlock window, specify which search sites to utilize for the search, and begin the search. Sherlock displays the matches it finds. You can then click a match to view the corresponding page.

## To search the Internet with Sherlock

1. In the Finder, choose File > Find (**Figure 67**), press ⌘ F, or choose Apple menu > Sherlock.

2. In the Sherlock window that appears, click the Search Internet tab to display its options (**Figure 68**).

3. Enter a search word or words in the Words box at the top of the window (**Figure 69**).

4. Toggle the check marks in the Search part of the window to specify the search sites you want to utilize for the search.

5. Click Search.

6. Sherlock searches the specified search sites for information matching the search criteria you entered. After a moment, it displays the Items Found window. A list of found items appears in the top half of the window; click an item to display a summary with a link in the bottom half (**Figure 70**).

7. To visit the Web page in the summary, click the blue underlined link. Internet Explorer launches and displays the page.

## ✔ Tip

■ When entering words in step 3, enter at least two or three words you expect to find in documents about the topic you are searching for. This helps narrow down the search, resulting in more useful matches.

# Personal Web Sharing

Personal Web Sharing is a feature of Mac OS that enables you to create your own Web server. With it, you can use Web pages to share information with others on your network.

Here's how it works. First create one or more Web pages with the information that you want to share. Place them in a folder on your hard disk. Then use the Web Sharing control panel (**Figure 71**) to specify the Web folder and home page, set privileges, and enable Web sharing. When another network user uses his Web browser to open your IP address, the home page you specified appears.

**Figure 71** Use the Web Sharing control panel to configure and enable Personal Web Sharing.

## ✔ Tips

- To use Personal Web Sharing, you must be connected to a TCP/IP network and have an IP address. I tell you about TCP/IP earlier in this chapter.

- Personal Web Sharing is automatically installed as part of a basic Mac OS 8.6 installation. I tell you about installing Mac OS in **Chapter 1**.

- Instructions for creating Web pages are far beyond the scope of this book. If you're looking for a program that makes creating Web pages easy and a book to make using the program easy, try Adobe PageMill 3.0 and *PageMill 3 for Macintosh & Windows: Visual QuickStart Guide.*

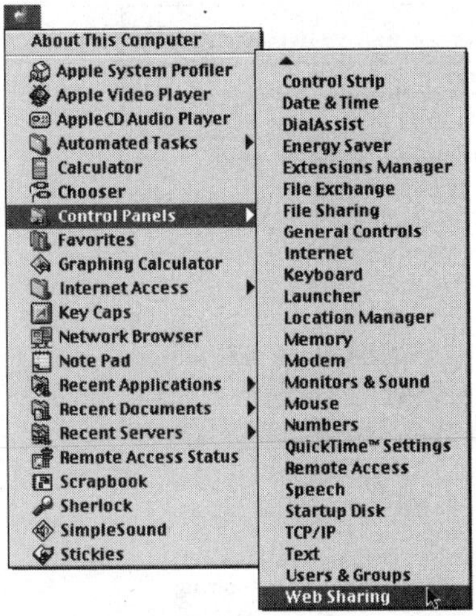

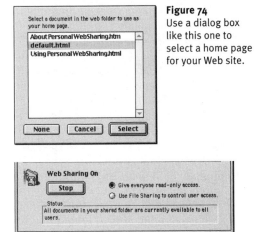

**Figure 72** Choose Web Sharing from the control panels submenu under the Apple menu.

**Figure 73** Use a standard Open dialog box to locate and select the Web folder.

**Figure 74**
Use a dialog box like this one to select a home page for your Web site.

**Figure 75** The words *Web Sharing On* appear in the bottom part of the Web Sharing control panel.

## To configure & enable Personal Web Sharing

1. Choose Apple menu > Control Panels > Web Sharing (**Figure 72**). The Web Sharing control panel appears (**Figure 71**).

2. To specify the location of the folder containing your Web pages, click the Select button beside Web Folder. Then use an Open dialog box (**Figure 73**) to locate and select the folder.

3. To specify the home page for your Web site, click the Select button beside Home Page. Then use the dialog box that appears (**Figure 74**) to select the document for your home page.

4. Select a radio button to either give everyone who accesses your Web site read-only access or use file sharing privileges to control access.

5. Click Start. After a moment, the words *Web Sharing On* appear in the bottom half of the Web Sharing control panel (**Figure 75**).

## ✔ Tips

■ Mac OS includes a folder on your hard disk called Web Pages. Inside it, you'll find sample Web pages to get you started.

■ I tell you how to use an Open dialog box in **Chapter 5** and how to set File Sharing privileges in **Chapter 11**.

CONFIGURING & ENABLING WEB SHARING

## To connect to a personal Web site

1. Choose Apple menu > Internet Access > Connect To (**Figure 49**).

2. In the dialog box that appears, enter the URL for the site to which you want to connect (**Figure 76**) and click Connect. After a moment, the page appears in your Web browser (**Figure 77**).

## ✔ Tip

- The URL for a personal Web site consists of the characters *http://* followed by the IP address for the computer (**Figure 76**).

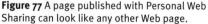

**Figure 76** Enter the URL for the site to which you want to connect.

**Figure 77** A page published with Personal Web Sharing can look like any other Web page.

# CUSTOMIZING MAC OS 8.6

## Customizing Mac OS 8.6

One of the great things about Mac OS is the way it can be customized to look and work the way you want.

Throughout this book, I show you ways to change settings so things work the way you need them to. In this chapter, I provide a closer look at the system software that extends or customizes the system—extensions, control panels, and fonts—and show you some other ways to customize Mac OS 8.6.

## ✔ Tips

- Some customization options explored elsewhere in this book that are not repeated here include:

  - ▲ Window views, in **Chapter 3**.

  - ▲ Finder preferences and the Info window, in **Chapter 4**.

  - ▲ The Info window in **Chapter 5**.

  - ▲ The Apple Menu Items control panel, Note Pad, Scrapbook, and SimpleSound, in **Chapter 7**.

  - ▲ File Exchange in **Chapter 9**.

  - ▲ Chooser and desktop printers, in **Chapter 10**.

  - ▲ AppleTalk, File Sharing, Users & Groups, Modem, and Remote Access control panels, in **Chapter 11**.

  - ▲ TCP/IP, Remote Access, and Internet control panels, in **Chapter 12**.

  - ▲ Balloon Help, in **Chapter 14**.

  - ▲ PowerBook-specific control panels, in **Appendix B**.

- You can usually customize the operation of a specific application by using its Preferences or Options dialog box. Check the application's Edit menu for a Preferences or Options command or consult its documentation for details. I tell you more about applications in **Chapter 5**.

## The System Folder

The software that makes up Mac OS 8.6 resides in the System Folder on your hard disk (**Figure 1**). The system software consists primarily of the System file, Finder file, and the following types of items:

◆ **Extensions** are files that add features or extend the functionality of the system. Their features are preset and cannot be modified—just install them and they work. You can find them in the Extensions folder.

◆ **Drivers** are files that enable your computer to use hardware devices such as printers and CD-ROM drives. Like extensions, their features are preset and cannot be modified—install them and the devices they control become available for use. You can find them in the Extensions folder.

◆ **Control panels** are files that either add features to the system or enable you to set system options. They offer an interface you can use to modify their settings. You can find them in the Control Panels folder.

◆ **Fonts** are typefaces that are used to display text on screen and in printed documents. When you install them properly, they're available for use in every application that can access fonts. You can find them in the Fonts folder.

◆ **Startup Items** are items that open when you start your computer. You can find them in the Startup Items folder, which is empty by default.

◆ **Shutdown Items** are items that open when you shut down your computer. You can find them in the Shutdown Items folder, which is empty by default.

**Figure 1**
The standard contents of a Mac OS 8.6 System Folder.

## ✔ Tips

■ As shown in **Figure 1**, there are more items in the System Folder than what I've listed here. The ones I discuss in this chapter are the ones you can use to customize your system.

■ Do not remove any item from your System Folder or a folder within it unless you know what you are doing or are instructed by someone who knows what he or she is doing. Removing a required item in error could prevent your computer from starting!

■ To prevent extensions, control panels, and startup items from loading, hold down (Shift) while the computer is starting up.

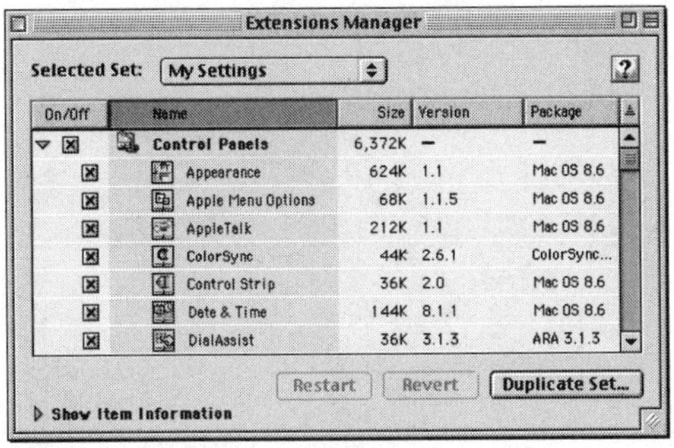

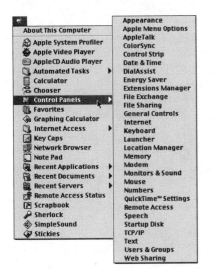

**Figure 2** The Extensions Manager control panel.

**Figure 3** The Control Panels submenu under the Apple menu offers many customization options.

# Extensions Manager

Extensions Manager (**Figure 2**) is a control panel that enables you turn individual extensions, drivers, control panels, startup items, and shutdown items on or off. An item that is turned off does not load at startup so it is disabled.

Extensions Manager also lets you create sets of item settings. By creating a variety of sets for different purposes, you can change settings quickly and easily by selecting a menu item.

## ✔ Tip

- After making changes in the Extensions Manager control panel, you must restart your computer for the changes to take effect.

## To open Extensions Manager

Choose Apple menu > Control Panels > Extensions Manager (**Figure 3**).

## To open Extensions Manager during startup

Hold down (Spacebar) while the computer is starting up. Do not release (Spacebar) until the Extensions Manager window appears (**Figure 2**).

## ✔ Tip

- If you open Extensions Manager during startup and make changes, it is not necessary to restart your computer for the changes to take effect. The changes take effect as the startup process finishes after you close Extensions Manager.

**OPENING EXTENSIONS MANAGER**

## To toggle item settings

1. Open the Extensions Manager control panel (**Figure 2**).

2. Click the check box to the left of an item name to turn it on or off (**Figure 4**).

3. Repeat step 2 for each item whose setting you want to toggle.

### ✔ Tip

■ To start over with the settings that were in the Extensions Manager window when you first opened it, click Revert.

## To turn all items on or off

1. Open the Extensions Manager control panel (**Figure 2**).

2. To turn all items on, choose Edit > All On (**Figure 5**).

   *or*

   To turn all items off, choose Edit > All Off (**Figure 5**).

## To save settings

To save the settings and immediately restart your computer, click Restart.

*or*

To save your settings without restarting your computer, close the Extensions Manager window.

### ✔ Tips

■ If you opened Extensions Manager while the computer was starting up, click Continue; there is no Restart button.

■ You can also save settings to the current set by switching to another set. I tell you about sets next.

*Folder with some items turned on and others turned off*

*Item turned off*

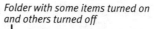

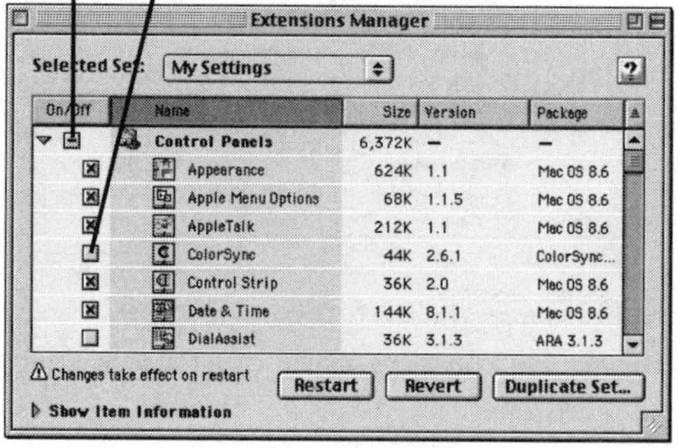

**Figure 4** Click a check box to toggle its setting.

**Figure 5** Use the All On or All Off commands under the Edit menu to quickly turn all items on or off.

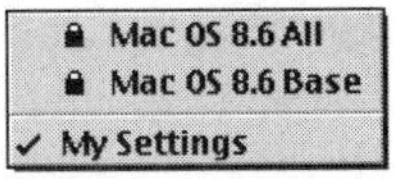

**Figure 6** The Selected Set pop-up menu lists all settings.

**Figure 7**
The File menu includes commands to create, duplicate, rename, and delete sets.

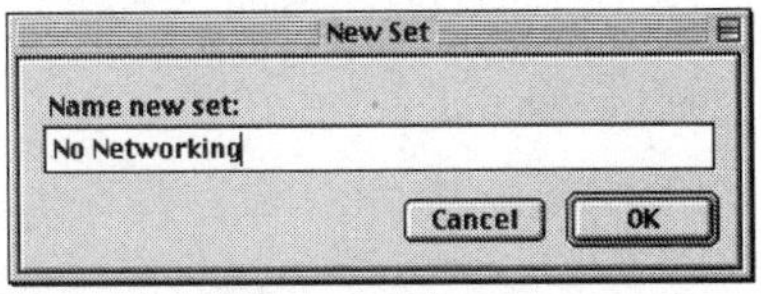

**Figure 8** Enter a name for the set in the New Set dialog box.

## To choose a set

In the Extensions Manager control panel (**Figure 4**), choose the set that you want from the Selected Set pop-up menu (**Figure 6**). The settings for the set are applied.

## ✔ Tips

- Extensions Manager comes configured with three sets:

  - ▲ **Mac OS 8.6 All** consists of all the Mac OS 8.6 items that are installed.

  - ▲ **Mac OS 8.6 Base** consists of the items that make up a basic Mac OS 8.6 system.

  - ▲ **My Settings** starts with all items turned on but can be changed.

- You cannot change the settings in or delete the Mac OS 8.6 All or Mac OS 8.6 Base sets.

## To create a set

1. Open the Extensions Manager control panel (**Figure 2**).

2. Choose File > New Set (**Figure 7**).

3. Enter a name for the set in the New Set dialog box that appears (**Figure 8**), and click OK. The name of the set appears in the Select Set pop-up window.

4. Toggle item check boxes as desired for the set.

## ✔ Tip

- Other commands under the File menu (**Figure 7**) let you delete, rename, and duplicate the currently selected set.

**WORKING WITH SETS**

## To show information about items

Click the Show Item Information triangle in the Extensions Manager window (**Figure 4**). The window expands. When you select an item, its description appears in the expanded area (**Figure 9**).

## ✔ Tip

■ You can click the Hide Item Information triangle in the Extensions Manager window (**Figure 9**) to hide information about selected items.

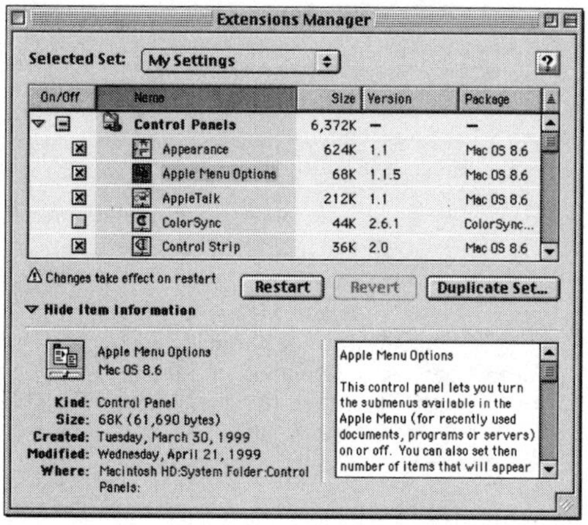

## To sort items

In the Extensions Manager window (**Figure 4**), click the heading at the top of the column by which you want to sort. The item order changes (**Figure 10**).

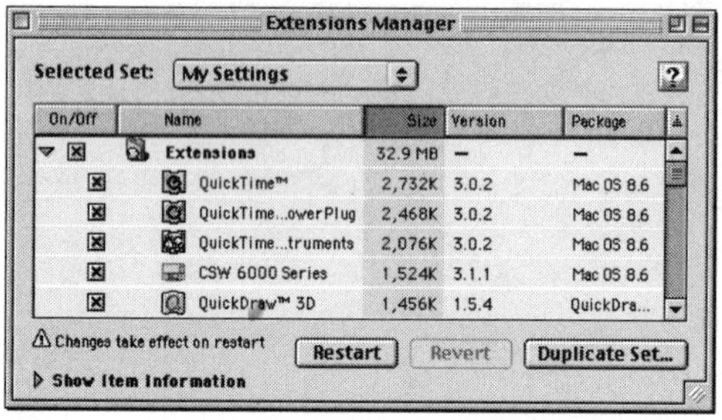

## To hide the items in a folder

In the Extensions Manager window (**Figure 4**), click the triangle to the left of the folder whose items you want to hide. The items disappear (**Figure 11**).

## ✔ Tip

■ You can click the triangle to the left of a folder with hidden items in the Extensions Manager window (**Figure 11**) to display the items.

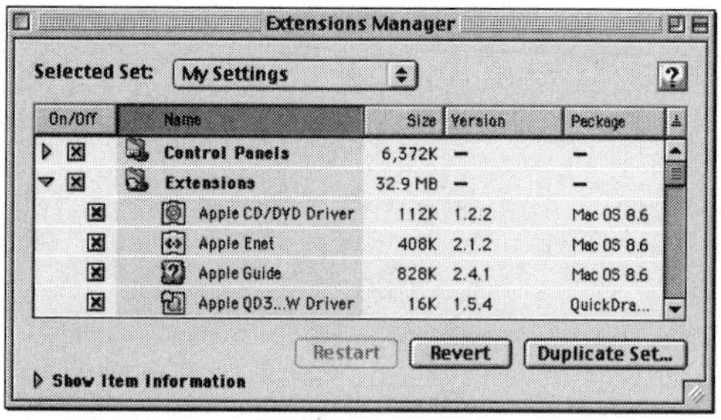

**Figure 9** When you expand the Extensions Manager window, information about a selected item is displayed in the expanded area.

**Figure 10** Click a heading to sort by its contents.

**Figure 11** Click the triangle to the left of a folder to hide its items.

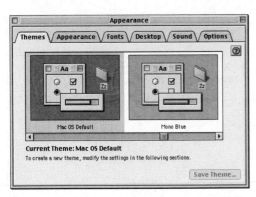

**Figure 12** The Themes tab of the Appearance control panel.

# Appearance

The Appearance control panel includes six tabs you can use to set options that determine how your Mac looks and sounds:

◆ **Themes (Figure 12)** enables you to select a group of predefined settings that combine all other appearance options.

◆ **Appearance (Figure 13)** enables you to choose an appearance option, highlight color, and variation color.

◆ **Fonts (Figure 16)** enables you to choose the fonts for menus, headings, explanatory text, labels, lists, and icons. It also enables you to turn on *anti-aliasing*, to smooth the appearance of fonts on screen.

◆ **Desktop (Figure 20)** enables you to select a desktop pattern or picture.

◆ **Sound (Figure 24)** enables you to choose a sound track—a group of sound effects for common tasks. It also enables you to disable sounds for certain tasks.

◆ **Options (Figure 25)** enables you to set scroll bar and window collapsing options.

## ✔ Tip

■ Mac OS 8.6 comes with a number of built-in themes, sound sets, and desktop pictures and patterns. Others are available from Apple and third-party developers.

## To open the Appearance control panel

Choose Apple menu > Control Panels > Appearance (**Figure 3**).

THE APPEARANCE CONTROL PANEL

## To select a theme

1. In the Appearance control panel, click the Themes tab to display its options (**Figure 12**).

2. Use the scroll bar in the window to scroll through the available themes.

3. When you see a theme you like, click it to select it.

4. Close the Appearance control panel to save your selection.

## ✔ Tips

- Themes include the appearance, fonts, desktop pattern or picture, sound, and window options settings in the Appearance control panel.

- To customize a theme, select it, make changes in the other tabs of the Appearance control panel, and click the Save Theme button in the Themes tab. Use the dialog box that appears to name and save your custom theme.

## To set appearance options

1. In the Appearance control panel, click the Appearance tab to display its options (**Figure 13**).

2. Choose an option from the Appearance pop-up menu to set the overall appearance of menus, icons, windows, and controls.

3. Choose a color from the Highlight Color pop-up menu (**Figure 14**) to set the color of highlighted text.

4. Choose a color from the Variation pop-up menu (**Figure 15**) to set the accent color of menus and controls.

5. Close the Appearance control panel to save your settings.

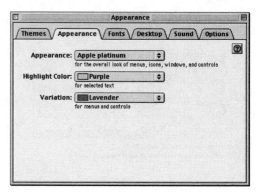

**Figure 13** The Appearance tab of the Appearance control panel.

**Figure 14**
The Highlight Color
pop-up menu.

**Figure 15**
The Variation
pop-up menu.

## ✔ Tip

- If you choose Other from the Highlight Color pop-up menu (**Figure 14**), you can use a color picker dialog box to select a custom color. I tell you about the color picker in **Chapter 3**.

SETTING THEME & APPEARANCE OPTIONS

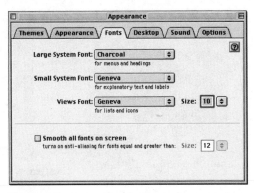

**Figure 16** The Fonts tab of the Appearance control panel.

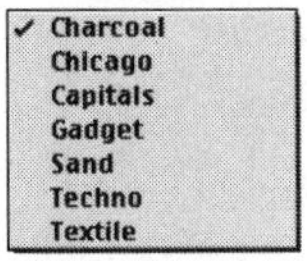

**Figure 17**
The Large System
Font pop-up menu.

**Figure 18**
The Views Font
pop-up menu.

## To choose system fonts

1. In the Appearance control panel, click the Fonts tab to display its options (**Figure 16**).

2. Choose a font from the Large System Font pop-up menu (**Figure 17**) to set the font for menus and headings.

3. Choose a font from the Small System Font pop-up menu to set the font for explanatory text and labels.

4. Choose a font from the Views Font pop-up menu (**Figure 18**) to set the font for lists and icon names. You can also enter a size for the font in the Size edit box beside the pop-up menu.

5. To enable anti-aliasing, turn on the Smooth all fonts on screen check box and enter a minimum font size for anti-aliasing in the Size edit box beside it.

6. Close the Appearance control panel to save your settings.

## ✔ Tip

■ **Figures 19a** and **19b** show examples of on-screen text with anti-aliasing turned off and on.

CHOOSING SYSTEM FONTS

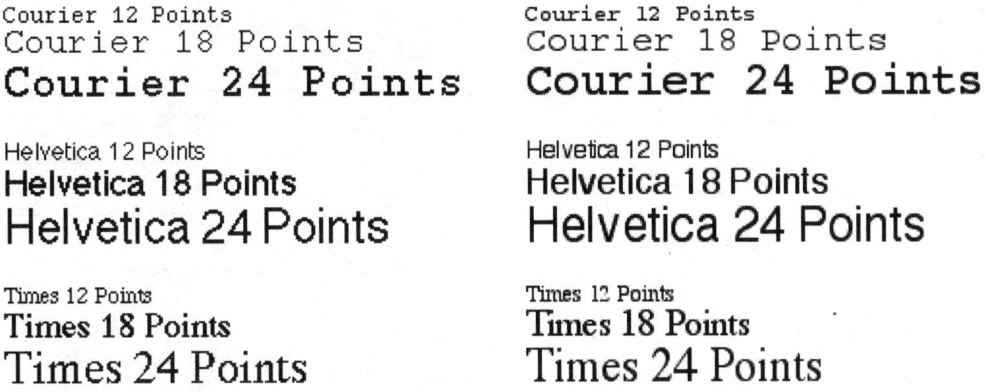

Courier 12 Points
Courier 18 Points
**Courier 24 Points**

Helvetica 12 Points
**Helvetica 18 Points**
**Helvetica 24 Points**

Times 12 Points
**Times 18 Points**
Times 24 Points

Courier 12 Points
Courier 18 Points
**Courier 24 Points**

Helvetica 12 Points
**Helvetica 18 Points**
**Helvetica 24 Points**

Times 12 Points
**Times 18 Points**
Times 24 Points

**Figures 19a & 19b** Examples of on-screen text with anti-aliasing turned off (left) and on (right).

## To set the Desktop pattern

1. In the Appearance control panel, click the Desktop tab to display its options (**Figure 20**).

2. Click each of the items in the Patterns scrolling list to see a preview in the left side of the window.

3. When you have selected a pattern you like, click the Set Desktop button. The pattern is applied to the desktop.

## To set the Desktop picture

1. In the Appearance control panel, click the Desktop tab to display its options (**Figure 20**).

2. Click the Place Picture button. An Open dialog box showing the contents of the Desktop Pictures folder appears (**Figure 21**).

3. Use the dialog box to locate and select the picture you want.

4. Click Choose. The picture appears in the sample area inside the Desktop tab of the Appearance control panel (**Figure 22**).

5. Choose a positioning option from the pop-up menu beneath the Remove Picture button (**Figure 23**).

6. When the picture is just the way you want it, click the Set Desktop button. The picture is applied to the desktop.

## ✔ Tips

- In step 3, you can click the Show Preview button to see what a selected picture looks like before you choose it.

- A desktop picture appears in place of any desktop pattern.

- You can remove a desktop picture by clicking the Remove Picture button in the Desktop tab of the Appearance control panel (**Figure 22**).

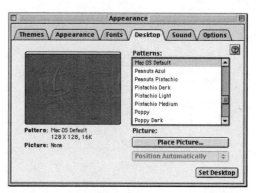

**Figure 20** The Desktop tab of the Appearance control panel.

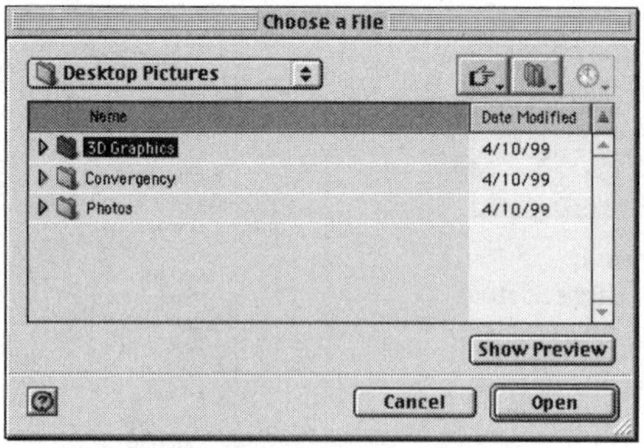

**Figure 21** The Open dialog box shows the contents of the Desktop Pictures folder.

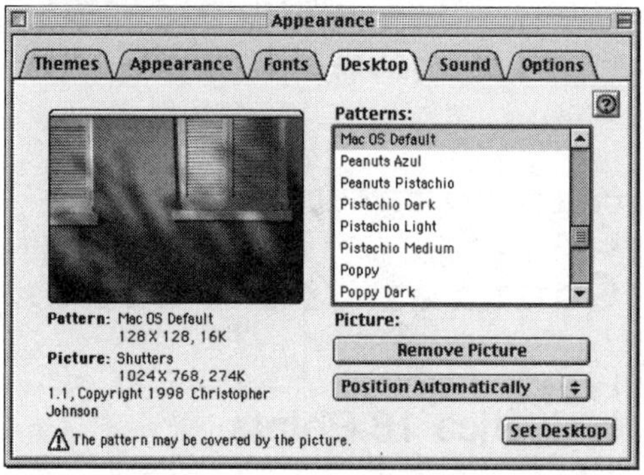

**Figure 22** When you choose a picture, it appears in the Desktop tab of the Appearance control panel.

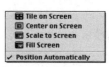

**Figure 23**
Choose a positioning option for the picture from this menu.

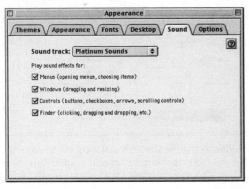

**Figure 24** The Sound tab of the Appearance control panel.

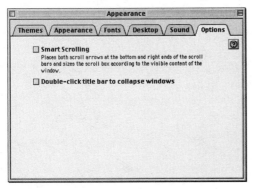

**Figure 25** The Options tab of the Appearance control panel.

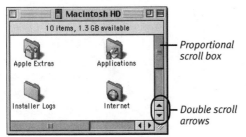

*— Proportional scroll box*

*— Double scroll arrows*

**Figure 26** Here's what the scroll bars in a window look like with Smart Scrolling turned on.

## To set sound options

1. In the Appearance control panel, click the Sound tab to display its options (**Figure 24**).

2. To turn on system sounds, choose an option from the Sound track pop-up menu.

3. Click to toggle check boxes on or off to select the events for which you want to hear sounds.

4. Close the Appearance control panel to save your settings.

## ✔ Tip

■ To disable sounds, choose None from the Sound track pop-up menu.

## To set window options

1. In the Appearance control panel, click the Options tab to display its options (**Figure 25**).

2. To display double-scroll arrows and pro-portional scroll boxes in the scroll bars of windows, turn on the Smart Scrolling check box. **Figure 26** illustrates a window with this option turned on.

3. To collapse or expand a window by double-clicking its title bar, turn on the Double-click title bar to collapse windows check box.

4. Close the Appearance control panel to save your settings.

# Monitors & Sound

The Monitors & Sound control panel enables you to set options for video and sound:

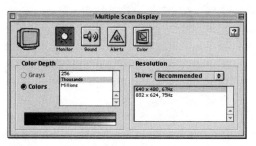

**Figure 27** Use the Monitors options of the Monitors & Sound control panel to set up your monitor. This illustration shows options for a Sony Multiscan 100ES monitor.

◆ **Monitor** (**Figure 27**) enables you to set the color depth, resolution, contrast, and brightness.

◆ **Sound** (**Figure 28**) enables you to set sound input, output, and volume options.

◆ **Alerts** (**Figure 29**) enables you to select and change the volume of alert sounds.

## To set monitor options

1. Choose Apple menu > Control Panels > Monitors & Sound (**Figure 3**).

2. If necessary, click the Monitor button in the window that appears (**Figure 27**).

3. Select a color depth from the list in the Color Depth area. If you choose 256, you can select the Grays radio button to switch to grayscale.

4. Select a resolution from the list in the Resolution area. The higher the resolution, the more information displays on screen.

5. Close the window to save your settings.

## ✔ Tips

■ The options that appear in **Figure 27** vary depending on the type of monitor and amount of VRAM (video RAM) installed in your computer. If other options are available, set them as desired.

■ If the options in the Monitors & Sound control panel look very different from what you see here, check the documentation that came with your monitor.

SETTING MONITOR OPTIONS

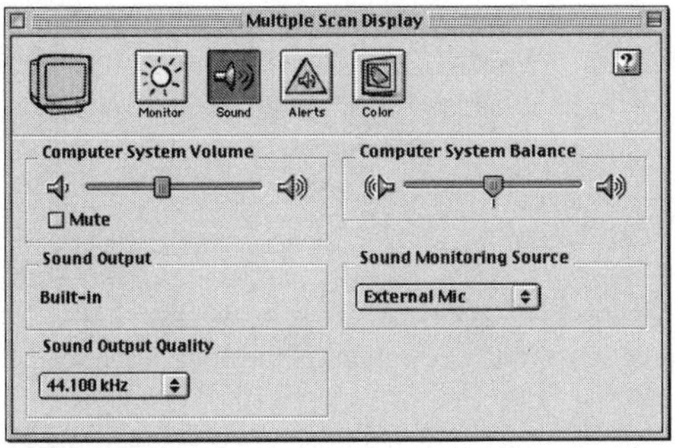

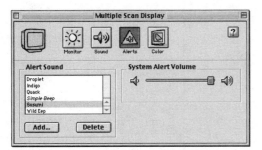

**Figure 28** Use the Sound options of the Monitors & Sound control panel to change volume and select input and output devices. This illustration shows options for a Power Mac 8500/180.

**Figure 29** Use the Alerts options of the Monitors & Sound control panel to select the alert sound and set its volume.

## To set sound options

1. Choose Apple menu > Control Panels > Monitors & Sound (**Figure 3**).

2. If necessary, click the Sound button in the window that appears (**Figure 23**).

3. Use the Computer System Volume slider to change the computer's sound volume.

4. If desired, choose options from pop-up menus to set other sound options.

5. To instruct your computer to listen for voice recognition commands, turn on the Listen check box.

6. Close the window to save your settings.

## ✔ Tips

- The options that appear in **Figure 28** vary depending on your computer model and connected devices.

- Voice recognition is included with Mac OS 8.6 but must be installed using a custom installation. I tell you about installing Mac OS 8.6 in **Chapter 1**.

## To set alert sound options

1. Choose Apple menu > Control Panels > Monitors & Sound (**Figure 3**).

2. If necessary, click the Alerts button in the window that appears (**Figure 29**).

3. Select the sound that you would like to hear as your alert sound from the Alert Sound list.

4. Use the System Alert Volume slider to change the volume of the alert sound.

5. Close the window to save your settings.

## ✔ Tip

- You can click the Add button (**Figure 29**) to record your own sounds. I explain how to use the Recording dialog box in **Chapter 7** when I tell you about SimpleSound.

**SETTING SOUND & ALERT OPTIONS**

# Speech

The Speech control panel enables you to set options for speech synthesis:

◆ **Voice** options (**Figure 30**) control the voice and speech rate.

◆ **Talking Alerts** options (**Figure 32**) controls whether your computer reads alert dialog boxes to you.

## To set voice options

1. Choose Apple menu > Control Panels > Speech (**Figure 3**).

2. If necessary, choose Voice from the Options pop-up menu at the top of the Speech window that appears (**Figure 30**).

3. Choose a voice from the Voice pop-up menu (**Figure 31**).

4. If desired, use the slider to change the speaking rate.

5. Close the window to save your settings.

## ✔ Tip

■ To hear what the selected voice sounds like, click the speaker icon to the right of the Voice pop-up menu (**Figure 30**).

## To set talking alerts options

1. Choose Apple menu > Control Panels > Speech (**Figure 3**).

2. If necessary, choose Talking Alerts from the Options pop-up menu at the top of the Speech window that appears (**Figure 32**).

3. To hear your computer speak a phrase instead of playing an alert sound, turn on the Speak the phrase check box. Then choose a phrase from the pop-up menu (**Figure 33**).

4. To hear your computer speak the text in alert dialog boxes, turn on the Speak the alert text check box.

5. If desired, use the Wait before speaking slider to set a delay.

6. Close the window to save your settings.

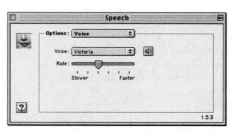

**Figure 30** The Voice options of the Speech control panel.

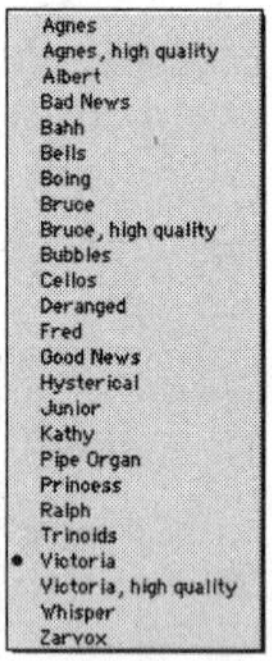

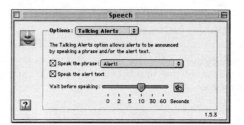

**Figure 31**
Choose a voice from the Voice pop-up menu.

**Figure 32** The Talking Alerts options of the Speech control panel.

**Figure 33**
Choose a phrase from the Speak the phrase pop-up menu.

## ✔ Tip

■ To hear a demo of the talking alerts settings, click the icon beside the Wait before speaking slider (**Figure 32**).

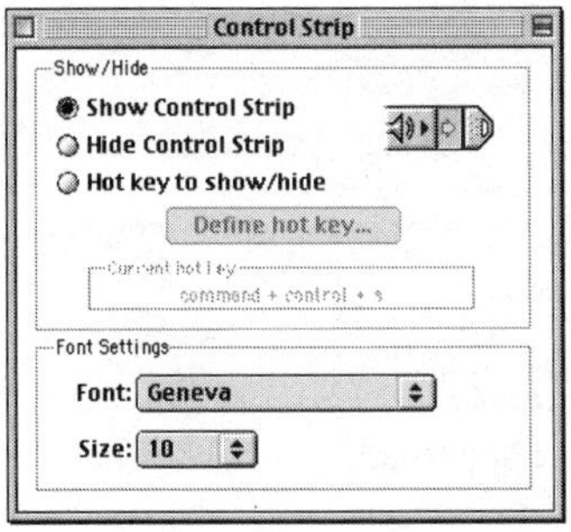

**Figure 34**
The Control Strip control panel window.

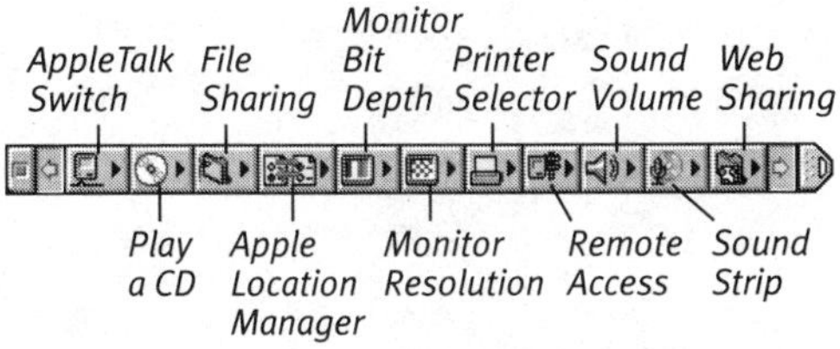

**Control Strip**

The Control Strip control panel (**Figure 34**) enables you to set options for the control strip that appears at the bottom of your screen (**Figure 35**).

### ✔ Tips

■ The control strip consists of *modules* that display pop-up menus for quick and easy access to many Mac OS features. The modules that appear on your control strip vary depending on your computer model and Mac OS options installed. Additional control strip modules are available from third-party developers.

■ You can collapse and expand the control strip by clicking the tab at its right end.

AppleTalk File   Monitor Bit Printer Sound Web
Switch Sharing Depth Selector Volume Sharing

Play   Apple   Monitor   Remote Sound
a CD   Location Resolution Access   Strip
       Manager

**Figure 35** The control strip. The modules that appear on your control strip may differ from these.

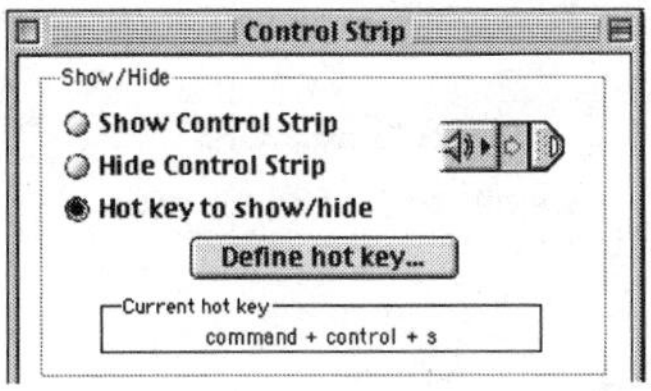

**Figure 36** If you select the Hot key to show/hide radio button, you can click Define hot key...

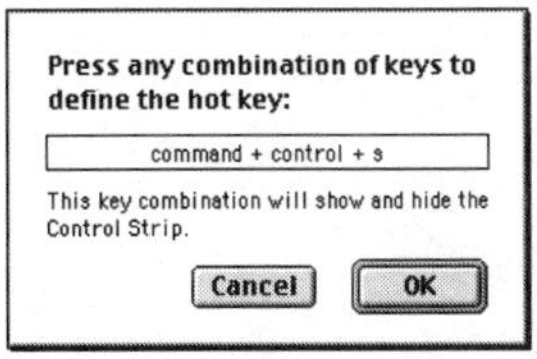

**Figure 37** ...to display this dialog box. Then change the hot key to show and hide the control strip.

### To set control strip options

1. Choose Apple menu > Control Panels > Control Strip (**Figure 3**). The Control Strip control panel appears (**Figure 34**).

2. Select a Show/Hide radio button:

 ▲ **Show Control Strip** displays the control strip.

 ▲ **Hide Control Strip** does not display the control strip.

 ▲ **Hot key to show/hide** enables the Define hot key button (**Figure 36**), which you can click to display a dialog box for changing the hot key (**Figure 37**). Pressing the keystroke in this dialog box toggles the display of the control strip.

3. Choose a font from the Font pop-up menu (**Figure 18**).

4. Choose a font size from the Size pop-up menu.

5. Close the window to save your settings.

SETTING CONTROL STRIP OPTIONS

# Energy Saver & Auto Power On/Off

Energy Saver is a control panel that enables you to set energy saving options:

◆ **Sleep Setup** (**Figures 38** and **39**) enables you to specify when your system, display, and hard disk should sleep.

◆ **Scheduled Startup & Shutdown** (**Figure 40**) enables you to set the days and times for your computer to automatically start up and shut down.

Computer models that do not support the sleep options do not support Energy Saver. On these computers, the Mac OS 8.6 installer installs Auto Power On/Off (**Figure 43**), a control panel that offers the same functionality as the Scheduled Startup & Shutdown options of Energy Saver.

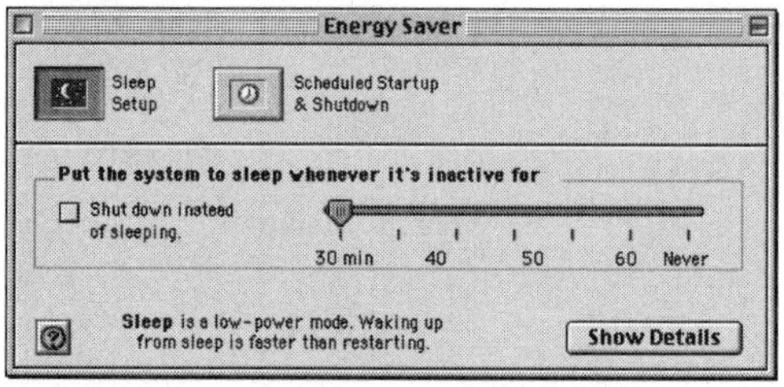

## To set automatic sleep options

1. Choose Apple menu > Control Panels > Energy Saver (**Figure 3**).

2. If necessary, click the Sleep Setup button at the top of the Energy Saver window that appears (**Figure 38**).

3. Use the slider to set the amount of idle time before the computer goes to sleep.

4. To set the computer so it shuts down instead of going into sleep mode, turn on the Shut down instead of sleeping check box.

5. To set different timing options for display (monitor) sleep and hard disk sleep, click Show Details. The window expands to show two additional sliders. Turn on the check box beside the sliders that you want to set and set the sliders (**Figure 39**).

6. Close the window to save your settings.

## ✔ Tip

■ I tell you about sleep mode and shutting down the computer in **Chapter 2**.

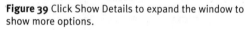

**Figure 38** The Sleep Setup options of the Energy Saver control panel window.

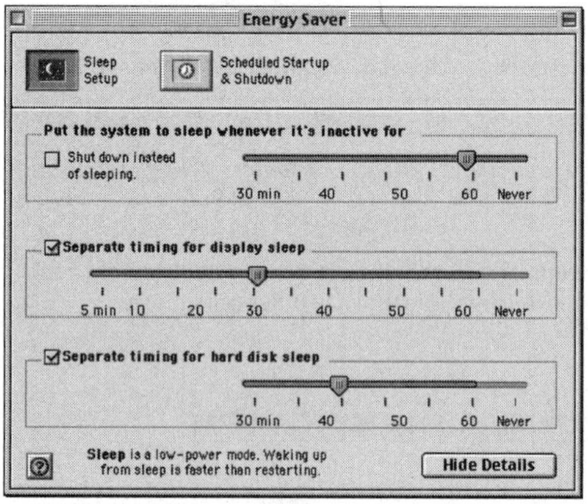

**Figure 39** Click Show Details to expand the window to show more options.

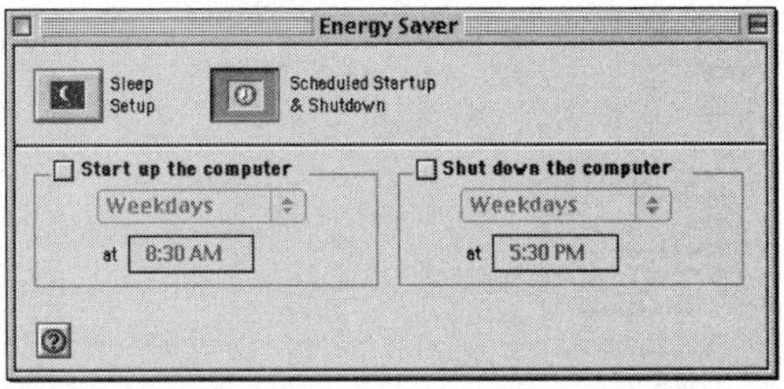

**Figure 40** The Scheduled Startup & Shutdown options of the Energy Saver window.

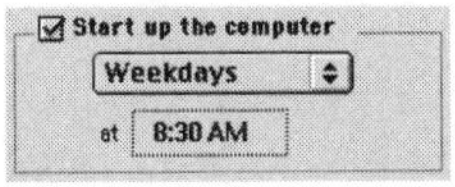

**Figure 41** Turn on the Start up the computer check box to choose a day and time.

**Figure 42**
Choose a day or group of days from the pop-up menu in the dialog box.

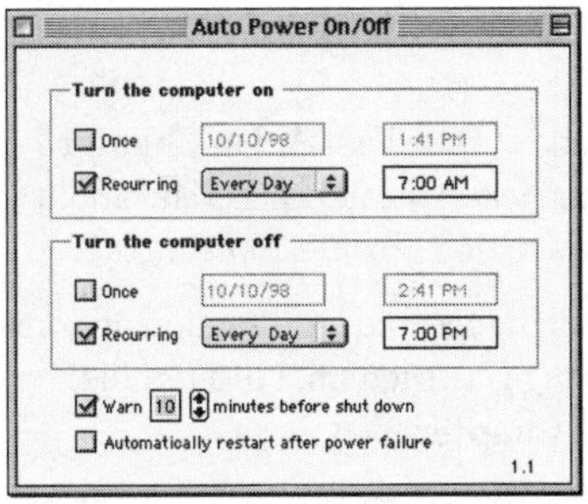

**Figure 43** The Auto Power On/Off control panel window.

## To schedule start up & shut down times

1. Choose Apple menu > Control Panels > Energy Saver (**Figure 3**).

2. If necessary, click the Scheduled Startup & Shutdown button at the top of the Energy Saver window that appears (**Figure 40**).

3. To start the computer at a specific time, turn on the Start up the computer check box (**Figure 41**). Use the pop-up menu beneath it (**Figure 42**) to select the day or days on which the computer should automatically start. Enter a time in the at edit box beneath the pop-up menu.

4. To shut down the computer at a specific time, turn on the Shut down the computer check box. Use the pop-up menu beneath it (**Figure 42**) to select the day or days on which the computer should automatically shut down. Enter a time in the at edit box beneath the pop-up menu.

5. Close the window to save your settings.

## ✔ Tips

- You can use this feature to start your computer before you arrive at work so it's ready and waiting for you.

- You can also use this feature to automatically shut down at a certain time so you don't work too long.

- If your computer has Auto Power On/Off installed rather than Energy Saver, choose Apple menu > Control Panels > Auto Power On/Off. Then set options in the Auto Power On/Off control panel (**Figure 43**). The interface is slightly different from Energy Saver but works the same way.

SCHEDULING START UP & SHUT DOWN TIMES

# General Controls

The General Controls control panel (**Figure 44**) enables you to set a variety of options that affect the way your Mac works.

## To set General Controls control panel options

1. Choose Apple menu > Control Panels > General Controls (**Figure 3**). The General Controls window appears (**Figure 44**).

2. To display the icons on your Desktop while other applications are active, turn on the Show Desktop when in background check box.

3. To automatically display the Launcher control panel when the computer starts, turn on the Show Launcher at system startup check box.

4. To have your computer inform you at start up when it was shut down improperly, turn on the Warn me if computer was shut down improperly check box. Enabling this option also instructs Disk First Aid to automatically check your hard disk when you start up after an improper shut down.

5. To keep items in the System Folder or Applications folder from being renamed or removed, turn on the appropriate check boxes in the Folder Protection area.

6. To set the rate at which the insertion point blinks, select a radio button in the Insertion Point Blinking area. The sample to the left of the radio buttons shows you the effect of your change.

7. To set the number of times a selected menu item blinks before the menu disappears, select a Menu Blinking radio button.

8. To set the default folder location in a Save As dialog box, select a Documents radio button.

9. Close the window to save your settings.

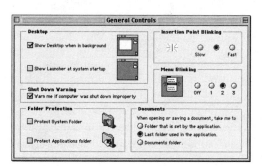

**Figure 44** The General Controls control panel window.

SimpleText

**Figure 45** With folder protection enabled, item icons include tiny padlocks...

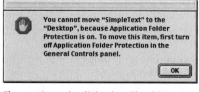

You cannot move "SimpleText" to the "Desktop", because Application Folder Protection is on. To move this item, first turn off Application Folder Protection in the General Controls panel.

OK

**Figure 46** ...and a dialog box like this appears when you try to move one.

## ✔ Tips

- I tell you about Disk First Aid in **Chapter 7**, about Launcher on the next page, and about the Save As dialog box in **Chapter 5**.

- You cannot change folder protection options if file sharing is turned on. I discuss file sharing in **Chapter 9**.

- With folder protection turned on, icons in protected folders appear with tiny padlocks beside them (**Figure 45**). A dialog box like the one in **Figure 46** appears if you try to move something out of a protected folder.

- If you select Documents folder in step 8 but do not have a Documents folder, Mac OS creates one for you.

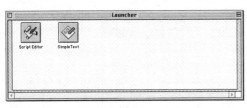

**Figure 47** The Launcher window appears at the bottom of the screen.

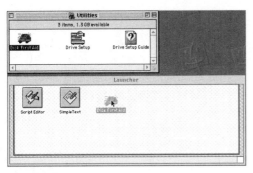

**Figure 48** Hold down ⌃⌘ while clicking in the Launcher window to display a menu of button sizes.

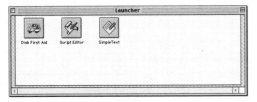

**Figure 49** To add an item, drag its icon into the Launcher window.

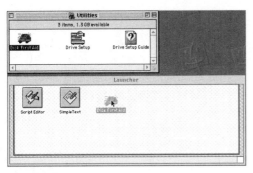

**Figure 50** A button for an alias of the item is added to the Launcher window.

# Launcher

Launcher displays a special window with buttons you can click to open specific items. You can add and remove items as desired to include only the items you access frequently.

## ✔ Tip

■ Launcher works with aliases, which I discuss in **Chapter 4.**

## To open Launcher

Choose Apple menu > Control Panels > Launcher (**Figure 3**). The Launcher window appears (**Figure 47**).

## ✔ Tips

■ To have Launcher automatically appear at start up, turn on the Show Launcher at system startup check box in the General Controls control panel (**Figure 44**). I discuss General Controls on the previous page.

■ To change the size of the buttons in the Launcher window, hold down ⌃⌘ while clicking in the window to display a menu of button sizes (**Figure 48**). Choose the size you want.

## To add items to Launcher

Drag the icon for an item that you want to include in Launcher into the Launcher window (**Figure 49**). When you release the mouse button, a button for the item appears in the Launcher window (**Figure 50**). The original item remains where it was.

## To remove items from Launcher

Hold down (Option) while dragging the item to the Trash.

**USING LAUNCHER**

# Keyboard

The Keyboard control panel (**Figure 51**) enables you to select keyboard layouts to appear on the Keyboard menu and to set key repeat options for keyboard operation.

## ✔ Tip

■ The Keyboard menu is displayed when WorldScript, a multilanguages feature of Mac OS, is installed. WorldScript is not installed with Mac OS 8.6; you can obtain it from Apple Computer, Inc.

## To set Keyboard control panel options

1. Choose Apple menu > Control Panels > Keyboard (**Figure 3**). The Keyboard window appears (**Figure 51**).

2. Turn on the check box to the left of each keyboard layout that you want to include on the Keyboard menu.

3. Use the Key Repeat Rate slider to set how fast a key repeats when held down.

4. Use the Delay Until Repeat slider to set how long a key must be pressed before it starts to repeat.

5. Close the window to save your settings.

## ✔ Tips

■ You can use the keyboard layout feature to type using the keyboard layout for another language.

■ At least one keyboard layout must be selected. That's why the check box for U.S. is gray in **Figure 51**.

■ You can click the Options button (**Figure 51**) to set additional options for using multiple keyboard layouts.

■ Key Repeat settings are especially useful for heavy-handed typists.

**Figure 51**
The Keyboard control panel window.

**Figure 52**
The Mouse control panel window.

# Mouse

The Mouse control panel (**Figure 52**) enables you to set options that control the way the mouse works.

## To set mouse options

1. Choose Apple menu > Control Panels > Mouse (**Figure 3**). The Mouse control panel window appears (**Figure 52**).

2. To set the speed of the mouse movement on your screen, select a Mouse Tracking radio button.

3. To set the amount of time between each click of a double-click, select a Double-Click Speed radio button. The radio button on the left is for longer time between clicks while the radio button on the right is for shorter time between clicks.

4. Close the window to save your settings.

## ✔ Tip

- If you're just learning to use a mouse, you may find it helpful to set the mouse speed and double-click rates to slower than the default settings shown in **Figure 52**.

# Memory

The Memory control panel (**Figure 53**) enables you to set options that determine how RAM is used in your computer. On most computers, it controls the following three options:

◆ **Disk cache** is RAM set aside for storage of frequently used computer instructions. The recommended disk cache setting is 32 kilobytes (K) of cache for each megabyte of installed RAM.

◆ **Virtual memory** is hard disk space used as RAM. For efficient performance on a computer with a PowerPC processor, virtual memory should be turned on and set to 1 megabyte (M) more than installed RAM.

◆ **RAM disk** is RAM used as disk space. If set up and used properly, it can benefit Power-Book users by reducing the computer's power consumption, thus increasing battery life.

## ✔ Tips

■ I tell you more about RAM in **Chapter 5**.

■ The options that appear in the Memory control panel vary depending on the computer model.

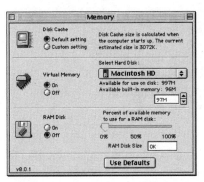

**Figure 53** The Memory control panel window.

**Figure 54** About This Computer tells you about the amount of RAM that is installed and in use.

## To set memory options

1. Choose Apple menu > Control Panels > Memory (**Figure 3**). The Memory control panel window appears (**Figure 53**).

2. To set the disk cache size, select the Custom setting ratio button. If a warning dialog box appears, click Custom to dismiss it. Then click the arrows beside the Size after restart edit box that appears in the Memory control panel window to change the value.

3. To turn virtual memory on or off, select the appropriate Virtual Memory radio button. If you select On, choose a hard disk from the pop-up menu and click the arrows beside the edit box to set the total amount of RAM that you want.

4. To turn a RAM disk on or off, select the appropriate RAM Disk radio button. If you select On, use the slider to set the RAM disk size.

5. Close the window to save your settings.

6. If you changed settings in the Memory window, restart your computer.

## ✔ Tips

- Don't change the memory options unless you know what you are doing or are following detailed instructions provided by someone who knows what he or she is doing. These are powerful options that can negatively affect your computer's performance if set improperly. When in doubt, click the Use Defaults button to use the default settings for your computer.

- You can learn how much RAM is installed in your computer by choosing Apple menu > About This Computer (when the Finder is active). A window like the one in **Figure 54** appears. It specifies the amount of installed (built-in) RAM, virtual memory, and largest unused block of RAM as well as the amount of RAM in use by applications.

# Startup Disk

The Startup Disk control panel enables you to specify which disk or volume should be used to start the computer.

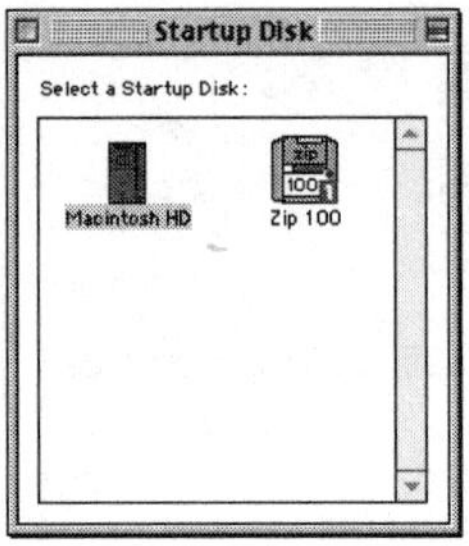

**Figure 55**
The Startup Disk window shows all bootable high-capacity media.

## ✔ Tips

- Any *bootable disk*—a disk with a correctly configured System Folder on it—can be a startup disk.

- You don't need to use the Startup Disk control panel to start from a bootable floppy disk (like a Disk Tools disk). Just insert the disk before starting up.

## To set the startup disk

1. Choose Apple menu > Control Panels > Startup Disk (**Figure 3**). The Startup Disk window appears (**Figure 55**).

2. Select the icon for the disk that should be used as the startup disk the next time the computer is started.

3. Close the Startup Disk window.

## ✔ Tip

- The Startup Disk control panel window displays all mounted bootable disks.

## To start from a bootable CD

Hold down Ⓒ right after hearing the computer's startup tone. You can release this key when you see the Welcome to Mac OS window. It is usually not necessary to use the Startup Disk control panel to start from a bootable CD.

**SETTING THE STARTUP DISK**

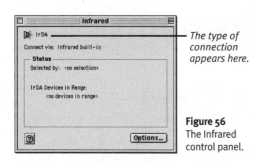

Figure 56
The Infrared
control panel.

*The type of connection appears here.*

Figure 57
The Options
dialog box for the
Infrared control
panel, which is
only available if
your computer
supports both
IrDA and IRTalk.

Figure 58
The AppleTalk
control panel.

Figure 59 Select Infrared Port
(IrDA) from the Connect via
pop-up menu.

Figure 60
The Infrared
control panel
indicates
connection
status.

## ✔ Tip

■ The Infrared control panel also displays the
status of the IrDA connection (**Figure 60**).

# Infrared

Some Mac models, including most PowerBooks
and the original iMac, have infrared communication capabilities. If you have one of these
computers, you can use the infrared port to
communicate with other computers or devices
that have infrared networking capabilities,
using one of the following infrared options:

◆ **IrDA** enables you to connect to a network
using infrared communication. This option
is available on all Mac models with infrared
capabilities.

◆ **IRTalk**, a proprietary Apple protocol,
enables you to exchange files with another
Macintosh computer that that has infrared
capabilities and supports IRTalk.

## To set up IrDA

1. Choose Apple menu > Control Panels >
Infrared. The Infrared control panel appears
(**Figure 56**).

2. If IrDA does not appear in the upper left
corner of the window, click Options. Select
the IrDA radio button in the Options dialog
box (**Figure 57**) and click OK.

3. Close the Infrared control panel. Click Save
or OK in any confirmation or warning
dialog boxes that appear.

4. Choose Apple menu > Control Panels >
AppleTalk (**Figure 3**) to display the Apple-
Talk control panel (**Figure 58**).

5. Select Infrared Port (IrDA) from the Connect
via pop-up menu (**Figure 59**).

6. Close the AppleTalk control panel. Click
Save or OK in any confirmation or warning
dialog boxes that appear.

7. Position the infrared port on your computer
within 3 feet of the LAN access device. You
can now utilize network services.

SETTING UP IRDA

## To set up IRTalk

1. Choose Apple menu > Control Panels > Infrared. The Infrared control panel appears (**Figure 56**).

2. If IRTalk does not appear in the upper left corner of the window, click Options. Select the IRTalk radio button in the Options dialog box (**Figure 57**), and click OK.

3. Close the Infrared control panel. Click Save or OK in any confirmation or warning dialog boxes that appear.

4. Choose Apple menu > Control Panels > AppleTalk (**Figure 3**) to display the Apple-Talk control panel (**Figure 58**).

5. Select Infrared Port (IRTalk) from the Connect via pop-up menu (**Figure 61**).

6. Close the AppleTalk control panel. Click Save or OK in any confirmation or warning dialog boxes that appear.

7. Open the Apple IR File Exchange folder in the Apple Extras folder on your hard disk (**Figure 62**).

8. Double-click the Apple IR File Exchange application icon. You are now ready to send and receive files via IRTalk.

**Figure 61** Select Infrared Port (IRTalk) from the Connect via pop-up menu.

**Figure 62** The contents of the Apple IR File Exchange folder.

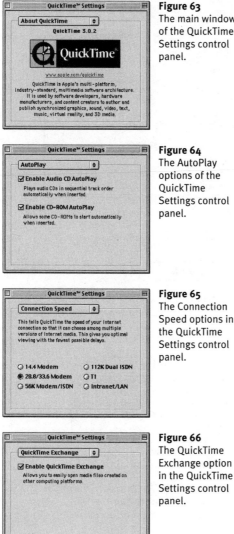

**Figure 63**
The main window of the QuickTime Settings control panel.

**Figure 64**
The AutoPlay options of the QuickTime Settings control panel.

**Figure 65**
The Connection Speed options in the QuickTime Settings control panel.

**Figure 66**
The QuickTime Exchange option in the QuickTime Settings control panel.

# QuickTime Settings

The QuickTime settings control panel (**Figure 63**) controls the way QuickTime and your CD-ROM drive work. In this section, I explain how to set some commonly used options.

## ✔ Tips

- You can also use the QuickTime Settings control panel to register your copy of QuickTime Pro. I tell you more about QuickTime Pro in **Chapter 8**.

## To set CD & QuickTime options

1. Choose Apple menu > Control Panels > QuickTime Settings (**Figure 3**). The Quick-Time Settings control panel appears (**Figure 63**).

2. To set CD autoplay options, choose Auto-Play from the pop-up menu at the top of the window to display the AutoPlay options (**Figure 64**). Toggle check box settings as desired:

   ▲ **Enable Audio CD AutoPlay** automatically plays audio CDs when they are inserted.

   ▲ **Enable CD-ROM AutoPlay** automatically starts CD-ROM discs when they are inserted.

3. To set the connection speed for playing back QuickTime files over the Web, choose Connection Speed from the pop-up menu at the top of the window. Then select the radio button for your usual Internet connection speed (**Figure 65**).

4. To easily open QuickTime-compatible media files created on any platform, choose QuickTime Exchange from the pop-up menu at the top of the window. Then turn on the Enable QuickTime Exchange check box (**Figure 66**).

5. Close the window to save your settings.

## ✔ Tips

- Not all CD-ROM discs utilize the CD-ROM autoplay feature.

- Some Mac OS users have reported computer virus problems when enabling the CD-ROM autoplay feature. If your computer does not have virus protection, consider keeping this option turned off.

**SETTING CD & QUICKTIME OPTIONS**

# Date & Time

The Date & Time control panel (**Figure 67**) enables you to set the date, time, and time zone for your computer. If you have Internet access, you can also use a network time server to set your computer's clock to the exact time.

## To manually set the date & time

1. Choose Apple menu > Control Panels > Date & Time (**Figure 3**). The Date & Time control panel window appears (**Figure 67**).

2. To change the date, click the numbers that make up the date and use the arrow buttons to change them.

3. To change the time, click the numbers that make up the time and use the arrow buttons to change them (**Figure 68**).

4. Close the window to save your settings.

## To use the time server

1. Choose Apple menu > Control Panels > Date & Time (**Figure 3**). The Date & Time control panel window appears (**Figure 67**).

2. Turn on the Use a Network Time Server check box.

3. Click the Server Options button.

4. In the Server Options dialog box that appears (**Figure 69**), select one of the Update the time radio buttons:

   ▲ **Automatically, when the system clock is different from the time server** changes the time when you are connected to the Internet and your computer's time is different from the time server's time.

   ▲ **Every** enables you to set the number of hours, days, weeks, or months between updates.

   ▲ **Manually** updates the time when you click the Set Time Now button.

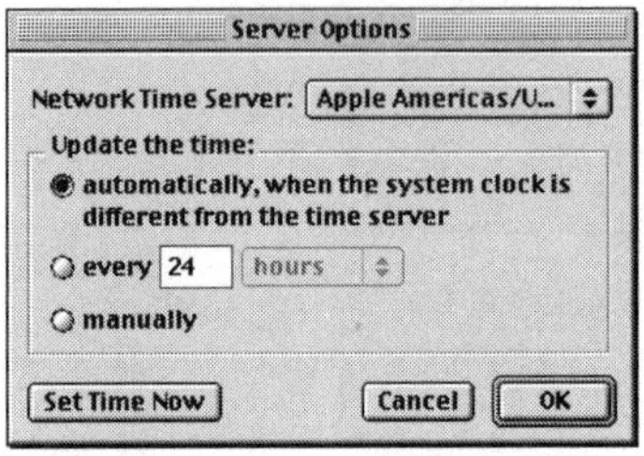

**Figure 67** The Date & Time control panel window.

**Figure 68** Click the digits that you want to change, then click the arrow buttons to change them.

**Figure 69** Use the Server Options dialog box to set options for using a time server.

5. Click Set Time Now to update the time immediately. (Your computer will connect to the Internet if necessary.)

6. Click OK to save the Server Options settings.

7. Close the Date & Time window to save your settings.

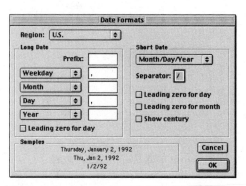

Figure 70 The Date Formats dialog box lets you customize date formats.

**Figure 71**
Use the Region pop-up menus to choose one of the preconfigured date, time, and number formats.

**Figure 72**
Choose a long date component from this menu.

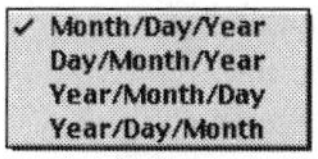

**Figure 73**
Choose a short date format from this pop-up menu.

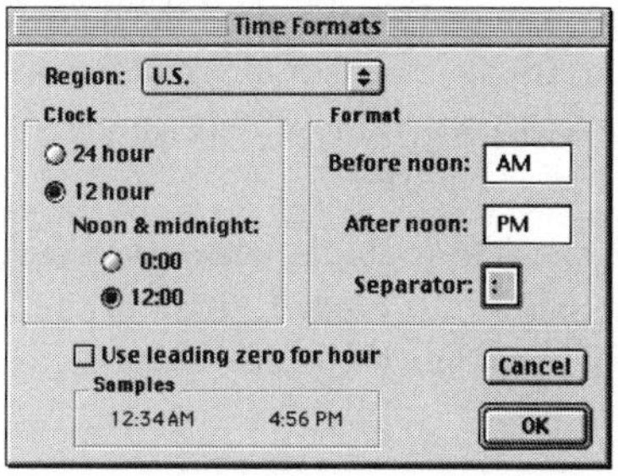

**Figure 74**
The Time Formats dialog box lets you customize the time format.

## To set date & time formats

1. Choose Apple menu > Control Panels > Date & Time (**Figure 3**). The Date & Time control panel window appears (**Figure 67**).

2. To change the date format, click Date Formats. The Date Formats dialog box appears (**Figure 70**).

3. Choose an option from the Region pop-up menu (**Figure 71**).

4. Modify the long date format by choosing options from the Long Date pop-up menus (**Figure 72**) and entering punctuation in the edit boxes. If desired, turn on the Leading zero for day check box.

5. Choose a short date format from the Short Date pop-up menu (**Figure 73**). If desired, change the separator character and turn on check boxes to include a leading zero for the day, a leading zero for the month, and the century as part of the year.

6. Click OK to save your changes.

7. To change the time format, click Time Formats. The Time Format dialog box appears (**Figure 74**).

8. Choose an option from the Region pop-up menu (**Figure 71**).

9. Select radio buttons in the Clock area to set clock preferences.

10. If desired, change the suffixes and separator in the Before noon, After noon, and Separator edit boxes and turn on the Use leading zero for hour check box.

11. Click OK to save your changes.

12. Close the Date & Time window to save your settings.

## ✔ Tip

■ You can check the custom formats you create by looking at the sample area in the Date Formats and Time Format dialog boxes (**Figures 70** and **74**).

## To set time zone options

1. Choose Apple menu > Control Panels > Date & Time (**Figure 3**). The Date & Time control panel window appears (**Figure 67**).

2. Click Set Time Zone. A dialog box like the one in **Figure 75** appears. Select a city in your time zone and click OK.

3. Set check boxes in the Time Zone area:

    ▲ **Set Daylight-Saving Time Automatically** enables your computer to automatically adjusts the clock for daylight saving time twice a year.

    ▲ **Daylight-Saving Time is in effect**, which is only available when the Set Daylight-Saving Time Automatically check box is turned off, enables you to manually specify whether daylight saving time is in effect.

4. Close the window to save your settings.

## To set menu bar clock options

1. Choose Apple menu > Control Panels > Date & Time (**Figure 3**). The Date & Time control panel window appears (**Figure 67**).

2. Select a Menu Bar Clock radio button to display (On) or hide (Off) the menu bar clock.

3. If you choose On, click the Clock Options button to display the Clock Options dialog box (**Figure 76**). Set options as desired, and click OK.

4. Close the window to save your settings.

## ✔ Tips

- The menu bar clock appears near the right end of the menu bar (**Figure 77**).

- If you use another program which also puts a clock in the menu bar, set the Menu Bar Clock option to Off in the Date & Time window (**Figure 67**).

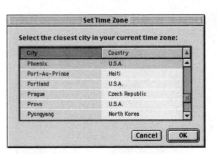

**Figure 75** Use this dialog box to select a city in your time zone.

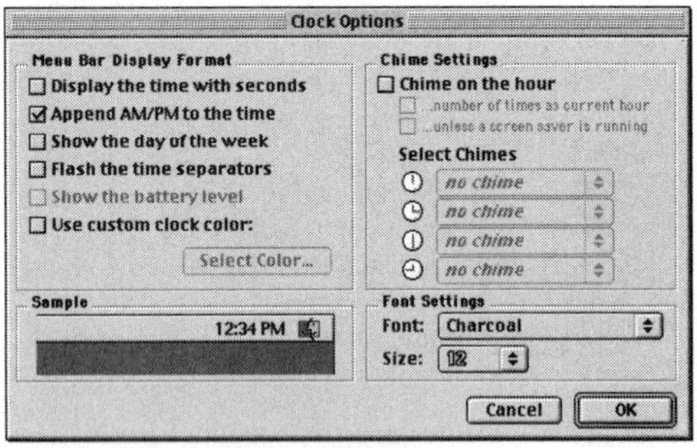

**Figure 76** Use the Clock Options dialog box to configure the menu bar clock.

**11:46 AM** 🖥 **Finder**

**Figure 77** The menu bar clock appears at the far-right end of the menu bar, just to the left of the Application menu.

**Figure 78**
You must turn on the Chime on the hour check box to set Chime Settings options.

- You must turn on the Chime on the hour check box in the Clock Options dialog box (**Figure 76**) to set options in the Chime Settings area (**Figure 78**).

- You can check the Sample area of the Clock Options dialog box (**Figure 76**) to see the results of your changes before saving them.

SETTING TIME ZONE & MENU BAR CLOCK

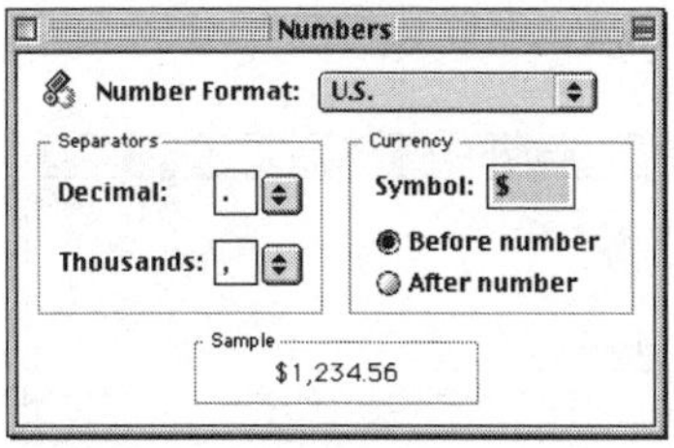

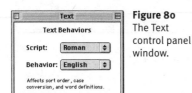

**Figure 79** The Numbers control panel window.

**Figure 80**
The Text
control panel
window.

**Figure 81**
Text behaviors
are based on
languages.

# Numbers & Text

The Numbers control panel enables you to set formatting options for numbers. The Text control panel enables you to set text behaviors for WorldScript and sorting. Both control panels are designed primarily for localization settings.

## To set number formats

1. Choose Apple menu > Control Panels > Numbers (**Figure 3**). The Numbers control panel window appears (**Figure 79**).

2. Choose a region from the Number Format pop-up menu (**Figure 71**).

3. If desired, customize the format by changing the contents of the edit boxes and selecting a different Currency radio button.

4. Close the window to save your settings.

## ✔ Tip

■ You can check a custom number format you create by looking at the sample area in the Numbers control panel (**Figure 79**).

## To set text behavior

1. Choose Apple menu > Control Panels > Text (**Figure 3**). The Text control panel window appears (**Figure 80**).

2. Choose an option from the Behavior pop-up menu (**Figure 81**).

3. Close the window to save your settings.

## ✔ Tip

■ The Script pop-up menu may offer options when WorldScript, a multiple language feature of Mac OS, is installed. WorldScript is not automatically installed with Mac OS 8.6; you must perform a custom installation of the International features to install it. I tell you about installing Mac OS 8.6 in **Chapter 1**.

# Location Manager

The Location Manager control panel (**Figure 82**) enables you to create *locations*—groups of computer settings for a specific place or purpose.

The settings you can include in a location depend on Location Manager modules installed in your computer. The modules that come with Mac OS 8.6 let you include the following settings:

◆ **AppleTalk & TCP/IP** switches between configurations of AppleTalk and TCP/IP (**Chapter 12**).

◆ **Auto-Open Items** are the items to open at startup (**Chapter 13**).

◆ **Default Printer** is the default printer (**Chapter 10**).

◆ **Extension Set** is the name of the Extension Manager set (**Chapter 13**).

◆ **File Sharing State** is the on or off setting for File Sharing (**Chapter 11**).

◆ **Internet Set** is the Internet control panel setting (**Chapter 12**).

◆ **Remote Access** is the Remote Access configuration (**Chapter 10**).

◆ **Sound Level** is the sound out volume in the Monitors & Sound control panel (**Chapter 13**).

◆ **Time Zone** is the time zone setting in the Date & Time control panel (**Chapter 13**).

## To open Location Manager

Choose Apple menu > Control Panels > Location Manager (**Figure 3**). Location Manager's window appears (**Figure 82**).

## ✔ Tip

■ To toggle the display of editing options in the Location Manager control panel window, click the triangle beside Edit Locations (**Figure 82**).

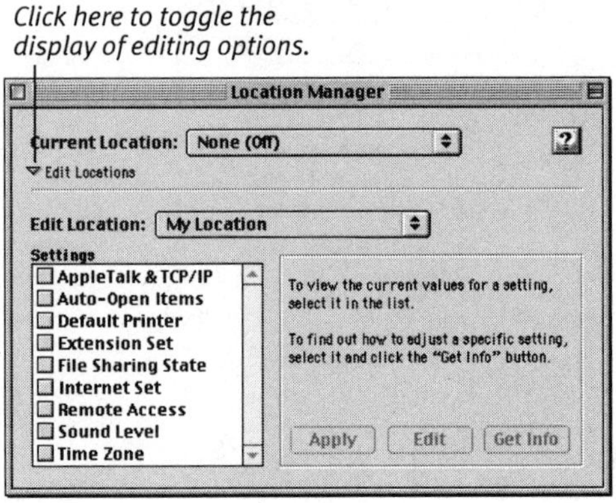

*Click here to toggle the display of editing options.*

**Figure 82** The Location Manager control panel with editing options displayed.

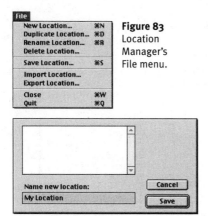

**Figure 83**
Location
Manager's
File menu.

**Figure 84** Enter a name for the new location and click the Save button.

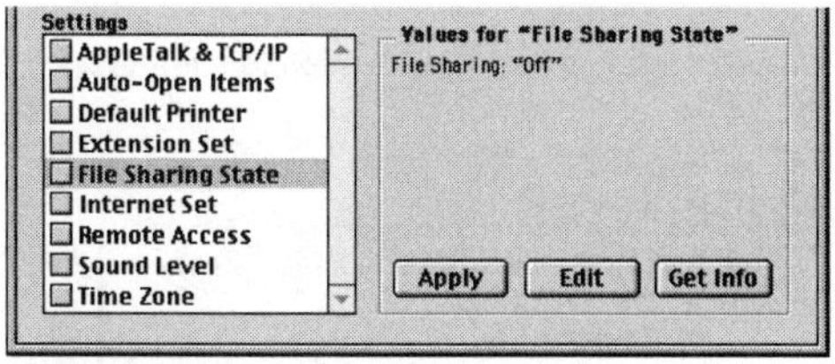

**Figure 85** When you select a setting, its current values appear in the right side of the Location Manager window.

**Figure 86** The Get Info button displays additional information about a setting.

**Figure 87** Follow the instructions in dialog boxes like this one to change settings, then apply changes to the location being edited.

## To create a location

1. Choose File > New Location (**Figure 83**).

2. In the dialog box that appears (**Figure 84**), enter a name for the Location and click the Save button.

   The Location Manager window expands to show editing options for the Location you added (**Figure 82**).

## ✔ Tip

- Commands under the File menu (**Figure 83**) also enable you to Duplicate, Rename, Delete, Import, and Export locations.

## To edit a location

1. If necessary, click the Edit Locations triangle in the Location Manager window to display editing options (**Figure 82**).

2. Choose the location that you want to edit from the Edit Location pop-up menu.

3. Turn on the check boxes beside the settings that you want to include.

4. Choose File > Save Location (**Figure 83**) to save the location's settings.

## ✔ Tips

- To display the value for a setting, click its name to select it. Its value appears on the right side of the window (**Figure 85**).

- To learn more about a setting, click its name to select it, then click the Get Info button. A dialog box with additional information appears (**Figure 86**).

- To edit a setting, click its name to select it, then click the Edit button. Follow the instructions in the dialog box that appears (**Figure 87**).

## To switch to a location

1. In the Location Manager window, choose a location from the Current Location pop-up menu (**Figure 88**).

2. A dialog box like the one in **Figure 89** appears. It indicates the progress of switching from one location to another. When it's finished (**Figure 90**), you can scroll through the comments in the window to review the changes made.

3. Click OK to dismiss the dialog box.

## ✔ Tip

■ If switching to another location requires switching to a different Extensions Manager set, you must restart the computer for the new set of extensions and control panels to load.

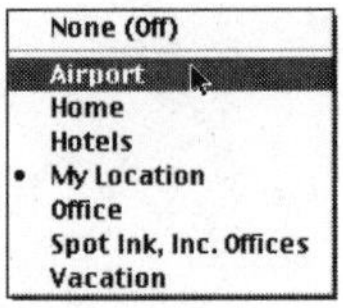

**Figure 88**
Choose a location to switch to from the Current Location pop-up menu.

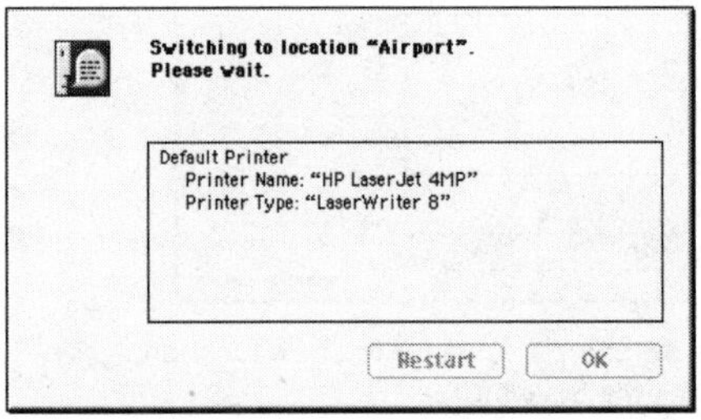

**Figure 89** Location Manager displays this dialog box as it switches from one location to another...

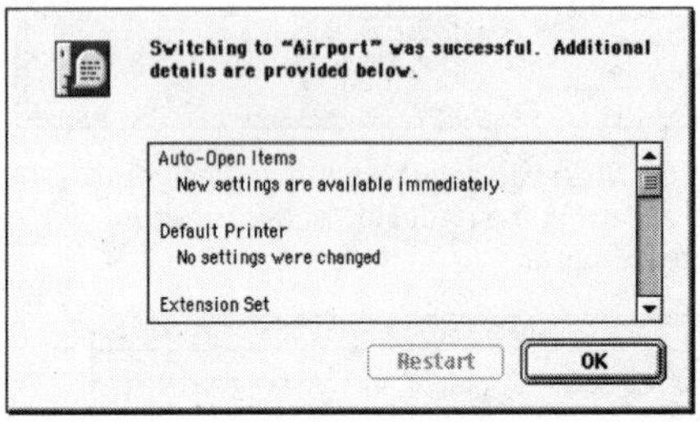

**Figure 90** ...and it tells you when it's finished switching so you can review the changes made.

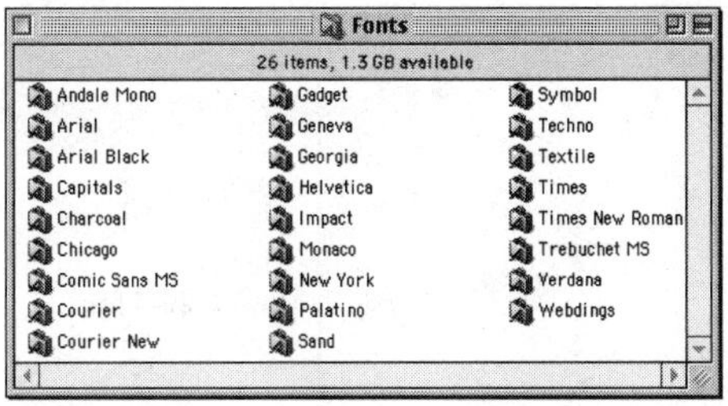

Figure 91 The TrueType fonts that are installed with Mac OS 8.6 can be found in the Fonts folder.

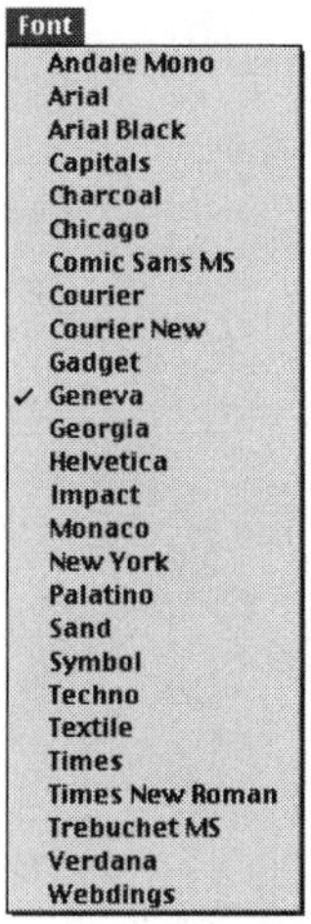

**Figure 92**
SimpleText's Font menu is just one of the menus that lists installed fonts.

**Figure 93**
Fonts can come in suitcases or as individual font files.

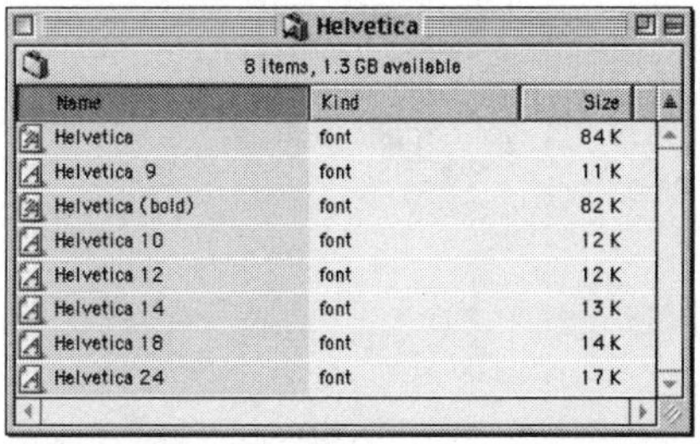

Figure 94 This suitcase contains both TrueType and bitmapped fonts.

# Fonts

*Fonts* are typefaces that appear on screen and in printed documents. When properly installed in the Fonts folder inside the System Folder (**Figure 91**), they appear on all Font menus (**Figure 92**).

There are three kinds of fonts:

◆ *TrueType fonts* are scalable fonts that appear clear on screen and in print, no matter what size or printer you use. They come in suitcase files (**Figure 91**).

◆ *Bitmapped fonts* are single-size fonts that appear clear on screen only when used in the correct size. They also come in suitcase files (**Figures 93** and **94**).

◆ *PostScript fonts* are scalable fonts that appear clear in print when printed on a PostScript printer, no matter what size you use. With the help of a utility called Adobe Type Manager (ATM), PostScript fonts can also appear clear on screen and in print no matter what size or printer they use. They come in individual font files but must be accompanied by a corresponding bitmapped font (**Figure 93**) to appear on Font menus.

## ✔ Tips

■ You can open a suitcase file to view the fonts inside it (**Figure 94**). Bitmapped fonts names include numbers.

■ You can open a font file within a suitcase to see a sample of the font's characters (**Figures 95** and **96**). Bitmapped fonts display only one size while TrueType fonts display three sample sizes.

■ If you're interested in learning more about fonts than what's on these two pages, check out these two Peachpit Press books: *How to Boss Your Fonts Around, Second Edition* and *The Macintosh Font Book, Third Edition.*

**FONTS**

## To install a font

1. Drag all suitcases and files that are part of the font onto the System Folder icon. When the System Folder becomes highlighted (**Figure 97**), release the mouse button.

2. A dialog box like the one in **Figure 98** appears to inform you that fonts must be stored in the Fonts folder. Click OK.

## ✔ Tips

- You can see a freshly installed font in the Font menu of an application like Simple-Text (**Figure 99**) or your favorite word processor. You can also view the characters in any installed font using Key Caps, which I discuss in **Chapter 7**.

- If an application is running when you install a font, you'll have to quit the application and restart it to see the font in that application's Font menu.

## To uninstall a font

1. Quit all applications.

2. Drag all suitcases and files that are part of the font out of the Fonts folder in the System Folder.

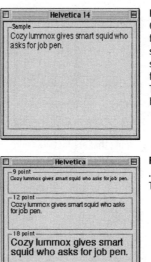

**Figure 95**
Open one of the font files inside a suitcase to see a sample of the font's characters. This is a bitmapped font...

**Figure 96**
...and this is a TrueType font.

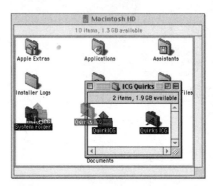

**Figure 97** Drag all of the font's files onto the System Folder icon.

These items need to be stored in the Fonts folder in order to be available to the computer. Put these items into the Fonts folder?

Cancel     OK

**Figure 98** Click OK when this dialog box appears.

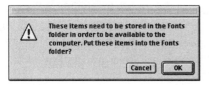

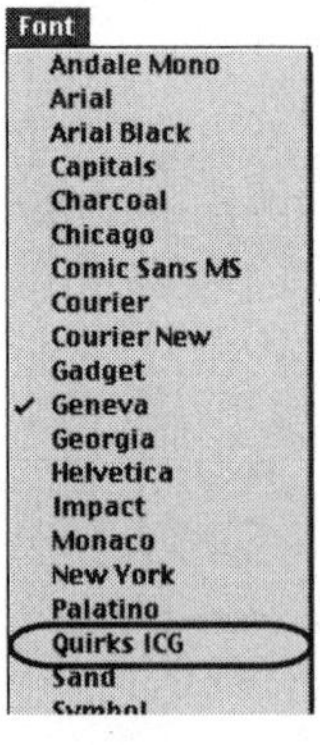

**Figure 99**
The font you installed appears on the Font menus of your applications.

# Startup & Shutdown Items

The System Folder includes two folders you can use to automatically open items:

◆ **Startup Items** automatically open right after your computer starts up.

◆ **Shutdown Items** automatically open just before your computer shuts down.

## ✔ Tips

■ Need some ideas for using the Startup Items and Shutdown Items folders? Try these:

▲ Put an alias of your calendar or to-do list document in the Startup Items folder so your calendar or to-do list opens when you're ready to get to work.

▲ Put a sound file in the Startup Items folder so your computer can greet you with a recorded sound.

▲ Put an alias of your backup application in the Shutdown Items folder so you're automatically given an opportunity to back up your work before quitting for the day.

■ It's a good idea to use aliases instead of original items in the Startup Items and Shutdown Items folder. This helps keep originals where they're easy to find and back up. I tell you about aliases in **Chapter 4**.

## To set an item to automatically open at start up or shut down

Drag the item (or an alias of the item) into the Startup Items or Shutdown Items folder inside your System Folder.

# GETTING HELP & TROUBLESHOOTING 14

**Figure 1** The Finder's Help menu.

## Getting Help

Mac OS offers several ways to get additional information and answers to questions while you work with your computer:

- ◆ **Balloon Help** identifies screen items as you point to them.

- ◆ **Help Center** provides information about using installed Mac OS components, such as Mac OS and AppleScript.

- ◆ **Mac OS Help** provides information about using Mac OS.

- ◆ **Guide help** provides information about using specific applications.

- ◆ **Application online help**, which is included in many third-party applications, provides information about the application.

All of these help features can be accessed using commands on the Help menu (**Figure 1**). In this chapter, I tell you how to get help when you need it.

# Balloon Help

Balloon Help identifies screen elements that you point to by providing information in cartoon balloon-shaped windows (**Figures 2**, **3**, and **4**).

## ✔ Tips

■ Although Balloon Help might be too annoying to keep turned on all the time, you might find it useful when first starting out with Mac OS 8.6 or a new software application.

■ Balloon Help works in the Finder, all applications and utilities that come with Mac OS 8.6, and many third-party applications.

## To turn on Balloon Help

Choose Help > Show Balloons (**Figure 1**).

## To use Balloon Help

Point to an item for which you want more information. A balloon appears with information about the item (**Figures 2**, **3**, and **4**).

## To turn off Balloon Help

Choose Help > Hide Balloons (**Figure 5**).

**Figure 2** Balloon Help displays a cartoon balloon with information about items you point to.

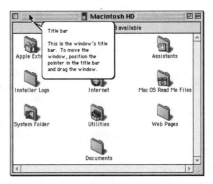

**Figure 3** With Balloon Help turned on, you can learn about almost anything on your screen, including window parts...

**Figure 4** ...and menu commands.

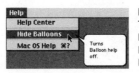

**Figure 5**
To turn off Balloon Help, choose Hide Balloons from the Help menu.

**Figure 6** The Help Center is a centralized starting point for getting help about Mac OS components.

**Figure 7** The Mac OS Help main window.

# The Help Center & Mac OS Help

The Help Center (**Figure 6**) offers access to information about Mac OS components installed on your computer. Mac OS Help (**Figure 7**) offers information and step-by-step instructions for using Mac OS. Both of these help features are displayed using Apple's Help Viewer application, so they work similarly.

You can use these features in two ways:

◆ Click blue underlined links to browse help topics and learn more about a topic that interests you.

◆ Search for a specific word or phrase to display a list of topics that discuss that word or phrase. Then click blue underlined links to learn more about the topic that interests you.

## To open the Help Center

Choose Help > Help Center (**Figure 1**). The Help Center window appears (**Figure 6**).

## To open Mac OS Help

Choose Help > Mac OS Help (**Figure 1**), or press ⌃ ⌘ ?.

*or*

Click the Mac OS Help link in the Help Center window (**Figure 6**).

The Mac OS Help main window appears (**Figure 7**).

OPENING & BROWSING THE HELP CENTER

## To browse Mac OS Help topics

1. On the left side of the Mac OS Help window (**Figure 7**), click an underlined topic link.

2. On the right side of the Mac OS Help window, click an underlined topic link (**Figure 8**).

3. Information about the topic appears in a window (**Figure 9**). Read the window's contents to learn more about the subtopic.

## ✔ Tips

■ When viewing information about a topic, you can click underlined links to learn about related topics.

■ You can use the navigation buttons at the top of the Mac OS Help window to view windows you have already seen:

  ▲ **Back** displays the previous window.

  ▲ **Forward** displays the next window.

  ▲ **Home** displays the Help Center window.

## To search Mac OS Help topics

1. Enter a search word or phrase in the edit box at the top of the Mac OS Help window (**Figure 10**).

2. Click Search.

3. After a moment, the Mac OS Help window fills with a list of search results (**Figure 11**). Click an underlined link to display information about the topic in a window (**Figure 9**).

## ✔ Tips

■ The asterisks to the left of a topic name in the Search Results list indicate how well the topic matches your search criteria.

■ You can search for help from the Help Center Window, too. Just follow these instructions in that window.

**Figure 8** Clicking the Memory link on the left side of the window displays memory topics on the right.

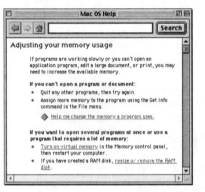

**Figure 9** Clicking a topic in the right side of the window displays a window full of information about the topic.

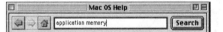

**Figure 10** Enter a search word or phrase in the edit box at the top of the window.

**Figure 11** Search results appear in a window like this.

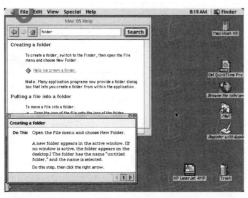

**Figure 12** The first step for creating a folder tells you to choose New Folder from the File menu, which is circled in red.

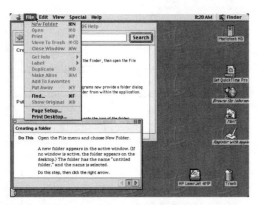

**Figure 13** The New Folder command appears in red and underlined.

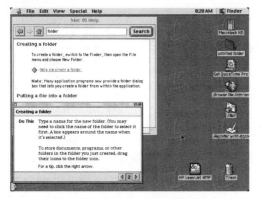

**Figure 14** The second step tells you to rename the folder you created and drag files into it.

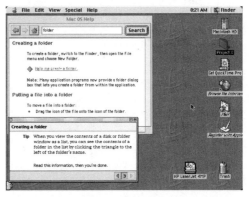

**Figure 15** The last step explains how you can see the contents of a folder in list view.

## To follow step-by-step instructions

1. In a topic's information window (**Figure 9**), click a link beginning with the words *Help me*.

   A window with instructions appears. Red circles or lines may also be drawn on screen to help you locate items referenced in the instructions. You can see all this in **Figure 12**.

2. Follow the instructions that appear in the window and click the right-pointing triangle at the bottom of the window to advance to the next step. **Figures 12** through **15** show the three steps for creating a folder.

3. Repeat step 2 until the task has been completed.

## ✔ Tip

■ Step-by-step instructions are created using Apple Guide technology.

# Guide Help

Apple Guide technology forms the basis for help within specific applications, including most applications and utilities that come with Mac OS 8.6. Opening an application's Guide Help offers information and step-by-step instructions similar to what's available in Mac OS Help but for a specific application.

## ✔ Tip

- I tell you all about Mac OS Help on the previous few pages.

## To open Guide Help for an application

Choose Help > *Application* Guide (**Figures 16a** and **16c**) or Help > *Application* Help (**Figure 16b**). The program's Guide Help window appears (**Figures 17a**, **17b**, and **17c**).

## ✔ Tips

- As shown in **Figures 16a**, **16b**, and **16c**, the exact name of the command to open Apple Guide depends on the application name.

- Most Guide Help windows enable you to browse topics, browse an index, or search for specific information. If a Guide Help window does not include Topics and Index buttons (**Figure 17c**), you can browse only the displayed help phrases.

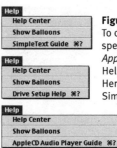

**Figures 16a, 16b, & 16c**
To open Guide Help for a specific application, choose *Application* Guide or *Application* Help from the Help menu. Here are the Help menus for SimpleText (top), Drive Setup (middle), and AppleCD Audio Player (bottom).

**Figures 17a, 17b, & 17c**
Here are the corresponding Guide Help windows: SimpleText Guide (top), Drive Setup Help (middle), and AppleCD Audio Player Guide (bottom).

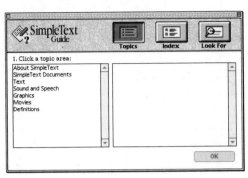

**Figure 18** When you click the Topics button, a list of topics appears on the left side of the window.

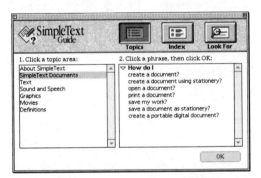

**Figure 19** When you click a topic, a list of help phrases appears in the right side of the window.

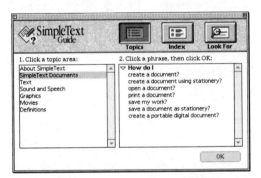

**Figure 20** Click a help phrase and click OK to display information about the phrase.

## To browse Guide Help topics

1. Click the Topics button in the Guide Help window (**Figures 17a** and **17b**).

2. In the list of topics that appears on the left side of the window (**Figure 18**), click the topic that interests you.

3. In the list of help phrases that appears in the right side of the window (**Figure 19**), click the phrase for the explanation you're looking for.

4. Click OK.

5. Read the explanation or follow the instructions in the window that appears (**Figure 20**).

6. If necessary, click the right-pointing triangle to advance through the help windows.

7. When you're finished reading help information, click the window's close box to dismiss it.

**BROWSING GUIDE HELP TOPICS**

## To browse the Guide Help index

1. Click the Index button in the Guide Help window (**Figures 17a** and **17b**).

2. On the alphabetical index bar that appears (**Figure 21**), click the letter for the term that interests you.

3. In the list of terms that appears in the right side of the window (**Figure 22**), click the term that interests you.

4. In the list of help phrases that appears in the right side of the window (**Figure 23**), click the phrase for the explanation you're looking for.

5. Click OK.

6. Read the explanation or follow the instructions in the window that appears (**Figure 24**).

7. If necessary, click the right-pointing triangle to advance through the help windows.

8. When you're finished reading help information, click the window's close box to dismiss it.

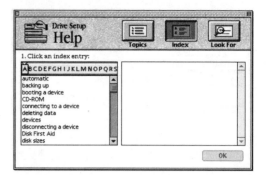

**Figure 21** When you click the Index button, an alphabetical index bar and term list appear.

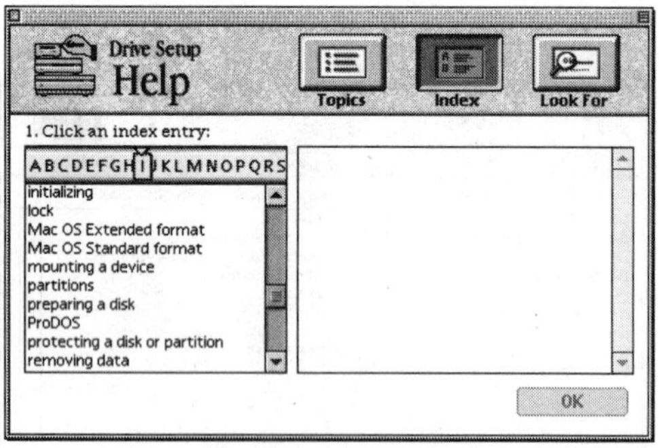

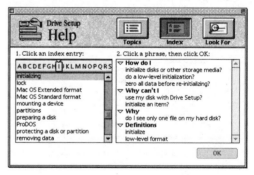

**Figure 22** Click a letter to display terms beginning with that letter.

**Figure 23** Click a term to display a list of phrases.

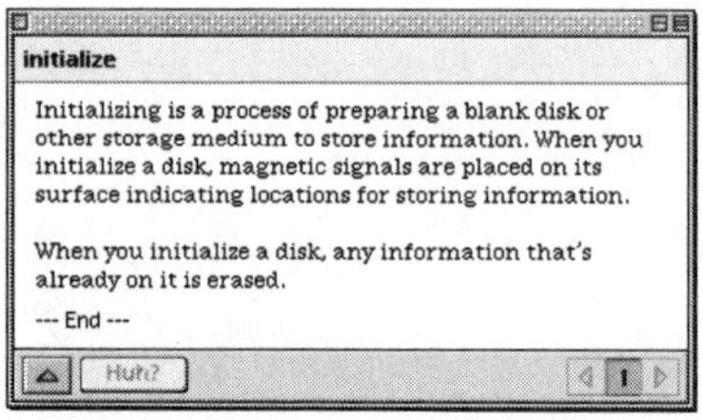

**Figure 24** Click a phrase and click OK to display information.

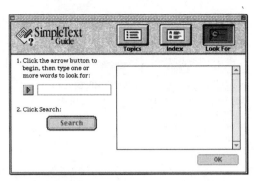

**Figure 25** When you click the Look For button, a search form appears.

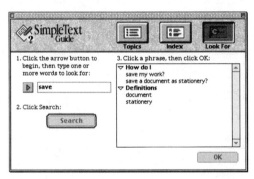

**Figure 26** Enter a search word or phrase in the edit box and click Search to display a list of help phrases.

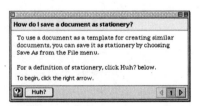

**Figure 27** Click a phrase and click OK to display information.

## To search Guide Help

1. Click the Look For button in the Guide Help window (**Figures 17a** and **17b**).

2. Click the right pointing triangle on the left side of the dialog box (**Figure 25**).

3. Enter a search word or phrase in the edit box beside the triangle.

4. Click Search.

5. In the list of help phrases that appears in the right side of the window (**Figure 26**), click the phrase for the explanation you're looking for.

6. Click OK.

7. Read the explanation or follow the instructions in the window that appears (**Figure 27**).

8. If necessary, click the right-pointing triangle to advance through the help windows.

9. When you're finished reading help information, click the window's close box to dismiss it.

# Application Help

Many applications include extensive online help. The help features of various applications look and work differently, so I can't cover them in detail here. I can, however, tell you how to access help in other applications and assure you that most online help features are easy to use.

**Figures 28a & 28b**
The Help menus for FileMaker Pro 4.1 (left) and Microsoft Word 98 (right) offer a variety of online help options.

## ✔ Tips

- Some applications, like the Microsoft Office suite of products, include an entire online manual that is searchable and printable.

- Not all applications include online help. If you can't locate an online help feature for an application, check the documentation that came with the application to see if it has one and how you can access it.

## To access an application's online help

Choose a command from the Help menu within that application (**Figures 28a** and **28b**).

*or*

Click a Help button within a dialog box.

# Troubleshooting

Occasionally, you might experience problems using your Mac. Here are some examples:

◆ An error message appears on screen when you attempt to perform a task.

◆ An application "unexpectedly quits" while you are using it.

◆ An application simply won't work correctly.

◆ You can't open a certain file.

◆ Your computer "freezes" or "locks up"— either at startup or while working with an application— making it impossible to move the mouse pointer, quit an application, or even properly restart the computer.

These are examples of problems you might experience. Although these problems may be caused by any number of things, there are some techniques you can use to narrow down the cause and fix the problem. That's what troubleshooting is all about.

This part of the chapter will provide some basic troubleshooting information you can use to diagnose and solve many problems on your Macintosh.

## ✔ Tip

■ Although the information in this section can solve many problems, it can't solve all of them. For a thorough guide to troubleshooting Macintosh hardware and software problems, check out *Sad Macs, Bombs, and Other Disasters, Third Edition*, a Peachpit Press book by Ted Landau.

■ For more troubleshooting information, including late-breaking information about specific compatibility problems, visit these Web sites:

▲ **MacFixIt** http://www.macfixit.com/

▲ **MacInTouch**
http://www.macintouch.com/

## The First Nine

I used to teach a two-day Macintosh trouble-shooting course written by John Bradley. The first thing the course covered was what John called "The First Six"—the first six things you should try when you encounter problems on your Macintosh. I added three things to the list. Here are all nine of these techniques, in the order I suggest trying them:

◆ **Restart.** This can solve RAM-related problems.

◆ **Rebuild the Desktop.** This can solve orphan document problems.

◆ **Restart with extensions disabled.** This can identify conflict problems.

◆ **Trash application preferences.** This can solve problems that occur when an application's preferences file is corrupted.

◆ **Zap the PRAM.** This can solve missing hardware or network device problems.

◆ **Use diagnostic software.** This can identify and repair disk-related problems.

◆ **Reinstall the Application.** This can solve problems related to corrupted application files.

◆ **Reinstall the system software.** This can solve problems related to corrupted system software. Be sure to do a clean installation!

◆ **Upgrade software or hardware.** This can solve problems related to incompatibilities between an application and the installed system software or your computer itself.

I've found that one or more of these nine techniques will solve 90 percent of the problems you encounter with your Macintosh.

## ✔ Tip

■ The rest of this chapter provides further explanations for these problems and techniques.

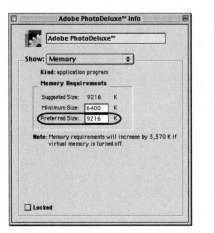

**Figure 29** Sometimes you can solve memory errors that occur with a specific application by changing the Preferred Size in the Memory area of the Info window for the application. The inclusion of a Note in this window identifies this application as PowerPC-native.

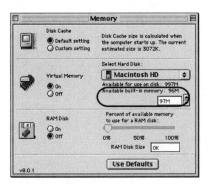

**Figure 30** In this illustration of the Memory control panel, Virtual Memory is properly set for best performance with most PowerPC-native applications: Virtual Memory is set to 97 M, which is 1 M more than the Available built-in memory of 96 M.

# Memory Problems

Some problems, including "Not Enough Memory" and "Application has Unexpectedly Quit" error messages, are caused by memory problems. Here are some possible causes:

◆ Your Macintosh may not have enough memory to run an application. Check the system requirements to make sure your computer meets them. If you don't have enough RAM, consider upgrading or using virtual memory. (I tell you about virtual memory in **Chapter 13**.)

◆ Your computer's RAM may be *fragmented*— a situation that occurs when you launch and quit many applications during a work session. Restarting your computer clears out RAM and solves this problem.

◆ The application may require more RAM than what is set in its current memory settings. This happens sometimes when you attempt to open very large or complex documents. Try increasing the value in the Preferred Size edit box of the Info window (**Figure 29**). I explain how in **Chapter 5**.

## ✔ Tips

■ The term *memory* almost always refers to RAM (Random Access Memory)—*not* hard disk space. I tell you more about RAM in **Chapters 5** and **13**.

■ In general, you can get good performance and minimize the amount of RAM used by *PowerPC-native* applications—those written specifically to take advantage of a Power Macintosh's PowerPC processor—by turning on virtual memory and setting it to 1 M more than installed memory. You do this in the Memory control panel (**Figure 30**), which I cover in **Chapter 13**. You can identify a PowerPC-native application by whether a Note appears in the Memory area of its Info window (**Figure 29**).

## Disk & File Corruption Problems

Some problems, including system "freezes" and files that won't open, may be caused by disk or file corruption:

◆ All kinds of problems can be caused by disk corruption. This can occur when the computer is improperly shut down—especially if the computer was writing a file to disk when the shutdown occurred. Although you can avoid this by always using the Shut Down command to shut off your Macintosh, it's tougher to prevent improper shutdowns due to power outages. Use a program like Disk First Aid (discussed in **Chapter 8**) or Symantec's Norton Utilities for Macintosh to diagnose and repair disk corruption problems.

◆ Problems with a specific application can be caused by corrupted application or prefer-ences files. Try trashing the preferences files for the application first. If the problem doesn't go away, try reinstalling the appli-cation from original installation disks.

◆ Problems with many applications can be caused by corrupted system software. Try trashing the Finder Preferences file and restarting. If that doesn't work, try doing a clean installation of the system software as discussed in **Chapter 1**.

◆ If double-clicking a document icon won't open the document with the correct application when the application is proper-ly installed on disk the disk's invisible Desktop files may be corrupted. To rebuild the Desktop for your internal hard disk, hold down ⌃ ⌘ Option while restarting the computer. Keep those keys held down until a dialog box like the one in **Figure 31** appears. Click OK, and wait while the Desktop is rebuilt.

◆ An "Error 39" or "Error 43" message when opening a file indicates that the file is corrupted. You'd better have a backup copy!

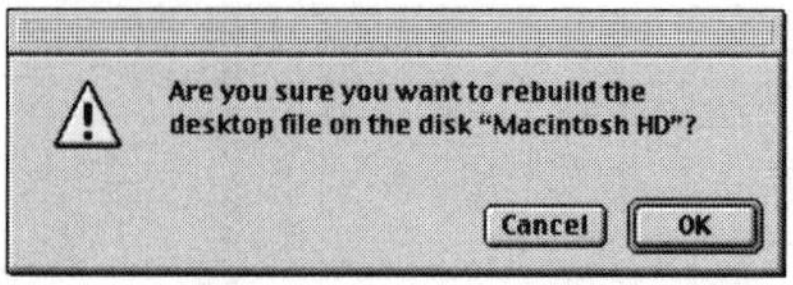

**Figure 31** This dialog box appears when you hold down ⌃ ⌘ Option while starting up or inserting a disk.

## ✔ Tips

■ You can usually find preferences files in the Preferences folder inside your System Folder.

■ You can rebuild the Desktop on removable media by holding down ⌃ ⌘ Option while inserting the disk.

## Conflict Problems

Conflicts between two or more installed software products or software and hardware can prevent your computer or certain applications from running properly.

◆ If, after installing new software, problems start occurring, chances are the new software conflicts with the system software or some other software in your computer. Remove the new software to see if the problem goes away.

◆ "Init" conflicts are caused by items installed in your Extensions or Control Panels folder conflicting with other software. These conflicts can cause all kinds of problems with your system and applications. You can test for these conflicts by restarting your Macintosh with Shift held down, thus disabling all extensions and control panels (as well as certain other System Folder items). If the problem goes away with extensions and control panels disabled, one of your extensions or control panels is causing the problem.

◆ If an application simply won't run on your Macintosh, it may not be compatible with your computer or Mac OS 8.6.

◆ If you believe a software product conflicts with other software or Mac OS 8.6, check with the software developer to learn about updates. *Always* obtain and install free updates to software products when they are available—you can find them on a software developer's Web site. If an upgrade requires a fee, be sure you understand what the revised software can do for you. Then decide whether the improvements are worth the upgrade fee.

## Hardware Problems

Hardware problems—such as severely damaged disks and bad computer components—can be a real nightmare because things may not work at all.

◆ If certain peripheral devices don't work properly and you're sure that all device drivers are properly installed, begin by shutting down the computer and checking all cable connections. Then restart. If that doesn't work, zap the PRAM (parameter RAM) by pressing ⌃ ⌘ Option P R while restarting the computer. Release the keys after the startup tone has sounded twice.

◆ A question mark icon at startup means your Mac can't find a bootable disk. This could be caused by a severely damaged or "crashed" hard disk or corrupted system files. Restart the computer from an emergency disk (a Disk Tools floppy or the system software CD-ROM disc). If you can see your hard disk icon on the Desktop, breathe a sigh of relief—it hasn't crashed. Use Disk First Aid to diagnose and repair any problems; if that doesn't solve the problem, reinstall the system software, doing a clean installation as discussed in **Chapter 1**.

◆ If you can't see your hard disk icon on the desktop, try using Drive Setup to update the disk's driver. Restart to see if the disk reappears. If the hard disk icon does not appear, even after trying all of the techniques listed in The First Nine on page 292, you should probably bring the computer to your local Apple dealer for servicing.

## ✔ Tip

■ Zapping the PRAM clears out parameter RAM, forcing your computer to check all connected devices. You may have to reset certain monitor and network settings after zapping the PRAM.

# Help & Troubleshooting Advice

Here's some additional advice for getting help with and troubleshooting problems.

◆ **Join a Macintosh user group.** Joining a user group and attending meetings is probably the most cost-effective way to learn about your computer and get help. You can find a users' group near you by consulting the User Group page at Apple's Web site (http://www.apple.com/usergroups/) or calling 1-800-SOS-APPL.

◆ **Visit Apple's Web site.** If you have access to the Web, you can find a wealth of information about your computer right online. Start at http://www.apple.com/ and follow links or search for the information you need.

◆ **Visit the Web sites for the companies that develop the applications you use most.** A regular visit to these sites can keep you up to date on updates and upgrades to keep your software running smoothly. These sites can also provide technical support for problems you encounter while using the software. Learn the URLs for these sites by consulting the documentation that came with the software.

◆ **Read Macintosh magazines.** A number of magazines, each geared toward a different level of user, can help you learn about your computer: *Macworld*, *Mac Addict*, *Mac Today*, and *Mac Home Journal* are the most popular. Stay away from PC-centric magazines; the majority of the information they provide will not apply to your Macintosh and may confuse you.

◆ **Check out *Macintosh Tips & Tricks*.** This freely distributable newsletter from Giles Road Press is available on the Web at http://www.gilesrd.com/.

# MENUS & KEYBOARD COMMANDS

## Menus & Keyboard Commands

This appendix illustrates all of the Mac OS 8.6 Finder's menus—both Simple Finder (left) and standard Finder (right)—and provides a list of keyboard commands you can use with the Mac OS 8.6 Finder.

To use a keyboard command, hold down the modifier key (usually ⌘), while pressing the keyboard key for the command. The only keyboard command that works when Simple Finder is turned on is ⌘? (Help).

I tell you all about using menus and keyboard commands in **Chapter 2**.

## File Menu

| | |
|---|---|
| ⌘N | New Folder |
| ⌘O | Open |
| ⌘P | Print |
| ⌘Del | Move to Trash |
| ⌘W | Close Window |
| ⌘ Option W | Close All Windows |
| ⌘I | Get Info (General Information) |
| ⌘D | Duplicate |
| ⌘M | Make Alias |
| ⌘Y | Put Away |
| ⌘F | Find |
| ⌘R | Show Original |

### File (Simple Finder)
- New Folder
- Open
- Close Window
- Duplicate
- Find...

### File (standard)
- New Folder ⌘N
- Open ⌘O
- Print ⌘P
- Move To Trash ⌘⌫
- Close Window ⌘W
- Get Info ▶
  - General Information ⌘I
  - Sharing...
  - Memory
- Label ▶
- Duplicate ⌘D
- Make Alias ⌘M
- Add To Favorites
- Put Away ⌘Y
- Find... ⌘F
- Show Original ⌘R
- Page Setup...
- Print Window...

### File (with Label submenu)
- New Folder ⌘N
- Open ⌘O
- Print ⌘P
- Move To Trash ⌘⌫
- Close Window ⌘W
- Get Info ▶
- Label ▶
  - ✓ None
  - Essential
  - Hot
  - In Progress
  - Cool
  - Personal
  - Project 1
  - Project 2
- Duplicate ⌘D
- Make Alias ⌘M
- Add To Favorites
- Put Away ⌘Y
- Find... ⌘F
- Show Original ⌘R
- Page Setup...
- Print Window...

## Edit Menu

| | |
|---|---|
| ⌘ Z | Undo |
| ⌘ X | Cut |
| ⌘ C | Copy |
| ⌘ V | Paste |
| ⌘ A | Select All |

## View Menu

(no command keys)

## Special Menu

| | |
|---|---|
| ⌘ E | Eject |

## Help Menu

| | |
|---|---|
| ⌘ ? | Help |

## Other Command Keys

| | |
|---|---|
| ⌘ Shift 1 | Eject floppy disk |
| ⌘ Shift 3 | Create picture of screen |
| ⌘ Shift 4 | Create picture of selection |

# PowerBook Considerations

## PowerBook Considerations

There are a number of differences between the components of Mac OS 8.6 installed on a desktop Mac and the components installed on a PowerBook. These differences fall into three categories:

◆ **Minor Differences.** Some software that is installed on all computers may offer different options on PowerBooks. The AppleTalk, Modem, and Monitors & Sound control panels offer either more or fewer options when installed on a PowerBook.

◆ **Major Differences.** Some software that is installed on all computers will offer completely different options on PowerBooks. The Energy Saver control panel is a good example.

◆ **Additional Software.** Some software is installed on PowerBooks only. This includes the File Synchronization, Password Security, PowerBook SCSI Disk Mode, and Trackpad control panels.

In this appendix, I cover all of these differences and explain how you can use PowerBook-specific software.

## ✔ Tip

■ Mac OS 8.6 components installed on a PowerBook also vary depending on the features supported by the PowerBook model. For example, a PowerBook without an internal modem will not display options for an internal modem in the Modem control panel. The Mac OS 8.6 installer is smart enough to know what software your PowerBook supports, so it installs only the software and options you need. I discuss the Mac OS 8.6 installer in **Chapter 1**.

# Minor Software Differences

In some instances, the software installed on your PowerBook may offer more or fewer options than the same software installed on a desktop Mac. Here's a quick summary of the differences you can expect to encounter.

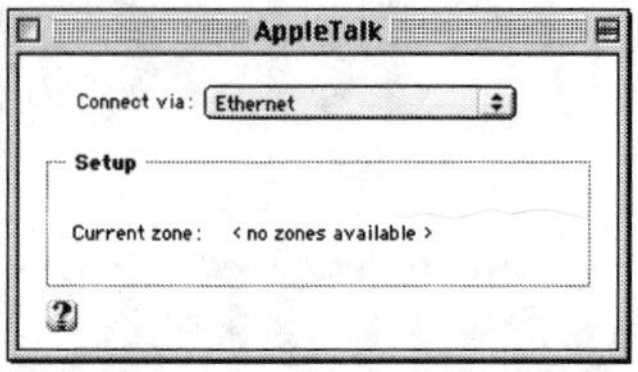

## AppleTalk

The AppleTalk control panel (**Figure 1**) offers different options under its Connect via pop-up menu (**Figure 2**):

◆ **Modem/Printer Port** refers to the single serial port on most PowerBook models. Use this for networking with LocalTalk connectors.

◆ **Infrared Port** is supported by many PowerBook models (and some desktop models) for networking or exchanging files via infrared communication.

I discuss the AppleTalk control panel in **Chapter 11** and Infrared communications in **Chapter 13**.

## Modem

The Modem control panel (**Figure 3**) offers different options under its Connect via pop-up menu (**Figure 4**):

◆ **Internal modem** is the PowerBook internal modem installed on many PowerBook models. With this option selected, you simply connect a phone cable to the phone jack on the back of your PowerBook to use its modem.

◆ **Modem/Printer Port** refers to the single serial port on most PowerBook models. Use this for connecting an external modem.

I discuss the Modem control panel in **Chapter 11**.

**Figure 1** The AppleTalk control panel on a PowerBook 3400c...

**Figure 2** ...offers different Connect via options than what's found on a desktop Mac.

**Figure 3** The Modem control panel on a PowerBook 3400c...

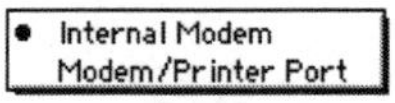

**Figure 4** ...also offers different connect via options than what's found on a desktop Mac.

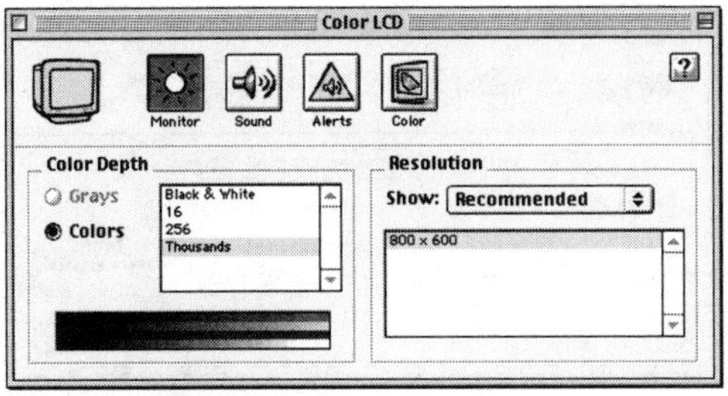

**Figure 5** The Monitor options in the Monitors & Sound control panel on a PowerBook 3400c.

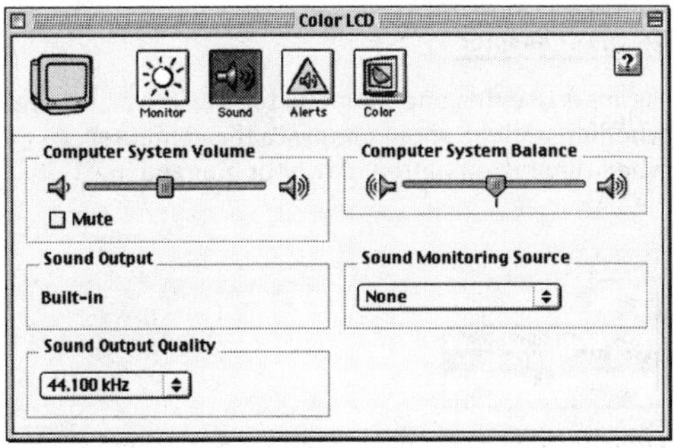

**Figure 6** The Sound options in the Monitors & Sound control panel on a PowerBook 3400c.

## Monitors & Sound

The Monitors & Sound control panel (**Figures 5 and 6**) offers different options:

◆ **Monitor** options (**Figure 5**) are limited based on the capabilities of the LCD monitor on your PowerBook.

◆ **Sound** options (**Figure 6**) may vary depending on the sound features built into the PowerBook model.

I discuss the Monitors & Sound control panel in **Chapter 13**.

## ✔ Tip

■ Additional Monitor options and Sound options may become available when you connect your PowerBook to an external monitor, projection device, or sound system, depending on the features of the device or system.

MONITORS & SOUND CONTROL PANEL

# Energy Saver

The Energy Saver control panel (**Figures 7, 10, 11,** and **12**) offers many different options when installed on a PowerBook. The reason: Power consumption is a major concern of PowerBook users who often depend on batteries for power.

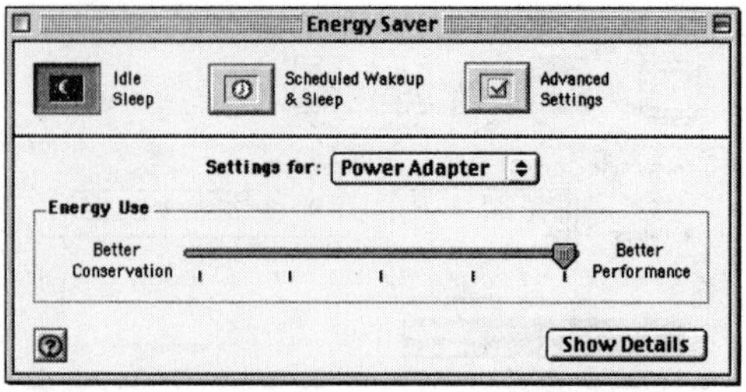

## ✔ Tips

- The PowerBook version of the Energy Saver control panel replaces the PowerBook control panel in versions of Mac OS prior to 8.5.

- The Energy Saver control panel maintains two settings: one for when the PowerBook is plugged in and one for when it isn't. These are referred to as the Power Adapter and Battery settings (**Figure 8**).

- To return Energy Saver settings to default values, choose Return to Defaults from its File menu (**Figure 9**).

- I discuss the Energy Saver control panel in **Chapter 13**.

## To set general energy use options

1. Choose Apple menu > Control Panels > Energy Saver.

2. If necessary, click the Idle Sleep button and the Hide Details button in the Energy Saver control panel that appears so the control panel window looks like the one in **Figure 7**.

3. Choose an option from the Settings for pop-up menu (**Figure 8**) to specify which setting should be modified.

4. Drag the slider in the Energy Use area to a desired position between Better Conservation (less power consumption) or Better Performance (more power consumption).

5. Close the control panel window to save your settings.

**Figure 7** Basic Idle Sleep options in the Energy Saver control panel on a PowerBook.

**Figure 8** Use this pop-up menu to specify whether settings should apply to the computer when running on battery power or plugged in.

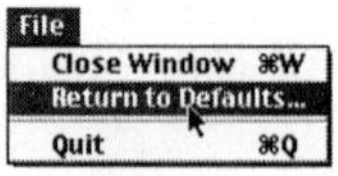

**Figure 9** To restore Energy Saver control panel settings to default values, choose Return to Defaults from the File menu.

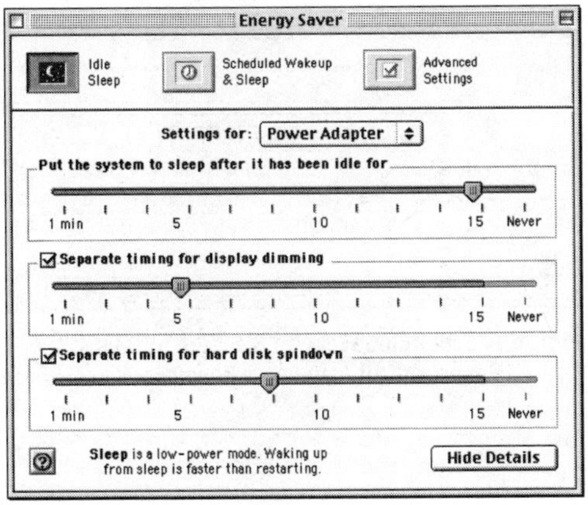

**Figure 10** Detailed Idle Sleep options in the Energy Saver control panel on a PowerBook.

## To set specific energy use options

1.  Choose Apple menu > Control Panels > Energy Saver.

2.  If necessary, click the Idle Sleep button and the Show Details button in the Energy Saver control panel that appears so the control panel window looks like the one in **Figure 10**.

3.  Choose an option from the Settings for pop-up menu (**Figure 8**) to specify which setting should be modified.

4.  To set system sleep timing, drag the top slider to the number of minutes of idle time before the computer goes into sleep mode.

5.  To set display dimming timing, turn on the Separate timing for display dimming check box and drag its slider to the number of minutes of idle time before the screen dims.

6.  To set hard disk spindown timing, turn on the Separate timing for hard disk spindown check box and drag its slider to the number of minutes of idle time before the hard disk stops spinning.

7.  Close the control panel to save your settings.

## ✔ Tips

■   The second two sliders can never be dragged past the rightmost position of the top slider.

■   If you use your PowerBook for presentations, set the first two sliders to Never. Otherwise, your presentation could go blank while you're giving a lengthy explanation of a slide.

SETTING DETAILED ENERGY USE OPTIONS

## To set scheduled wakeup & sleep options

1. Choose Apple menu > Control Panels > Energy Saver.

2. If necessary, click the Scheduled Wakeup & Sleep button in the Energy Saver control panel that appears to display wakeup and sleep options (**Figure 11**).

3. Choose an option from the Settings for pop-up menu (**Figure 8**) to specify which setting should be modified.

4. To automatically wake the computer at prescheduled days and times, turn on the Wake up the computer check box. Then set options in the area below the check box.

5. To automatically put the computer in sleep mode at prescheduled days and times, turn on the Put the computer to sleep check box. Then set options in the area below the check box.

6. Close the control panel to save your settings.

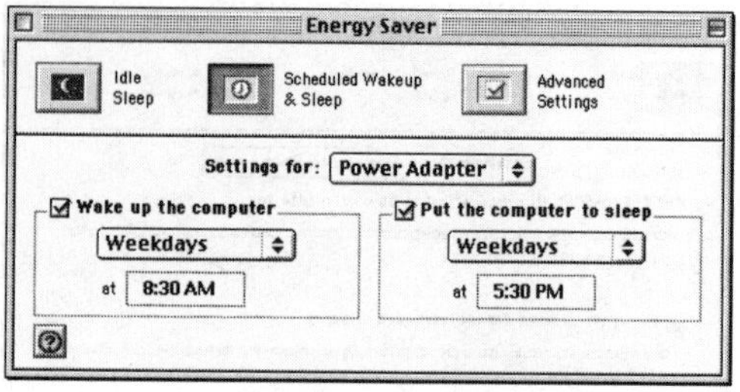

## ✔ Tips

■ These options work very much like the scheduled startup and shutdown options in the Energy Saver control panel on desktop Macs. Consult **Chapter 13** for details on setting these options.

■ If you schedule an automatic wake up time, be sure to leave the PowerBook open. The PowerBook will not be able to start if its cover is down.

**Figure 11** Scheduled Wakeup & Sleep options in the Energy Saver control panel on a PowerBook.

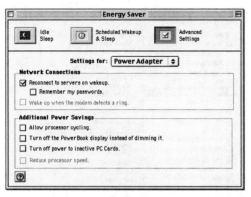

**Figure 12** Advanced Settings options in the Energy Saver control panel on a PowerBook.

## To set advanced options

1. Choose Apple menu > Control Panels > Energy Saver.

2. If necessary, click the Advanced Settings button in the Energy Saver control panel that appears to display advanced options (**Figure 12**).

3. Choose an option from the Settings for pop-up menu (**Figure 8**) to specify which setting should be modified.

4. Set Network Connections options as desired by toggling check boxes:

   ▲ **Reconnect to servers on wakeup** automatically reconnects to any servers to which the PowerBook was connected when it went to sleep.

   ▲ **Remember my passwords** reconnects to servers without prompting you for a password.

   ▲ **Wake when the modem detects a ring** wakes the computer when its modem detects an incoming call. This option is not supported by all PowerBook models.

5. Set Additional Power Savings options as desired by toggling check boxes:

   ▲ **Allow processor cycling** switches your PowerBook's processor to a reduced power mode when idle.

   ▲ **Turn off the PowerBook display instead of dimming it** shuts off the display when idle for the amount of time specified for display dimming.

   ▲ **Turn off power to inactive PC Cards** cuts power to installed PCMCIA cards that are not in use.

   ▲ **Reduce processor speed** saves power by changing the processor speed. This option is not supported by all Power-Book models.

6. Close the control panel to save your settings.

SETTING ADVANCED ENERGY SAVER OPTIONS

# PowerBook SCSI Disk Mode

The PowerBook SCSI Disk Mode control panel (**Figure 14**), which is available only on Power-Book computers, enables you to set the SCSI ID number assigned to the PowerBook when it is attached to another computer via a SCSI cable.

## ✔ Tip

- This feature does not affect the PowerBook in any way if it is not connected to another computer via a SCSI cable.

- The PowerBook SCSI Disk Mode control panel replaces the PowerBook Setup control panel that was part of previous versions of Mac OS.

## To set the PowerBook's SCSI ID number

1. Choose Apple menu > Control Panels > PowerBook SCSI Disk Mode (**Figure 13**). The PowerBook SCSI Disk Mode control panel appears (**Figure 14**).

2. Select the radio button for the SCSI ID number that you want.

3. Close the control panel to save your settings.

## ✔ Tips

- When attaching your PowerBook to another computer via SCSI cable, it's vital that the PowerBook's ID number be different than all other connected SCSI devices.

- You must turn off password protection when attaching your computer to another computer via SCSI cable. I tell you about password protection next.

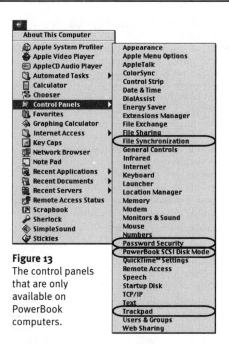

**Figure 13**
The control panels that are only available on PowerBook computers.

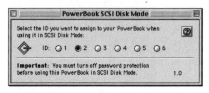

**Figure 14** The PowerBook SCSI Disk Mode control panel.

**Figure 15**
The Password
Security control
panel.

**Figure 16** Use the Password Security Setup dialog box
to configure password protection.

# Password Security

The Password Security control panel (**Figure 15**)
protects your PowerBook from unauthorized
use. You can set it up to require a password for
access when starting up and waking from sleep
mode.

## To set up password protection

1.  Choose Apple menu > Control Panels >
    Password Security (**Figure 13**). The Password
    Security control panel appears (**Figure 15**).

2.  Click the Setup button to display the
    Password Security Setup dialog box
    (**Figure 16**).

3.  Enter the same password in the top two
    edit boxes.

4.  Enter a hint for remembering the password
    in the third edit box.

5.  To also require a password for access when
    the computer wakes, turn on the Also ask
    when waking from sleep check box.

6.  To display your name and contact informa-
    tion in the dialog box that prompts for a
    password, turn on the Show ownership
    information check box. Then fill in the edit
    boxes to provide contact information.

7.  Click OK.

8.  Close the window to save your settings.

## ✔ Tip

■ You may be prompted to enter a password
  (**Figure 17**) in steps 2 and 7. Enter the
  password, and click OK to continue.

## To enable password protection

1. Choose Apple menu > Control Panels > Password Security (**Figure 13**). The Password Security control panel appears (**Figure 15**).

2. Select the On radio button.

3. In the Password dialog box that appears (**Figure 17**) enter your password to confirm that you know it and click OK.

4. Close the window to save your settings.

5. If password protection is configured to require a password when the computer wakes, restart the computer.

## To access a password-protected PowerBook

1. Start or wake the PowerBook.

2. A password dialog box like the one in **Figure 17** appears. Enter your password, and click OK.

## ✔ Tips

- If you enter an incorrect password, a dialog box like the one in **Figure 18** appears. Click OK, and try again.

- If you do not enter a password within a minute or so, the computer automatically shuts down or goes back to sleep.

## To disable password protection

1. Choose Apple menu > Control Panels > Password Security (**Figure 13**). The Password Security control panel appears (**Figure 15**).

2. Select the Off radio button.

3. In the Password dialog box that appears (**Figure 17**) enter your password to confirm that you know it and click OK.

4. Close the window to save your settings.

5. If password protection was configured to require a password when the computer wakes, restart the computer.

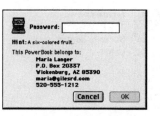

**Figure 17** Use this dialog box to enter your password when prompted.

**Figure 18** If you enter an incorrect password, this dialog box tells you.

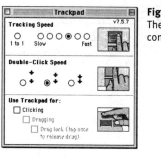

**Figure 19**
The Trackpad control panel.

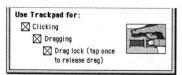

**Figure 20** To turn on the Dragging and Drag lock check boxes, you must turn on the check boxes above them.

# Trackpad

The Trackpad control panel (**Figure 19**) lets you change the way the trackpad works.

## To set Trackpad options

1. Choose Apple menu > Control Panels > Trackpad (**Figure 13**). The Trackpad control panel appears (**Figure 19**).

2. To change the speed at which the mouse pointer moves, select a Tracking Speed radio button.

3. To change time between double-click clicks, select a Double-Click Speed radio button. The one on the left is for more time between double-clicks and the one on the right is for less time.

4. To use the trackpad for clicking, dragging, and drag lock, turn on the appropriate check boxes in the Use Trackpad for area.

5. Close the control panel window to save your settings.

## ✔ Tips

- To turn on the Dragging or Drag lock check box, you must turn on the check box above it (**Figure 20**).

- To use the trackpad dragging feature, tap the item you want to drag, then tap and move your finger on the trackpad to drag it. When Drag lock is enabled, you must tap again to release the item.

SETTING TRACKPAD OPTIONS

# File Synchronization

The File Synchronization control panel (**Figure 21**) enables you to synchronize specific items or the contents of specific folders that exist on both a desktop computer and a PowerBook. This helps ensure that you are always working with the most current version of files.

## ✔ Tips

- File Synchronization requires that you have a network connection between your Power-Book and desktop computer. I tell you about networks in **Chapter 11**.

- To make the most of File Synchronization, you should use it every time you return from a trip with your PowerBook and every time you prepare to leave for a trip with your PowerBook.

- The File Synchronization control panel replaces the File Assistant application that was part of versions of Mac OS prior to 8.5.

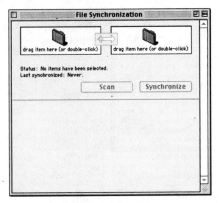

**Figure 21** The File Synchronization control panel window.

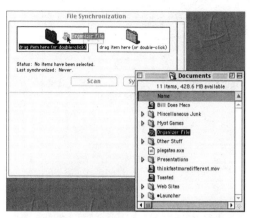

**Figure 22** Drag the icon for the item you want to synchronize to the File Synchronization area.

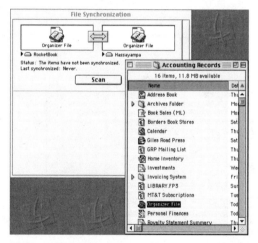

**Figure 23** The icon for the second file that you dragged appears beside the first.

**Figure 24**
Use the Synchronize menu to select a synchronization direction and choose other synchronization options.

## To set up a synchronization

1. Establish a network connection to the desktop computer's hard disk.

2. Choose Apple menu > Control Panels > File Synchronization (**Figure 13**). The File Synchronization control panel appears (**Figure 21**).

3. If necessary, choose File > New or press ⌃⌘N to create an empty synchronization pair.

4. Drag the icon for a file or folder on the PowerBook to the left side *drag item here (or double-click)* area of the File Synchronization window (**Figure 22**). Its icon appears where you dragged it.

5. Drag the icon for the corresponding file or folder on the desktop computer to the right side *drag item here (or double-click)* area of the File Synchronization window. Its icon appears where you dragged it (**Figure 23**).

6. Choose a synchronization direction for the file from the Synchronize menu (**Figure 24**):

   ▲ **In Both Directions** (the default selection) updates either file in the pair when the other file changes.

   ▲ **Left to Right** only updates the file on the right when the file on the left changes.

   ▲ **Right to Left** only updates the file on the left when the file on the right changes.

7. Repeat steps 3 through 6 for each synchronization pair you want to create.

## ✔ Tips

■ If desired, you can double-click the folder icon in steps 4 and 5 to use a standard Open dialog box for locating and selecting files to synchronize.

■ With In Both Directions synchronization selected, if both files change, File Synchronization cannot synchronize them.

## To synchronize files

1. Establish a network connection to the desktop computer's hard disk.

2. Choose Apple menu > Control Panels > File Synchronization (**Figure 13**). The File Synchronization control panel appears (**Figure 21**).

2. Choose Synchronize > Synchronize (**Figure 24**), or press ⌃ ⌘ G.

3. Wait while the files are synchronized. The Synchronizing dialog box appears (**Figure 25**) to indicate the synchronization progress.

4. When synchronization is complete, a dialog box like the one in **Figure 26** appears. Click OK.

   The synchronization date and time appear in the File Synchronization window (**Figure 27**).

## ✔ Tips

- To synchronize just one pair of files, click the Synchronize button beneath them (**Figure 27**).

- If there is an error during synchronization, a dialog box appears to report it.

- To automatically synchronize files every time your PowerBook connects to the desktop computer while File Synchronization is open, choose Synchronize > Automatic (**Figure 24**) or press ⌃ ⌘ T. This turns on automatic synchronization.

**Figure 25** The Synchronizing dialog box appears while files are being synchronized.

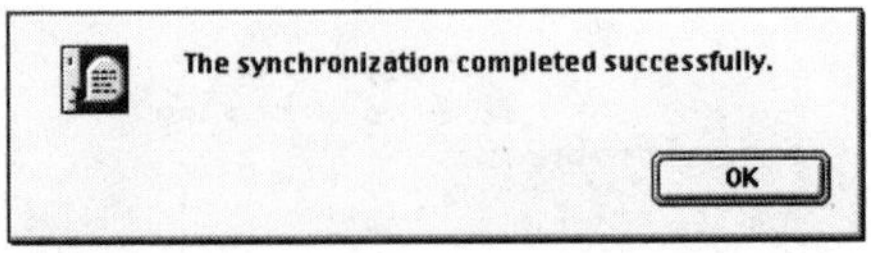

**Figure 26** A dialog box like this appears when synchronization has been successfully completed.

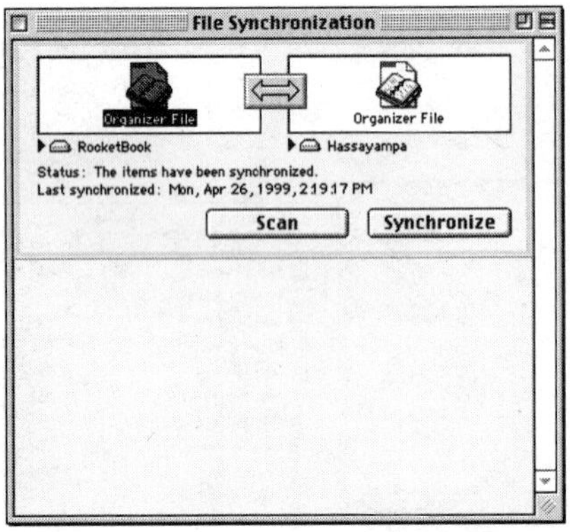

**Figure 27** The date and time of the last synchronization appears in the File Synchronization window for each pair of files.

# iMac & Blue G3 Considerations

## iMac & Blue G3 Considerations

Apple's iMac computer and the new blue-and-white Power Macintosh G3 represent a radical change in computer design. These machines not only look different but have several interface elements that set them apart from older Macintosh models.

Generally speaking, the differences between the new Macs and older Mac models fall into two categories:

◆ **Minor Software Differences.** Some software that is installed on all computers may offer different options on the iMac and blue G3. The AppleTalk, Modem, and Monitors & Sound control panels are examples.

◆ **Hardware Differences.** The iMac and blue G3 lack a number of hardware devices and connections found on other Macintosh models: floppy disk drive, SCSI port, and serial port. Instead, these models have a built-in CD-ROM drive, USB ports, and an Ethernet port.

In this appendix, I cover all of these differences.

### ✔ Tip

■ Throughout this appendix, when distinguishing between the original and new iMacs, I refer to them as the *bondi blue iMacs* and the *fruit-flavored iMacs* respectively. I refer to the blue-and-white G3 as simply the *blue G3*.

# Minor Software Differences

In some instances, the software installed on an iMac or blue G3 may offer more or fewer options than the same software installed on other Macs. Here's a quick summary of the differences you can expect to encounter.

## AppleTalk

The AppleTalk control panel (**Figure 1**) offers different options under its Connect via pop-up menu (**Figure 2**):

◆ **Infrared Port** is supported by the original bondi blue iMac, many PowerBooks, and some other Mac desktop models for networking or exchanging files via infrared communication.

◆ **Modem Port** and **Printer Port** are not offered because neither the iMac nor the blue G3 has these serial ports.

I discuss the AppleTalk control panel in **Chapter 11** and Infrared communications in **Chapter 13**.

## Infrared

The Infrared control panel (**Figure 2**), which is installed on an original bondi blue iMac, offers fewer options than the version installed on some PowerBooks and other desktop Macs. Specifically, it does not include an option to switch to IRTalk.

I discuss Infrared communications in **Chapter 13**.

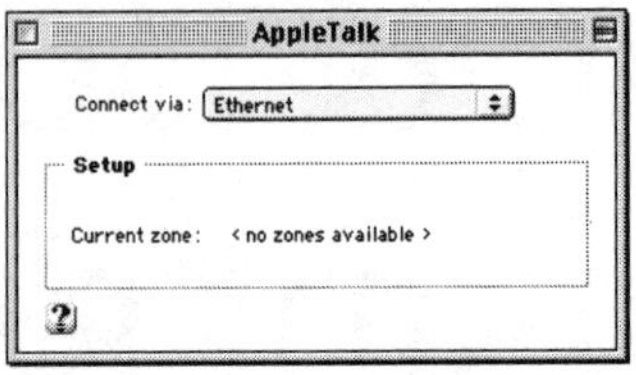

**Figure 1** The AppleTalk control panel on an iMac or blue G3...

**Figure 2** ...offers different Connect via options than what's found on other Macs. The Infrared Port option only appears on original iMac models.

**Figure 3** The Infrared control panel on a bondi blue iMac does not have an Options button for switching between IrDA and IRTalk.

**APPLETALK, INFRARED**

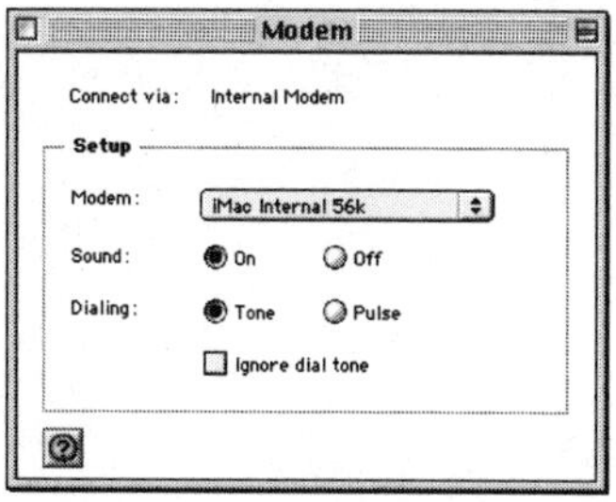

**Figure 4** The Modem control panel on an iMac does not have a Connect via pop-up menu.

**Figure 5** The Monitor options in the Monitors & Sound control panel on an iMac.

## Modem

The Modem control panel on an iMac (**Figure 4**) does not enable you to switch connection options. This is because the iMac does not have any serial ports—just an internal modem.

I discuss the Modem control panel in **Chapter 11**.

## Monitors & Sound

The Monitors & Sound control panel on an iMac (**Figures 5 and 6**) offers different options:

◆ **Monitor** options (**Figure 5**) are based on the capabilities of the built-in iMac monitor. You can change the color depth, resolution, brightness, and contrast as you can on most Mac models.

◆ **Sound** options (**Figure 6**) include support for 3D stereo surround sound—which really does sound good!

I discuss the Monitors & Sound control panel in **Chapter 13**.

**Figure 6** The Sound options in the Monitors & Sound control panel on an iMac.

# Hardware Differences

Possibly the most significant differences between the iMac and blue G3 and older Mac models are their lack of traditional Mac input and output ports.

## ✔ Tip

- The following discussion concentrates on hardware differences. It omits input and output ports found on all Mac models, such as Sound In and Sound Out.

## What the iMac & blue G3 don't have

The following is a list of devices and ports that you won't find on an iMac or blue G3, along with a brief description of what that item does on other Macs:

- **Floppy disk drive** enable Macs to read from and write to 3-1/2 inch floppy disks.

- **Serial ports** enable Macs to connect to LocalTalk networks, printers, external modems, and other serial devices.

- **SCSI ports** enable Macs to connect to storage devices such as external hard disks, Zip and Jaz drives, and CD-ROM drives. They are also widely used for connecting to scanners.

- **ADB ports** enable Macs to connect to input devices such as a keyboard, mouse, or graphics tablet. The iMac does not include this port; the blue G3 does.

## ✔ Tip

- SCSI stands for *Small Computer System Interface*. ADB stands for *Apple Desktop Bus*.

## What the iMac & blue G3 do have

After reading what the iMac and blue G3 don't have, you may be thinking that they're missing out on a lot. But they do have some things most other Mac models don't have:

◆ **USB ports** enable iMacs and blue G3s to connect to a wide range of external devices, including floppy disk drives, printers, external storage devices, scanners, keyboards, mice, and graphics tablets.

◆ **FireWire ports** enable new (fruit-flavored) iMacs and blue G3s to connect at high speeds to a number of external devices, including hard drives, storage devices, and video cameras.

◆ **Internal 56Kbps modem**, which comes standard on the iMac and is offered as an option on the blue G3, enables the computer to connect to other computers and the Internet at high speeds without attaching an external modem.

◆ **100BaseT Ethernet port** enables iMacs and blue G3s to transfer data at high speed over high-speed Ethernet networks. But don't worry—if you connect either machine to a 10BaseT Ethernet network, it'll work just fine.

◆ **Infrared port** enables the bondi blue iMac to connect to a network via infrared connection. Although some other Mac models include this type of port (notably PowerBooks), most don't.

# More about USB

USB, which stands for *Universal Serial Bus*, is an industry standard that has been supported by Wintel computers for a number of years. The bondi blue iMac was the first Mac OS computer to include USB ports; all iMacs and blue G3s include these ports, as will future Mac models.

The main benefit of USB over serial and ADB ports is speed—it can move data much faster than either of these ports. That means your computer can communicate with a printer, scanner, or other USB device faster than it could communicate with the same device using serial or ADB connections.

Another benefit of USB is the ability to connect up to 127 USB devices to a single Mac. This isn't done with *daisy-chaining*—connecting one device to another the way SCSI devices are connected. It's done with USB hubs, which are similar to network hubs. You attach a hub to your computer, then attach devices to the ports on the hub. And there's no need to set addresses, like you must do with SCSI device chains. USB can handle all that for you.

## ✔ Tips

- Check Apple's USB Web page (`http://www.apple.com/usb/`) for more information about USB, including a list of currently available USB devices.

- Because USB has been available for PCs for some time, many USB devices are available. To use them with a Mac, however, you must have a Mac version of the device's driver, which, if available, can be obtained from the device's manufacturer.

- You can purchase an adapter that makes it possible to connect serial and ADB devices to an iMac or blue G3. This makes it possible to use devices you already have with an iMac or blue G3.

# More about FireWire

FireWire, which was developed by Apple Computer, is a high-speed peripheral standard that is quickly gaining popularity in both Mac OS and Wintel platforms. The fruit-flavored iMacs and blue G3 were the first Macs to include FireWire ports; all future Mac models will also include them.

The main benefit of FireWire over serial and SCSI ports is speed—it can move data many times faster. It can even move data about 30 times faster than USB! That means your computer can communicate with a hard disk, printer, scanner, digital camera, or other FireWire device faster than it could communicate with the same device using serial, SCSI, or USB connections.

Another benefit of FireWire is the ability to connect up to 63 FireWire devices in a peer-to-peer bus. The FireWire bus can include not only FireWire peripherals but other computers, thus enabling several computers to share devices. The bus is created by connecting one device to another, the way SCSI devices are connected. But there's no need to set addresses, like you must do with SCSI device chains. FireWire handles addressing for you.

## ✔ Tip

- Check Apple's FireWire Web page (`http://www.apple.com/firewire/`) for more information about FireWire, including a list of currently available FireWire devices.

# INDEX

INDEX

# Other Visual QuickStart Guides for Mac OS Users

## Word 98 for Macintosh: Visual QuickStart Guide

*Maria Langer*

With the release of Word 98, Word promises to not only remain but continue to grow as the leading word processor on the Macintosh platform. It's been dramatically reworked to more fully utilize and integrate with the Mac OS user interface and functionality. Now more powerful and friendly than ever, Word 98 enables users to create a wide range of documents, from simple, one-page letters to complex multifile reports with figures, table of contents, and index to Web pages with hyperlinks and graphics.

*Word 98 for Macintosh: Visual QuickStart Guide* will introduce new and experienced Word users alike to the host of new features and improved Web integration and functionality. Using concise steps and numerous illustrations, the book covers everything from word processing basics and formatting fundamentals to desktop and Webtop publishing techniques. This is a comprehensive introduction to the powerful capabilities of Word 98.

260 pages • ISBN 0-201-35354-7 • $17.95

## Excel 98 for Macintosh: Visual QuickStart Guide

*Maria Langer*

Excel is the spreadsheet of choice for home users and business workers. With it you can create anything from a simple chart to an advanced worksheet with graphics and more, based on just about any data you can enter into a Macintosh. Excel 98 is the latest version of the most popular spreadsheet for the Mac. New features include the Natural Language Formula, Range Finder, and Formula AutoCorrect features to write and edit formulas; the free rotation, merge cells, AutoSize Text, and Conditional Formatting features; enhanced Internet features that let you include links in documents and convert Excel 98 documents to Web pages; and the new Office Assistant.

The fast-paced and easy-to-read *Excel 98 for Macintosh: Visual QuickStart Guide* helps both new and experienced Excel users get up-to-speed quickly on all of Excel's new and improved features. This book uses the power of pictures to guide readers through the software, with plentiful screen captures and succinct, to-the-point instructions. Numerous tips and tricks throughout the book make this an excellent reference to the versatility and power of the program.

262 pages • ISBN 0-201-35360-1 • $17.95

## AppleWorks 5 for Windows & Macintosh: Visual QuickStart Guide

*C. Ann Brown*

With a simple name change and some modified screen elements, ClarisWorks 5 becomes AppleWorks, the integrated package that encompasses word processing, database, spreadsheet, graphics, and telecommunications modules, all of which allows users to create sophisticated documents quickly. Apple is so sold on its program that it has included AppleWorks on all new iMacs, the consumer Internet Macs for home, small business and school, a market that has already embraced ClarisWorks. And what better match for an Internet Mac than a product rich with Internet capabilities and multimedia features, making it easy for users of all levels to add pictures, sound, and even QuickTime movies to their projects.

*AppleWorks for Windows & Macintosh: Visual QuickStart Guide* is a great tool for mastering the best of the "Swiss Army knife" applications. The Visual QuickStart Guide's simple-to-follow instructions, hundreds of screenshots, and loads of tips will help the beginner navigate Appleworks' many facets with confidence, and more seasoned users will value it as a useful reference.

224 pages • ISBN 0-201-35403-9 • $17.99

## PageMill 3 for Macintosh & Windows: Visual QuickStart Guide

*Maria Langer*

With PageMill 3, creating Web pages has never been easier. No need to learn HTML or master complex applications—a WYSIWYG interface provides a familiar environment for creating colorful, dynamic Web pages. PageMill 3.0 uses drag-and-drop simplicity for adding and manipulating text, images, and hyperlinks. This allows for quick and easy integration with your current office and graphics applications. By taking away all the scary technical details, PageMill allows users to focus on content and design.

*PageMill 3 for Macintosh & Windows: Visual QuickStart Guide* is a richly illustrated, step-by-step guide that gets readers up and running quickly. In no time at all readers are designing and creating Web pages and effectively utilizing all the features of PageMill. Hundreds of screenshots accompanied by clear instructions and loads of helpful tips guide readers through basic editing techniques, applying styles, working with graphic images and links, and finally, to testing and enhancing their new Web pages.

253 pages • ISBN 0-201-35443-8 • $17.99

**To order these and other Peachpit Press books, visit our Web site at http://www.peachpit.com/ or call toll-free 1-800-283-9444**

# About Giles Road Press

Giles Road Press is a small Web publishing organization that provides the following information to Macintosh and Windows users:

♦ **Companion Web sites for recent books by Maria Langer.** These sites include information about books, sample chapters, sample files used throughout the books, corrections and clarifications, tips and tricks, and news links of interest to book readers.

♦ **Discounts and special offers on books and software.** Giles Road Press offers all recent books by Maria Langer at a discount to site visitors. You can even get an autographed copy! Links to other computer and non-computer books available through Amazon.com make it easy to find books that interest you without dealing with cryptic search engines. Occasionally, visitors will also find special offers on clearance and other items offered by Giles Road Press's Web partners.

♦ **Macintosh Tips & Tricks.** This newsletter, which is issued periodically, provides a wealth of information for Macintosh users. Recent issues covered topics such as HFS+ and choosing an Internet Service Provider (ISP).

♦ **Links to other Web sites.** The Giles Road Press site includes links to other sites of interest to Macintosh and Windows users and writers.

There is no charge for accessing the Giles Road Press Web site or any of its information. No membership or registration is required.

For more information about Giles Road Press, including information on how you can become a site sponsor, visit the site or send an e-mail message to **info@gilesrd.com**.

---

### Get on Our Mailing List!

To get on the Giles Road Press mailing list and learn about major changes to the site and special offers, send an e-mail message to info@gilesrd.com with the word *ADD* in the subject line. You will receive confirmation that you have been added, along with instructions for being removed from the list. The Giles Road Press mailing list seldom sends out more than four messages in a month and is not shared with any other organization.

---

## Visit Giles Road Press at http://www.gilesrd.com/